GENDER <u>IN</u> H

Series editors:
Lynn Abrams, Cordelia Beattie, Pam Shar

The expansion of research into the history of women and gender since the 1970s has changed the face of history. Using the insights of feminist theory and of historians of women, gender historians have explored the configuration in the past of gender identities and relations between the sexes. They have also investigated the history of sexuality and family relations, and analysed ideas and ideals of masculinity and femininity. Yet gender history has not abandoned the original, inspirational project of women's history: to recover and reveal the lived experience of women in the past and the present.

The series Gender in History provides a forum for these developments. Its historical coverage extends from the medieval to the modern periods, and its geographical scope encompasses not only Europe and North America but all corners of the globe. The series aims to investigate the social and cultural constructions of gender in historical sources, as well as the gendering of historical discourse itself. It embraces both detailed case studies of specific regions or periods, and broader treatments of major themes. Gender in History titles are designed to meet the needs of both scholars and students working in this dynamic area of historical research.

Catholic nuns and sisters in a secular age

MANCHESTER
1824

Manchester University Press

CATHOLIC NUNS AND SISTERS IN A SECULAR AGE

BRITAIN, 1945–1990

—— Carmen M. Mangion ——

Manchester University Press

Published by Manchester University Press
Altrincham Street, Manchester M1 7JA
www.manchesteruniversitypress.co.uk

British Library Cataloguing-in-Publication Data
A catalogue record for this book is available from the British Library

ISBN 978 1 5261 4046 3 hardback

First published 2020

The publisher has no responsibility for the persistence or accuracy of URLs for any external or third-party internet websites referred to in this book, and does not guarantee that any content on such websites is, or will remain, accurate or appropriate.

This book is produced with the generous assistance of a grant from Isobel Thornley's Bequest to the University of London.

Typeset by Newgen Publishing UK
Printed in Great Britain
by TJ International Ltd, Padstow

In memory of
Iris Mary (née Theuma) Mangion (1934–2017)
Eva Bourgeois (1907–1985)

Contents

Figures

Tables

Preface and acknowledgements

I have a rather unusual admission: this was not a book I wanted to write. This was a book I thought should be written. I waited for someone else to write it. But no one did. I spent the first decade of my career doing research on nineteenth-century women religious. My research in convent archives often included tea-time breaks with sisters and nuns who were more often than not somewhat befuddled by my seemingly myopic interest in their nineteenth-century forebears. They would tell me their stories of the 1950s and 1960s and 1970s and I would think 'someone needs to write these stories'. That someone was not supposed to be me – but the awareness that the generation that had lived through such dramatic changes in religious life was fast disappearing meant it became me. That window of opportunity for capturing the voices of women who had lived through the dramatic changes of religious life was slowly closing. So I took the plunge and immersed myself in the twentieth-century post-war world with all its complexities. I have found myself, so many times, feeling as if I was falling into the abyss that is twentieth-century history. Despite initial reservations on the immensity of a twentieth-century historiography and the complexities of oral testimony and memory, it has been an immense pleasure doing the research for this book. I have been supported in this academic journey by so many people along the way, friends and colleagues, sisters and scholars (and some sister-scholars) but above all, what I have enjoyed most is listening to each life story. I could have spent a lifetime listening to stories about childhoods, novitiates and the ups and downs of religious life. Eventually, though, I had to stop listening and begin writing.

So here I am, finally.

I am indebted to so many who have supported me over the last five years. It is a great privilege to belong to such a generous and collaborative academic community. First, the sisters whom I interviewed – thank you for the gift of your stories. No story was as 'ordinary' as you made out – I am so grateful for your time and trust. You were the best part of the project (even more fun than the archives – and that says a lot because I love the archives). I hope you see your contribution to this history. To the religious institutes who gave their permission to do research in their archives and to interview their community members; and to the archivists who opened their doors to me I owe a special thanks. I am grateful to the Benedictines of Stanbrook (now Wass), Canonesses Regular of the Holy Sepulchre, the Congregation of Jesus, the Poor Clare

Communities of Much Birch, York, Arundel, Lynton and Hollington, the Sisters of Charity of Our Lady Mother of Mercy, the Sisters of Mercy of the Union and the Institute, the Society of the Sacred Heart, the Religious of La Retraite, the Syon Bridgettines and the Vocation Sisters. Researching recent history requires a special trust, and I can't say thank you enough to archivists and others I have bombarded with requests and questions, especially Sister Mary Bede, Kathryn Byrne, Joseph Chinnici, Marianne Cosgrave, Chris Dols, Robert Finnegan, Lilianne Hecker, Barbara Jeffery, Naomi Johnson, Christina Kenworthy-Browne, CJ, Patricia Harriss, CJ, Pauline McAloone, Margaret Phelan, RSCJ, Sister Benignus O'Brien, Peter O'Brien, Annie Price, Dan Regan, Magdalen Roskell, CRSS, Fr Nicholas Schofield, Fr John Sharp, Marian Short, Jenny Smith, Anne Smyth, OssS, Hazel State, Hannah Thomas, Barbara Vesey and Meg Whittle. I am very grateful to have been given access to the personal archives of Francis Pullen OSC and Elizabeth Rendall by her nieces Diana, Jane and Vanessa Rendall. Then there were those very clever academic colleagues, some near, some far, who have offered support on more than just the book: Caroline Bowden, Kathleen Sprows Cummings, Marjet Derks, Patrick Hayes, Mary Lyons, RSM, Sue Morgan, Anselm Nye and Joos van Vugt. I belong to the best home team in the world: thanks to Jen Baird, Joanna Bourke, Sean Brady, Becky Briant, Matt Cook, Rosie Cox, Serafina Cuomo (you're still on the home team to me), Jasmine Gideon, Louise Hide, Leslie McFadyen and Jessica Reinisch. Academic colleagues read and commented on sometimes pretty chaotic prose and reminded me of what I was trying to say. Thank you, Madisson Brown, Mary Beth Fraser Connolly, Alana Harris, Kathleen Keane, LCM, Maria Power, Maggie Scull, Ruth Slattery and Stephanie Spencer; and of course my very special reading group, Lucy Bland, Clare Midgley, Alison Oram, Krisztina Robert and Katharina Rowold. The listserv members of the Historians of Women Religious of Britain and Ireland (H-WRBI) were generous, as always, with responses to my many questions. One special person read each and every chapter and was a guiding light: thank you, Susan O'Brien. Your incisive and perceptive work remains my inspiration. I am fortunate to have a very special husband who always thinks my work is important: love you, Rich Wagner. And special thanks to my parents, Iris and Saviour, who were my first 'practice' interviewees. I was privileged to interview them both about their lives; their experience of the 1960s was coloured by their immigration from Malta to Detroit with two small children in the midst of the Detroit race riots. I am dedicating this work to my mother because although I know she had a good life, I am aware of what she gave up.

She trained as a teacher; it was a vocation she loved and lost when she married in 1959 and had to resign because of the marriage bar. Those years at Mater Dei teacher training college and the lasting friendships of her teacher friends became a part of who she was though she never returned to the profession that she loved. And I have also dedicated this work to Eva Bourgeous. She and her husband Lee adopted my family when we moved to the United States. They showed us the best of what it was to be American, to welcome and accept the foreigner in their hearts. But Eva did more for me, she listened to my childhood dreams, celebrated my academic accomplishments and convinced me I could be and do anything. It was a gift to last a lifetime.

I have travelled near and far to do this research, had transcribed many an interview (thanks to Sue Lovell-Greene and Susan Nicholls) and organised many a conference, and the financing of this has come from a host of funders who deserve credit for filling the funding breach: the Notre Dame Global Collaboration Initiative, the Scouloudi Historical Awards, the Catholic Record Society (The David Rogers Research Fund), the English Catholic Historical Society, the Catholic Family History Society, a Peter R. D'Agostino Research Travel Grant and Birkbeck, University of London. This book is produced with the generous assistance of a grant from Isobel Thornley's Bequest to the University of London.

While I learned much from those who have offered me their generous feedback, the interpretations, and any errors, are my own.

Introduction

Religious sisters and nuns, known collectively as women religious,[1] have always operated in a liminal place in church and popular culture. Nuns for centuries maintained a spiritual capital that gave them a special role in the life of the Catholic Church. Though some individual abbesses may have wielded significant power, women religious were never canonically members of the clergy. They had, however, in popular understanding, a 'higher calling'.[2] Through the institutions they managed, female religious had enormous influence in shaping generations of Catholics. They were, by the nineteenth century,

---

1   The term religious life refers to a form of life where men or women take three vows, of poverty, chastity and obedience, and are members of a particular religious institute which is governed by a rule and constitution. Catholic religious life has traditionally been divided into two main categories: orders of contemplative nuns whose work is prayer of the Divine Office inside the cloister and 'active' congregations of religious sisters whose ministry or apostolate (traditionally teaching, nursing and social welfare) is outside the cloister. The terms sisters and nuns were are often used interchangeably, although with the codification of Canon Law in 1917 the term sister came to define women who took simple vows and worked outside the cloister and the term nun came to refer to contemplatives who took solemn vows and lived a life of prayer behind cloister walls. Catholic religious sisters and nuns are often referred to collectively as women religious. The *Annuarium Statisticum Ecclesiae* dated 2017 reported 659 thousand women religious worldwide. https://translate.google.com/translate?hl=en&sl=it&u=https://press.vatican.va/content/salastampa/it/bollettino/pubblico/2018/06/13/0440/00957.html&prev=search, accessed 30 October 2018.

2   In 1964, the Dogmatic Constitution on the Church (*Lumen Gentium*) made explicit that vowed religious were categorised as laity (§43). (Papal documents originating in Latin are named after the first few words of the document so the Dogmatic Constitution of the Church is also known as *Lumen Gentium*.) Some scholars argue that this was explicitly intended to reduce the power and authority of women religious. Mary Jo Weaver, *New Catholic Women: A Contemporary Challenge to Traditional Religious Authority* (San Francisco: Harper & Row, 1985), p. 72.

integral to the development of Catholic social welfare systems that often ran in parallel with those of the state. Despite, or maybe because of their utility, nuns and sisters were often caricatured and essentialised, both from within the Catholic Church and without. At different times, they have been imagined as obedient pawns of the church, saintly virtuosos, naïve young innocents, cruel shrews, disobedient heretics and sadistic abusers – and most recently 'radical feminists'. And today, though numbers of women religious decline in the 'Global North' (and increase in the 'Global South'), they continue to attract media attention, though almost always as 'other'.

Since the 1950s, a profusion of books has been published in Britain and Ireland and elsewhere recounting personal experiences by nuns and about nuns. The genre of 'nuns talking' presents a disparate range of experiences. In Britain, Karen Armstrong's gripping and widely cited 1960s memoir explores a complex young woman's experience of a stifling convent regime and her eventual exodus.[3] Sister Giles' story of parting is gentler and less well known; she left religious life after almost twenty-five years in an enclosed monastery but continued her faith journey, still connecting with her former monastery.[4] Journalist Mary Loudon gathered together the stories of faith and transition of ten nuns and sisters in England in *Unveiled: Nun's Talking*.[5] Camillus Metcalfe framed her interviews of ten Irish women religious psychoanalytically, emphasising what she identified as the repressive nature of Irish religious life.[6] In addition to these British and Irish voices, there are volumes of published interviews of North American and Australian former and current women religious. The stories they tell are often polarised into 'strong women' who worked through repressive pre-conciliar regimes to do great things and 'angry women' who left, enraged and unable to countenance what they saw as the hypocrisy of religious life and the Catholic Church.[7]

---

3   Karen Armstrong, *Through the Narrow Gate: A Nun's Story* (London: Flamingo, 1981) and its sequel *The Spiral Staircase* (London: William Collins, 2004).
4   Sister Giles, *The End and the Beginning* (Stanhope: The Memoir Club, 2007).
5   Mary Loudon, *Unveiled: Nuns Talking* (London: Chatto & Windus, 1992).
6   Camillus Metcalfe, *For God's Sake: The Hidden Life of Irish Nuns* (Dublin: The Liffey Press, 2014).
7   Carole G. Rogers, *Habits of Change: An Oral History of American Nuns* (New York: Oxford University Press, 2011); Mary Ryllis Clark, Heather O'Connor and Valerie Krips (eds), *Perfect Charity: Women Religious Living the Spirit of Vatican II* (Australia: Morning Star Publishers, 2015); Anne Patrick Ware (ed.), *Midwives of the Future: American Sisters Tell Their Story* (London: Sheed and Ward, 1985); Marie Therese Gass, *Unconventional Women: 73 Ex-Nuns Tell Their Stories* (Clackamas, OR: Sieben Hill, 2001).

Stories about women religious by those they educated are equally divergent. The feminist press Virago published *There's Something about a Convent Girl* in 1991. Its founder, Carmen Callil, a convent girl in 1940s Australia, was so scarred by her experiences she wanted the world to know what it was like to be traumatised by nuns.[8] But not all the twenty-four recollections authored by former convent girls educated in convent schools in England, Ireland, Australia and Rome from the 1930s to the 1960s emphasised trauma. Katie Boyle's experience was of sisters who were 'understanding, so broadminded, so worldly, and yet not at all worldly'.[9] These 'love them' or 'hate them' stories were perplexing. And I became even more confounded when meeting female religious in the course of my research. They were – well – quite ordinary women. I found it difficult to see them as either the 'evil nun' or the 'holy nun'. The stories both current and former religious told me of their experiences of religious life were also contradictory. Some felt damaged by their novitiate experience; others loved every moment of it. What was universal, however, was that they experienced a dramatic change in the way religious life was lived. I wanted to understand how these women had experienced the complex, sometimes metamorphic, changes of religious life. This book in exploring nuns and sisters in a secular age provides a lens with which to decipher these complex, diverse stories of female religious life.

At the heart of the transformations in religious life was the discipline of obedience and the way its practice had changed. St Augustine's often-quoted maxim, *Roma locuta est, causa finita est* (Rome has spoken; the case is finished), underscored the power of the Holy See, which expected blind obedience to conciliar and papal decision-making where no questioning, no rebuttal and no recourse to conscience was brooked.[10] Religious institutes had become 'little Romes' with authority centralised under a superior general or abbess.[11] When these leaders of congregations and orders spoke, *causa finita est*! For much of the nineteenth and the twentieth centuries, the Holy See with its centralising remit expected universality (the church of all peoples) to be maintained through uniformity. According to its way of thinking, the spirit of

8   Jackie Bennett and Rosemary Forgan (eds), *There's Something about a Convent Girl* (London: Virago, 1991), p. 56. This book was later made into a television programme and the book was reissued in 2003 as *Convent Girls*.
9   *Ibid.*, p. 43.
10   This Latin statement (and its English translation) from St Augustine's Sermon 131, §10 references the power and authority of the Holy See.
11   In this volume, 'religious institutes' encompasses religious orders, congregations and societies of apostolic life.

the world, modernity, led to worldliness and sorrow – and was to be dismissed or condemned.[12] From the 1940s, in a noticeable shift, the Holy See spoke with words that urged an engagement with the modern world: adaptation, renewal and change. Female religious in Britain, weighed down by the reification of centuries of tradition, responded hesitantly. Then the 1960s: in the Church and in the world, ideas that had been slowly simmering began to bubble and sputter. The *zeitgeist* of the times was one of action. Expectations of a better world generated a radicalisation, religious and secular, explored and lived by laity, religious and priests. The Second Vatican Council (1962–1965) re-enforced that *zeitgeist*. New, more urgent words were added to the religious lexicon: *aggiornamento, ressourcement,* collegiality and experimentation. These words were intended to encourage religious to rethink the essence of the aims and objectives of the religious institutes in which they lived. This rethinking could be radical, sweeping away much of what was familiar to insiders and outsiders of religious life. Renewal was a source of new-found energy for some, but for others, loss, of what they had known, believed, understood and loved about their vocation and about their Church. Change, in communities with hallowed traditions that had stood the test of time for hundreds of years, was difficult, confusing and painful. *Catholic Nuns and Sisters in a Secular Age* tells the story of the excitement of the renewal of religious life. It also tells the story of the despair of that same renewal.

The post-war world is this book's starting point, as the Second World War provided an important watershed, launching a new world order where the social and cultural landscape shifted dramatically for Britons.[13] The war years were disruptive for Catholic nuns and sisters: privations, cohabitations and evacuations altered relationships within and without the convent.[14] From this, there was no turning back. This story of change

---

12   Bruno M. Hagspiel, 'The Religious Life in the U.S. Is on the Decline Both in Men's and Women's Orders', *Sponsa Regis*, 28:2 (1956), 29–41; Adrian Hastings, 'Catholic History from Vatican I to John Paul II', in Adrian Hastings (ed.), *Modern Catholicism: Vatican II and After* (New York: Oxford University Press, 1991), p. 3; Patrick Pasture, 'Religion in Contemporary Europe: Contrasting Perceptions and Dynamics', *Archiv für Sozialgeschichte*, 49 (2009), 328.

13   Arthur Marwick, *The Sixties: Cultural Revolution in Britain, France, Italy, and the United States, c. 1958–c. 1974* (Oxford: Oxford University Press, 1998), pp. 5, 806.

14   As Monique Luirard and others suggest, the Second World War in particular interrupted the stability of convent life and introduced what appears as an unprecedented interaction with the larger world. Monique Luirard, *The Society of the Sacred Heart in the World of Its Times 1865–2000* (St Louis, MO: iUniverse, 2016),

begins as the Second World War ends, when British women were no longer conscripted and were free to enter religious life. Young women were changed by their experiences of the war years, and the modifications in religious life that began in these pre-conciliar years reflected a new modernity. The Second Vatican Council collated many shifts in Church thinking in the sixteen documents that it published. What followed their publication was an unprecedented rethinking and restructuring of religious life as women religious obediently (some with great enthusiasm, others with a heavy heart) reimagined religious life into the 1970s and 1980s. This book ends in 1990: for many religious institutes this was another turning point. By the 1990s, the years of experimenting had coalesced into more stable processes of decision-making, consultation and leadership. Many communities now thought more strategically and realistically about their future and their ministries and were able to look back on the previous thirty years and assess this history with greater detachment.

This study examines the changes in religious life for women religious in Britain from 1945 to 1990, identifying how community and individual lives were altered. Though the project considers both secular and Catholic events that occurred in the post-war world, it pivots on the Second Vatican Council, and considers pre- and post-Vatican II social, cultural and religious events and social movements as influencers in these changes. It frames the new ways of living religious life in two important ways. First, it interrogates 'lived experience' by examining the day-to-day lives of women religious, responding to historian Joseph Komonchak's reflection that 'to give a sense of what Vatican II was as experienced and what it means as an event, the documents are inadequate'.[15] In doing this, it also addresses historical theologian Massimo Faggioli's critique that it is time to move past the event of the Second Vatican Council and focus on its afterlife.[16] Second, Catholic religious institutes were national and global Catholic institutions and this project is influenced by their transnational interactions. Though rooted in the experiences of women religious in Britain, the project probes the relationships and interconnectivities between women religious within and across national

p. 370. Outside of individual convent histories, there is little published of religious life in Britain during the first half of the twentieth century.

15 Joseph A. Komonchak, 'Vatican II as Ecumenical Council: Yves Congar's Vision Realized', Commonweal, 22 November 2002, p. 14.

16 Massimo Faggioli, Vatican II: The Battle for Meaning (Mahwah, NJ: Paulist Press, 2012), p. 139.

divides as they move from institutions embedded in uniformity to the acceptance of cultural plurality.

Catholic Nuns and Sisters in a Secular Age also engages with the histories of the social movements of the long 1960s. For too long, religion has been relegated to its own silo, unlinked to the 'radical sixties' and depicted as ultimately obstructionist to 'new thinking and freer lifestyles'. The doyen of 1960s scholarship Arthur Marwick insisted the Catholic Church acted as a centre of opposition to 'all the great movements aiming towards greater freedom for ordinary human beings'.[17] To contest this, female religious life is examined as a microcosm of change in the Catholic Church, pointing to the 'new thinking and freer lifestyles' that allowed for the questioning of institutional cultures and the introduction of personal autonomy that had its parallels in the larger British society.

Why is this research important? First, it promotes a better understanding of the changing role of religion in modern society in the post-war twentieth century by expanding our understanding of how religious bodies interacted with society. Despite the decline of religious belief in the Global North, religion remains inescapably relevant, as any review of recent newspaper headlines demonstrates. Religion, in many of the social and cultural histories of Britain in the 1960s, if addressed at all, has often been portrayed as a stagnant, obstructionist force. This research displays Catholicism as a living, dynamic faith tradition interacting with and being influenced by the changing nature of British society and culture. Balancing religious principles with modernity had its perils; it has resulted in a difficult and often contentious journey. This is not a story of 'progress', but a complex history of the individual and institutional efforts towards readjusting Catholicism to the 'modern world'. It does not deny the uncomfortable stories of kyriarchy or the 're-positioning and self-historicising' that occurred in some communities.[18]

Second, this is a women-centred, lived history. It uses material from the archives as well as oral testimony to tell a gendered story. Women's voices in many of the major religions have been relegated as subsidiary (if not invisible) in published histories. The women who have participated

---

17 Marwick, *The Sixties*, p. 34.

18 Margaret Susan Thompson, 'Circles of Sisterhood: Formal and Informal Collaboration among American Nuns in Response to Conflict with Vatican Kyriarchy', *Journal of Feminist Studies in Religion*, 32 (2016), 63–82. See also Marit Monteiro, Marjet Derks and Annelies Van Heijst, 'The Stories the Religious Have Lived by since the 1960s', in R. Ruard Ganzevoort, Maaike de Haardt and Michael Scherer-Rath (eds), *Religious Stories We Live by: Narrative Approaches in Theology and Religious Studies* (Leiden: Brill, 2014), p. 223.

in this study often engaged with the world as religious catechists and evangelists and as educators, social workers or nurses. In these roles, they influenced the lives of Catholics and non-Catholics. This project reminds us of the significance of women in the larger history of religion and analyses their subjectivities as well as their interactions with society and the church. Third, this project raises the standard of knowledge about Catholicism by telling the story of social change in a different way, through lived history. It complements the event-based histories of the Second Vatican Council and the scores of theological or sociological studies of the Council and its aftermath, by utilising social and cultural history methodologies to evaluate the changes in religious life as part of the social movements of the 1960s, but like other social movements with a noteworthy prehistory and afterlife.

This research explores female religious life through lived experience in order to understand the changing nature of women's communities from the mid-1940s to the 1980s. It does not scrutinise the theology undergirding Vatican decrees but links their usage and understanding to the experiences of women religious. It acknowledges the meanings these women have ascribed to the changing dimensions of religious life. It asks questions about the changes that took place in terms of structural (e.g. community, decision-making), relational (e.g. family and friends), professional (e.g. training and ministry) and visible (e.g. religious habits, the grille) shifts. How were these changes communicated and implemented? Examining this time period through the debates of 'continuity versus rupture' (as the pre-conciliar and post-conciliar terminology suggests) denies earlier developments in thinking and praxis and suggests that Catholics resided in an impermeable Catholic silo. *Catholic Nuns and Sisters in a Secular Age* in moving outside the Catholic world acknowledges that women religious were influenced by the broader social movements of the long 1960s.

Despite this broad remit, there is much this book does not do. As already mentioned, it does not delve into the theology or the event of the Second Vatican Council. There are numerous publications that do this.[19] This is not a history of the spirituality of women religious, though

19 Giuseppe Alberigo (ed.), *History of Vatican II*, 5 vols, English version edited by Joseph A. Komonchak (Maryknoll, NY: Orbis, 1995–2006); Matthew L. Lamb and Matthew Levering (eds), *Vatican II: Renewal within Tradition* (Oxford: Oxford University Press, 2008); M. Lamberigts and L. Kenis (eds), *Vatican II and Its Legacy* (Leuven: Leuven University Press, 2002); Richard John Neuhaus, *The Catholic Moment: The Paradox of the Church in the Postmodern World* (San Francisco: Harper & Row, 1987).

it recognises the centrality of their relationship to the Divine and the spiritual journey that was also part of the changes in religious life. God-centredness was integral to the stories sisters and nuns told of why they entered religious life and why they remained. This work does not explore explicitly why women left religious life in great numbers as they did in the 1970s and 1980s. There are publications that address this more fully.[20] Nor is this a history that takes up a position alongside 'liberal' or 'traditional' histories that either exalt or denounce the changes that came out of the Second Vatican Council. Many pundits have weighed in on the consequences of the Second Vatican Council in print and social media, arguing either that the Second Vatican Council has destroyed Catholicism or that 'progressive' changes have not gone far enough. As with any story of change, this one is complicated. Lastly, this is not the last word on women religious and Vatican II. Each woman and each archive told unique stories of institutional and personal change. Even within the same congregation or order, change was experienced and lived differently. There are more themes to be addressed, more deep analysis to be completed and other facets of this story to be written.[21] This monograph offers one interpretation of what is a complicated set of events and experiences. Like the Council of Trent, this was a game-changing council.

Historical approaches and sources

Catholic Nuns and Sisters in a Secular Age draws on a variety of original material using both documentary sources and oral testimonies. Material from the archives of religious institutes were heavily weighted to explaining the structures of religious life, and offered a more institutional and less experiential history. The bureaucratising of religious life

---

20   Christine Gervais, *Beyond the Altar: Women Religious, Patriarchal Power, and the Church* (Waterloo: Wilfrid Laurier University Press, 2018); Helen Rose Ebaugh, Jon Lorence and Janet Saltzman Chafetz, 'The Growth and Decline of the Population of Catholic Nuns Cross-Nationally, 1960–1990: A Case of Secularization as Social Structural Change', *Journal for the Scientific Study of Religion*, 35 (1996), 171–83; Helen Rose Fuchs Ebaugh and Paul Ritterband, 'Education and the Exodus from Convents', *Sociology of Religion*, 39 (1978), 257–64.

21   It is with some regret that I did not tackle the subject of lay sisters in this book. I was unable, within the wordcount of this book, to do justice to the complex and vexed issues developing out of the phasing out of the lay category of religious life in the 1940s and 1950s. It is the subject of a forthcoming journal article entitled ' "The Lay Sister Problem": Social Class and Power in Post-War British Catholic Convents'.

resulted in a rapid expansion of committees (local, provincial, national and international) and reporting necessary to communicate decision-making. Here I encountered Eric Hobsbawm's 'unmanageable excess of primary sources' and a degree of sifting and targeted reading was necessary.[22] Much of the extant documentary evidence, correspondence, instructions, questionnaires and reports were generated from the central motherhouse. These institutional materials were offset by sources from individual convent archives that included house diaries, newsletters or correspondence that reflected local responses and the interaction between the centre and the periphery. Autonomous communities contained similar material, though on a smaller scale. They also often liaised with those outside their monastery via correspondence with ecclesiastical officials and local, national and international leaders of their religious family. Diocesan archives across Britain also provided rich material. Bishops and clergy responded and advised on both personal and canonical issues. I was also privileged to have access to personal archives, which offered candid insights, through family letters and spiritual notebooks. Also consulted were the various papal encyclicals and most importantly the sixteen documents that came out of the Second Vatican Council that were the impetus to these changes to religious life. The emergent industry of religious life studies became an important source too. The growing numbers of memoirs by religious and former religious from the 1940s exploded into the 1970s and 1980s with more theologically, spiritually or sociologically infused works focused on the disruption of and new opportunities for religious life. Print and television media played an increasingly important role in disseminating news of religious life. Reporting in Catholic newspapers such as *The Tablet*, *The Universe*, the *Catholic Herald* and the *Catholic Pictorial* revealed both excitement and discomfort at unfolding developments. Editorials and correspondence columns offered a public space to air emotive reactions from laity and religious. Other Catholic monthly publications such as *Blackfriars*, *Doctrine and Life* and *Review for Religious* offered more theological reflections on a changing Catholic world. This was not simply an insular Catholic development. The Second Vatican Council was enacted on a world stage – its aftershocks were of interest to a mass public. Religious life and its reframing proved to be a magnet for the local and national press too, with visual displays of vocations exhibitions and nuns in 'short skirts' providing newsworthy copy from the 1950s. Despite

22   E. J. Hobsbawm, 'The Present as History: Writing the History of One's Own Times', Creighton Lecture, University of London, 1993, pp. 17–18.

the competing social movements of the long 1960s, religious life was also an extraordinary feature of the 'radical sixties'.

Documents do not tell us everything we need to know about the past, though they often identify events, official decision-making and institutional ideologies. The 'turn to self' which legitimated (in some circles) the engagement with life stories (particular autobiography and oral history) in academic studies has been influential to scholars working on cohorts marginalised or missing from documentary sources. Oral histories can transfer focus from the institution and the 'exceptional' (founders or leaders) to the 'ordinary' individual. The vast majority of the sisters and nuns in Britain today entered religious life in the 1950s and 1960s and went through a period of profound personal and institutional change.[23] Many interviewees initially claimed an ordinariness that suggested I was mistaken in interviewing them. These were precisely the women who often leave very little trace in archival documents and whose oral testimonies reflect lived and subjective experiences that complicate an institutional top-down narrative which identified a sense of progress seemingly implicit in the renewal of religious life.[24]

Oral testimonies have multiple layers. To focus on subjectivities, the meanings, emotions and attitudes so central to the construction of self, requires being alert to more than just the 'facts'.[25] Interview narratives reflect a re-envisioned life history. These stories are embedded in each individual's personal background, developed first from the formative experiences as children, then of their religious life, especially their novitiate, and also their experiences as professed religious in the pre- and post-conciliar world. Some self-reflections appeared spontaneous and unexpected even to the narrator. Others sounded well rehearsed; perhaps they had been planned out or told to other audiences. The narrator's relationship with the wider social and cultural discourses is present in the selection and omission of stories within their narrative and can reflect the need for composure. Being alert to coherent and comfortable stories is important to considering meanings and discursive origins.[26]

23   Compass Project, 'Religious Life in England and Wales' published by the National Office for Vocation of the Roman Catholic Church in England (2010).

24   Some interviewees have agreed to make their oral audiorecordings available to a wider public as part of the British Library Life History collection.

25   Alessandro Portelli, 'The Peculiarities of Oral History', *History Workshop Journal*, 12 (1981), 96–107.

26   Lynn Abrams, *Oral History Theory* (London: Routledge, 2010), pp. 41–2, 67; Lynn Abrams, 'Liberating the Female Self: Epiphanies, Conflict and Coherence in the Life Stories of Post-War British Women', *Social History*, 39 (2014), 14–35.

Individual memory is influenced by its relationship to a transient cultural world. Cultural historian Alessandro Portelli reminds us: 'Oral sources tell us not just what people did, but what they wanted to do, what they believed they were doing, and what they now think they did.'[27] The world of sisters and nuns was one where self-examination was an integral feature of a disciplined, spiritual religious life and introspection became even more commonplace for women religious by the 1970s as psychoanalysis developed into an important means of making sense of the disruption many faced. Teasing apart these layers allowed me a glimpse into women-centred communities and the 'social and material framework within which they operated, the perceived choices and cultural patterns they faced, and the complex relationship between individual consciousness and culture.'[28] Religious life is a relational life and oral history provides a relational means for exploring how women religious explained, rationalised and made sense of their past. As one of the catalysts of oral history, Alistair Thomson, has recognised, oral history is not simply 'the voice of the past' but it is 'a living record of the complex interaction between past and present within each individual and in society.'[29] The stories women religious told had been influenced not only by their lived experience but by the intervening years of workshops and seminars, reading and discussions of religious life. Representations of women religious in popular culture such as film, television and media influenced memories also. Rebecca Sullivan has argued that American filmmakers drew on contemporary issues which suggested both elements of radicalism and traditionalism.[30] Films such as *The Nun's Story* (1959), *The Sound of Music* (1965) and *In This House of Brede* (1975) were featured on the big screen. Television series such as *The Flying Nun* (1967–1970) invited substantial interest. These sources not only added women's voices

27   Alessandro Portelli, *The Death of Luigi Trastulli and Other Stories: Form and Meaning in Oral History* (New York: State University of New York Press, 1991), p. 50.

28   Joan Sangster, 'Telling Our Stories: Feminist Debates and the Use of Oral History', *Women's History Review*, 3 (1994), 6.

29   Alistair Thomson, 'Unreliable Memories? The Use and Abuse of Oral History', in William Lamont (ed.), *Historical Controversies and Historians* (London: UCL Press, 1998), p. 28.

30   Rebecca Sullivan, 'Celluloid Sisters: Femininity, Religiosity, and the Postwar American Nun Film', *Velvet Light Trap*, 46 (2000), 56; see also, Penny Summerfield, 'Public Memory or Public Amnesia? British Women of the Second World War in Popular Films of the 1950s and 1960s', *Journal of British Studies*, 48 (2009), 935–57. For more on representations of women religious in films see Maureen Sabine, *Veiled Desires: Intimate Portrayals of Nuns in Postwar Anglo-American Film* (New York: Fordham University Press, 2013).

to social and cultural histories but also influenced the project's research agenda. The chapter themes of *Catholic Nuns and Sisters in a Secular Age* come out of many hours of conversations and the narrators' emphasis on the relational nature of religious life.

My own subjectivity was relevant too; as was my insider/outsider status. The intersubjectivity that results from my interaction with each narrator created a unique oral testimony. My outsider status was evident on numerous levels: as an academic, as a married woman and as a foreigner easily identified by an American accent. But in some respects I was an insider also. I was known to many archivists and religious. I began doing research on nineteenth-century religious life in 2000 and throughout my PhD and subsequent research I had on numerous occasions interacted with women religious in their convent archives and refectories, kitchens and sitting rooms where they offered me tea and biscuits and generously answered my many queries. Some of the sisters I had met on previous archive visits agreed to be interviewed. My positionality was linked to my professional relationships with archivists and sisters through my past research on nineteenth-century religious life. The stories I was told were dependent on intersubjectivities, positionalities and interpersonal dynamics and as such, can only be a partial history.[31]

It is subjectivity that gives oral sources value, but also leaves them open to questions of the reliability, authenticity and representativeness of memory, which suggests infallibility, inaccuracy and bias (as do other source types).[32] Methodological challenges include memories of a 'golden age', the meanings of discrepancies, uncertainties about dates and forgetfulness of events. To address these issues, scholars have urged a rethinking of oral testimony. Rather than testimony being simply a source of factual statements, it can be considered as an 'expression and representation of culture' which includes 'dimensions of memory, ideology and subconscious desires'.[33] Taking into account the implications of silences is important too. These elements of 'subjective reality' are useful to thinking through the diverse ways in which social change was recognised and received, and to consider their contemporary resonance.

31 For more discussions on intersubjectivities see Penny Summerfield, 'Dis/Composing the Subject: Intersubjectivities in Oral History', in Tess Cosslett, Celia Lury and Penny Summerfield (eds), *Feminism and Autobiography* (London: Routledge, 2000), pp. 91–106.

32 The same can be said, of course, of documentary sources.

33 Luisa Passerini, 'Work Ideology and Consensus under Italian Fascism', *History Workshop Journal*, 8 (1979), 84, 86.

The communities in which women religious lived were institutional as well as social cultures, with a strong, explicit corporate identity often related to an institute's charism and the story of the institution's founding and founder.[34] A religious institute's functional objectives, such as teaching or nursing, or praying the Divine Office also influenced corporate identity. Women's religious institutes were very conscious mnemonic communities, communities that influenced individual socialisation. The formal socialisation process, that training period of religious life (the postulancy and novitiate) was rigorous.[35] Religious communities as commemorative communities were linked to historical traditions, customs and myths.[36] As such, communities created a shared collective memory transmitted from sister to sister, highlighting selectively features of their past.[37] Maurice Halbwachs argued that 'The individual calls recollections to mind by relying on the frameworks of social memory.'[38] These frameworks provided a means of identifying with a version of the religious institute's collective and corporate past. For example, the foundation story was often linked to the identity of a religious institute, used to build community and influence its self-perception. Collective memory was experiential but is also linked to the historicising of the past. It provided a means of uniting individuals and creating cohesive communities with a very specific corporate identity.

34 Charism is often understood as a gift given by God through the Holy Spirit to a founder of a religious institute that orients its activities of building up the church to a particular spiritual emphasis. Margaret Susan Thompson, '"Charism" or "Deep Story"? Toward a Clearer Understanding of the Growth of Women's Religious Life in Nineteenth-Century America', *Review for Religious*, 28 (1999), 230–50.

35 Until the 1960s, most women went through a two-part formation process, first as a postulant then as a novice, with each stage punctuated by milestones celebrated by ceremonies. After six months to a year as a postulant, women were clothed with a religious habit. They then entered the novitiate, undergoing a second phase of formation which lasted one to two years; then took their first vows. After this, they operated as 'young professed' for two to three years until they took their final vows. The stages of this process varied over time and according to the religious institute.

36 Monteiro, Derks and Van Heijst have argued that within some Dutch religious communities, foundation stories were reinterpreted and remade in the 1960s becoming ahistorical in the process. Monteiro *et al.*, 'The Stories the Religious Have Lived by', pp. 235–6.

37 Jan Assman, 'Collective Memory and Cultural Identity', *New German Critique*, 65 (1995), 125–33; Michael G. Kenny, 'A Place for Memory: The Interface between Individual and Collective History', *Comparative Studies in Society and History*, 41 (1999), 421.

38 Lewis A. Coser (ed.), *Maurice Halbwachs on Collective Memory* (Chicago: University of Chicago Press, 1992 [1952]), p. 182.

Despite the prominence of collective memory, individual memory remained influential, particularly to the cohort being interviewed. Interviews often pointed to different and conflicting meanings rather than generalisable experiences.

Interview cohort

In popular understanding, two forms of religious life stand out: enclosed contemplative (sometimes monastic) religious orders and active (now more often called apostolic) religious congregations. Enclosed religious orders such as Benedictines, Bridgettines and Poor Clares through their recitation of the Divine Office offered prayers for the Church and the world. The nuns residing in these typically autonomous communities were enclosed, and women resided and typically remained attached to one monastic home. Religious congregations evolved from the seventeenth century to work in the mission field at home or abroad. Their form of prayer was active: their aim was to catechise and this often required movement outside the enclosure. Sisters from congregations such as the Sisters of Mercy or the Institute of the Blessed Virgin Mary[39] taught, nursed or provided forms of social welfare outside the cloister. They had more freedom of movement than contemplative nuns but they also embraced some rules of enclosure. Some groups like the Augustinian Canonesses of the Holy Sepulchre and the Society of the Sacred Heart self-identified more with the 'mixed life', where they followed rules of enclosure, prayed the Divine Office and taught in schools. Many congregations, such as the Religious of La Retraite or the Sisters of Charity of Our Lady, Mother of Mercy, became very large, centralised and international congregations. Then as now, the differences between these categories of religious life were in many ways constructed. Some enclosed nuns have 'active' apostolates such as retreat-giving or hospitality and they now have more leeway to leave the cloister to attend meetings, retreats and seminars. Active sisters often have a significant contemplative life. In many ways

---

39 This congregation has operated under a number of names. In 1609, Englishwoman Mary Ward founded the congregation that became known as the Institute of English Ladies on the continent. In the nineteenth century, the congregation was based in York and called itself the Institute of the Blessed Virgin Mary, which was the name under which it received its final approbation by Rome in 1877. In 2004, in honour of Mary Ward's founding vision, the Roman branch of the congregation was renamed the Congregation of Jesus.

women religious all live a 'mixed life' if we think of religious life on a spectrum with 'contemplation' on one end and 'action' on the other.

The nine international women's religious institutes named above agreed to participate in this project.[40] Table 0.1 suggests some of the diversity of these religious institutes, in terms of enclosure, apostolate, place of foundation and governance. There is no representative form of religious life, and the value of this selection of case studies is reflected in its diversity.

The selection process of interviewees was not completely under my direct control. Once approval was given by the leadership team of the religious institute, I offered to interview any of its members. The offer was often communicated via the archivist or the leadership committee through correspondence or internal publications. Any sisters and nuns who contacted me had self-selected, and I interviewed every volunteer.[41] Though some of the women religious had been community leaders, most were 'ordinary' nuns and sisters. Interviews took place throughout England, typically in the sister's residence. Table 0.2 identifies the date of entry of the cohort of participants. It is important to note, given the majority of interviewees entered in the 1950s and 1960s, that the narrators were (in the main) not leaders and decision-makers during the tumultuous time of renewal. I also interviewed some former religious. I had initially planned to interview a larger group of women who had left religious life, but due to time constraints this proved logistically difficult. Four former religious were interviewed; their interview questions were identical to those asked of current sisters and nuns and thus were focused on the changing dimensions of religious life rather than why they left. The women religious interviewed were born in England, Ireland and Scotland. The nature of religious life is such that women religious were often transferred or relocated from one convent to another irrespective of national boundaries. Many of the Irish-born sisters entered religious life in England or Scotland and worked in England exclusively. This research does not examine the significance of national identities in religious life. It is a specifically British history as the religious institutes studied were

40 I approached three other religious institutes for this project, they were unable to participate.
41 The interviews with the sisters who entered in the 1990s and 2000s provided me with important context for writing the conclusion. However, these interviews have not been included in the demographic profiles discussed in this section as they were technically outside the temporal remit of this work.

Table 0.1 Religious institutes used as case studies

Religious institute	Foundation date	Founded in	Type	Date of first foundation in Britain	Primary ministry in 1960s	Community structure	Motherhouse
Poor Clares (OSC)[a]	1212	Assisi	enclosed	1795	Divine Office	autonomous	n/a
Bridgettines of Syon Abbey (OssS)	1415	Middlesex	enclosed	1415	Divine Office	autonomous	n/a
Benedictines of Stanbrook (OSB)	1623	Cambrai, Flanders	enclosed	1838	Divine Office	autonomous	n/a
Canonesses of the Holy Sepulchre (CRSS)	1642	Liège	mixed	1794	Divine Office; education	autonomous	n/a
Congregation of La Retraite (RLR)	1678	Brittany	active	1880	education; retreat work	centralised	Belgium
Sisters of Mercy (RSM)[b]	1831	Ireland	active	1839	education; nursing; social welfare	autonomous	n/a

Institute of the Blessed Virgin Mary (IBVM)[c]	1609	St Omer, Flanders	active	1669	education	centralised from 1953	Rome
Society of the Sacred Heart (RSCJ)	1800	France	mixed	1842	education	centralised	France
Sisters of Charity of Our Lady, Mother of Mercy (SCMM)	1832	Netherlands	active	1861	nursing; social welfare	centralised	Netherlands

Notes

a The Poor Clares operate as autonomous communities. Nuns from five communities were interviewed (Much Birch, York, Arundel, Lynton, Hollington).

b The Sisters of Mercy in Britain were originally autonomous convents. They are now organised into amalgamations. Sisters interviewed belonged to the Institute of Our Lady of Mercy and Sisters of Mercy of the Union of Great Britain.

c Renamed the Congregation of Jesus in 2002.

Table 0.2 Participants interviewed, decade of entry

Religious institute	Total interviewed	Decade of entry as postulant					
		1930s	1940s	1950s	1960s	1970s	1980s
Poor Clares	14		2	4	4	1	3
Bridgettines of Syon Abbey	1			1			
Benedictines of Stanbrook	4			1	1	1	1
Augustinian Canonesses of the Holy Sepulchre	17		3	4	4	3	3
Religious of La Retraite	3			3			
Sisters of Mercy	13		2	7	4		
Institute of the Blessed Virgin Mary	12		3	3	5	1	
Society of the Sacred Heart	17	1	4	4	7	1	
Totals	**81**	**1**	**14**	**27**	**25**	**7**	**7**
Percentage	*100*	*1*	*17*	*33*	*31*	*9*	*9*

located in England, Wales and Scotland; however, not all participants would have identified as British.[42]

The stories I heard were intensely personal and sometimes emotive, and some participants wished to remain anonymous so all the oral narratives have been anonymised for consistency, though in some cases (and with permission) I have identified the religious institute to which a narrator belonged.

I have used a life-cycle approach in order to acknowledge the significance of the larger context of these women's lives, not simply their lives in religion, but also their lives before entering and, in some cases, after leaving religious life. I introduced religion early on, asking about their experience of faith within their family. I had in front of me a menu

---

42 For more on the challenges of four nations histories see Naomi Lloyd-Jones and Margaret M. Scull, 'A New Plea for an Old Subject? Four Nations History for the Modern Period', in Naomi Lloyd-Jones and Margaret M. Scull (eds), *Four Nations Approaches to Modern 'British' History: A (Dis)United Kingdom?* (London: Palgrave Macmillan, 2018), pp. 3–31.

of questions, but allowed the interview to flow as the narrator wished. If prompts were needed to move things along, I gave them. I often let the narrator speak, interjecting only to further explore what had been said, or at an appropriate pause, taking the sister back to obtain more clarification on a particular episode in her life.

The interplay between the archival material and the oral histories allowed a deeper understanding of the lived experience of religious life to emerge. In combining documentary sources with personal narratives I was able to delve more deeply to explore the social changes negotiated by women religious in the period after the Second World War.[43] In keeping with Robert Orsi's work on 'lived religion', this methodology engages with the phenomenologically empiricist world of *doing* religious life.[44] The lived experience under examination is the quotidian of their daily lives: this includes the everyday practices of governance and hierarchy, relationships within and without the community, experiences of religious ministry; interactions with the modern world (where the interior meets the exterior) and becoming a woman. This approach tells us much about personal agency whilst acknowledging the messiness and subjectivity of identities. It also allows an interrogation of the nature of social movements, and the changing collective identity of women religious as they redefined their common interests and aims. These sources and methodologies allow this work to benefit from both the empirical and the experiential.

Themes

This work is grounded and linked by three core premises: women religious were influenced by and participated in the wider social movements of the long 1960s; women's religious institutes were transnational entities and part of a larger global happening; and the struggles of renewal were linked to competing and contradictory ideas of collective, institutional identities.

Social movements

Most of the women religious that contributed to this project lived through the transforming post-war British world of the 1940s and

43   Joan W. Scott, 'The Evidence of Experience', *Critical Inquiry*, 17 (1991), 773–97.
44   Robert Orsi, 'Everyday Miracles: The Study of Lived Religion', in David D. Hall (ed.), *Lived Religion in America: Toward a History of Practice* (Princeton, NJ: Princeton University Press, 1997), p. 7.

1950s and the social movements that have become emblematic of the long 1960s. They travelled from the ideological mentality of the 'fortress church' of the 1940s and 1950s to a more visible global church, particularly after the Second Vatican Council. They were a part of the social movements of their time, but also participated in their own social movement. Scholars of women's social movements argue that female-led movements exist when women organise 'as women' to make social change.[45] Social movements come out of the frustrations of current conditions and a shared belief that change is necessary.[46] Vowed religious life has a place in the larger social movements of the 1960s that fought for personal emancipation and participatory democracy and wrestled with social repression and the limitations of authoritative, hierarchical structures. Women religious experimented with alternative modes of living religious life when traditional ways did not seem to fit into a changing world. Though renewal was initiated from the top down at the request of the Holy See, women religious at all levels engaged with social change; some encouraged it, others obstructed it and countless were acquiescent. Like most social movements, there were periods of social and cultural disjuncture and sometimes schism. Many voiced their grievances and collectively (though not unanimously) charted forms of action that included, for some, leaving religious life. Collaborations occurred at all levels: in individual communities, at the provincial level and in the international motherhouse. Women's religious institutes began the process of renewing corporate structures and via them, religious identities. This work examines the changes in women's religious life as a women's social movement and questions how it developed within a specific social, cultural and religious milieu.[47]

45 Myra Marx Ferree and Carol McClurg Mueller, 'Feminism and the Women's Movement: A Global Perspective', in David A. Snow, Sarah A. Soule and Hanspeter Kriesi (eds), *The Blackwell Companion to Social Movements* (Chichester: John Wiley & Sons, 2008), p. 577.

46 Donatella della Porta and Mario Diani, *Social Movements: An Introduction* (Oxford: Blackwell, 1999), p. 4.

47 'New monastic movements' (for example the Community of St John or Franciscan Sisters of the Renewal) founded from 1960s are not within the remit of this book. Angela A. Aidala, 'Social Change, Gender Roles, and New Religious Movements', *Sociological Analysis*, 46 (1985), 287–314; Joanna Gilbert, 'Young People in Search of Religious Vocation', in Gemma Simmonds, CJ (ed), *A Future Full of Hope?* (Dublin: The Columba Press, 2012), pp. 92–105.

Transnationalism

Religious institutes operated within a globalising world. Examining the changes in religious life with an exclusively national lens is artificial and ignores the international ties that linked women religious. This social movement needs to be analysed in a transnational perspective, highlighting connections, transfers and reception of ideas between women of different cultural and national backgrounds within the same religious institutes. Understanding the 'movements and forces that cut across national boundaries', to use theorist Akira Iriye's definition of transnationalism,[48] is important for understanding the changes in religious life. The empirical and experiential details coming out of the documents and the oral testimonies lent themselves to a transnational approach. From the beginning of this project, the links between motherhouse, sisterhouses and daughterhouses at home and abroad were relevant. Even enclosed orders, often holding tight to their autonomy, made links with communities within their religious families in other national contexts. These links grew stronger over time. This work pays close attention to the places where transnational communities intersected at a time of great social change. Transnational history reflects cross-national influences, and the questions I ask are intended to illuminate just how the relationship between ideals and praxis (how religious life was enacted, practised, embodied and/or realised) functioned across national borders and the ways that praxis might be mediated by particular cultural contexts.

Identities

Women's religious institutes rethought sometimes centuries of shared beliefs and practices, redefining and renewing religious identities. The traditional role of religious sister and nun into which many women had been socialised failed to make sense within an emerging socio-cultural modernity that reflected a secular age. Not all felt this way, some clung to the socialisation that had formed them and had given them a life-giving corporate identity that extolled a uniformity, lived internally and externally, with the religious institute to which they belonged. It was a uniformity that was intended to suppress others identities of social class, ethnicity, family, gender and sexuality. A shared identity remained

48   Akira Iriye, 'Transnational History', *Contemporary European History*, 13 (2004), 213.

essential to religious life,[49] but uniformity became out of place within the processes of renewal and adaptation to a modern world.

Interlinking worlds: post-war Britain, Catholics, Vatican II

Much of the material in the upcoming chapters, because of the international and transnational nature of religious life, will resonate with historians of women religious from other national contexts. However, this research is grounded in a particular British context and contextualises the changing dimensions of women's religious life in Britain within the historiographies of post-war Britain, Catholicism in Britain and the Second Vatican Council, exploring how religious bodies engaged in modernisation and reinvigorated (or not) their global presence. The aftermath of the Second World War led to a slow and cautious reconstruction, an austerity Britain with rationing and queues and the introduction of the welfare state. Full employment, growing affluence, youth culture, educational opportunities and increased mobility became emblematic of 'progress' after the more ascetic war years. This new world order was celebrated by Harold Macmillan's 'most of our people have never had it so good' in 1957.[50] Women's lives changed. Young and old were integral to the work force and war efforts. Waged work was plentiful for most young women in the 1950s, and though typically interrupted by motherhood, work was often returned to in later life.[51] Women religious were a part of this world. Many of the women who entered religious life after the war had experience of waged employment; as religious, they acknowledged women's waged work was important while still promoting the 'greatest work' of motherhood.[52] Though women's suffrage was achieved in 1928, rectifying social, economic and political inequalities remained on the agenda of both feminist and non-feminist organisations. Women's groups were actively involved in efforts to improve

49   Verta Taylor and Nancy E. Whittier, 'Collective Identity in Social Movement Communities: Lesbian Feminist Mobilization', in Aldon D. Morris and Carol McClurg Mueller (eds), *Frontiers in Social Movement Theory* (New Haven, CT: Yale University Press, 1992), pp. 104–29.

50   Peter Hennessy, *Having It So Good: Britain in the Fifties* (London: Allen Lane, 2007), p. 1. The 'most' in this phrasing is telling. Macmillan goes on to say in this speech that not everyone was sharing in this prosperity.

51   Bill Osgerby, *Youth in Britain since 1945* (Oxford: Blackwell, 1997), p. 52; Selina Todd, *Young Women, Work, and Family in England 1918–1950* (Oxford: Oxford University Press, 2005), p. 52.

52   Sister Mary Laurence, OP, *Nuns are Real People* (London: Blackfriars Publications, 1955), p. 8; 'The Successful Woman', *Poor Soul's Friend*, 9:5 (1961), p. 137.

equitable access to state pensions, health care, family allowances, improved housing and maternity services. Conservative organisations, both religious and secular, also played a role in enhancing women's lives even without an explicit link to feminism.[53] Religion was relevant to and influenced by the post-war world. Hugh McLeod points to a national Christian identity that both the Second World War and the Cold War encouraged in Western nations. He highlights continued church-building, Christian socialisation in schools and confessional identities into the 1960s.[54] Church attendance, though, was declining; this religious world appeared in competition with an affluent 1950s and 1960s culture and its materialistic world of leisure and consumerism.[55]

The narratives of the 1950s as a time of prosperity and social cohesion stand in marked contrast to the popular tales of social change and generational dissonance of the 1960s. Arthur Marwick's influential tome *The Sixties: Cultural Revolution in Britain, France, Italy, and the United States, c. 1958–c.1974* (1998) argues that:

> [M]inor and rather insignificant movements in the fifties became major and highly significant ones in the sixties; that intangible ideas in the fifties became powerful practicalities in the sixties; that the sixties were characterised by the vast number of innovative activities taking place simultaneously, by unprecedented interaction and acceleration.[56]

He cites numerous examples of major movements, including youth culture, consumerism, civil rights, women's liberation and gay rights. However, more recent scholarship about the 1950s has challenged this vision of a 'radical sixties', emphasising more continuities than ruptures with the 1950s and the 1970s.[57] Religion is often ignored in this historiography; Marwick

---

53 Caitríona Beaumont, *Housewives and Citizens: Domesticity and the Women's Movement in England, 1928–64* (Manchester: Manchester University Press, 2013); Maggie Andrews, *The Acceptable Face of Feminism: The Women's Institute as a Social Movement* (London: Lawrence and Wishart, 1997).
54 Hugh McLeod, *The Religious Crisis of the 1960s* (Oxford: Oxford University Press, 2007), p. 59.
55 Callum G. Brown, *Religion and the Demographic Revolution: Women and Secularisation in Canada, Ireland, UK and USA since the 1960s* (Woodbridge: Boydell Press, 2012), p. 220.
56 Marwick, *The Sixties*, p. 7.
57 Heiko Feldner, Clare Gorrara and Kevin Passmore (eds), *The Lost Decade? The 1950s in European History, Politics, Society and Culture* (Newcastle upon Tyne: Cambridge Scholars Press, 2011), p. 2. See also N. Thomas, 'Will the Real 1950s Please Stand Up? Views of a Contradictory Decade', *Cultural and Social History*, 5:2 (2008), 227–8; Selina Todd and Hilary Young, 'Baby-Boomers to "Beanstalkers" Making the

along with many feminist historiographies had little sympathy for religion in their rendition of the radical 1960s.[58] Marwick claims that religion, though an 'important force' behind some movements, was ultimately obstructionist to 'new thinking and freer lifestyles'.[59] Yet Catholicism had its own sphere of progressive activism. Scholars Gerd-Rainer Horn and Emmanuel Gerard have demonstrated in *Left Catholicism* how a 'brief flowering' of the Catholic left in the 1940s and 1950s became a 'powerful challenge' that influenced European society and politics.[60] Such political involvement grounded by theology and ministry is also entrenched in Horn's *The Spirit of Vatican II*, which situates Europe's liberal Catholicism within the long 1960s.[61] These works address the politicisation and radicalisation of Catholics, particular Catholic laity and clergy, but hardly acknowledge the efforts of male and female religious.[62] In addition, this 'Europe' often does not include Britain.

A 'secular age' is often discussed as a by-product of the radical 1960s, and secularisation dominates the histories of religion of post-war Britain.[63] In his interpretation of Rowntree and Lavers's study, historian Alan D. Gilbert finds a continuity of belief but a 'negligible commitment coupled with a nominal acceptance of prevailing belief and social

---

Modern Teenager in Post-War Britain', *Cultural and Social History*, 9 (2012), 451–67; Gillian A. M. Mitchell, 'Reassessing "the Generation Gap": Bill Haley's 1957 Tour of Britain, Inter-Generational Relations and Attitudes to Rock "n" Roll in the Late 1950s', *Twentieth Century British History*, 24 (2013), 573–605.

58   Weaver, *New Catholic Women*, p. x.

59   Marwick, *The Sixties*, p. 34.

60   Gerd-Rainer Horn and Emmanuel Gerard (eds), *Left Catholicism 1943–1955: Catholics and Society in Western Europe at the Point of Liberation* (Leuven: Leuven University Press, 2001), p. 14; See also Martin Conway's chapter in this volume, 'Left Catholicism in Europe in the 1940s: Elements of an Interpretation', p. 278.

61   Gerd-Rainer Horn, *The Spirit of Vatican II: Western European Progressive Catholicism in the Long Sixties* (Oxford: Oxford University Press, 2015). Jay P. Corrin's work *Catholic Progressives in England after Vatican II* (Notre Dame, IN: University of Notre Dame Press, 2013) discusses the less influential politics of the English Catholic left movements. Belinda Davis also briefly mentions the influence of Catholicism on women's movements in 'What's Left? Popular Political Participation in Postwar Europe', *American Historical Review*, 113 (2008), 377.

62   McLeod, *The Religious Crisis of the 1960s*, pp. 141–60; see also Horn and Gerard, *Left Catholicism*, p. 43; Gerd-Rainer Horn, *The Spirit of '68: Rebellion in Western Europe and North America, 1956–1976* (Oxford: Oxford University Press, 2007), pp. 74–92; Horn, *The Spirit of Vatican II*; and Corrin, *Catholic Progressives*.

63   Steve Bruce, *Religion in Modern Britain* (Oxford: Oxford University Press, 1995); Steve Bruce (ed.), *Religion and Modernisation: Sociologists and Historians Debate the Secularization Thesis* (Oxford: Oxford University Press, 1992).

habits'.[64] One of the dominant voices in the debate, Callum Brown, made the connection between gender and secularisation central to his study, *The Death of Christian Britain* (2001), contentiously arguing that women 'broke their relationship to Christian piety in the 1960s and thereby caused secularisation'.[65] Hugh McLeod's investigation of the 'religious crisis' of the 1960s contends that church association remained strong into the 1970s, though church attendance and membership of church youth groups declined.[66] Scholars have questioned the dominance of the secularisation thesis. Religious issues were 'hotly and enthusiastically debated' and rebels and nonconformists had influence out of proportion with their numbers.[67] Grace Davie in her work questions the methods of measuring religiosity.[68] More recently, the contributors to *Redefining Christian Britain: Post-1945 Perspectives* argue that scholars need different lenses from which to measure modern Christian dynamism, moving away from statistics of decline to examining Christianity's transformation and its continued cultural influence.[69] Timothy Jones's intervention suggests the 'teleology of decline' may be a Eurocentric norm rather than a global standard and considers a post-secular view that returns to considering religion as a category of analysis and asking, as this research does, new questions of religious change.[70] Secularisation

64 Alan D. Gilbert, *The Making of Post-Christian Britain: A History of the Secularization of Modern Society* (London: Longman, 1980), p. 122. B. Seebohm Rowntree and G. R. Lavers, *English Life and Leisure* (London: Longman, Greens and Co, 1951).

65 Callum G. Brown, *The Death of Christian Britain: Understanding Secularisation, 1800–2000* (London: Routledge, 2001), pp. 10–13. Those who argue against his premise include Jeremy Morris, 'The Strange Death of Christian Britain: Another Look at the Secularization Debate', *Historical Journal*, 46 (2003), 963–76.

66 McLeod, *The Religious Crisis of the 1960s*, p. 59. Perhaps too, as Brewitt-Taylor argues, a discursively constructed secularisation was more influential. Sam Brewitt-Taylor, 'The Invention of a "Secular Society"? Christianity and the Sudden Appearance of Secularization Discourses in the British National Media, 1961–4', *Twentieth Century British History*, 24:3 (2013), 327–50.

67 Dominic Sandbrook, *White Heat: A History of Britain in the Swinging Sixties* (London: Little, Brown, 2006), p. 432; Hugh McLeod, 'The 1960s', in Ira Katznelson and Gareth Stedman Jones (eds), *Religion and the Political Imagination* (Cambridge: Cambridge University Press, 2010), p. 254.

68 Grace Davie, *Religion in Britain since 1945: Believing without Belonging* (Oxford: Blackwell, 1994).

69 Jane Garnett, Matthew Grimley, Alana Harris, William Whyte and Sarah Williams, *Redefining Christian Britain: Post-1945 Perspectives* (London: SCM Press, 2006), pp. 289, 291.

70 Timothy W. Jones, 'Postsecular Sex? Secularisation and Religious Change in the History of Sexuality in Britain', *History Compass*, 11 (2013), 919.

debates became a major discourse, in the Church, in the press and in universities. Women religious were operating in this secular age.

The twentieth-century Catholic world in Britain was deeply wedded to a tradition that espoused separateness and what has been called a 'fortress church' mentality.[71] This was a church that created an alternate infrastructure running in parallel with Protestant institutions (schools, social clubs, newspapers, etc.) in order to maintain its own moral authority and mandate conformity in belief and behaviour. Women religious were very complicit in this project of separation. However, what to outsiders may have appeared as a unified body was a complicated mix of ethnicities and social classes that did not always gel in matters of politics or practices of faith. Catholics in Britain characterised themselves with a range of identities: as 'recusant' Catholics; English, Irish, Scottish or Welsh Catholics; convert Catholics; and from the 1950s European and colonial immigrant Catholics. Social class divides were a part of this mix. The extent of this 'fortress church' can be debated, but there is little disagreement that the disintegration of a separate Catholic subculture was hastened after the Second World War.[72]

Catholicism remains almost invisible in post-war British histories. Social and cultural histories of the 1960s often ignore the developments of the local, national and global Catholic Church.[73] McLeod only briefly addresses the impact of the Second Vatican Council in *The Religious Crisis*, simply noting it was a vital catalyst to religious change more broadly.[74] Even explicitly Catholic histories skirt around the influence of the Second Vatican Council. Kester Aspden's *Fortress Church* is an ecclesial history that takes us only to 1963.[75] Editors V. Alan McClelland and Michael Hodgetts introduce a useful overview of 150 years of Catholicism in England but not one chapter focuses on the reception

---

71   Kester Aspden, *Fortress Church: The English Roman Catholic Bishops and Politics 1903–1963* (London: Gracewing, 2002); Michael P. Hornsby-Smith, *Roman Catholics in England: Studies in Social Structure since the Second World War* (Cambridge: Cambridge University Press, 1987), p. 21.

72   Corrin, *Catholic Progressives*, pp. 56–7; Hornsby-Smith, *Roman Catholics in England*, pp. 6–7.

73   There are some exceptions, including the Oxford-based project '1968: Activism, Networks, Trajectories'. www.history.ox.ac.uk/research/project/around-1968-activism-networks-trajectories.html, accessed 17 June 2014. See Robert Gildea, James Mark and Anette Warring (eds), *Europe's 1968: Voices of Revolt* (Oxford: Oxford University Press, 2013), pp. 231–2, which includes work on the Catholic worker-priest movement.

74   McLeod, *The Religious Crisis of the 1960s*, p. 10.

75   Aspden, *Fortress Church*.

of the Second Vatican Council.[76] Michael Hornsby-Smith's extensive
sociological interpretations offer the most sustained analysis of post-
war Catholic identities and of the extent of tradition and change.[77] It
is unfortunate that a robust lived history of the after-life of the Second
Vatican Council in any of the four nations in Britain has yet to be written.
There is progress though. James Hagerty's recent biography of Cardinal
John Carmel Heenan addresses many challenges faced by Heenan,
particularly those associated with the Second Vatican Council and its
reception in England.[78] Jay P. Corrin's *Catholic Progressives in England
after Vatican II* (2013) offers a much-needed spotlight on the Catholic
left.[79] David Geiringer's interventions on post-war Catholic religious
change suggest that Church authorities and Catholic laity engaged with
secular ideas and recategorisation of certain religious beliefs.[80] Alana
Harris's work on post-war Catholicism and the family utilises 'lived
experience' to explore the continuity within English Catholic cultures of
beliefs, devotional practices and identities.[81] Like many of these works,
Catholic Nuns and Sisters in a Secular Age connects with the social and
cultural context of the post-war British world and questions the 'rupture'
of the post-conciliar Catholic world.

The term *aggiornamento*, employed to signal an opening of windows
that let in fresh air, was the keyword behind the spirit of the Second
Vatican Council opened by Pope John XXIII (1881–1963) on 11 October

76 V. Alan McClelland and Michael Hodgetts (eds), *From without the Flaminian Gate: 150 Years of Roman Catholicism in England and Wales, 1850–2000* (London: Darton, Longman & Todd, 1999). Vatican II is mentioned in several chapters including the last one, entitled 'Faith in Crisis: From Holocaust to Hope, 1943–2000'.

77 For example, Hornsby-Smith, *Roman Catholics in England*; Michael P. Hornsby-Smith, *Roman Catholic Beliefs in England* (Cambridge: Cambridge University Press, 1991); Michael P. Hornsby-Smith (ed.), *Catholics in England 1950–2000: Historical and Sociological Perspectives* (London: Cassell, 1999).

78 James Hagerty, *Cardinal John Carmel Heenan: Priest of the People, Prince of the Church* (London: Gracewing, 2012).

79 Corrin, *Catholic Progressives*.

80 David Geiringer, '"At Some Point in the 1960s, Hell Disappeared": Hell, Gender and Catholicism in Post-War England', *Cultural and Social History*, 15 (2018), 1–17; David Geiringer, 'Catholic Understandings of Female Sexuality in 1960s Britain', *Twentieth Century British History*, 28 (2017), 209–38.

81 Alana Harris, *Faith in the Family: A Lived Religious History of English Catholicism, 1945–1982* (Manchester: Manchester University Press, 2013); Alana Harris, '"A Paradise on Earth, a Foretaste of Heaven": English Catholic Understandings of Domesticity and Marriage, 1945—65', in Lucy Delap, Ben Griffin and Abigail Wills (eds), *The Politics of Domestic Authority since 1800* (London: Palgrave Macmillan, 2009), 155–81.

1962.[82] He acceded to the pontificate in 1958, then aged 76, and was expected to be a caretaker pope who maintained the status quo. Instead, he called for a Council which began the movement to make Catholicism more relevant to the modern world. This was a pastoral council, concerned with ecclesiology and the nature and mission of the church. By the close of the Council on 8 December 1965, the primary published outputs of the council, sixteen decrees and encyclicals, had already begun to bring about changes in (amongst other things) liturgy; in the responsibilities of the laity and clergy; in relationships with other faith groups; in the role of an informed conscience in making moral decisions; in the revision of Canon Law; and, of course, in the lived experience of religious life. The interpretation of council documents changed the look and feel of Catholicism. These changes were enthusiastically welcomed by those who felt the Catholic Church had lost touch with the modern world, and disparaged by others who felt the changes went too far. The Council allowed the public discussion of issues that had previously been consigned to so-called 'progressive' Catholic circles.

Theologians have long dominated the conversation of the Second Vatican Council, with debates revolving around continuity and rupture.[83] Theologian and (at the time) Lutheran Richard John Neuhaus's reflection on the aftershocks of the Second Vatican Council twenty-five years after they had begun are as relevant today as they were in 1987: 'the contest over the interpretation of Vatican II constitutes a critical battlefront in our society's continuing cultural wars'.[84] The political and ideological conflicts over the interpretation of the Second Vatican Council remain deeply emotive and personal. Some like parish priest Dermot A. Lane saw Vatican II as 'a radical turning point in the self-understanding of the Catholic Church which included an embrace of the modern world, the initiation of a fresh dialogue between the Church and the world, a desire to bring about Christian unity among the Churches, and an appreciation of the value of other religions'.[85] Others found the concept of rupture

---

82 Pope John XXIII died within nine months of the opening of the council and newly elected Pope Paul VI took the helm on 21 June 1963.

83 The historiography of Vatican II is vast. For a summary of the historiographical debates see Faggioli, *Vatican II*. The most influential interpretations of the Second Vatican Council were published by the Bologna Group under the leadership of Giuseppe Alberigo in the magisterial five-volume *History of Vatican II* (the volumes were published from 1995 to 2006).

84 Neuhaus, *The Catholic Moment*, p. 61.

85 Dermot A. Lane, 'Vatican II: The Irish Experience', *The Furrow*, 55 (2004), 69.

dangerously erroneous and suggested Pope Benedict XVI's discourse of 'reform in continuity'.[86]

Research on female religious life by Susan O'Brien, Deirdre Raftery, Karly Kehoe, Caitriona Clear, Barbara Walsh and my own contributions addressed the agency and authority of women religious, highlighting their substantial role in the growth and dynamism of the nineteenth-century Church in Britain and Ireland.[87] The historiography of British and Irish women religious in the twentieth century is scant compared to that of North America and Europe.[88] Yvonne McKenna documents the lives of twentieth-century Irish women religious in *Made Holy: Irish Women Religious at Home and Abroad* (2006), which highlights identity, migration and diaspora and addresses the changes to religious life coming out of the Second Vatican Council in an Irish context.[89] A number of congregation-specific histories provide rich illustrations of the specificities of the responses to the Second Vatican Council.[90] The work of Susan O'Brien has been particularly valuable as it goes beyond the corporate activities of one religious institute to engage with

86 Matthew L. Lamb and Matthew Levering (eds), *Vatican II: Renewal within Tradition* (Oxford: Oxford University Press, 2008), p. 8.
87 Susan O'Brien, '"Terra Incognita": The Nun in Nineteenth-Century England', *Past and Present*, 121 (1988), 110–40; S. Karly Kehoe, *Creating a Scottish Church: Catholicism, Gender and Ethnicity in Nineteenth-Century Scotland* (Manchester: Manchester University Press, 2010); Barbara Walsh, *Roman Catholic Nuns in England and Wales, 1800–1937: A Social History* (Dublin: Irish Academic Press, 2002); Caitriona Clear, *Nuns in Nineteenth-Century Ireland* (Dublin: Gill and Macmillan, 1987); Deirdre Raftery, 'Rebels with a Cause: Obedience, Resistance and Convent Life, 1800–1940', *History of Education*, 42 (2013), 1–16.
88 Carol K. Coburn, 'An Overview of the Historiography of Women Religious: A Twenty-Five-Year Retrospective', *US Catholic Historian*, 22 (2004), 1–26. Some recent examples include Mary Beth Fraser Connolly, *Women of Faith: The Chicago Sisters of Mercy and the Evolution of a Religious Community* (New York: Fordham University Press, 2014); Barbra Mann Wall, *Into Africa: A Transnational History of Catholic Medical Missions and Social Change* (London: Rutgers University Press, 2015); Jazon Zuidema (ed.), *Understanding the Consecrated Life in Canada: Critical Essays on Contemporary Trends* (Waterloo: Wilfrid Laurier University Press, 2015); Rosa Bruno-Jofré, Heidi McDonald and Elizabeth Smyth, *Vatican II and Beyond: The Changing Mission and Identity of Canadian Women Religious* (Toronto: McGill-Queen's University Press, 2017).
89 Yvonne McKenna, *Made Holy: Irish Women Religious at Home and Abroad* (Dublin: Irish Academic Press, 2006).
90 Mary Lyons, *Governance Structures of the Congregation of the Sisters of Mercy: Becoming One* (Lampeter: Edwin Mellen Press, 2005); Louise O'Reilly, *The Impact of Vatican II on Women Religious: Case Study of the Union of Irish Presentation Sisters* (Newcastle upon Tyne: Cambridge Scholars Publishing, 2013); Anselm Nye, *A Peculiar Kind of Mission: The English Dominican Sisters, 1845–2010* (Leominster: Gracewing, 2011).

both the theological and the wider transnational and social context.[91] Fifty years on from 'the beginning of the beginning' of *aggiornamento*, the experiential outcomes of the Council still need to be addressed, particularly in the British context.[92] Alana Harris by examining the lived religious experiences of English Catholic devotional life has begun this work.[93] *Catholic Nuns and Sisters in a Secular Age* joins this experiential bandwagon with its focus on women religious.

Structure

This brief summary of the histories and historiographies in which the research is situated suggests several points. First, that scholars are far more interested in secularisation than they are in matters of religious belief and religious responses to the social movements of the 1960s. Second, that the history of social movements of the long 1960s is rarely gendered. Third, that Church and Catholic historians focus more on institutional than experiential matters. *Catholic Nuns and Sisters in a Secular Age* embeds the history of women religious within the social movements of the long 1960s, informing this historiography with a Catholic and women-centred study. Decentring these traditional historiographies of the 1960s disrupts the usual scripts of social and cultural transformations that are male and secular. It is time to add to the past studies of a centrist and bureaucratised church by investigating the convolutions of the living church. By examining the lives of women religious in the period 1945 to 1990, we can reflect on the continuities and discontinuities of lived religious life. This work suggests these changes in religious life in Britain were more evolutionary than revolutionary; modest experiments of the 1940s and 1950s informed the post-conciliar experiments that were ongoing through to the 1980s and suggest a longer time frame for the implementation of changes in religious life. *Catholic Nuns and Sisters in a Secular Age* tells the complicated story of post-war Catholic women religious in a nuanced way, acknowledging that though women religious grounded their experiments in the need for authenticity, such authenticity was always contested.

91 Susan O'Brien, *Leaving God for God: The Daughters Charity of St Vincent de Paul in Britain, 1847–2017* (London: Darton, Longman & Todd, 2017); Anselm Nye, *A Peculiar Kind of Mission: The English Dominican Sisters, 1845–2010* (London: Gracewing, 2013).
92 Karl Rahner, *The Church after the Council* (New York: Herder and Herder, 1966), p. 20.
93 Harris, *Faith in the Family*.

Chapter 1 provides a snapshot of the Catholic Church engaging with the modern world in the 1940s and 1950s. It looks at both the global and the national church and is in part the backstory to the remaining chapters, asserting a significant prehistory to the Second Vatican Council as it pertains to religious life. It surveys young women's place in the modern world of the 1940s and 1950s, considering their opportunities and their decision to enter religious life through an analysis of the 'vocation story'. It links the specificities of their life histories to the growing global, national and institutional awareness that fewer women were saying 'yes' to religious life. The 1950s was often remembered as a golden age 'when novitiates were bursting'. The archives suggest a different story that features the paucity of women crossing the monastic threshold. This phenomenon was addressed in various ways. Pope Pius XII's apostolic constitution *Sponsa Christi* (1950) and subsequent international congresses advocated a renewal of religious life. Modern approaches were employed to develop a more sophisticated means of vocation promotion that was direct, public-facing and professional. The new religious discourse on the 'modern world' acknowledged that religious life must modernise to become more relevant and attractive to Catholic women.

In Chapter 2 the discourse on the post-war Modern Girl takes centre stage and the chapter investigates how she influenced the boundaries of female religious life in British congregations and orders from the 1940s to the 1960s. It identifies the predominant themes developed by the cultural trope of the Modern Girl, which reflected certain orthodoxies regarding perceived social and moral swings and then demonstrates how these were incorporated within the Catholic discourse of youth culture in general, but more particularly the Catholic Modern Girl. It interrogates how the institutional church along with female religious congregations and orders reacted to this discourse and what steps were taken (or not taken) to restructure the lived experience of religious life to accommodate the Modern Girl.

Chapter 3 explores the ways in which religious life was reconfigured in regard to governance and obedience, leading to the elimination of, as one sister put it, 'a Victorian attitude'. It genders our knowledge of the global 1968 movements by exploring an emancipatory movement led, sustained and spread by women. The female leaders of religious institutes rethought governance and replaced deeply embedded structures where the mother superior or abbess and her council made decisions for all members of the community. The result: more women participated in governance, as delegates to General Chapters or as members of provincial structures; more voices were heard via questionnaires and consultative meetings. At the local level, changes in governance practices were experienced by each and every member of a community. Renewal released a social movement that gave voice to grievances and concerns about religious life and unleashed collective action that changed, in many communities, the lived experience of community life. And yet, this was in no way a straightforward story of progress. These changes polarised women religious in groups that were 'for change' and 'against change' and were highly contentious.

Prescriptive and promotional convent literature portrayed community life as an unchanging oasis of serenity grounded in fictive familial bonds. Homosocial relationships within the convent were more complicated, particularly during and after the structural changes of religious life discussed in the previous chapter. Chapter 4 addresses the changing tenor of the relationships within monastic and convent female homosocial spaces as a move from the formal to the relational. Women's experiences of religious life are analysed to understand how relationships were understood and lived. The first section considers the 'common life', communal ways of inhabiting the social spaces of the convent that held religious life together. As the horarium which regulated the religious day was altered, the permission-centred model of religious life became one that allowed for personal responsibility. The formal structures of the common life provided a unity that was now questioned and relationships grounded in formerly rigid structures were renegotiated. The second section addresses the complex, relational nature of these shifts and questions the language of generations used to identify those for and against change. The convent, often imagined as a conservative site of religious piety, became a place of radical activism and generational dissonance when a discourse of personal and shared responsibility challenged matriarchal social hierarchies.

The nun in the modern world and the modern world inside the convent is the subject of Chapter 5. Some considered adaptations to a secular age as a dangerous move towards religious secularisation. Others saw this as a necessary antidote to the evils of modernity. This engagement with the world, faintly visible in archival sources from the 1940s, quickened with the publication of council documents *Perfectae Caritatis* (Adaptation and Renewal of Religious Life, 1965) and *Lumen Gentium* (Dogmatic Constitution on the Church, 1964) which emphasised (or so it seemed) a radical activism embedded in a secular world. That acceptability to engaging with the modern world on its own terms in its own language exemplifies this new relationship with modernity. By the 1960s and 1970s, the questioning of institutional barriers to ministry and bolstering of individual autonomy was reflective of the larger 1960s mentality that emphasised individual expression, links between people and the removal of boundaries. Becoming part of the world was a response to both religious and secular social movements. For many sisters and nuns, it was not a sudden thrust into the world; but a gradual shift. It was not always a welcome shift when it disrupted patterns of living and beliefs about the sacred/secular divide.

Chapter 6 questions how religious institutions re-examined their ministries in the 1970s and 1980s, influenced by a discourse of social justice grounded in solidarity with those marginalised by society and in line with a voluntary sector re-energised by the social movements of the long 1960s. In addressing the role of women religious as purveyors of religion, it suggests a rethinking of the spiritual and corporal works of mercy which realigned them with the politics of mercy. Alternate ministries were both local and global, but united by their focus on those marginalised by society. Whether working as parish sisters, in convent schools or in the *barriadas* of Peru, female religious held on to this larger objective of social justice that was not narrowed by geography. What linked these ministries was a more global thinking of their role as religious: their work revealed both a local mission done globally and a global mission done locally. Added to these shifts in ministries is the complexities of the realisation that the decline in numbers would not be reversed and institutional work running large schools and hospitals needed to be rethought.

Chapter 7 engages with the ideas coming out of the 1970s women's movement and their influence on the identities of women religious. Encouraged by the *Nun in the World* (1963) and feminist theologians, nuns and sisters experienced a more thorough grounding in theology that acknowledged their womanhood and sexuality and linked it to a deeper understanding of their faith. They questioned the 'charged symbols' of religious life. Enclosed nuns opened their non-cloistered spaces more readily, and some began to see the grille that separated them from the world as an unnecessary impediment to their ministry. The other loaded symbol of religious life, the religious habit, was being modified and in some communities was seen as a barrier to new ministries. For some, these unchanging symbols of religious life signified tradition, security and the authenticity of religious life. For others, the need for modernity, to meet the modern world in different ways, offered a 'renewed' way to be an authentic religious. Women religious, like feminists, claimed for themselves the right to define their own place in both secular society and the Catholic world. This chapter demonstrates that both religious and secular ideas shaped these women's awareness of their womanhood.

The Conclusion encapsulates the changes enacted from 1945 to 1990, considering both the voices heard and the voices not heard in this study, and acknowledging the pain of change. It examines the three core premises: religious life as a social movement influenced by secular social movements, transnational influences and changing identities setting these in the more international frame of religious life, identifying what made British religious life distinctive. In addressing the global nature of these changes, it reminds us of the internationality of religious life and the transnational encounters that informed women's understanding of religious change. It then links this historical study with the continued complexity of contemporary religious life: a time of diminishment and innovations, revelations of abuse and new religious movements.

This history of Catholic nuns and sisters in a secular Britain begins in the following chapter with an acknowledgement of the significance of the 'modern world' of the 1940s and 1950s and an examination of the vocation stories of women who entered religious life.

1

Before the Council: post-war modernity and religious vocations

In this crisis of vocations, be watchful lest the customs, the way of life or the asceticism of your religious families should prove a barrier or be a cause of failures.[1]

Introduction

Thirty-something Catholics Edna John and Doris Andrews met while working at the Catholic Truth Society. In 1936, they realised they had something in common: both felt drawn to a vocation to religious life but were hindered by family responsibilities and poor health. During the Second World War, like many civilians, they 'did their bit' and became air raid wardens. In between their waged employment and war work, they sketched a plan to support women such as themselves, women waiting to enter religious life. They obtained episcopal approval in 1942 to form the Helpers of Our Lady of Good Counsel, a lay religious society aimed at developing strong female vocations from 'weak' ones. Twenty years on, this lay society became a religious congregation known as the Vocation Sisters.[2] Dressed in forest green A-line dresses and simple veils, they represented the modern face of religious life. This was more than a new look; their ministry used contemporary approaches to tackle vocation recruitment. In a piece that appeared in the British press in the 1960s, the Vocation Sisters were introduced as a 'modern' element of the Church. Their ministry was described as transitioning 'would-be nuns to the life

1   Abbé Gaston Courtois (ed.), *The States of Perfection* (Dublin: Gill, 1961), p. 217.
2   'A Short Account of the Beginnings of the Work of the Daughters of the Mother of Good Counsel'. Sent to author by Vocation Sister Marian Short. They became a diocesan congregation in 1962 and took the name *Filiae matris boni consilii* (Daughters of the Mother of Good Counsel) but were known as the Vocation Sisters.

behind the veil', and 'selling' vocations to the public. The article asserted that they 'act very much like public relations officers, giving talks and film shows, advising, teaching, answering questions and helping girls to acquire a general knowledge of the life of a nun'.[3] They used modern technologies to reinvigorate the vocations of those who 'needed just a little encouragement and assistance; those who lived with a family having [an] anti-Catholic atmosphere, unsympathetic surroundings – in Catholic homes even vocations were not always encouraged'.[4] In 1948, their religious adviser, Benedictine Ambrose Agius, intimated that religious institutions had become stagnant in their recruiting efforts. He chided religious institutes with 'I respectfully invite a wider and intenser [sic] co-operation in the work on the part of the many convents in this country. The time has gone by when it is sufficient to sit still and twiddle our thumbs and wait for vocations to drop into our lap.'[5]

Why did vocation promotion seem so crucial from the late 1940s? Some religious institutes reported experiencing a boost in postulants after the war, but for many, this was short-lived. And many more religious institutes, both enclosed and active, acknowledged a shortage of vocations. The discourse on the decline in vocations, both religious and clerical, became more pronounced in the 1950s. Was this vocation shortage simply a response to the greater needs of a growing Catholic population? Or was this indicative of a decline in entrants into religious life? This chapter addresses these questions, first, through an examination of the decision-making process of women entering religious life in the 1940s and 1950s. Next, through an analysis of discursive and quantitative data which demonstrates that some congregations and orders were experiencing a decline in vocations. Lastly, it addresses two top-down responses to this decline. The response from the Holy See was Pope Pius XII's apostolic constitution *Sponsa Christi* (1950) and the subsequent international congresses encouraging 'adaptation' and 'modernisation'. In Britain, the response was the development of a more direct, public-facing and professional form of vocations promotion: vocations exhibitions. This chapter acknowledges the growing global, national and institutional awareness that fewer women were saying 'yes' to religious life in the 1940s and 1950s.

---

3   West Sussex Record Office, Vocation Sisters (henceforth WSRO): 292, untitled press article, hand-dated 1960, pp. 74–5.

4   WSRO: 14, 'Filiae matris boni consilii', typescript dated 15 August 1947, p. 4.

5   WSRO: *Magister te Vocat*, 3:1 (January 1948), p. 3. This journal was published from 1946 to 1951.

Modernity is often marked by a shifting social, cultural, economic and political environment and a questioning of the past.[6] Women entering religious life in the 1940s and 1950s were in the midst of a post-war British world feeling the push and pull of modernisation. They experienced life differently from their mothers and grandmothers; the post-war modern world held the potential for new encounters and worldviews. Women of all social classes during the war had experienced diverse forms of war work, more financial independence and greater occasion for relationships with men and women inside and outside their social class.[7] Women's rights campaigner Vera Douie observed:

> In one way, perhaps, the war may have made a permanent difference to life in Britain. Women have moved in a wider world, and mingled with men and women of every type.[8]

The feminine ideal that centred on home and domesticity did not disappear but women experienced meaningfully serving their nation as workers, citizens and political actors.

Post-war, career options for young women were expanding. Flipping through the pages of *Girl* magazine, a 'New Super Colour Weekly for Every Girl' launched in 1951, readers found an exciting array of options for careers in the 'I Want To Be' section. These included traditional female roles of nanny, nurse and secretary and more extraordinary options, such as kennel-maid, plastics designer and architect.[9] The magazine *My Home* also included a series on 'careers with a future' reflecting the rising proportion of women in long-term employment.[10] Financial means gave

6   Martin Daunton and Bernhard Rieger (eds), *Meanings of Modernity: Britain from the Late-Victorian Era to World War II* (Oxford: Berg, 2001), p. 1.
7   Gerry Holloway, *Women and Work in Britain since 1840* (London: Routledge, 2005), p. 193. Gail Braybon and Penny Summerfield, *Out of the Cage: Women's Experiences in Two World Wars* (London: Pandora, 1987), pp. 185, 196–204; Selina Todd, *Young Women, Work, and Family in England 1918–1950* (Oxford: Oxford University Press, 2005), p. 52.
8   Vera Douie, *Daughters of Britain* (Oxford: privately printed, 1949), p. 158.
9   *Charm School: Advice for the Thoroughly Modern Girl* (London: Prion, 2007).
10   Judy Giles, *The Parlour and the Suburb: Domestic Identities, Class, Femininity and Modernity* (Oxford: Berg, 2004), p. 158. In 1951, 43 per cent of women aged between thirty-five and fifty-nine were employed (compared to 26 per cent in 1931). Also see Stephen Brooke, 'Gender and Working Class Identity in Britain during the 1950s', *Journal of Social History*, 34 (2001), 778–80; Stephanie Spencer, 'Women's Dilemmas in Postwar Britain: Career Stories for Adolescent Girls in the 1950s', *History of Education*, 29 (2000), 329–42, for more on the complex nature of women, work and femininity.

young women a degree of autonomy and consumer power. Historian Claire Langhamer suggests that many young women from the 1920s to the 1950s experienced their pre-marriage youth as a 'golden age' of leisure and independence.[11] The materialism of the world often discussed in this period suggests the enticement of recreational culture. The 1950s anxiety about 'the problem of leisure' came about as more statutory holidays and shorter working hours led to increasing consumption of activities such as television, cinema, sport and holidays. Historian Brian Harrison has written that 'technological change, improved transport, growing affluence, and (for many) reduced working hours, were opening up hitherto unimaginable cultural and recreational opportunity'.[12]

And yet, despite this bevy of career options, many women ended their waged working lives just before or shortly after their wedding day.[13] More women were likely to marry in the 1940s, 1950s and 1960s than in the 1920s and 1930s. Age of first marriage for women was also consistently dropping each decade, from 25.5 in 1921 to 22.6 in 1971.[14] Historian Pat Thane has claimed a new 'normality' of a long-lasting marriage. Marriages became almost universal with an average of two children the norm. Family and a home-centred society was one central feature of the 1950s and Britons were bombarded with ideals of marriage, home and family which reinforced the primacy of the role of wife and mother. Wage dependability and social welfare policies encouraged family stability and security.[15] Both middle- and

11   Claire Langhamer, 'Leisure, Pleasure and Courtship: Young Women in England 1920–60', in Mary Jo Maynes, Birgitte Soland and Christina Benninghaus (eds), *Secret Gardens, Satanic Mills: Placing Girls in European History, 1750–1960* (Bloomington: Indiana University Press, 2005), p. 280.

12   Brian Harrison, *Seeking a Role: The United Kingdom, 1951–1970* (Oxford: Clarendon Press, 2009), p. 401.

13   Women often returned to waged work when children were older, though this later employment was not always career-oriented. Selina Todd's statistics show that adult females (over age twenty-four) occupied in paid employment increased from 23 per cent in 1921 to 28 per cent in 1951. This can be compared to young females' (aged between fifteen and twenty-four) employment, which increased 63 per cent to 72 per cent in the same time period. Todd, *Young Women*, pp. 20, 158–9.

14   The shift in percentages of women marrying is staggering. In 1921 and 1931, 55.2 and 54.7 per cent of women married. In 1941, 74.5 per cent of women married; by 1961 this figure had moved up to 83.0 per cent and by 1971 97.9 per cent. Jane Lewis, 'Marriage', in Ina Zweiniger-Bargielowska (ed.), *Women in Twentieth-Century Britain* (London: Longman, 2001), p. 71.

15   Pat Thane, 'Family Life and "Normality" in Postwar British Culture', in Richard Bessel and Dirk Schumann (eds), *Life after Death: Approaches to a Cultural and Social History of Europe during the 1940s and 1950s* (Cambridge: Cambridge University Press, 2003),

working-class families believed their children could improve in social status and education.[16] Home life for women was still labour-intensive, but improved housing, smaller family sizes, modern labour-saving conveniences and the potential of creating homely interior spaces led to a domesticity with room for self-fulfilment.[17] Motherhood was also less isolating for the post-war mother; a growing number of women combined being wives and mothers with waged employment. In the years before Betty Friedan's *Feminine Mystique* (1963), the future looked brighter for women who married.[18]

The post-war Catholic 'fortress church' was changing too. Fuelled (again) by immigration, the Catholic Church appeared ascendant as mass attendance rose, requiring the building of new schools and churches. This was particularly striking alongside a public discourse of secularisation, with Protestants battling declining church turnout.[19] Catholic self-confidence, fuelled by its growing numbers of adherents in Britain, also came out of influencing national legislation.[20] Yet, there was little time for complacence. Ecclesial reactions to the post-war world with its state-supplied health care and social welfare were negative; bishops feared the long arm of the state would damage Catholic family life by removing parental (and clerical) authority. Kester Aspden's study of English Catholic bishops suggested parochialism, where fears of

pp. 193–210. Claire Langhamer, 'The Meanings of Home in Postwar Britain', *Journal of Contemporary History*, 40 (2005), 341–62.

16   Jeremy Seabrook, *Working Class Childhood* (London: Victor Gollancz, 1982), pp. 210–11; Thane, 'Family Life', pp. 206–7.

17   Langhamer, 'The Meanings of Home'.

18   Caitríona Beaumont, '"What Is a Wife"? Reconstructing Domesticity in Postwar Britain before *The Feminine Mystique*', *History of Women in the Americas*, 3 (2015), 76.

19   James Sweeney, *The New Religious Order* (London: Bellew, 1994), p. 46; Ross McKibbin, *Classes and Cultures: England 1918–1951* (Oxford: Oxford University Press, 1998), p. 285. Catholic adherents continued to rise until the 1990s. Callum G. Brown, *Religion and Society in Twentieth-Century Britain* (Harlow: Pearson Longman, 2006), p. 25.

20   In 1950, Catholics in England, Wales and Scotland totalled 3,499,374, compared to 1,847,998 members of the Church of England who attended Easter Services (though 2,958,840 were on the electoral rolls). Robert Currie, Alan D. Gilbert and Lee Horsley, *Churches and Churchgoers: Patterns of Church Growth in the British Isles since 1700* (Oxford: Clarendon Press, 1977), pp. 129, 153. James Hagerty, *Cardinal John Carmel Heenan: Priest of the People, Prince of the Church* (London: Gracewing Publishing, 2012), p. 108; Kit Elliott, '"A Very Pushy Kind of Folk": Educational Reform 1944 and the Catholic Laity of England and Wales', *History of Education*, 35 (2006), 91–119.

leakage, materialism and intellectualism led to increasing clericalism and *nil sine episcopo* (nothing without the bishop).[21] Despite this antipathy, the Catholic laity were benefiting from these initiatives and becoming more educated, more socially active and more questioning.[22] An educated middle-class Catholic milieu was growing in number and finding its place in the church and the professions.[23] The Holy See's emphasis of a lay apostolate from the 1920s was slow to take hold in England, but the Catholic laity was flexing its muscles. Some Catholic social organisations such as the Newman Society, Catholic Action and the Catholic Women's League provided places for like-minded Catholics to address the needs of the larger world. Sociologist Michael Hornsby-Smith has queried the homogeneity of the Catholic community by emphasising its heterodoxy in relation to doctrinal and moral beliefs and practices.[24] Alana Harris's research establishes also that in the 1940s and 1950s the 'lived experience' of Catholicism was of a diverse, thinking and feeling Catholicism which might (or might not) fall into line with the Church hierarchy on matters of doctrine and morality.[25] Increasingly, Catholics were interacting with non-Catholics on the front lines and the home front and in educational institutions.[26] The persistent denunciations against 'mixed marriages' suggests these long-term liaisons also perpetuated fears of the breakdown of a Catholic subculture.[27] The Catholic laity was growing in numbers and diversity from the 1940s with an influx of Catholics, converts and immigrants from Ireland, Eastern Europe and the colonies.

---

21 Kester Aspden, *Fortress Church: The English Roman Catholic Bishops and Politics 1903–1963* (London: Gracewing, 2002), pp. 264–303. See also Peter Coman, *Catholics and the Welfare State* (London: Longman, 1977), p. 67.

22 Hugh McLeod, *Religion and the People of Western Europe: 1789–1970* (Oxford: Oxford University Press, 1981), p. 130.

23 James Pereiro, 'Who Are the Laity?', in V. Alan McClelland and Michael Hodgetts (eds), *From without the Flaminian Gate: 150 Years of Roman Catholicism in England and Wales, 1850–2000* (London: Darton, Longman & Todd, 1999), p. 179; Kit Elliott, '"A Very Pushy Kind of Folk": Educational Reform 1944 and the Catholic Laity of England and Wales', *History of Education*, 35 (2006), 94.

24 Michael P. Hornsby-Smith, *Roman Catholics in England: Studies in Social Structure since the Second World War* (Cambridge: Cambridge University Press, 1987), p. 30.

25 Alana Harris, *Faith in the Family: A Lived Religious History of English Catholicism, 1945–1982* (Manchester: Manchester University Press, 2013), pp. 260–2.

26 John Hickey, *Urban Catholics: Urban Catholicism in England and Wales from 1829 to the present day* (London: Geoffrey Chapman, 1967), pp. 162–3.

27 Aspden, *Fortress Church*, pp. 264–6; Coman, *Catholics and the Welfare State*, p. 100. In 1945–1949, 55.1 per cent of Catholic marriages were classified as mixed marriages.

Vocation story

How did this changing social world influence the young women who entered religious life? This section examines young women's attitudes towards their religious vocation, their decision-making process and the reactions of families and friends to suggest that the push and pull of the modern world was influential in the lives of these young women. They were making a very active choice when saying 'yes' to religious life. It also suggests that contemporary fears that many young women were saying 'no' to the sacrifices of religious life were well founded.

Vocations recruitment in the 1940s and 1950s was, as it had been in the nineteenth century, an organic process operating within Catholic circles. Young women who felt they had a vocation often gravitated towards religious institutes that were local or that had educated them. In some families, vocations to religious life were a family tradition and young women followed their siblings or aunts into particular religious houses. Sometimes the local Catholic priest was a useful sounding board and would direct young women to one religious community or another. He may have consulted published works on women's religious life, such as Francesca Steele's *The Convents of Great Britain* (1901)[28] or Hermann Hohn's *Vocations: Conditions of Admission, etc., into the Convents, Congregations, Societies, Religious Institutes, etc.* (1912). Ireland continued to be a source of vocations. Women religious visited Ireland on recruiting drives and enlisted schoolgirls in Irish convent schools to enter communities in England.[29] The reasons for entering contemplative communities were very particular to that form of life, and often related to a devotion to a particular saint such as St Francis of Assisi (Poor Clares) or St Thérèse (Carmelites).[30] Vocation stories of the fifty-one women who entered religious life prior to 1960 suggest that vocation was linked to Catholic circles of socialisation. Convent school education was particularly relevant. Of the seventeen Augustinian Canonesses of

28 Francesca M. Steele, *The Convents of Great Britain* (London: Sands and M. H. Gill, 1902).

29 Carmen M. Mangion, *Contested Identities: Catholic Women Religious in Nineteenth-Century England and Wales* (Manchester: Manchester University Press, 2008), pp. 190–1.

30 Paul Gerrard interviewed forty Poor Clares in the 1990s and observed that many entrants were motivated by devotion to Franciscan saints. Few of my narrators discussed their attraction to religious life as coming from a devotion to a particular saint or founder of a religious institute. Explaining this difference is difficult as Gerrard's dissertation was not completed and this important archive of oral history interviews has not been located. Paul Gerrard, '"The Lord Said 'Come'": Why Women Enter a Religious Order', *Oral History*, 24 (1996), 54–8.

CATHOLIC NUNS AND SISTERS IN A SECULAR AGE

the Holy Sepulchre interviewed, twelve were schoolgirls at New Hall, the school the sisters managed. A similar pattern can be found with those interviewed from the two other congregations with a focus on education, the Institute of the Blessed Virgin Mary and the Society of the Sacred Heart.[31] But socialisation, as vocation stories make clear, was not all that was at work here.

Call from God

The vocation story was evolving. This anonymous handwritten poem found in the files of the archives of the Sisters of Mercy dated (likely by an archivist) 'c. 1900' illustrates characteristics expected of vocation stories.

Vocation
I hear a voice, how deep the sound,
Just like the murmur of the sea,
And in my heart that echo found
The words were these 'Come follow me.'

Place not thy hopes in earthly joys,
Ambition, dreams, or family;
These are as frail as children's toys,
Forsake them all 'Come Follow Me.'

You must forsake them from thy heart;
Ere I my secrets tell to thee,
Then sorrow from thee will depart,
Will thou consent? 'Come follow me.'

Ah Yes! It was my Saviour's voice,
I heard Him sweetly say to me,
I or the world which thy choice
My God! My God! I'll follow thee.[32]

In these verses, a vocation to religious life was interpreted as a call from God. The request 'come follow me' was followed by a ready response

---

31 Ten of twelve interviewees belonging to the Institute of the Blessed Virgin Mary attended IBVM convent schools. Only seven of the seventeen Religious of the Sacred Heart interviewed attended RSCJ convent schools, though an additional six attended one of the Society's teacher training colleges. Interestingly, only two of the nine Sisters of Mercy interviewed attended Mercy convent schools.

32 Archive, Institute of Our Lady of Mercy (henceforth IOLM), IOLM/BER/12/2/7: 'Life of Venerable Mother Anne of St Bartholomew', c. 1900, handwritten poem, 'Vocation', found inside front cover of volume. No author. Anne of St Bartholomew (1550–1626) was a Discalced Carmelite born in Spain.

despite the sacrifice of 'Ambition, dreams, or family'. Personal sacrifice was rewarded by an intimate union with God represented as a higher calling. What was not highlighted was the discernment and interior struggle some women experienced.

Vocation stories recounted by interviewees were more unpredictable than this poem. Some of the sisters and nuns who entered in the 1940s and 1950s gave an unembellished narrative: they realised they had a vocation, they entered religious life. But, more often than not, vocation stories implied some wavering and a discernment of options. One English sister told her vocation story succinctly:

> Right at the end of the sixth form, we'd just taken Highers, and suddenly it just came. As a young girl religious life was in the horizon when I was ten and 11, then it went right away, teenage rebellion, not in a big way but certainly [pause] not the thing I want to do. And then it suddenly came to me that this was a call and I thought well, if this is what God wants, I'll see. The only way to tell is to actually do it.[33]

This sister's vocation appeared and disappeared rapidly in her teenage years. When it reappeared, her response was a measured 'I'll see'. Many of the spoken testimonies indicated caution, indecision and obstacles to 'the call', suggesting that young women found it difficult to leave the world for religious life. One narrator reported that after telling her parish priest 'I think I ought to be a nun', he proposed the Poor Clares and gave her an address. She wrote to them and after a visit entered that community one month later. When prompted to explain what appears to be a sudden decision, she paused and recalled how a few years earlier:

> I'd been thinking about it and I'd spoken to a Jesuit at the university, but he said forget about it and if it's meant it'll come back. So that's right, for a couple of years I was doing, living a double life, being normal and then also having this thing at the back of my mind which I didn't get rid of ...[34]

So, what begins as a very straightforward tale of vocation to religious life has a prehistory; this young woman completed her university studies while still considering her vocation. Most narrators readily acknowledged hearing a 'call from God', but admitted to a waiting period. They took

33 Anonymised interview. The stories I heard were intensely personal and sometimes emotive, and some participants wished to remain anonymous so all the oral narratives have been anonymised for consistency, though in some cases (and with permission) I have identified the religious institute to which a narrator belonged.

34 Anonymised interview.

time for serious discernment, balancing the 'call' for religious life and a life in the world. One woman who entered an enclosed order in the 1950s enthused 'I just knew that God wanted me to join' but also admitted:

> I was appalled because we had grilles in those days, you know, bars and black curtains, and it was everything I thought was horrible, absolutely horrible. I was completely gob-smacked, I thought it's horrible, I could see nothing attractive about it. So, there was a bit of a tussle between me and the Almighty. But of course he is Almighty, so guess who won? And at that time I could only see the price I was paying for this, you know, my career, marriage, which I wanted to do. All these things I wanted to do, I wasn't, I just couldn't reconcile. Anyway, I had to do it.[35]

Aged twenty-one at the time, she had intended on a career and marriage, and some of the features of enclosed religious life in the 1950s were, to her, distinctly unattractive. Her decision to enter an enclosed order was not a ready 'yes' but a 'tussle', though she ultimately followed her heart to enter religious life. Another nun acknowledged the difficulty of leaving her family:

> Well, you know, when I was fifteen I knew God was, I knew I had a vocation but I didn't want to follow it because I loved my mother and father and my family and it was going to break my heart to leave them. And I went out dancing and enjoyed life. I said, ooh, how am I going to give all – I was only fifteen then – and I said, goodness. So I let it go by for a number of years until I was eighteen, but it kept nagging at me and it was so clear to me that God wanted me for the religious life.[36]

Young women in the 1940s and 1950s were attracted to religious life, but there were other options equally enticing: family, work and social life. Their 'yes' was not always immediate; they thoughtfully balanced their options between 'Ambition, dreams, or family' and religious life.

Family responses

Post-war family life was becoming more romanticised. More men and women were marrying in the 1940 and 1950s and at a younger age than their parents. Companionate marriage was a much-discussed ideal.[37]

---

35   Anonymised interview.
36   Anonymised interview. She was twenty when she finally entered religious life.
37   Leonore Davidoff, Megan Doolittle, Janet Fink and Katherine Holden, *The Family Story: Blood, Contract and Intimacy, 1830–1960* (London and New York: Longman, 1999), p. 191.

Family sizes were smaller and parenting styles shifted as parents became younger and 'egalitarian family dynamics' led to a less authoritarian style of parenting. The mothers of the 1950s envisaged their daughters would lead a better life than they had, with more modern conveniences and increased opportunities for leisure. They still expected, though, that their daughters would become mothers and lead a home-centred life.[38]

So perhaps, with the weight of these expectations, it is not so unexpected that Catholic parents' reaction to their daughter's decision to enter religious life was sometimes ambiguous.[39] Some sisters declared that their parents were 'very happy. Oh yes they were very happy.'[40] But many more had parents who were not united in their response. One sister revealed:

> Well, they were very hesitant and my father said I would prefer you to finish your education first properly, but he said, well I won't stand in your way. But my mother was quite enthusiastic really.[41]

Many recounted their Catholic parents and family seeing their choice as a 'waste'. One sister entering in the 1950s recounted:

> Erm … they weren't pleased. My mother was in France with my sister and I wrote them a letter and I said, you'd better sit down when you read this, or words to that effect. And well, I think they both thought it was an awful waste of a life because I wasn't … there was no ambition in it at all.[42]

Another reflected on her mother's response with:

> She was appalled. Appalled and very angry … she'd been very much an intellectual in London …[43]

Even parents who were 'good Catholics' found themselves troubled by their daughter's decision. One sister confessed:

---

38   Elizabeth Roberts, *Women and Families: An Oral History 1940–1970* (Oxford: Blackwell, 1995), p. 39.

39   Even in the nineteenth century, parents in England and Wales were not always enthusiastic about a daughter's vocation to religious life. Mangion, *Contested Identities*, pp. 75–7.

40   Anonymised interview.

41   Anonymised interview.

42   Anonymised interview.

43   Anonymised interview.

> My parents were both good Catholics and in theory their daughter
> wanting to be a nun was wonderful, until I told them I wanted to be
> one, and my father in particular found it devastating.[44]

'Devastating' suggests the powerful emotiveness of this father's response and
the sacrifice expected of a daughter and her family. Many women religious
reflected on the emotional reaction of their parents. One sister disclosed
that her parents were 'both behind me', but:

> [T]he day I was coming, when we left in the afternoon, my mum and dad
> and a friend took us in the car, I just happened to walk in the bathroom,
> mum was crying. And I hadn't realised till that point the way she was
> feeling, because I'd always had encouragement ... I suppose it was only
> natural that she'd be upset about me going, isn't it? Dad was as proud as
> punch.[45]

Many narrators after recounting their story offered something similar to
this nun's reflection: 'it was just a very big sacrifice for them. You don't
think when you're young, no'.[46] Another sister recalled 'for my mother to
give me up was more of a sacrifice than it was for me to go and enter the
convent'.[47] Until the 1960s, such sacrifice was expected of daughters and
their parents.[48] Those entering anticipated having limited and monitored
access to their family and friends. Sister Prue Wilson writes of her early
years as a Sacred Heart sister: 'we knew that we would never again see
our homes'.[49] Some, like former religious Karen Armstrong, suffered
from the artificial nature of her relationship with her parents, recalling
her correspondence with them: 'This letter, I thought, was not a natural
letter at all. I was retreating from my family behind a screen of stilted
words and phrases. It was so painful.'[50] One sister admitted, 'But, you
know, there was great emphasis in those days on individuals making a

---

44 Anonymised interview.

45 Anonymised interview.

46 Anonymised interview.

47 Archief Congregatie Zusters van Liefde, Tilburg (henceforth SCMM-Tilburg): SCMM
    003 interviewed by Annemiek van der Veen (2003).

48 See also Chapter 5. By the 1960s these rules had begun to change and women religious
    were seeing their families more often. There were exceptions by community: see
    Carmen M. Mangion, '"It Took a Little While to Get It Right": Women Religious and
    Family Relationships, 1940–1990', *Catholic Ancestor*, 16:2 (2016), 60–8.

49 Prue Wilson, *My Father Took Me to the Circus* (London: Darton, Longman & Todd,
    1984), p. 31.

50 Karen Armstrong, *Through the Narrow Gate: A Nun's Story* (London: Flamingo, 1981),
    p. 108.

sacrifice, and that is what we thought we were doing ... that is what we bought into.'[51] Many of the narrators acknowledged as commonplace that this 'higher life' required 'sacrifice, and charity'.[52]

Some narrators suggested their family expected their vocation was a fleeting whim that would be abandoned after a few days in the convent. One nun explained the reaction of her father as: 'You won't settle there, you know, you've got all your life in front of you.'[53] Many parents gave their daughters leeway to return home: 'I remember my father saying to me, oh well, you'll be safe if you go to the convent, but if it's not right, you come out.'[54] Another father gave his daughter a return ticket and money for a taxi for her return home.[55] Some parents insisted on delaying what they hoped was an impetuous decision. One sister who entered in the late 1940s described her own grief when her parents made her wait until she was twenty-one.

> Well, I left [school] just before the end of the war, I must have been just on eighteen, and I'd hoped to enter, but my parents both said no, not until you're twenty-one, and that was the age at that stage. And I thought that was terrible, oh, bitter tears. But it was the best thing, much the best thing. I got some experience, you know, became less of a schoolgirl and much better equipped to enter.[56]

Women who converted to Catholicism as young adults faced even greater opposition. One daughter of atheists recounted her father's response:

> [M]y father sent a psychologist to interview me. Um he didn't say he was a psychologist he said he was a diagnostician but I gathered from the questions he was asking about 'How do you feel about religious

---

51   Anonymised interview. Yvonne McKenna in her interviews of Irish women religious also identifies the theme of sacrifice as significant. Yvonne McKenna, *Made Holy: Irish Women Religious at Home and Abroad* (Dublin: Irish Academic Press, 2006), p. 60.
52   WSRO: 103, *Quo Vadis* (1950), p. 17.
53   Anonymised interview.
54   Anonymised interview.
55   Anonymised interview.
56   Anonymised interview. This 'experience' was not unusual. Forty-one of the eighty-one sisters interviewed were employed or had attended university before they entered religious life. Sister Mary Laurence, writing of her experience as a Dominican noted: 'Nowadays it is an exception for girls not to be trained for career: we have ex-teachers, bank clerks, secretaries, dispensers, gardeners, university educated and served in armed forces.' Sister Mary Laurence, OP, *Nuns are Real People* (London: Blackfriars Publications, 1955), p. 8. Notably, ten of the thirteen Irish-born Sisters of Mercy entered after leaving school without work or university experience.

life' and um and in the end I said well if I want to discuss my religious life I will discuss it with people who know something about it. So he, I didn't see him again [laughs].[57]

One woman's recounted how her uncle 'took immense trouble to create a dossier, which was about an inch thick, I mean it was an appalling document, of the incidence of mental health in religious orders to try and persuade me that this was not a good idea'.[58] Another young woman entered 'knowing that I was leaving devastation at home and, in particular, a totally grief-stricken father. My becoming a Catholic had been bad enough – for his father, Roman Catholics were not Christians.'[59] Anti-Catholicism was muted (sometimes), but still commonplace in the last half of the twentieth century.[60] B. Seebohm Rowntree and G. R. Lavers writing on religious practice in England in the 1950s spoke with sociological authority linking the Catholic faith to 'spiritual totalitarianism':

> Its success to-day is gained by removing from individual minds all sense of fear, doubt and uncertainty, and by giving instead a feeling of security. Like totalitarian organizations in other fields of human activity, spiritual totalitarianism can produce satisfactory results over a considerable period of time.[61]

Broadcaster George Scott recounts being told in the 1960s 'There are undoubtedly some people – it is impossible to quantify – to whom a Catholic is automatically a doubtful character, people for whom, if they accept you, it is very much despite your being a Catholic.'[62] Even today, journalist Dennis Sewell maintains that Catholics are considered a 'stealth minority, undetectable by conventional social radar' and not quite like 'ordinary people'.[63]

57   Anonymised interview.
58   Anonymised interview.
59   Sister Patricia Harriss, 'Looking Back on my Religious Life' (2014; in Sister Patricia's possession).
60   McKibbin, *Classes and Cultures*, pp. 292–3.
61   B. Seebohm Rowntree and G. R. Lavers, *English Life and Leisure: A Social Study* (London: Longmans Green and Co., 1951), pp. 373–4.
62   George Scott, *The R.C.s: A Report on Roman Catholics in Britain today* (London: Hutchinson, 1967), pp. 33, 14–35.
63   Dennis Sewell, *Catholics: Britain's Largest Minority* (London: Penguin Books, 2001), p. 2. See the review of his book by Hugo Young: www.theguardian.com/education/2001/jun/09/socialsciences.highereducation, accessed 24 August 2017.

Vocation stories of Irish-born sisters offered some significant variants on those of English sisters.[64] They were less likely to voice hesitancy about entering religious life and their parents were more likely to encourage a religious vocation. Ireland's strong Catholic identity, socio-economic pressures and kin participation in religious life suggest possible explanations.[65] One Irish-born sister who entered in the 1950s recounted:

> So when I'd finished my education then, I felt this longing was throbbing there all the time, so I thought, got to do something about it, so I told my parents. My mother was delighted. My father was delighted too, but my father didn't want me to come to England, he wanted me to stay in Ireland. But for me, I felt that England was more of a missionary country, that there was more need for religious in England, so that's why I came to England.[66]

Many sisters, like this one, also acknowledged the pull of the missions. Irish women religious were a distinctive subset of the worldwide Irish diaspora and their border-crossing was an important development of the

64 Irish-born sisters entered convents in England and Wales in great numbers. Data suggests that in the nineteenth century 41 per cent of religious were born in Ireland. Extant analysis for the twentieth century also suggests a similar dominance of Irish-born nuns. Susan O'Brien notes that two-thirds of the Daughters of Charity of St Vincent de Paul in the 1920s were Irish-born; by the 1940s, this had increased to 75 per cent. Barbara Walsh's work suggests that in the first quarter of the twentieth century, Irish-born sisters accounted for 63 per cent of the Sisters of St Paul the Apostle, 81 per cent of the Sisters of the Sacred Heart of Jesus and Mary and 15 per cent of the Sisters of Notre Dame de Namur. This variance can be linked to institutional recruiting strategies. In my sample of interviewed sisters, ten of the eighty-one sisters were Irish-born; the majority entered the Sisters of Mercy, which heavily recruited in Ireland. Mangion, *Contested Identities*, p. 191; Susan O'Brien, *Leaving God for God: The Daughters of Charity of St Vincent de Paul in Britain, 1847–2017* (London: Darton, Longman & Todd, 2017), p. 277; Barbara Walsh, *Roman Catholic Nuns in England and Wales, 1800–1937: A Social History* (Dublin: Irish Academic Press, 2002), p. 184
65 Yvonne McKenna writes extensively of the attraction to religious life based on interviews of women who entered Irish congregations and became missionaries between 1930 and 1970. Unsurprisingly, given her cohort, they often reference the excitement of the foreign missions, a theme not mentioned often in my interviews. She also describes parental responses as 'ambiguous' but mentions the symbolic capital of having a daughter in religious life in Ireland. McKenna, *Made Holy*, pp. 55–71.
66 Anonymised interview. According to Tranter, Irish parents were likely to protest when their daughters were sent to faraway missions to North America and Australia. Janice Tranter, 'The Irish Dimension of an Australian Religious Sisterhood: The Sisters of Saint Joseph', in Patrick O'Sullivan (ed.), *Religion and Identity* (London: Leicester University Press, 1996), p. 249.

nineteenth-century transnational exchanges that were part and parcel of religious life. From the nineteenth century, they followed Irish migrants to mission territories, meeting their spiritual needs through Catholic education, health care and social welfare.[67] The economic struggles of the 1940s and 1950s led to yet another mass migration of Irish.[68] Women were a significant constituent of this wave. Irish historian Caitriona Clear argues that women's emigration should be understood in an additional context: 'the coming of age of a generation of women who wanted to change their lives'. She highlights the harsh realities of married life in Ireland and suggests mothers may have discouraged their daughters from marrying.[69] The discourse of a religious vocation underscored the spiritual advantages of a 'higher calling'; in addition, religious life could offer distinct economic, professional and social advantages for families as well as young women.[70]

Yet, like many English-born women religious, even Irish sisters vacillated, thinking:

> And I knew then when my vocation was really, really strong, felt really strong, if I don't go soon, I'll never go because I'll be persuaded out of it. You know, there were lots of reasons why I shouldn't do it.[71]

Some women hurriedly joined religious communities as they feared they would be enticed by all the modern world had to offer. Others entered reasoning: 'I thought I won't stick it out, I'll come home. I know I wasn't

67   For example, Deirdre Raftery, 'Teaching Sisters and Transnational Networks: Recruitment and Education Expansion in the Long Nineteenth Century', *History of Education*, 44 (2015), 717–28; Colin Barr and Rose Luminiello, '"The Leader of the Virgin Choirs of Erin": St Brigid's Missionary College, 1883–1914', in Timothy G. McMahon, Michael de Nie and Paul Townend (eds), *Ireland in an Imperial World: Citizenship, Opportunism, and Subversion* (London: Palgrave Macmillan, 2017), pp. 155–78; McKenna, *Made Holy*.
68   Enda Delaney, 'The Vanishing Irish? The Exodus from Ireland in the 1950s', in Dermot Keogh, Finbarr O'Shea and Carmel Quinlan (eds), *The Lost Decade: Ireland in the 1950s* (Cork: Mercier, 2004), pp. 82–3; Caitriona Clear, '"Too Fond of Going": Female Emigration and Change for Women in Ireland, 1946–1961', in Dermot Keogh, Finbarr O'Shea and Carmel Quinlan (eds), *The Lost Decade: Ireland in the 1950s* (Cork: Mercier, 2004), p. 135.
69   Clear, '"Too Fond of Going"', pp. 136, 142–3. Miriam Rooney, 'Our Block', in John A. O'Brien (ed.), *The Vanishing Irish: The Enigma of the Modern World* (London: W. H. Allen, 1954), p. 197.
70   Also discussed in McKenna, *Made Holy*, pp. 55–62; Yvonne McKenna, 'Embodied Ideals and Realities: Irish Nuns and Irish Womanhood, 1930s-1960s', *Éire-Ireland*, 41 (2006), 45, 49.
71   Anonymised interview.

the only one who said that, other religious have said it too.'[72] The process of becoming a vowed religious was a long one, with a postulancy and novitiate that lasted at least three years (and later longer); women who entered were aware they could leave during this formation process if they did not have a vocation.

These oral narratives draw out the thoughtfulness with which women entered religious life. Their initial response to the call from God was not always an enthusiastic and automatic 'Yes!'. The women interviewed recounted their vocation story in ways that emphasised their agency as young women to follow a call from God. It was a choice they made, often after some discernment, and sometimes in opposition to their own inclinations and desires for career and family. In some cases, women displayed discomposure at the pain their decision gave their family. Many narrators ended these reflections with stories of reconciliation, underscoring that their parents 'did come to accept it in the end'.[73] But, for those interviewed, their committed 'yes' was one of awareness of the sacrifice of career and marriage. These stories also suggest that contemporary fears that many young women were saying 'no' to the sacrifices of religious life were credible. The next section investigates this rejection of religious life through the discourse of a 'vocations crisis'.

Vocations crisis

National concerns

Edna John and Doris Andrews initially established the Helpers of Our Lady of Good Counsel to aid 'weak' vocations. It developed into the Vocation Sisters, a religious congregation that addressed national concerns over shrinking vocations to the female religious life. In the 1949 issue of their quarterly magazine *Magister te Vocat*, the Vocation Sisters wrote: 'Owing to the war we may count seven years lost as regards vocations – ALL Orders are crying out for them.'[74] The brochure 'A Clarion Call to Young Women', aimed at encouraging vocations, asked its readers:

> [D]o we ever give a thought to the religious Orders, how they have been depleted and how there is more need for their work than ever before?

72 Anonymised interview.
73 Harriss, 'Looking back on my religious life'.
74 WSRO: *Magister te Vocat* 2:1 (January 1947), p. 4; also 'A Great Need', *Magister te Vocat*, 1:2 (July–September 1949), pp. 1–2.

It then exhorted: 'Contemplative and active' are 'crying out for Vocations'.[75] Were the Vocation Sisters alone in this battle cry? Some enclosed orders were reporting declining numbers.[76] *The Poor Soul's Friend*, the publication of the Bridgettines of Syon Abbey, revealed in 1948 that they were praying to St Jude, patron of hopeless causes, for postulants; a year on they were still waiting: 'Now we have plenty of choir Stalls empty for Postulants.' 'Are there none of our Readers who have daughters or friends willing to consecrate themselves to the life of Praise of the Holy Mother of God?'[77] Though twenty-one postulants entered Syon in the years subsequent to 1949, only five women were professed, the last one in 1965.[78] One Benedictine prioress writing in 1956 protested:

> Nothing is done to help the Contemplative Orders, yet we are constantly asked for the prayers of our Community and unless we get novices to carry on our good work of the Perpetual Adoration and Divine Office our prayers will be of little avail as many of our small number are already old, therefore we need recruits.[79]

Active congregations had similar concerns about declining entrants. Susan O'Brien suggests it is time for a rethinking of a pre-conciliar 'golden age' of religious life. She questions the commonly voiced assumption that decline in vocations in Europe and North America occurred after the Second Vatican Council.[80] Her demographic analysis of the Daughters of Charity of St Vincent de Paul, one of England's largest female religious institutes, reveals that a 1920s spike in entrants was followed

75 WSRO: 14, 'A Clarion Call to Young Women', undated.

76 The Poor Clare community of Leyland which had opened in the diocese of Liverpool in 1930 was disbanded in 1957. They had not received a postulant in ten years. Archdiocese of Liverpool Archives (henceforth ALA): A/26, 'Poor Clares Formby and Leyland'.

77 'Syon Notes', *Poor Soul's Friend* 54 (1948), p. 65; 'Syon Notes', *Poor Soul's Friend* 55 (1949), p. 183; E. A. Jones, *Syon Abbey 1415–2015: England's Last Medieval Monastery* (London: Gracewing, 2015), pp. 128–9.

78 A complete register of twentieth-century postulants or professed Bridgettines was not extant. The Syon database was created by me from archival sources and census data. Postulant data was collected from visitation reports found in Plymouth Diocesan Archives (henceforth PDA) and Exeter University Library (henceforth EUL). PDA: CMB 3.1, Syon Abbey, Blue Folder: canonical visitations, 1933–1962, Visitation of Syon Abbey 4–5 February 1953; EUL: MS 389/2487, Folder 'Visitations'.

79 ALA: GHC/S1/1/B/12, Letter from Sister Mary OSB, Prioress, to Archbishop of Westminster, William Godfrey, dated 10 June 1956.

80 O'Brien, *Leaving God for God*, pp. 274–5. Anne O'Brien finds a similar decline from the 1920s in Australia. Anne O'Brien, 'Catholic Nuns in Transnational Mission, 1528–2015', *Journal of Global History*, 11 (2016), 400–1.

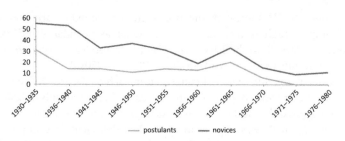

Figure 1.1 Postulants and novices, Institute of the Blessed Virgin Mary, 1930–1980

by a decline from the 1930s and an ageing demographic profile from the 1940s.[81] Community numbers may have remained high, but this was an ageing community. This trend was replicated elsewhere in other active congregations. The statistics of the numbers of novices and postulants entering the Institute of the Blessed Virgin Mary from 1930 to 1980 demonstrate a downward trend from the 1930s (see Figure 1.1). Despite a steady stream of postulants from the mid-1930s to the late 1950s, they do not translate into novices. The numbers of novices continues to decline during this period, suggesting that women who entered did not find what they were looking for. Many religious anecdotally report a post-war bulge of postulants representing those women who would have entered during the war years but were likely employed in war work or were conscripted. The slight upward trend from the mid-1950s aligns too with Callum Brown's demographic analysis, which suggests the 1950s as a 'decade of intense, and arguably intensifying, religious culture'.[82] The Canonesses of the Holy Sepulchre were at their largest, fifty-seven canonesses, in

81 O'Brien, *Leaving God for God*, pp. 274–81. For examples of publications that indicate decline occurs in the years after the Second Vatican Council: Gerald A. Arbuckle, *Strategies for Growth in Religious Life* (Middlegreen, Slough: St Paul Publications, 1986), p. 3; Rodney Stark and Roger Finke, 'Catholic Religious Vocations: Decline and Revival', *Review of Religious Research*, 42 (2000), 125–45.

82 Callum G. Brown, *Religion and the Demographic Revolution: Women and Secularisation in Canada, Ireland, UK and USA since the 1960s* (Woodbridge: Boydell Press, 2012), p. 53. This is explored in more detail in Alana Harris and Martin Spence, '"Disturbing the Complacency of Religion"? The Evangelical Crusades of Dr Billy Graham and Father Patrick Peyton in Britain, 1951–54', *Twentieth Century British History*, 18 (2007), 481–513.

1871 and 1872.[83] Thereafter, the size of the community started slowly declining, though women continued to enter as postulants and were professed through to the 1990s. The English Dominicans experienced a distinct decline in new recruits in the 1940s and 1950s.[84]

Even a large international congregation such as the Dutch Sisters of Charity of Our Lady, Mother of Mercy, which had four convents in Britain, also recognised this decline in numbers of postulants. The largest class of novices, 155 in all, was in place in 1938. The subsequent drop in novices can be explained somewhat by the Second World War, but by 1949, the novice class had halved to seventy-five, and thereafter until 1962, ranged from twenty-nine to sixty-eight, averaging fifty novices a year. The numbers of professed sisters reached an all-time high in 1950, at 3,951, and by 1962 had dropped to 3,447.[85] Other international congregations note a similar pre-conciliar decline in numbers. Though the Society of the Sacred Heart continued to grow in the number of communities from the 1940s to the late 1950s, 'vocations were waning while the age level was rising'.[86] The Faithful Companions of Jesus had their largest membership in 1925.[87]

In the 1950s and 1960s, the reasons given for vocation decline looked outward rather than inward. The Institute of the Blessed Virgin Mary in their five-year annual reports submitted to Rome for both 1953–1957 and 1958–1962 acknowledged declining vocations with: 'The lack of vocations in England is attributed to the materialistic outlook and the present social conditions and the weakness of family life.' The biggest obstacle they mentioned was: 'the opposition of their parents'.[88] Syon Abbey's quinquennial report of 1959 documented as obstacles to vocations: 'the pleasure-loving atmosphere of to-day' as well as 'the great freedom and facilities allowed to girls in the business world of to-day,

---

83 They primarily lived in one community, though in 1946 they opened a school at Goodings which moved to Denford Park and closed in 1967.

84 The Stone community had been an ageing community since 1929. Anselm Nye, *A Peculiar Kind of Mission: The English Dominican Sisters, 1845–2010* (Leominster: Gracewing, 2011), pp. 153, 186–7, 195.

85 These figures were not available for England and Wales. My own calculations indicate that the English province was at its largest in 1962, when numbers peaked at ninety-seven sisters.

86 Margaret Williams, *The Society of the Sacred Heart: History of a Spirit 1800–1975* (London: Darton, Longman & Todd, 1978), p. 230.

87 Teresa White, *A Vista of Years: History of the Society of the Sisters Faithful Companions of Jesus 1820–1993* (privately printed, 2013), pp. 178, 204. They had 1,291 members in 1925.

88 Archives of the English Province of the Congregation of Jesus (henceforth ACJ/EP): C/35/b/i, 'English Province, Five-Yearly Report January 1st 1953 to December 31st 1957', p. 5; 'English Province, Five-Yearly Report January 1st 1958 to December 31st 1962', p. 5.

and lack of encouragement by parents'.[89] Similar statements were made elsewhere. The author of *Our Eternal Vocation*, published in 1948, explained this 'conception of a vocation as a calamity' was 'the result no doubt of living in a non-Catholic country' and claimed this response of family and friends 'to be both false and shallow'.[90] Figure 1.2, published in the *Catholic Pictorial*, intimates that this disparagement of vocations was present in the 1960s. Many were convinced that 'ever growing distractions, materialism, etc., in the world to-day' enticed young women to ignore the call to religious life.[91] Women who became sisters and nuns, as this image in the *Catholic Pictorial* published in 1962 suggests, were seen to have wasted their lives.[92] The national Catholic press did not report on these concerns about female religious life in the 1940s and 1950s, perhaps because overall numbers in female congregations and orders were still robust.[93] The fall-off of postulants and novices could easily be hidden by a still large, but ageing population of sisters and nuns.

The Catholic press did, however, voice concern over priestly vocations. Nationally all appeared well. The number of priests in England and Wales increased from 5,642 to 6,643 in the 1940s, but priests were being recruited from Ireland and elsewhere in large numbers.[94] *The Tablet* reported that ordinations in 1952 were 100 shy of the numbers in 1937, which was a 'peak year' for ordinations.[95] Some of the seminaries in England were full (Ushaw, Oscott and Wonersh), but bishops were concerned they would not meet the needs of a then growing Catholic population.[96] Another worry that surfaced a decade later was the increasing drop-out rate: 'There has always been a high rate of loss, but there used to be an expectation that of four boys started on their course at fourteen one would persevere to ordination, while two would have dropped off before beginning at the senior seminary. Now it is more like one in ten.'[97] The decline in numbers entering the English seminaries

---

89   PDA: CMB 3.1 Syon Abbey, Taupe Folder: Constitutions and Quinquennial Report, 1959 Quinquennial Report.

90   A Carmelite Nun, *Our Eternal Vocation* (London: Sands & Co., 1948), p. 129.

91   WSRO: 14, 'Helpers of Our Lady of Good Counsel', Typescript; undated.

92   *Catholic Pictorial* (10 June 1962), p. 4.

93   This shortage was reported in more specialist publications. See for example, John Berry, CSsR, 'Why so Few?', *Novena*, 6:8 (December 1956), 262–4.

94   Denis Gwynn, 'Growth of the Catholic Community', in George Andrew Beck (ed.), *The English Catholics, 1850–1950* (London: Burns Oates, 1950), p. 436.

95   That year 251 priests were ordained; 170 of them were diocesan clergy, and the remainder were male religious.

96   The seminarians in English seminaries were likely English-born.

97   'Vocations for Tomorrow', *The Tablet* (3 July 1965), p. 4.

Figure 1.2 'I hear she's going into the convent – what a waste', *Catholic Pictorial*
(10 June 1962), p. 4

was blamed on socio-economic factors: assimilated second-generation
Irish immigrants, mixed marriages, smaller family sizes, free secondary
education and the emergence of a Catholic middle class. The 'materialism
of this age' was linked to 'commercial entertainment' and families
reluctant to foster vocations. These were results, the author noted, of
a 'post-Christian society'.[98] Growing dioceses found this particularly
challenging. The *Catholic Pictorial* reported that the Liverpool diocese
ordained 306 secular priests between 1927 and 1947; in the following

---

98   John FitzSimons, 'Ministering to Growing Numbers', *The Tablet* (4 July 1953), p. 5.
     Joachim Schmiedl writes of similar concerns articulated in Belgian pastoral letters
     blaming a 'worldly atmosphere' for declining vocations. Joachim Schmiedl, 'Reception
     and Implementation of the Second Vatican Council Religious Institutes', in Leo Kenis,
     Jaak Billiet and Patrick Pasture (eds), *The Transformation of the Christian Churches in
     Western Europe (1945–2000)* (Leuven: Leuven University Press, 2010), p. 297.

two decades (1948–1967) only 185 were ordained. During that same period, the population of Catholics in Liverpool increased from 373,885 to 529,995 (1927–1967).[99] The language used in the press of a 'shortage of vocations' was ambiguous; sometimes it referenced the rising demands for priests due to a larger population of Catholics but it also acknowledged fears about decline in ordinations of British-born men.[100]

The concept of modernity often suggests a grand narrative of progress but in Catholic discourse the 'modern world' was a negative trope that linked to the materiality, rather than the spirituality, of the modern world. It suggested that young men and women were enamoured of leisure and pleasure and the enticements of 'materialism' and resisted their vocation to religious life.

Global response

Europe was also facing a 'crisis' of vocations. Religious communities were, like many social groups, unsettled by wartime upheavals and austerities. Enclosed nuns appeared most affected by both poverty and a waning interest in religious life. The autonomous governance structures of contemplative orders such as the Poor Clares, Benedictines and Bridgettines encouraged a seclusion and self-sufficiency that nourished a contemplative lifestyle. Each community was financially and operationally self-supporting, ruled by an abbess and lived behind cloistered walls. Some relied on dowries, others on benefactions and alms; and as much as possible they depended on their own labour, farming plots of land for sustenance, making their own clothing and maintaining the structural fabric of their monastic abode.[101] The potential problems with such isolation were becoming increasingly visible. Pope Pius XII drew attention to the poverty and 'near starvation' of enclosed communities.[102] His concerns led to the apostolic constitution *Sponsa Christi* (1950),

---

99 'What Can Be Done about Priest Shortage', *Catholic Pictorial* (26 February 1967), p. 1.

100 'The Need for Vocations', *The Tablet* (13 June 1953), p. 22; 'Great Shortage of Priests', *Catholic Herald* (20 April 1951), p. 7.

101 Carmen M. Mangion, 'Syon Abbey's "Second Summer", 1900–1950', in Elin Andersson, Claes Gejrot, E. A. Jones and Mia Akestam (eds), *Continuity and Change: Papers from the Birgitta Conference at Dartington, 2015* (Stockholm: Kungl. Vitterhets historie och antikvitetsakademien, 2017), pp. 382–3.

102 'News, Notes and Texts', *The Tablet* (4 July 1953), p. 20. This article notes that 700 hundred convents of enclosed nuns in Spain were 'in the direst misery'. *Audience Invisible: Broadcast Address of His Holiness Pius XII by Divine Providence Pope to the Cloistered Nuns of the World* (London: Catholic Truth Society, 1958), p. 25.

directed towards enclosed contemplatives, which addressed issues such as federations, solemn vows, papal enclosure, monastic work and ministry with the aim of re-energising and refinancing religious life. He was suggesting the creation of stronger transnational networks in the form of regional and international collaborations and exchanges. Some orders such as the Syon Bridgettines contemplated joining a federated body with their sister Bridgettines on the continent but this did not materialise.[103] Significantly, *Sponsa Christi* also used the word 'adaptation', encouraging religious orders to modify or remove outmoded religious practice:[104]

> We find in the institutions of women religious elements which are, of themselves, unnecessary and bring no advantages, but, being merely external and of historic interest, are due to circumstances in the past that are now fundamentally altered. These are no longer of use, and may even impede a greater good: there is no reason for their preservation.[105]

Eight years later in a special radio broadcast to 'Cloistered Nuns of the World', Pius XII again encouraged modernisation, asking nuns to 'collaborate with the Ecclesiastical Authorities, so as to help forward that vivifying adaptation and development which the Church seeks to promote'.[106] The very need for this broadcast, which was later translated and printed in English, implied that religious orders had not rushed to make these changes. Contemplative orders in Britain were aware of *Sponsa Christi* and listened to the broadcasts but some recalled *Sponsa Christi* as addressing a European problem, not a British one.[107]

Active congregations were also being encouraged to modernise. In the 1950s, several international congresses were organised by the Holy See to discuss matters pertaining to active women religious. Days after the announcement of *Sponsa Christi*, the First International Congress of Religious was held in Rome attended by superiors general from all over the world. The Congress was consultative and delegates discussed elimination of and modifications to regulations.[108] Such international

---

103 Jones, *Syon Abbey*, p. 128.

104 In Latin, *accommodationes*. *Sponsa Christi* (1950), §25.

105 'Books of the Week', *The Tablet* (12 September 1953), p. 256. Review of *La Vie Spirituelle* by Albert Plé.

106 *Audience Invisible*, p. 24.

107 Anonymised interview. Durham University Library and Special Collections, GB-033-CHS (henceforth DUL CHS): A3a, *Simul in Unum* (1953), Sister Mary Veronica, 'Notes on the Religious Vocation Exhibition', p. 26; D2a, Chantress Book, Volume 15, 19–20 July 1958.

108 'Eugenio Pacelli, Pope Pius XII', *The Tablet* (11 October 1958), p. 4.

events encouraged discussion and exchange at a new level; transnational exchanges would now occur more regularly across religious institutes as opportunities where congregation leaders could meet to learn from each other increased.[109] Mother Campion Davenport's notes of the meeting were relayed to her community, the Institute of the Blessed Virgin Mary. She highlighted how superiors general with their councils would collaborate 'in the holy movement of revitalizing the religious spirit in conformity with the need of the Church and of the world at this historic moment'.[110] One conference speaker, Jesuit Riccardo Lombardi, stressed that 'outmoded rules should be discarded without any false reverence' though 'innovations must be excluded'. *L'Osservatore Romano* made reference to *'l'aggiornamento del Religiosi'.*[111] The term *aggiornamento* would become, twenty years later, the rallying cry of the Second Vatican Council.

The first International Congress of Religious Teachers, held in Rome in September 1951, encouraged further professional and theological education of women religious.[112] The following year, the first International Congress of Mothers-General was attended by 700 religious from Europe, North America, India and Australia. This Congress directed sisters to address the 'changed condition of the world today' by a 'revitalizing of religious life in accordance with its basic constitutions and the particular rules and regulations of the various religious communities'.[113] Pope Pius XII addressed the 'crisis of vocations' and directed women religious to adapt their ways of living to the modern girl:

> For your part, this is what We counsel: make sure that nothing in your customs, your manner of life or your ascetical practices raises a barrier or causes loss of vocations. We have in mind certain usages which were, no doubt, suited to the times and surroundings in which they were instituted but are out of place today, so that even a good girl with courage would find them an obstacle to her vocation ... To sum up, then: in all that is not essential, make the adaptations called for by reason and well-ordered charity.[114]

---

109 This was aided by the founding of the Roman Union in 1952 and the International Union of Superiors General in 1965.

110 ACJ/EP/C/17/28, 'First Congress of Superiors General', p. 1.

111 'Religious Orders in Conference', *The Tablet* (16 December 1950), p. 5.

112 Courtois (ed.), *The States of Perfection*, pp. 199–200. Pope Pius XII 'Discourse to Teaching Sisters' dated 13 September 1951.

113 'News, Notes and Texts', *The Tablet* (20 September 1952), p. 16.

114 ACJ/EP/C/17/26, 'Address given by the Holy Father', 15 September 1952, p. 11.

Jesuit Joseph Gallen, writing in *Review for Religious*, elaborated on the meaning of adaptation:

> [A]daptation is change. A law, regulation, custom, practice, observance or manner of thinking and acting should be changed when it has become harmful or useless for the end for which it was intended … the law of life is gradual change and a mixture of the old and the new.[115]

The decline of religious vocations was perceived as a national and global issue. Many religious institutes were experiencing declining numbers in the 1940s and 1950s. The Holy See, through the apostolic constitution *Sponsa Christi*, the radio broadcasts that followed and the congresses and conferences held in the 1950s, addressed structural issues within religious life and spurred women's religious institutes to change with the times.[116]

A national response

In Britain, Edna John and Doris Andrews sensed the need for a fresh approach to vocations recruitment and their Vocation Sisters offered alternative means of encouraging vocations. First, they offered women time, space and information which enabled them to discern whether they had a vocation. Next, they organised the first national, public-facing vocations exhibition. In doing this, the Vocation Sisters took on the role of vocation promoters on a national level.

The Vocation Sisters initially aimed their efforts at three sorts of young women:

1   Those who are not sure whether they have vocations are able to discern in quiet and undisturbed atmosphere.
2   Those who feel they have a vocation but not decided which community to join.
3   Those who have chosen their order but owing to circumstances at home are unable to follow the call.[117]

Within these three cohorts was an acknowledgement of the changed circumstances of the post-war world: women had more options to consider than their mothers and grandmothers. This included expanded

---

115   Joseph F. Gallen, SJ, 'Renovation and Adaptation', *Review for Religious*, 14 (November 1955), 293–4.
116   These structural changes will be addressed in Chapter 3.
117   WSRO: 14, Filiae matris boni consilii, typescript dated 15 August 1947, p. 5.

opportunities for further education, waged employment and the 'new normality' of family life with room for self-fulfilment. The Vocation Sisters provided a quiet space where those with potential religious vocations could obtain information about religious life and women's religious institutes. By 1937, there were 175 religious congregations and orders in England and Wales to choose from.[118] The Vocation Sisters became an intermediary, replacing, or perhaps alongside, the parish priest or spiritual adviser who had that role in the nineteenth century. Their well-stocked library in both Pimlico, London and at Hallaton Hall (from 1951), near Market Harborough in Leicestershire, included biographies of founders, published histories of religious institutes, brochures and films.[119] Potential postulants dropped by after work or on their days off and spent time reading or meeting with the Vocation Sisters.[120] Monthly vocation talks in Pimlico were attended by twenty to twenty-five women. The Vocation Sisters had the requisite knowledge to direct women to particular religious institutes according to their circumstances and interests. They offered membership to a Vocation Club which initiated women into religious life. Each Wednesday they had lessons in French, plain chant, Church Latin, the Little Office of Our Lady, dramatics, needlework and domestic science.[121] These lessons gave young women a taster of religious life. This pre-formation proved valuable. The Vocation Sisters reported:

> [S]ome Nuns have written that it is a real asset to postulants to have joined [the Vocations Club] before entering, as they receive a clearer idea of the meaning of religious life, and even of certain essentials of external behaviour in the Novitiate – getting out of the habit of crossing her legs, of monopolising a conversation, or talking too loudly, etc. etc.[122]

The third category of young woman was personal to John and Andrews, who were aware that some women could not enter religious life because of family responsibilities or family opposition. The good Catholic home was the presumed 'cradle of vocations',[123] yet oral testimony suggested what religious and clergy claimed: parental opposition to religious life.

---

118 Walsh, *Roman Catholic Nuns in England and Wales*, p. 171.
119 WSRO: 14, 'Report on Development of the Work of Filiae Matris Boni Consilii', 1951, p. 5. In Hallaton Hall they offered retreats.
120 WSRO: 14, Filiae matris boni consilii, typescript dated 15 August 1947, p. 5.
121 WSRO: 14, 'Report on Development of the Work of Filiae Matris Boni Consilii', 1951, p. 1; also 103, *Quo Vadis*, 1:1 (April 1949), p. 11.
122 WSRO: 14, 'Report on Development of the Work of Filiae Matris Boni Consilii', 1951, p. 2.
123 WSRO: 14, Filiae matris boni consilii, typescript dated 15 August 1947, p. 6.

So, the Vocation Sisters promoted religious life to parents. They spoke to the Guild of Catholic Mothers on the 'privilege of a vocation in the home and how it can be fostered there'. In 1951, they produced the vocation film *The Master Calleth Thee*. After its first showing at Westminster Cathedral Hall in 1949, the sisters went on 'vocation tours' with the film to schools and church halls.[124] In the 1960s they launched a support group for parents of religious and priests. This 'Circle' emphasised that parents

> share in the Vocations of their children. If every parent would join this Circle and say even one Hail Mary daily, that all parents may come to appreciate the privilege it is to have a child completely dedicated to Christ, we feel that one cause of the lack of Vocations would be eliminated.[125]

The Vocation Sisters through this ministry were at the forefront of promoting, directing and initiating women into the world of female religious life by offering connected ways to disseminate knowledge about religious institutes to both women and their families.

Vocation exhibitions

In 1947, the Vocation Sisters organised a meeting in Westminster Cathedral Hall to discuss means of increasing vocations. This meeting, attended by 232 women religious representing 112 religious institutes, was one of the first occasions where women religious met together nationally to discuss matters of common interest.[126] One meeting outcome was the organisation of the first of many national vocation exhibitions.[127] Exhibitions, for example the Ideal Homes exhibitions and the Festival of Britain, had become a key means of promoting and disseminating modern ideas to the masses.[128] The first two exhibitions were organised

---

124 WSRO: 14, 'Report on Development of the Work of Filiae Matris Boni Consilii', 1951, p. 2.
125 DUL CHS: C1a 2, Letter to Reverend Mother/Sister Superior from Vocation Sisters undated, 1967.
126 The Conference of Religious was established in 1959 as the Council (or Conference) of Major Religious Superiors with separate men's and women's sections. In 1979 the first joint meeting took place and since then has been one Conference.
127 Local vocation exhibitions were also convened. For example parishioners of St Matthew held a vocation exhibition in their parish. 'Home for Week-End', *Catholic Pictorial* (6 May 1962), p. 20.
128 Claire Langhamer, 'The Meanings of Home in Postwar Britain', *Journal of Contemporary History*, 40 (2005), 353–4; Peter Scott, 'Marketing Mass Home Ownership and the Creation of the Modern Working-Class Consumer in Inter-War Britain', *Business History*, 50 (2008), 4–25.

Figure 1.3 Mother M. Joseph (Vocation Sisters foundress) and sisters

by the Vocation Sisters in Blackburn in 1949 and Birmingham in 1950 (see Figure 1.3). Fourteen additional national vocation exhibitions were held in ten major British cities, the last in London in 1969; these were organised by a committee of religious and clergy.[129]

Vocation exhibitions allowed clergy, religious and lay institutes the time and space to showcase their ministries to a larger public. Seventy-seven religious institutes of men and women exhibited at the June 1951 Manchester religious vocation exhibition, which welcomed 80,000 attendees, of whom 65,000 were children. The vocation exhibition moved north the following year to Glasgow's Kelvin Hall and received 200,000 visitors.[130] *The Tablet* commended some of the more striking booths of the 1953 vocation exhibition in London:

> Good marks for an ingenious display went also to the Sisters of Charity of St. Paul the Apostle, up in the gallery; who had reproduced a hospital ward with home-made dolls strapped to their beds in readiness for the most frightening operations. From a little model of the convent church

129 'A "Vocational Exhibition" in London', *The Tablet* (27 September 1952), p. 15.
130 ALA: GHC/S1/1/B/12, Letter from the Archbishop of Liverpool to Sir Arthur Binns, CBE, Chief Education Officer in Preston, dated 5 January 1956.

at Selly Park one could learn about the four stages in a nun's life: dolls dressed as postulants, on their day of clothing, as novices and professed nuns, appeared in the church door, and entered as graciously as the mechanism permitted.[131]

Sisters designed and managed specially built stalls that promoted their religious institute, drawing attention to their ministries and religious life. These were lively events. One young woman who attended the Manchester 1959 vocation exhibition recalled the hustle and bustle:

> There were so many orders … it wasn't a conference centre, it was more like Wembley Stadium or something, a huge place, and all the different orders had their stalls and there were crowds and crowds of young people.[132]

Did the vocation exhibitions influence vocations? Most definitely. For some the vocation exhibition provided confirmation of their vocation. The young woman had already decided to enter the Franciscans and helped out at their stall. One convert was convinced she had a vocation to religious life but was unsure of which religious institute to enter:

> I looked through this vocations exhibition, which was like a catalogue of religious orders really. And when I came to this particular one in Berkshire, I just had this extraordinary sense I'd been hit on the side of my head and I can remember sitting there feeling dizzy and just knowing that was where I was supposed to go.[133]

And a few attributed the first stirrings of their vocation to the vocation exhibition. One attendee admitted:

> I went to the Manchester religious vocations exhibition with a group from school and became very interested … I think probably my concept of what I wanted to do later in life became focused on religious life. I had been very interested in liturgy at school, prayer, and there was a group called the Sodality of Our Lady, which I was part of. And at this exhibition I collected information and I think it came down to five, my recollection is five. I shoved them under the mattress for about a year and then I thought I'd better take these out, you know.[134]

---

131 'The Vocations Exhibition', *The Tablet* (11 July 1953), p. 20.
132 Anonymised interview.
133 Anonymised interview.
134 Anonymised interview.

One Notre Dame teacher training college student attending the 1960 vocation exhibition in Kelvin Hall, Glasgow related the very efficient way in which she and her friends had organised their time at the exhibition:

> [T]he morning we were given off lectures to come in, we wanted – my friends and I – we wanted to get through it as quickly as possible. It was a bit like a motor show or a modern homes exhibition and so they were all set out with lots of passages between. So we divided ourselves up; you go down there, I'll go down there, you go down there, and we'll collect all the literature and we'll share it around.[135]

She had not been seriously considering religious life, but:

> During the exhibition at Kelvin Hall there were all sorts of films going on in a cinema part of it and I felt drawn to go back to the exhibition and went to the cinema and somehow, during the course of that watching, I don't remember seeing much, but during the course of that watching I knew that I had to become a nun. It was very, very quick.

She chose two congregations to visit after the exhibition and entered one in September.[136]

Quantifying the effectiveness of the vocation exhibition on vocation promotion proved difficult. The 1963 Newcastle upon Tyne vocation exhibition was attended by eighty-five exhibitors and at least 106,000 attendees. Nine months afterwards, the exhibitors reported that of 383 young women who indicated a strong interest in religious life: five became aspirants, seven postulants and two were about to begin their novitiate.[137] These were dispiriting statistics, but they don't capture women who, like the sister who attended the 1959 Manchester exhibition, 'shoved them [the brochures] under the mattress for about a year'.[138] Vocation exhibitions initially raised the hopes of the episcopacy and religious institutes. The 1951 archdiocese of Liverpool's Low Week Meeting notes remarked on the success of the Manchester vocation exhibition in encouraging vocations by making the work of the clergy better known and removing 'many prejudices in the minds of parents and others'.[139] Organiser Father

---

135   Anonymised interview.
136   Anonymised interview.
137   Archives of the Archdiocese of Westminster (henceforth AAW): HE1/R2, 'Religious Vocation Exhibition', Newcastle upon Tyne, May 1963, written by Bernard P. Slevin, CSSp, dated 10 March 1964, p. 8.
138   Anonymised interview.
139   ALA: GHC/S1/1/B/12, 'Low Week Meeting', undated. 'Low Sunday' is the second Sunday of the Easter season in the Roman Catholic Church.

James Forrestall claimed that the Catholic Church in England was on the fringe of a 'great forward movement, and that in this movement the work of the Exhibitions would be important both by fostering vocations and by increasing the influence of the Religious Orders'.[140] Despite such optimism, vocations exhibitions did not stem the tide of the decline in numbers of women entering religious life.

Conclusion

The growing awareness that fewer women were saying 'yes' to religious life in the 1940s and 1950s was of immense concern. What is curious is that no one questioned the expectation that large numbers of women would continue to enter religious life. The Church had experienced dynamic growth in religious life since the restoration of the hierarchy in 1850, and as the numbers of Catholics were still growing, they needed great numbers of women religious to educate, nurse and operate the social welfare institutions that helped to maintain a 'fortress church'. The extraordinary growth of religious institutes in the nineteenth century was assumed to be normative. Yet, the longer history of religious life which covers two millennia is not one of continuous growth; its trajectory suggests an irregular pattern of rise and fall linked to socio-political events.[141]

In examining young women's place in the modern world of the 1940s and 1950s, this chapter has considered their opportunities and their decision to enter religious life through an analysis of the 'vocation story'. It linked the specificities of their stories to the growing global, national and institutional awareness that fewer women were saying 'yes' to religious life in the 1940s and 1950s. Susan O'Brien has problematised this 'golden age' construct which suggests the post-war years were a time 'when novitiates were bursting'.[142] The archives suggest another story which features the paucity of women crossing the monastic or conventual

---

140 DUL CHS: A3a, *Simul in Unum* (1953), Sister Mary Veronica, 'Notes on the Religious Vocation Exhibition', p. 26.

141 Jo Ann McNamara, *Sisters in Arms: Catholic Nuns through Two Millennia* (London: Harvard University Press, 1996); Elizabeth Rapley, *The Lord as Their Portion: The Story of the Religious Orders and How They Shaped Our World* (Cambridge: Wm. B. Eerdmans Publishing, 2011), pp. 321–5. Lawrence Cada, Raymond Fitz, Gertrude Foley, Thomas Giardino and Carol Lichtenberg, *Shaping the Coming Age of Religious Life* (New York: Seabury Press, 1979). Discussed in more detail in the Conclusion.

142 O'Brien, *Leaving God for God*, pp. 274–5; Anonymised interview.

threshold in some religious institutes from the 1930s. Scholarly and public attention needs to be redirected from the 1960s and 1970s as a time of vocation decline and departure to the 1940s and 1950s when the vocation shortage became evident.

This phenomenon was addressed in various ways. Pope Pius XII's apostolic constitution *Sponsa Christi* (1950) and subsequent international congresses advocated 'modernisation' of women's religious institutes. In Britain, the Vocation Sisters became central to the marketing of religious life using modern approaches to promote vocations. Vocation exhibitions became commonplace from the late 1940s, displaying religious life as modern, exciting and pertinent. There was acknowledgement, too, that religious life needed to become more relevant and attractive to Catholic women. These attempts at vocation promotion also spurred cooperation amongst women religious that led to international, national and regional collaborations. We will see, in subsequent chapters, how this language of adaptation, modernising and *aggiornamento* was interpreted by women religious as they made changes to religious life in response to the directives of the Holy See. Sister Mary L. Schneider, speaking of the American context, argues that it is 'precisely in this period that the seeds of change were planted, nurtured and began to grow'.[143] This chapter examined these 'seeds of change' in a British context, but what happened inside the convent? How was this message received? The next chapter probes the trope of the Modern Girl and her influence (or not) within the convent.

---

143 Mary L. Schneider, 'American Sisters and the Roots of Change: The 1950s', *US Catholic Historian*, 7 (1988), 55–72. Schneider points to movements within American congregations focusing on internal changes within communities, the professionalisation of sisters and the call to collaboration.

2

The Modern Girl and religious life

Introduction

In 1969, Abbess Mary Joseph regaled the Poor Clares of Darlington on her return from the vocations exhibition in Leeds with 'interesting and amusing' talks on religious life, 'especially on how to deal with the modern girl'. The following week, Poor Clare abbess Mother Mary Paula Smallwood of Baddesley Clinton visited Darlington and also 'entertained us with stories of the "antics" of modern postulants'.[1] The Modern Girl was a recurrent trope which featured even in religious life. Each generation laid claim to its modernity with a Modern Girl who was either heralded as a progressive and sparkling rendition of all that was new or, in a negative stereotype, reflected a tainted version of femininity when compared to rose-coloured imaginings of a bygone age. The abbesses' stories suggest the Modern Girl was a figure of fun, but she was also instrumental in the refashioning of female religious life in Catholic religious congregations and orders. This chapter examines her influence. It begins with a historiographical introduction to the Modern Girl and girlhood more broadly. It then reveals her relationship to modernity and to religious life through memoirs and vocation literature. Lastly, it identifies how religious congregations and orders reacted to the Modern Girl who entered religious life from the 1940s to the 1960s.

In this analysis of memoirs and vocation literature, the representation and display of the Modern Girl is more relevant than her actual lived experience. This is a constructed Modern Girl, one that is less complicated than lived experience would highlight and one that is, in the sources at least, easily typecast. She is an object rather than an individual and, as a

---

1   Archives of the Poor Clares Monastery, Much Birch, Herefordshire (henceforth OSC Much Birch): Chronicles of St Clare's Abbey, Darlington, 1969, pp. 22–3.

heuristic device, is intended to focus our perceptions on female youth.[2] Historian Timothy Burke sees the gap between representation and lived experience as meaningful and argues that representations of the Modern Girl influenced the way 'everyday life is shaped by human agents'.[3] This influence is important because, as this chapter will demonstrate, understandings of the Modern Girl influenced the actions of religious institutes.

The Modern Girl, is of course, a very familiar trope. She appears in social critic Eliza Lynn Linton's 1868 piece on the 'Girl of the Period' as self-absorbed and consumed by fad styles linked to 'this loud and rampant modernization'.[4] Women's Studies scholar Sally Mitchell points to the Modern Girls of the late nineteenth century as 'consciously aware of their own culture' recognising its 'discord with adult expectation'. These Modern Girls, she says, would 'mark out a new way of being in the world'.[5] The Modern Girl reappears with even more style and flair in the interwar period historiography. Social, cultural, economic and political transformations were fuelled by a developing leisure culture and an emergent advertising industry.[6] Research coming out of two collaborative, international projects points to an interwar Modern Girl sharing some characteristics in common: her visibility, her agency, her patterns of consumption and her associations with romance and sexuality.[7] She is identified as a localised global phenomenon

2   The Modern Girl around the World Research Group identifies the Modern Girl as a global construct. I will be following their practice of treating the Modern Girl as a proper noun that relates to a very specific model of femininity. Alys Eve Weinbaum, Lynn M. Thomas, Priti Ramamurthy, Uta G. Poiger, Madeleine Yue Dong and Tani E. Barlow (eds), *The Modern Girl around the World: Consumption, Modernity, and Globalization* (Durham, NC: Duke University Press, 2008), pp. 2–8.

3   Timothy Burke, 'The Modern Girl and Commodity Culture', in Weinbaum *et al.* (eds), *The Modern Girl around the World*, p. 363. See also, Joan W. Scott, 'The Evidence of Experience', *Critical Inquiry*, 17 (1991), 778.

4   Eliza Lynn Linton, 'The Girl of the Period', *Saturday Review* (14 March 1868), p. 340.

5   Sally Mitchell, *The New Girl: Girls' Culture in England, 1880–1915* (New York: Columbia University Press, 1995), pp. 3–4. The Modern Girl and the New Woman appear at similar times in the late nineteenth century and share some similar traits as they both threatened normative ideals of womanhood. The difference between the two can feel illusory, but scholars have argued that the Modern Girl has less political resonance than the New Woman.

6   Cheryl Krasnick Warsh and Dan Malleck (eds), *Consuming Modernity: Gendered Behaviour and Consumerism before the Baby Boom* (Vancouver: UBC Press, 2013), p. 2.

7   The Modern Girl around the World Research Group is based at the University of Washington in Seattle and its sister group, the Modern Girl and Colonial Modernity Research Group, is based in Tokyo.

who challenged conventional understandings of girlhood and thus destabilised the social order and the moral codes of the times.[8] Historian Sally Alexander emphasises the agency of 1930s English working girls at a time of declining working hours and increasing wage packets.[9] This working-class Modern Girl availed herself of leisure activities such as cinemas and dance halls; she spent her pay packet on the latest affordable fashions and cosmetics.[10] Perhaps this is why social critic J. B. Priestley (1894–1984), in his journeys throughout England in 1933, insisted that England's factory girls looked like actresses.[11] Lest we think this Modern Girl was a piece of frivolous fluff, Alexander touts the aspirations of modern working girls: some were active in trade unions and local government.[12] Some were sporty, and thus emblematic of youth and freedom.[13] English Modern Girls were more multidimensional than the historiography on consumption would have us believe; they were participants in the modern world.

Visual representations of this Modern Girl were ubiquitous in cinemas, magazines and advertisements linking her to popular culture through the lenses of social class, ethnicity, sexuality, femininity and age. Magazine covers emphasised 'youth, liberation, mobility, fun' attending to the female body as the site of modernity; articles and advertisements directed towards the Modern Girl addressed beauty, hair, skin and clothes.[14] As established in the previous chapter, the 1940s and 1950s Modern Girl had more diverse employment opportunities than her predecessors.[15] She was encouraged to find meaningful work: to teach, to

---

8   Weinbaum *et al.* (eds), *The Modern Girl around the World.*
9   Sally Alexander, 'Becoming a Woman in London in the 1920s and 1930s', in David Feldman and Gareth Stedman Jones (eds), *Metropolis London: Histories and representations since 1800* (London: Routledge, 1989), p. 247. See also Rebecca Conway, 'Making the Mill Girl Modern? Beauty, Industry, and the Popular Newspaper in 1930s' England', *Twentieth Century British History*, 24 (2013), 519–20.
10 Conway, 'Making the Mill Girl Modern?', p. 531; Ina Zweiniger-Bargielowska, *Managing the Body* (Oxford: Oxford University Press, 2010), 239–40; David Fowler, *The First Teenagers: The Lifestyle of Young Wage-Earners in Interwar Britain* (London: Woburn Press, 1995), pp. 98–102.
11 J. B. Priestley, *English Journey* (London: William Heinemann, 1934), p. 401.
12 Alexander, 'Becoming a Woman', p. 247.
13 Fiona Skillen, *Women, Sport and Modernity in Interwar Britain* (Bern: Peter Lang, 2013).
14 Penny Tinkler, *Constructing Girlhood: Popular Magazines for Girls Growing Up in England, 1920–1950* (London: Taylor & Francis, 1995), p. 153.
15 Stephanie Spencer, 'Women's Dilemmas in Postwar Britain: Career Stories for Adolescent Girls in the 1950s', *History of Education*, 29 (2000), 329.

nurse, to engage in social work.[16] Young women imbibed 'the egalitarian and collective sentiments of social welfarism' alongside the 'equally powerful discourse of individualism and personal responsibility'.[17] By the 1960s, the discourse of youth subcultures brought new terms: from the wide-ranging 'teenager' and 'teenybopper' to the more distinctive 'beat girl' and 'dolly bird'.[18] The press continued to report of female youth consumption patterns. One *Daily Mail* article dubbing her a 'Spendager', whilst others noted the newish trend for girls leaving home and living independently in bedsits.[19]

Convent sources also indulge in the trope of the Modern Girl, though by the mid-twentieth century this terminology is a bit dated. The catchword 'girl' was an ambiguous but recurring label identifying this cohort; it became noticeable in late nineteenth-century memoirs, advice books, magazines and club names.[20] Rather than a chronological age, girlhood represented a stage of life, typically that period between mandatory school-leaving (which increased from fourteen to fifteen in 1947[21] and then sixteen in 1972) and marriage (average age of marriage was 22.4 for women in 1951[22]). Potential candidates for religious life were rarely identified as 'women' but almost exclusively characterised as 'girls' despite having achieved the legal age of majority (twenty-one until 1970 when it dropped to eighteen). Women interviewed for the book entered religious life from age fifteen to fifty-eight, though with a median age of twenty-one.[23]

16   Helen McCarthy, 'Social Science and Married Women's Employment in Post-War Britain', *Past and Present*, 233 (2016), 269–305; Stephanie Spencer, '"Be Yourself": *Girl* and the Business of Growing up in Late 1950s England', in Krista Cowman and Louise A. Jackson (eds), *Women and Work Culture: Britain c. 1850–1950* (Aldershot: Ashgate, 2005), 150–3.

17   Judy Giles, *The Parlour and the Suburb: Domestic Identities, Class, Femininity and Modernity* (Oxford: Berg, 2004), p. 158.

18   Carol Dyhouse, *Girl Trouble: Panic and Progress in the History of Young Women* (London: Zed Books, 2013); Bill Osgerby, *Youth in Britain since 1945* (Oxford: Blackwell, 1997), pp. 50–63; Mark Abrams, *Teenage Consumers* (London: London Press Exchange, 1959), pp. 1–3.

19   *Daily Mail*, 1 October 1963, p. 9, cited in Dyhouse, *Girl Trouble*, pp. 161–2.

20   Mitchell, *The New Girl*, p. 6.

21   This was an outcome of the 1944 Education Act.

22   Michael Anderson, 'The Social Implications of Demographic Change' in F. M. L. Thompson (ed.), *The Cambridge Social History of Britain, 1750–1950* (Cambridge: Cambridge University Press, 1990), p. 32.

23   For the entire cohort of interviewees, the average age was twenty-four, with a mode of eighteen. In examining the cohort of fifty-one women that entered before 1960, the average, median and mode was twenty-one. The 1960s cohort was younger, with an average age of twenty, mode of eighteen, and median of nineteen. The 1970s and

The aspirant to religious life was often linked with the 'modern world', a post-war world, as noted in the previous chapter, that often fell short of Catholic ideals which centred on faith, family and the parish community.

Catholic Modern Girls in print

Nineteenth- and twentieth-century published histories of religious institutes or founder biographies were usually promotional, often triumphalist texts heralding the sacrifice, holiness and piety of women religious and reflecting religious life as the 'higher call' for women.[24] From the 1940s, additional genres were used to publicise religious life: nun memoirs, apologetic texts and vocation promotion literature. Though much of the vocation promotion literature was meant for a local audience; some of this print literature, particularly the memoirs, became transnational cultural products circulating around the English-speaking world. These works often muted national identity, telling a story of a Modern Girl that was relatable across national boundaries, reflecting larger cross-national influences.

Nun memoirs

Nun memoirs were particularly noteworthy from the 1940s.[25] The nun-author in these quasi-anthropological published works, in the first person, described ordinary life within a convent/monastery/abbey, addressing convent rituals, traditions and ways of behaving as a postulant, novice and professed sister. Post-war memoirs were often written to encourage vocations, but were also a response to works written by former nuns such as Monica Baldwin's *I Leap over the Wall* and Kathryn Hulme's

---

1980s cohort were markedly older, with an average age of thirty-five, mode of twenty-five, and median of thirty-three. Susan O'Brien's study of the Daughters of Charity in Britain shows a similar decline, from twenty-six to twenty-one, in average age from the decadal cohorts of the 1920s to the 1950s. Susan O'Brien, *Leaving God for God: The Daughters of Charity of St Vincent de Paul in Britain, 1847–2017* (London: Darton, Longman & Todd, 2017), pp. 277–8.

24 For more on the nineteenth-century literature see Carmen M. Mangion, *Contested Identities: Catholic Women Religious in Nineteenth-Century England and Wales* (Manchester: Manchester University Press, 2008), pp. 175–7. John Berry, CSsR., 'Why so Few?', *Novena*, 6:8 (December 1956), 262.

25 Prior to this time, biographies of nuns were more commonly written, as well as occasional 'memoirs' that were compilations of the writing of a notable figure in religious life.

The Nun's Story.[26] Three popular memoirs are analysed in this section: *A Right to be Merry* (1957), *The Nun's Answer* (1957) and *Barefoot Journey* (1961).[27] Written to reach an English-speaking audience and emphasising the perceived uniformity of religious life (especially for enclosed orders), this literature rarely acknowledged national identity.[28]

American Poor Clare Mary Francis Aschmann, author of *A Right to be Merry*, wrote her memoir as if a Poor Clare in the United States lived a more or less similar life to Poor Clares in other far-flung places. Her work accentuated how autonomous Poor Clare monasteries were 'bound closely together by genuine affection' and connected via epistolary communication. Aschmann recounted letters read out loud from Poor Clare abbesses living abroad on the feast days of founders St Clare and St Francis.[29] *A Right to be Merry* from the start was directed to an international audience. First published by Sheed and Ward in the United States and England in 1956, it remains a popular work, republished in a new edition in 2001 by Ignatius Press. It was well reviewed in the English-speaking Catholic press. The Irish periodical *Doctrine and Life* welcomed this book 'wholeheartedly', contrasting it to the flurry of 'How I came to leave the convent' books.[30] It was a particularly influential book, and motivated women to consider entering the Poor Clares. One

26 Monica Baldwin's *I Leap over the Wall: A Return to the World after Twenty-Eight Years in a Convent* (London: Hamish Hamilton, 1949) detailed Baldwin's traumatic re-entry into a secular world after twenty-eight years as an enclosed contemplative. Kathryn Hulme's quasi-fictional *The Nun's Story* (London: Pan Books, 1959) became a Hollywood classic staring Audrey Hepburn. It chronicles the story of a nun's decision to leave religious life.

27 Sister Mary Francis Aschmann, *A Right to Be Merry* (London: Sheed & Ward, 1957), A Carmelite Nun, *The Nun's Answer* (London: Burns, Oates, 1957) and Sister Felicity, *Barefoot Journey* (London: Darton, Longman & Todd, 1961). Other American nun memoirs published from the 1940s to the 1960s include Catherine Thomas, *My Beloved: The Story of a Carmelite Nun* (New York: McGraw-Hill, 1955), Madeline De Frees, *The Springs of Silence* (Kingston, Surrey: The World's Work 1913, 1954) and Sister M. Catherine Frederic, *... And Spare Me Not in the Making: Pages from a Novice's Diary* (London: Clonmore & Reynolds, 1955).

28 Carmen M. Mangion, '"Shades of Difference": Poor Clares in Britain', in Christian Sorrel (ed.), *Le Concile Vatican II et le monde des religieux (Europe occidentale et Amérique du Nord, 1950–1980)* (Lyon: LARHRA, 2019), pp. 317–29.

29 Aschmann, *A Right to be Merry*, p. 47. The Poor Clares are part of the international Franciscan family of religious established by Francis di Bernardone (1181/2–1226). They were named after their first abbess and founder Clare Offreducio (1194–1253).

30 F. H., 'Book Reviews', *Doctrine and Life* 7:5 (1957), p. 275 (725). I've been unable to locate publication figures for *A Right to be Merry*.

Hawarden Poor Clare in the documentary *Poor Clares, Rich Lives* (1993) recounted that:

> When I was sixteen, *The Nun's Story*, *I Leap over the Wall*, were very much the in thing, I remember thinking there must be some happy nuns somewhere. I looked around and found the book *The Right to be Merry* and that was about Poor Clares and I didn't know such things existed and it hit me tremendously.[31]

A reader of popular nun memoirs, she recalls her dissatisfaction with the two well-known works where unhappy nuns left religious life. She deliberately searches for 'happy nuns' and finds what she is looking for in *A Right to be Merry*.

The founding of a new community of Poor Clares in Roswell, New Mexico is the memoir's explicit storyline. Sister Mary Francis explains the traditions, customs and history of the Poor Clares but also skilfully weaves into this story the expected behaviour of women living enclosed lives. As the foundation team of nine Poor Clares travelled by rail from Chicago to Roswell, Sister Mary Francis explains that though outside the cloister, 'she is still a cloistered nun. She observes the spirit of her vow of enclosure where she is.' She clarifies precisely what this means: she doesn't 'wander about the train "Making friends" or striking up chance conversations. Neither would she stare about curiously at everything and everybody.'[32] She admits that independent Modern Girls who have earned their own living and ran their own lives will find convent obedience testing, but gradually the 'tight network of permission' will become understood and 'a postulant comes to take this kind of dependence for granted'.[33] She points out that the Modern Girls who enter and persist in contemplative religious life must have a sense of humour, because 'Without it, the enclosure can easily become a spiritual hothouse where every trifle marks a crisis ... A sense of humor is like a sweet, clean wind sweeping through our enclosed lives and purifying the small details of it.'[34] She depicts Poor Clare monasteries as 'gay and charming' even in their poverty.[35] She consistently alludes to the joy and happiness of consecrated virginity, telling her readers that 'one long look at the faces

---

31 British Film Institute (henceforth BFI): *Poor Clares, Rich Lives* (Open Space series, Tx 17.11.1993), Ty Mam Duw, Hawarden Poor Clares.
32 Aschmann, *A Right to be Merry*, p. 18.
33 *Ibid.*, pp. 58–9.
34 *Ibid.*, p. 37.
35 *Ibid.*, p. 54.

of nuns, one long listen to their laughter' will convince readers of the happiness of the virginal state.[36]

Dominican Sister Mary Jordan reviewed *A Right to be Merry* for the Catholic newspaper, *The Tablet*. Not convinced by its depiction of enclosed religious life, she elicited comments from three friends, enclosed nuns, who were 'representative of that much written about creature, the modern girl'. She précised their conversation:

> 'Another book,' I [Sister Mary Jordan] said, 'by a nun who writes from the sheer joy of being in a convent.' 'Aw, come off it!' said the first. 'What gets me,' said the second, 'is all this emphasis on the setting. If I bought a book about marriage I wouldn't expect it to go on and on about jam-making.' 'Books like this,' said the third and keenest-supporter of enclosed life, 'make me go hot under the collar.'

All three enclosed nuns were dismissive of *A Right to be Merry*. Sister Mary Jordan insisted that the main premise of the book, 'that girls of today, apart from certain differences of clothes and manners, are no different from their grandmothers', was 'palpably false'.[37] She identified the 1950s Modern Girl as one embedded in the culture of a certain time and place. She was influenced by post-war modernity and differed in thought and action from the young women who entered religious life in the 1930s.

Sister Mary Jordan also reviewed *The Nun's Answer*. This nun memoir was written by a very complicated, cerebral Modern Girl who believed she had a vocation, but did not desire it. She joins the Carmelites in October 1951, as an extern, to try out the life.[38] She finally enters the enclosure after six months. In total, this is 174 pages of indecisiveness influenced by the wisdom of 'dear Mother' (the Mother Superior) who 'sees *everything* supernaturally' though not, according to our nun-author, with excessive piety.[39] A strong religious message about the primacy of 'union with God' and 'acceptance of His will' permeated this work, but the notion of piety was severely underplayed in a pattern that was reflected throughout memoirs and vocation promotion literature as well as oral testimony.[40] Modernity was exhibited in many ways. The writer appears to be a well-educated young woman (though probably not university-educated), and

36   *Ibid.*, p. 96.
37   'Book Supplement', *The Tablet* (7 December 1957), pp. 509–10.
38   Externs were sisters who took simple vows and did not take a vow of enclosure and so were able to manage the external affairs (shopping, errands, etc.) of a convent.
39   *The Nun's Answer*, pp. 19–20.
40   *Ibid.*, p. 17.

perhaps a well-heeled one as she calls to mind attending the opera and the 'Constables' at home.[41] She revels in the great English outdoors. She recounts being told that she had 'none of that tiresome holiness about me' and that she was 'easy to talk to'.[42]

Midway through the book, she recounts the story of Amanda, another postulant. Cigarette-smoking and possibly hung-over, Amanda arrived at the convent alone in a taxi. Upon meeting one of the extern sisters, she decides to flee before crossing the monastic threshold. Our nun-author in an effort to convince this melodramatic Modern Girl to stay suggests the root of her discomposure:

> I pointed an accusing finger at her suddenly: 'Did you go to a farewell party last night?' I demanded. 'That's it: I knew you had. I always said that wasn't the way to come into Carmel, and it isn't. You can't do beautiful mediaeval things on nasty modern methods. I expect you have an awful headache, and you probably feel sick —'[43]

In contrasting the modern world and its 'nasty modern methods' with the 'beautiful mediaeval things' of Carmel, she reiterates the dominant trope that juxtaposed the 'modern world' in a negative light when compared to the ethereal beauty of religious life. Many of these published works argue that the modern worldview does not appreciate the value or understand the practices of enclosed religious life.[44] Amanda, unsurprisingly, crossed the monastic threshold and became a happy and contented Carmelite.

The Modern Girl, throughout this memoir, was consistently characterised unfavourably. The nun-author after a recreation with her fellow novices intimated:

> I had come to the conclusion that the present generation has rather an incoherent view of life. What we want is something to make sense of it all and hang it together. We have a vague idea that we are in a muddle, but we cannot altogether put our finger on the whys and wherefores.[45]

---

41   She is referring to the work of English landscape painter John Constable.

42   *The Nun's Answer*, p. 47.

43   She seems to be suggesting Amanda overindulged in alcohol, but later she says that Amanda became sick on salmon mayonnaise and cream cakes. *The Nun's Answer*, p. 54.

44   Carmen M. Mangion, 'Syon Abbey's "Second Summer", 1900–1950', in Elin Andersson, Claes Gejrot, E.A. Jones, and Mia Akestam (eds), *Continuity and Change. Papers from the Birgitta Conference at Dartington, 2015* (Stockholm: Kungl. Vitterhets historie och antikvitetsakademien, 2017), pp. 367–88.

45   *The Nun's Answer*, p. 94.

She discussed the Modern Girl with Reverend Mother, who pronounced:

> The mental age of all of them seems to me so much lower than it used to be … we were such full grown young women at eighteen, and now they are no more than babes at that age.

Our nun-author concurred, with 'I am afraid we aren't very adult'.[46] The Modern Girl, in this memoir, was persistently portrayed as incoherent, muddled and immature.

The reviews of *The Nun's Answer* were mixed. One reviewer noted that *The Nun's Answer*

> may not please all readers, but it is a human account of a vocation. It shows something of the prejudices, the misconceptions, as well as the ordinary picture of life in the enclosed order.[47]

Dominican Sister M. Mathias's assessments in the *Clergy Review* were scathing. She found the book 'inane', reflecting 'trite language and puny sentiments'. She recommended to readers who wanted to know about Carmel 'the more profound record of suffering in St Therese or Sister Elizabeth of the Trinity (both Carmelites) in place of this nun's answer'. Her response reflected her distaste for this new genre of nun memoirs, pointing to the more traditional rendering of religious life as suffering and, one suspects, a bit more piety.[48]

Sister Mary Jordan's *Tablet* review advocated that though the nun-author of *The Nun's Answer* exhibited 'some of the characteristics of her generation', she misrepresented the 1950s Modern Girl. Sister Mary Jordan asserted:

> Yet surely, neither she nor her kittenish and pliable companions are representative of present-day novices. Unless Carmel is peopled solely by survivals from a past age, and why should you suppose this, you have to conclude that the picture is misleading.[49]

She ends her review by defining the Modern Girl for *Tablet* readers as one of the

> mature, argumentative, sceptical young women of today, who question everything, thrive on logic, and find flippancy an

---

46   *The Nun's Answer*, p. 156.
47   'Book Reviews', *Clergy Review* 43:2 (1958), pp. 696–7, p. 696.
48   Sister M. Mathias, OP, 'Book Reviews', *Clergy Review* 8:1 (February–March 1958), p. 52.
49   'Book Supplement', *The Tablet* (7 December 1957), pp. 509–10.

indispensable covering for their serious enthusiasm. Reverence and receptivity are not usually their strongest points but they have an eye for fundamentals and therefore, in the long run, a deep capacity for obedience. A book of this kind, enlivened as it is by a delicate response to nature and to the human side of things, does valuable work in dispelling ignorance and prejudice against the enclosed orders. But it seems a pity that it should take so little account of the type of recruit on whom such orders will come to depend more and more for filling up their ranks.[50]

Sister Mary Jordan's Modern Girl was 'modern' but in the 'longer term' she had what it took to make a good religious: 'serious enthusiasm', 'an eye for fundamentals' and of great importance, the 'capacity for obedience'.

A few years later, another Poor Clare, Sister Felicity, reflected that 'religious life has not been given a square deal', so wrote *Barefoot Journey* as a 'little cheep or two' by someone who had 'found her spiritual and psychological level' and could be 'merry withal' in religious life.[51] She entered the Poor Clares in 1945, aged twenty-seven, having spent the war years with the Women's Auxiliary Air Force. While she included quite a bit of merriness, giggling and laughter in her rendition of convent life she was also forthright about the difficulties. She acknowledged her discomfort at using convent language such as 'humbly begging' when making requests. She admitted 'I thought the formula rather artificial and was secretly revolted.'[52] She found 'Kneeling to speak to Superiors' awkward.[53] Later she noted, 'I was by now growing more accustomed to all the ground kissing but at first it had irked me considerably.'[54] She was frank about her struggles in the novitiate: 'The fervour of the novitiate is spasmodic, erratic and subject to many disturbing fluctuations.'[55] She represented the convent and religious life as a challenging but joyful place.

All three participant memoirs were written by members of enclosed international religious orders and potentially had a large, global English-speaking audience. These books aspired to demystify religious life and encourage vocations. The memoirs were written using informal and colloquial language. They portrayed religious life as challenging

50   *Ibid.*
51   Sister Felicity, *Barefoot Journey*, pp. x–xi.
52   *Ibid.*, p. 36.
53   *Ibid.*, p. 37.
54   *Ibid.*, p. 54.
55   *Ibid.*, p. 127

spiritually as well as corporally, but focused more on everyday events and portrayed religious life as familial and joyful, often ignoring or lightly touching upon (sometimes dismissing) the complexities of demanding personalities as well as intergenerational and inter-class human relationships.

This genre of convent literature reflected a departure from past publications on religious life, pious works intended as prescriptive literature. Nun memoirs were important as a means of creating an understanding of enclosed religious life which in the mid-twentieth century was increasingly being seen by some as an anachronism.[56] In their more accessible language, the nuances of everyday life in the enclosed monastery were translated for the Modern Girl, who, nun-authors implied, could be successfully integrated into religious life.

Defending religious life

Apologetic texts that sought to inform and educate the Modern Girl on religious life both responded to objections and publicised convent living.[57] The works discussed below, published in the 1950s, were written to offer informal, and more accessible, dialogic apologetics. They disseminated knowledge whilst defending religious life. Sister Mary Laurence's trilogy and other short books based on her own correspondence were particularly well received.[58] The first volume, *She Takes the Veil* (1952), contained the epistolary conversation between shopgirl Doreen Neeves and Sister Mary Laurence. Twenty-five-year-old Neeves identified herself as a convert of six years who did not spend a lot of time in church and was 'not a bit pious, I go in for every kind of sport and dancing and theatre and love it all'. She was considering a vocation to religious life but suggested that as she liked to have 'a good time', she was not the nunnish type. In her response, Sister Mary Laurence proposed otherwise, explaining that

---

56 Mangion, 'Syon Abbey's "Second Summer", 1900–1950'.
57 I am using the term apologetic in this section as an adjective. There is a long history of Christian apologetics that is now addressed in the discipline of fundamental theology. These works would not be considered part of that theological discipline.
58 Sister Mary Laurence was probably an enclosed Dominican at Carisbrooke Priory, though her name was likely a pseudonym. The books were published individually and later compiled in an anthology, *The Convent and the World* (London: Blackfriars Publications, 1955). Her works were reviewed positively in the Catholic press. For example, 'Vocations Today', *The Tablet* (30 August 1952), p. 10; 'Leaping over the Wall', *Catholic Herald* (7 January 1955), p. 3.

she too liked to have a good time and as a young woman 'spent every evening in some form of amusement, dancing, skating, playing cards, theatre, etc'. Their correspondence becomes more serious as discussions centred on the essentials of contemplative religious life, its ministry and the horarium. The book's ending was predictable: Doreen Neeves entered the Dominicans and became Sister Mary Paul.[59]

In the second in the trilogy, *Within the Walls*, Sister Mary Laurence again became the recipient of a series of letters from a good friend of Doreen Neeves, another recent convert, Marjory Ferrans.[60] Ferrans operated a small business and her prominently displayed crucifix elicited queries from customers regarding Catholic practices.[61] She revelled in exercising her 'little apostolate' by responding to their questions, but turned to Sister Mary Laurence with the more difficult theological issues. Noting Ferrans seemed over-anxious to stress her status as a laywoman, Sister Mary Laurence assured her that despite the shortage of vocations, nuns were not 'out to grab any nice girl they come into contact with, and persuade her into entering their own particular Order'. By the end of the book Ferrans found her vocation too, when she met like-minded Michael, a Catholic man she eventually married.[62]

The third of the trilogy, *They Live the Life*, continued Sister Mary Laurence's conversations with Ferrans. Ferrans and Michael visited the 1953 vocations exhibition at Olympia with Michael's friend John, who asserted that religious life was anachronistic. Ferrans reported to Sister Mary Laurence that he insisted that 'young people, being the product of the age' would not be attracted to the restrictions of religious life, particularly the vow of obedience. Sister Mary Laurence responded, agreeing that religious life asked much of youth, but she noted that 'the modern girl *does* find happiness in this complete sacrifice of personal freedom for the love of God'.[63] Sister Mary Laurence in her apologetic

---

59   Sister Mary Laurence, OP, *She Takes the Veil* (London: Blackfriars Publications, 1952), pp. 1–2. The horarium, the timetable of religious life, will be discussed in more detail in Chapter 4.

60   Sister Mary Laurence may have chosen converts as her discussants in order to provide basic information without seeming to patronise cradle Catholics.

61   The openness with which she displayed her Catholicism was indicative of the confidence of Catholicism in the 1950s. James Sweeney, *The New Religious Order* (London: Bellew, 1994), p. 46.

62   Sister Mary Laurence, OP, *Within the Walls* (London: Blackfriars Publications, 1953), pp. 1–2, 35, 84–5.

63   Sister Mary Laurence, OP, *They Live the Life* (London: Blackfriars Publications, 1954), pp. 8, 12. This volume contains the complete trilogy.

texts, like the memoirs above, underscored the ordinariness of the Modern Girl who entered the convent, pointing out that 'we have ex-teachers, bank clerks, secretaries, dispensers, gardeners, girls just down from the universities, girls who have served in the Forces'. She '*is* just the ordinary, gay, lighthearted, normal girl *of her own period*, who does enter a Convent – and stay'.[64]

Such works also addressed the evolution of religious life. In 1959, Sister Mary Laurence admitted, in *One Nun to Another*, that religious life was at a crossroads, with 'people leaping over walls and the alleged seamy side of Convent life', as well as talk of 'new looks', the shortage of vocations and the 'crowded days of modern religious life'. She acknowledged religious were part of the modern world: 'reform' and 'change' were 'in the air' and 'it is right and good that they should be'. Adaptations could and would occur in the 'accidentals' of religious life without affecting 'essentials' and she was convinced that the Modern Girl of 1959 would continue to adjust to these essentials, as young women in the past had done.[65]

Vocation promotion: *Bride of a King*

This third genre used to publicise religious life consisted of the numerous pictorials, brochures and pamphlets published by religious institutes. Most, like the brochure *The Congregation of the Sisters of Charity of Our Lady Mother of Mercy: A Pictorial of the Houses and Work of the Order* (1949), were published specifically to make their own religious institute 'better known'.[66]

Bride of a King (c. 1958), a simply illustrated text that gave a visual as well as discursive story of a young woman entering religious life, was published for a larger audience of Modern Girls. It developed out of an earlier work by the Jesuit Daniel Lord (1888–1955), *Shall I Be a Nun?*, published in the United States in 1927. Lord was a prolific author, publishing over 500 pamphlets, plays and songs directed towards a

---

64 Sister Mary Laurence, OP, *Nuns Are Real People* (London: Blackfriars, 1955), pp. 5–8.
65 Sister Mary Laurence, OP, *One Nun to Another* (London: Blackfriars, 1959), pp. 1, 13, 28, 43. In referring to the 'seamy' side of religious life, she is likely referring to Rumer Godden's fictional *Black Narcissus* (1939; made into a film in 1947), which documents madness, sexuality and desire in the lives of five Anglican sisters missioned to the Himalayas.
66 Archives of the British Province of the Sisters of Charity of Our Lady, Mother of Mercy: Preston Diary, 17 September 1949.

Catholic, typically lay audience.[67] Though the text and images were originally published for an American audience in the 1950s, the book was reprinted and distributed in Britain in 1958 by the Vocation Sisters, which suggests the narrative was relatable to a British audience.[68] Texts like *Bride of a King* are rarely found in convent archives as they are typically ephemeral to the archive collections but this book was catalogued in the archives of the Sisters of Mercy in Handsworth.[69] The annotation on the front cover suggests teaching sisters lent the book to fourth-form students in their schools, so young girls aged thirteen or fourteen. It also appeared in another form, as a serial in the *Catholic Pictorial*, a weekly Catholic newspaper. Here, it was advertised as 'The True Fairy Tale – The Story of a Religious Vocation'.

The storyline of *Bride of a King* was simple: girl meets Christ, and after a bit of indecision says 'YES' and lives happily ever after, but the points made throughout her journey are instructive to understandings of the young women entering religious life. The first section of the book depicts the smartly dressed Catholic girl leaving her living quarters, in this case not her family home but a 'Young Ladies Hostel'.[70] The image suggests that as a Modern Girl, she was financially independent with a promising career. The next few pages identify themes from an ordinary young woman's life: music, dancing, children, male company and even a suggestion of a marriage proposal (see Figure 2.1). Her lively social life was a part of her life in the secular world. She was of the world: fashionable, sporty, sensible and kind. These traits were repeated again and again throughout the book.

67   Daniel A. Lord, *Shall I Be a Nun?* (St Louis, MO: The Queen's Work Press, 1927). This volume was reprinted by the Catholic Truth Society of Ireland in 1945. He also published *Shall My Daughter Be a Nun?* (1927), *Letters to a Nun* (1947) and *Who Can Be a Nun?* (1948).

68   I have not been able to identify the print run or the distribution of this work. The bishop of Nottingham gave his imprimatur for publication in England and Wales.

69   The Sisters of Mercy were one of the largest Catholic religious congregations worldwide, founded in 1831 by Catherine McAuley in Dublin. In 1957, they operated 1,500 convents worldwide, of which 115 were in England, Wales and Scotland. Archives of the Union Sisters of Mercy, Great Britain (Handsworth, Birmingham) (henceforth RSM Union): WOL/200/5/4, vocation brochure 'Congregation of Sisters of Mercy Archdiocese of Birmingham & Wales', p. 3.

70   *Bride of a King* (London: Daughters of Our Lady of Good Counsel, 1958), p. 16. For more on the 1950s Career Girl see Stephanie Spencer, 'Schoolgirl to Career Girl. The City as Educative Space', *Paedagogica Historica*, 39 (2003), 121–33.

Figure 2.1 Young woman leaving her hostel and dancing. Illustrations from *Bride of a King* (London: Daughters of Our Lady of Good Counsel, c. 1958), pp. 16–17

The 'call' to a vocation was not portrayed as a sudden 'lightning bolt' insight. Rather it was a 'slowly gathering conviction, vague or clearly defined … that religious life is best for them'.[71] But vocation calls could be 'rebuffed'. Though 'she follows Christ' and entered the convent, there was a hesitancy, an uncertainty that was portrayed as natural. This indecision quickly dissolved in the 'peace and a deep content' of religious life. Convent life was depicted as full of smiles, laughter, sporty recreation and music; the message here was that convent life too was modern. The everyday work of a religious sister, teaching, nursing, caring, at home and abroad, was represented as esteemed and respected. The enclosed, contemplative nun was barely addressed, perhaps because her spiritual role was more difficult to explain in this version of modernity. The message of this text was clear: ordinary Modern Girls, 'normal, natural young women' with a 'quite ordinary piety', had a place in religious life.[72]

Bride of a King represented the Catholic Modern Girl as a young woman with choices. It acknowledged the attractiveness of the modern world and the sacrifices she made when entering religious life. Its rose-coloured depiction of religious life was highly optimistic, avoiding any difficulties of adjustment to religious life and the demands of living with different personalities. The nun memoirs, apologetic texts and the *Bride of a King* demonstrate that the Modern Girl with a religious vocation had a place in religious life. She might, like Sister Felicity, be a bit uncomfortable with some convent practices, but those feelings would eventually dissipate and she would fit in. Discursive texts suggest that modern girls would be altered by religious life, but that religious life would remain static. Religious life, however, was remade by the Modern Girl. Writing from an English Carmelite monastery in 1948, the nun-author of *Our Eternal Vocation* (1948) acknowledged that a 'modern approach' to religious vocations was necessary because 'the postulant of to-day is a very different person mentally to her sister of say twenty years ago, although spiritually she may differ scarcely at all'.[73] As transnational products, these works circulated around the English-speaking world. Much more analysis needs to be done on their reception, but their message suggests the formation of women religious needed to be revised to fit a secular age.

---

71 *Bride of a King*, p. 58.
72 *Ibid.*, pp. 20, 22, 34, 36.
73 A Carmelite Nun, *Our Eternal Vocation* (London: Sands & Co., 1948), p. 137.

Educating the Modern Girl

This final section interrogates the 'modern approach' to religious vocations. The discourse of the Modern Girl was often linked with the anxiety about declining vocations discussed in the previous chapter.[74] Concerns about falling vocations were heard in Europe also, particularly from enclosed orders. In France, a series of symposia organised by the Dominicans in the 1950s examined the 'problems of the nun's vocation today'. The resulting edited volumes on religious life were published in French then translated into English by the London-based Blackfriars Press, whose editor argued that 'practical experiences' found in the volumes would be of interest to those in the Anglo-American world. These publications were part of the transnational literature on religious life that crossed national borders because of perceived commonalities. They were reviewed in the Catholic press and though pointing to a French context, often acknowledged the 'historical and theological' exposition that was of importance to both men and women religious.[75]

One *Tablet* reviewer of a 1953 volume of edited conference papers intimated that 'a partial cause of the shortage of religious vocations to the Orders and Congregations of women may well be their instinctive refusal to adapt themselves to modern conditions and ways of thought'. Quoting the volume's editor he advised that 'The modern girl does not abandon her personality', suggesting not only that religious life must adjust, but also that the training of the women entering religious life must be updated: 'In modern times a girl "has to be won" in order that she may be "trained interiorly."'[76] Redemptorist Edward Murphy, writing of the relationship between the teaching sister and her female students, argued that:

74 Although there were concerns about a vocation crisis for male religious and the priesthood, the Modern Girl trope does not have a parallel Modern Boy despite, as discussed in the previous chapter, reports that suggest the reasons for the 'crisis' in vocations for men and women were similar.

75 Albert Plé (ed.), *Authority in the Cloister: Obedience* (London: Blackfriars Press, 1953), p. v. At least ten other volumes of similar works edited by Albert Plé were translated and published by Blackfriars Press.

76 Plé (ed.), *Authority in the Cloister*, reviewed in 'Books of the Week', *The Tablet* (12 September 1953), p. 13. This French conference on female contemplative life was attended by secular and regular clergy and even members of the National Committee of Nuns.

Religious teaching thus assumes a co-operative character more essential and significant than ever before. To produce fruits that will abound and abide it requires a new relationship between pupil and teacher which is more in the nature of a partnership freely and mutually negotiated and sustained.[77]

The Catholic press weighed in also. In 1963, the *Catholic Pictorial*'s article on Cardinal Leon Jozef Suenens's book, *The Nun in the World* (1963), was blunt: 'fewer and fewer modern girls feel the call to the convent' and something must be done about it. The article continued: 'Some people think that if a girl is chosen by God, then she should be prepared to sacrifice everything for her vocation even to the acceptance of the bizarre or the repugnant.'[78] By implication, outmoded customs and traditions, which had been identified as impeding vocations by Pope Pius XII a decade earlier, had remained intrinsic to both enclosed and non-enclosed religious life.

In the 1950s, some religious institutes were rethinking the novitiate experience of the Modern Girl.[79] Young women entering religious life in the 1950s would have been the first generation to benefit from the post-1944 expansion of secondary, further and higher education. Bishops and clergy played a significant role in protecting and expanding Catholic schools but so did the growing numbers of upwardly mobile, informed and articulate Catholic laity.[80] Catholic-educated boys and girls were joining groups like the Young Christian Workers in the 1950s and being taught to engage with the secular world in Christian ways through the motto 'See Judge Act'.[81] Historian Alana Harris suggests that young women

---

77   Edward Murphy, 'The Teaching Sister and the Modern Girl', *The Furrow*, 9:9 (1958), 565.

78   'A New Era for Nuns', *Catholic Pictorial* (3 March 1963), p. 15. For more on the influence of *The Nun in the World*, see Chapter 7.

79   Women who entered religious life spent their first six months or so as postulants, and then entered the novitiate for one to two years. Sisters then took annual vows for two to three years and were known as Young Professed. Each novice received formal training in the novitiate in the spirituality, customs, practices and sometimes the works of the religious institute. The stages of this process varied over time and according to the religious institute.

80   Michael P. Hornsby-Smith, *Roman Catholics in England: Studies in Social Structure since the Second World War* (Cambridge: Cambridge University Press, 1987), p. 6; Kit Elliott, '"A Very Pushy Kind of Folk": Educational Reform 1944 and the Catholic Laity of England and Wales', *History of Education*, 35 (2006), 91–119.

81   British Library: 'The Young Christian Workers' (undated), p. 3. For more on the Young Christian Workers see Sylvia Collins and Michael P. Hornsby-Smith, 'The Rise and Fall of the YCW in England', *Journal of Contemporary Religion*, 17 (2002), 87–100.

were offered an alternative to the conservative model of femininity, one that advocated an equal discipleship along with 'emotional maturity, self-expression and intellectual independence'.[82] As discussed earlier and below, young Catholic women were likely to question and exercise their critical faculties. Dominican Conrad Peplar, in his introduction to the edited volume *The Education of the Novice*, a collection of lectures given to fifty novice mistresses in 1955, began by remarking that novitiates posed different problems from those of fifty years earlier. He noted that 'revolutionary changes' in society required novice mistresses to become a 'bridge' between the life of the secular world and the life of the cloister. Her role was to 'inculcate firmly the essentials of religious life while interpreting the particular customs and regulations of the convent to the mentality of the newcomers'. He referenced Modern Girls who had been brought up with

> an almost excessive frankness ... used to forming their own opinions and expressing them without hesitation ... The process of education to an age-old form of life is therefore more difficult than it was a century ago when the young women lived a more sheltered and protected life, developed by an education which was more or less exclusively concerned with the domestic virtues ... The novice-mistress then has to adjust herself to the new style of education of the girl without modifying any of the essentials in education for religious life.[83]

Peplar insisted that novice mistresses must understand the psychology of the Modern Girl in order to effectively educate them about religious life. The same emphasis can be found in Father Albert Plé's study days for novice mistresses in France in the early 1950s, whose lectures were published and later translated into English. Plé's influence led to the inclusion of psychological training for students studying theology and psychological testing for religious candidates in France. Pope Pius XII, once opposed to psychotherapy, gave it his approval, even welcoming the International Congress of Psychotherapy to Rome in 1953.[84] There is little evidence to suggest that psychology was used by sisters and nuns in Britain in the 1950s, but this awareness may have sown the seeds for the

---

82   Alana Harris, *Faith in the Family: A Lived Religious History of English Catholicism, 1945–1982* (Manchester: Manchester University Press, 2013), p. 143.

83   Conrad Peplar, 'Introduction', in Ambrose Farrell, Henry Saint John and F. B. Elkisch, *The Education of the Novice* (London: Blackfriars Publications, 1956), pp. vii–ix.

84   C. Kevin Gillespie, 'Review of Agnès Desmazières, *L'Inconscient au paradis. Comment les catholiques ont reçu la psychoanalyse (1920–1965)* (Paris: Payot, 2011)', *Catholic Historical Review*, 98 (2012), 596–98.

embrace of psychoanalysis in the late 1960s and 1970s.[85] This thinking replicated messages in the nun memoirs and *Bride of a King*: today's novice was different from her predecessor. It adds, however, an important innovation – the novice mistress in revising her teaching methods must 'adjust herself' and, by implication, the convent too must modernise.[86]

Religious could not stand at a distance from the world. They were being told to keep up with 'modern trends and problems'. At the Annual General Meeting of the Council of Major Religious Superiors in 1965, the Abbot of Ampleforth spoke on 'Some Problems among young Religious Today'. He stressed the importance of

> supernatural obedience in the religious life. Young religious are not only progressives, but are idealists in the right sense of that word. It is necessary for Superiors to keep up to date with modern trends and problems, so that when young religious come to talk out their difficulties, the Superiors know what they are talking about and are able to give sympathy and understanding when these are needed.[87]

Here, the onus was on superiors to be aware of the modern world. Still, as the language of the title of the presentation makes clear, the problem remained with the Modern Girl.

Slowly, religious institutes shifted their thinking away from changing the Modern Girl, to changing religious life. Each of the four convents of the Sisters of Charity of Our Lady, Mother of Mercy in England and Wales received a circular letter from Superior General Josephino van Dinter in 1957 insisting that religious life should be made 'attractive to the <u>modern girl</u>'. She proposed that as a congregation, when addressing the question of renewal, the sisters should consider eliminating some of the antiquated features of religious life.[88] And, by implication, to

---

85   The development of popular psychology in Britain is addressed in Mathew Thomson, 'The Popular, the Practical and the Professional: Psychological Identities in Britain 1901–1950', in G. C. Bunn, A. D. Lovie and G. D. Richards (ed.), *Psychology in Britain: Historical Essays and Personal Reflections* (Leicester: BPS Books, 2001), pp. 115–32. See also a discussion on psychoanalysis in David Geiringer, 'Catholic Understandings of Female Sexuality in 1960s Britain', *Twentieth Century British History*, 28 (2017), 209–38. Many sisters trained as psychoanalysts in the 1960s and 1970s and used their skills professionally to counsel religious.

86   Peplar, 'Introduction', p. ix.

87   Erfgoedcentrum Nederlands Kloosterleven, Sint Agatha, Archiefinventaris Zusters van Liefde (henceforth SCMM-ENK): 374, 'Minutes of the Annual General Meeting of the Council of Major Religious Superiors held at the convent of La Sainte Union, Highgate, on 5th and 6th March, 1965'.

88   SCMM-ENK: 88b, 'Uitleg en t…', letter of explanation for 1957 circular dated 29 May 1957, pp. 2–3.

make modifications. This they did. Ten years later, Margaret Williams's article in the *Liverpool Daily Post* displayed photographs of 'The nuns of Pantasaph' dubbed the 'nuns in short habits' riding bikes on the A55 in North Wales, playing tennis and cycling. She wrote 'For the girls – they're no more than that – in the modern nun's habits are the first to train at Britain's first noviciate' of the Dutch Sisters of Charity. Their 'quick witted novice mistress', Mother Anne Marie Newsham, at the time described the novice's timetable as work, study, prayer but with time for outdoor activity. In one of their promotion brochures, they described themselves as 'A Modern Active Order!'.[89] This thinking was controversial. One Poor Clare abbess speaking to a reporter from the *Birmingham Mail* noted 'Many of the modern orders are bending over backwards to attract modern girls. But I would think that many would-be nuns do not want this easing of their lot.'[90] The reporter of this article gushed about the 'steady flow of postulants' into this strict monastery: it had two juniors, three novices and a postulant.[91] Some enclosed communities remained convinced of new entrants' malleability. One Benedictine of Stanbrook writing in *The Tablet* praised the Modern Girl for her commitment to tradition:

> A few days ago, a girl of eighteen, making her farewell at Stanbrook before entering with the Cistercians at Stapehill, observed that their grille was of closer mesh than ours. 'Do you like the grille?' she was asked. 'Oh yes! It's a challenge. It shows that you have cut yourself off completely from the world. I have always wanted to do things wholeheartedly, and I want to give God my whole self.' This modern teenager's reply goes straight to the heart of the matter. The life we live is bound to be a sign of contradiction to the world until the end of time ... And the question we enclosed nuns have to answer at the present moment is this: shall we confront the contemporary world with a challenge, or a compromise?[92]

The idea of 'compromise', the alterations to long-held traditions and customs of religious life, was particularly vexing for enclosed communities.

---

89 SCMM-ENK: 2339, vocation brochure 'A Modern Active Order! Charity without Self-Love'.

90 Birmingham Archdiocesan Archives (henceforth BAA): CC/B/1/L/12, Maureen Messent, 'The Free Choice Made by a Nun' (undated).

91 Archive sources suggest an equally steady flow of postulants and novices who left before profession. The monastery closed in 2011.

92 Benedictine of Stanbrook, 'Freedom Behind the Grille', *The Tablet* (11 June 1966), p. 7.

Such traditions and customs were often linked to medieval foundations and as we'll see in Chapter 7 to traumatic histories of exile.

By the 1960s, more attention was being directed towards the training of the Modern Girl and the language of renewal was being embraced more seriously. At a 1965 retreat for religious attended by fifty-two sisters from numerous religious congregations, the discussion featured the value of change:

> It is a sign of growth. Change leads us to think fundamentally about our purpose as religious. It is a time of self questioning and finding concrete reasons for what we are and the things we do. Our times are changing rapidly so we must fit our ideals to the development of future committed Christians.[93]

This probing of the purpose of religious life corroborated a need to rethink the novitiate experience. On a training day held for novice mistresses organised by the Council of Major Religious Superiors, novice mistress Mother Mary Andrew FMDM, speaking to an audience of her peers, commented on youth in general, noting that 'horrifying outspokenness is not unusual and that a certain pride is taken by young moderns in immoral behaviour'. She observed the ' "general softening" of our age' and the 'loss of sense of sin': 'young people today see no need for asceticism'.[94] She characterised youth as containing: 'A certain immaturity that often goes hand in hand with a good brain and a good basic education.'[95] 'They have generally enjoyed very great freedom' but 'they are casual and critical, and are disinclined to accept what they cannot understand'.[96] Her remarks coincide neatly with Sister Mary Jordan's characteristics of the Modern Girl. Yet Mother Mary Andrew also pointedly observed: 'while a former generation might have liked quiet, mousy little yes-women around the convent ... today's Apostolate calls for the "mulier fortis" of the Gospel and we shall answer to God for sending Peter Pans on for Profession'.[97] Despite emphasising some unflattering characteristics of 'young moderns', Mother Mary Andrew concluded that some of these character traits were important for tackling 'present-day problems': 'The modern girl is critical. Shall our system blunt and mutilate her God-given

---

93 SCMM-ENK: 352, 15–22 April Retreat for Religious [no year].

94 SCMM-ENK: 374, 'Training to be Given in the Noviciate to Prepare Sisters to Meet Present Day Problems', report by Reverend Mother Mary Andrew, Novice Mistress, Franciscan Missionaries of the Divine Motherhood, pp. 5–6.

95 *Ibid.*, p. 16.

96 *Ibid.*, p. 21.

97 *Ibid.*, p. 16.

critical faculty? To do so will not fit her to meet present-day problems later on.'[98]

She ended with: 'Let us welcome the questioning spirit and accept the fact that today's youth is trained to this enquiring approach. We must use it for God.'[99] Others also noted the 'high ideals' of young women who wished to give their life 'to God for the salvation of souls'.[100] In a 1965 workshop entitled 'Training in Responsibility', Mother Aiden advised those training juniorate sisters:

> Now, the modern girl may be restless, impatient of restraint, somewhat critical and self-opinionated, and, though at the end of her two years of Novitiate, she may have thos[e] weeds under control, one can be sure they will sprout up again if given a chance. On the other hand, she is usually very honest, generous and responsive to the challenge of high ideals. Let her feel her responsibility for the Community by giving of her best for Christ's sake.[101]

So by the late 1960s, training in the novitiate was being rethought in light of the characteristics and needs of the Modern Girl. Mothers Mary Andrew and Aiden recommended that her more 'critical and self-opinionated' nature could be useful to the Church in the modern world.

Conclusion

As a cultural trope, the Modern Girl reflected certain orthodoxies regarding perceived social and moral shifts of youth in the 1940s and 1950s. This chapter has interrogated the discursive Catholic Modern Girl in order to pinpoint why she was perceived as a problem and why her modern views were seen as responsible for the decline in interest in female religious life. Memoirs and apologetic texts spoke directly to the Modern Girl, using a colloquial language to demystify and make accessible convent traditions and practices. Nun-authors sought to alleviate concerns, implying that once she entered the novitiate, the Modern Girl would acclimatise to religious life. Vocation brochures such as *Bride of a King* accepted the modernity of young women, and recognised their attraction to the modern world whilst suggesting that a religious vocation was 'The True Fairy Tale'. The Catholic Modern

---

98 *Ibid.*, p. 21.
99 *Ibid.*, p. 25.
100 Sister Mary Laurence, OP, *Nuns are Real People*, p. 11.
101 SCMM-ENK: 350, 'Training in Responsibility', paper read by Mother Aidan (Ursuline) at Conference for Juniorate Mistresses held at East Finchley, 19 April 1966, p. 5.

Girl discourse emphasised that the Modern Girl would adapt to fit into convent life, as generations before her had. Declining vocations were influential in convincing the Church and women religious that the Modern Girl was unlikely to change. Conference speakers and published texts in the late 1950s began to suggest that the novice mistress must alter her methods of training to reach the Modern Girl. She must have an understanding of the modern world in which the Modern Girl was formed. By the end of the 1960s, many congregations and orders were accepting (though perhaps not really celebrating) the critical faculties of their new entrants, proposing that her personal attributes would be necessary to address the needs of the secular age. These shifts over the 1940s to the 1960s demonstrate how understandings of the Modern Girl influenced the training of female religious in British congregations and orders. The institutional Church and female religious reacted to this discourse and took steps to restructure the lived experience of religious life to accommodate the Modern Girl.

The next chapter examines one of the ways this lived experience was altered through the change in governance structures demanded by the Council decree *Perfectae Caritatis* (Adaptation and Renewal of Religious Life, 1965) and the '1968' renewal chapters.

3

Governance, authority and '1968'

I knew there had to be changes but was amazed – I would say, even offended – at the haphazard manner in which information was made know[n] to the province at large. Authority disappeared, which made it difficult to find out for oneself. In short, turmoil reigned and two groups formed – 'for change' and 'against change'.[1]

Thinking back, this sister acknowledged the dramatic changes that were a part of her experience of the 1960s and 1970s as the congregation she had entered in the 1940s went through a re-engineering of how religious life was governed. The strong sense of hierarchy and the practice of obedience to authority that had prevailed in the congregation in which she had resided was replaced by more flexible structures alongside greater permissiveness. Where once the peace of conformity and uniformity reigned, the turmoil of change led to tensions between those who held opposing views of how 'authentic' religious life should be lived. Some women religious experienced the turmoil and pain of change, others found the renewal of religious life reinvigorated their inner spirituality and mission-related activities.

Changes in the way religious life was lived were introduced in some religious institutes from the 1940s, but it was during the Second Vatican Council (1962–1965), that religious were encouraged to live in

1   Society of the Sacred Heart, Archives of the Province of England and Wales (henceforth SSH ENW): 'RSCJ and 1967', Luirard survey, Remembrance 5. Sister Monique Luirard surveyed sisters worldwide asking them to recount their experiences of the changes in religious life for her book *The Society of the Sacred Heart in the World of Its Times 1865–2000*, published in French in 2009 and in English in 2016. Of the twenty typewritten and autograph responses from members of the Province of England and Wales, one was dated 2006 so it seems likely the responses were written around this time. The responses have been anonymised at the request of the congregation.

new, more radical and experimental ways. The worldwide, ecumenical council launched a 'reform' movement that was intended to modernise Catholicism while holding firm to 'essentials'. For many women's religious institutes, this necessitated a rethinking and oftentimes a reworking of the day to day praxis of religious life. The decree on the Adaptation and Renewal of Religious Life, *Perfectae Caritatis* (1965), gave religious institutes the impetus to revisit (amongst other things) how their institutes were governed and structured. Women's religious congregations and orders took on this challenge in ways which subsequently shocked and dismayed some of the ecclesiastical hierarchy, Catholic laity as well as their own constituents.

What did renewal mean for religious life? The menu of changes that renewal could encompass was wide ranging. It included alterations in liturgy, both in the global Church and in the day-to-day lived prayer life of the nuns and sisters. Relationships with family, friends, other religious and co-workers took on new dimensions. Ministry was rethought and some religious institutes moved away from the institutionally based work that had been so intrinsic to their mission and identity. A renewed emphasis on ecumenism reflected more openness and engagement with other forms of Christianity. These were some of the many revisions to religious life contested by various factions who were 'for change' or 'against change'.

This chapter examines another of these changes: governance and authority within convent spaces.[2] Religious communities reorganised themselves. The convent, considered by many Catholics and non-Catholics alike as a conservative site of religious piety, became a place of radical engagement, social change and dissonance when shifts from hierarchical to participatory governance challenged embedded feminine hierarchies and matriarchal structures. The context for the shifting parameters of religious life is the tumultuous landscape of the long 1960s and the emancipatory impulses of the events of '1968'.[3] Admittedly, this is not a completely apt analogy, and almost incongruous given the bottom-up impetus of the '1968' movements and the top-down directives from

---

2   Convent spaces are being defined very functionally: they were places where women religious reside. Convents can be anything from a specially built monastic structure to a two-up, two-down terraced house.

3   I am referring to '1968' as shorthand for the period of political activity and social unrest that begins around the mid-1960s and continues through the 1970s. Gerd-Rainer Horn, *The Spirit of '68: Rebellion in Western Europe and North America, 1956–1976* (Oxford: Oxford University Press, 2007), pp. 1–2.

the Second Vatican Council. Yet that energy unharnessed in the aftermath of the Council in these religious institutes embraced the essence of the secular challenges to authority in the long 1960s. Subsequent strains reflected in some cases schismatic disagreements over *How Far Can You Go?* in regard to organisational restructuring.[4]

'1968' has become synonymous with 'the movement', a shorthand for the collection of bottom-up mass protests, local, national and international, emerging out of student and worker movements, anti-nuclear and anti-war demonstrations and the civil, women's and gay rights rallies that took place from the late 1950s into the 1970s.[5] Protests gave voice to many who felt unrepresented in social and political spheres.[6] One scholar has suggested that the Cold War emphasis on freedom and democracy 'led [the] young to expect democratic institutions to live up to their democratic rhetoric'.[7] Many uprisings reflected a frustration and discontent, built up over time, about structures of representation managed by a very few that did not seem to engage with the desires of the many. Protesting students demanded involvement in university policy-making and management, free assembly and speech and student grants.[8] Working-class movements also featured as part of '1968'. Worker unrest led to coordinated action as workers went on strike to protest for better wages and a role in decision-making.[9]

The historiography of '1968', perhaps unsurprisingly, contains a tension between the myth and lived experience of such tempestuous events. Much of the early scholarship written by academic participant-observers and informed by their recollections and experiences emphasises the 'clash of contestation'; this contrasts with those that suggest some collaboration and 'measured judgement'. Arthur Marwick weighs in by emphasising the 'rational, tolerant' voices that contributed to the cultural

---

4   This refers to David Lodge's popular novel published in 1980, which introduces the tumultuous changes in Catholic thought and theology in England in the 1950s and 1960s. David Lodge, *How Far Can You Go?* (Harmondsworth: Penguin Books, 1981).

5   Andrew Hunt, '"When Did the Sixties Happen?" Searching for New Directions', *Journal of Social History*, 33 (1999), 147. For example, see Horn, *The Spirit of '68*.

6   Bruno Bonomo, '*Presa della parola*: A Review and Discussion of Oral History and the Italian 1968', *Memory Studies*, 6 (2013), 7–22.

7   Nick Thomas, 'Challenging Myths of the 1960s: The Case of Student Protest in Britain', *Twentieth Century British History*, 13 (2002), 293

8   Caroline M. Hoefferle, *British Student Activism in the Long Sixties* (Abingdon: Routledge, 2013), p. 9. See also Sylvia A. Ellis, '"A Demonstration of British Good Sense": British Student Protest during the Vietnam War', in Gerard J. DeGroot (ed.), *Student Protest: The Sixties and After* (London: Longman, 1998), pp. 54–69.

9   Horn, *The Spirit of '68*, pp. 93–130.

revolution of the long 1960s.[10] Historian Maud Anne Bracke suggests the 'memory battles' have led to a 'fetishization' of '1968'.[11] She suggests an overreliance on a series of national 1968s (situated in northwestern Europe and North America) which were cultural revolutions (à la Marwick) to the neglect of the political and social revolutions that were more dominant in countries such as Italy and France.[12] In addition, the '1968' generation did not speak with one voice. Anna von der Goltz writes of 'generation building' that has written out of German historiography members of the '1968' generation belonging to the moderate right.[13] The English '68' appears very moderate besides some other national 1968s; British students remained trusting in the parliamentary system and British politicians and police were less heavy-handed.[14]

Catholics were shaped by the social, cultural and political transformations of the 1960s. They participated in the student movements, radical workers' movements and civil rights rallies. They also initiated Catholic social movements such as worker-priest initiatives and base communities (often operating outside of traditional parish structures).[15] Catholics voted with their conscience in opposition to their Church's preference for political parties or conscientiously dissented from teachings such as those on birth control.[16] Catholic male and female

10   Arthur Marwick, 'The Cultural Revolution of the Long Sixties: Voices of Reaction, Protest, and Permeation', *International History Review*, 27 (2005), 780–806, pp. 781, 806.

11   Maud Anne Bracke, 'One-Dimensional Conflict? Recent Scholarship on 1968 and the Limitations of the Generation Concept', *Journal of Contemporary History*, 47 (2012), 638–9.

12   *Ibid.*, p. 642.

13   Anna von der Goltz, 'Generations of 68ers', *Cultural and Social History*, 8 (2011), 473–91, p. 485.

14   Sylvia A. Ellis, 'British Student Protest during the Vietnam War', in Gerard J. Degroot (ed.), *Student Protest: The Sixties and After* (London: Longman, 1998), 67–8. See also Keith Robbins, '1968: Identities – Religion and Nation in the United Kingdom', *Schweizerische Zeitschrift für Religions- und Kulturgeschichte / Revue suisse d'histoire religieuse et culturelle*, 104 (2010), 35–50.

15   Gerd-Rainer Horn, *The Spirit of Vatican II: Western European Progressive Catholicism in the Long Sixties* (Oxford: Oxford University Press, 2015).

16   For example, in Italy, not only were there developments in new Catholic movements, but also 'political pluralism' influenced the behaviours of Catholics who felt empowered to vote with their conscience rather than succumb to episcopal pressure to vote for the Christian Democratic party. Richard Drake, 'Catholics and the Italian Revolutionary Left of the 1960s', *Catholic Historical Review*, 94 (2008), 450–75; Massimo Faggioli, 'The New Elites of Italian Catholicism: 1968 and the New Catholic Movements', *Catholic Historical Review*, 98 (2012), 37–40; Daniela Saresella, 'Ecclesial Dissent in Italy in the Sixties', *Catholic Historical Review*, 102 (2016), 67–8; Alana Harris, '"The Writings of Querulous Women": Contraception, Conscience and Clerical Authority

religious in North America were active and visible participants in social movements such as the civil rights movements, anti-Vietnam protests and women's rights movements.[17] There was less Church and congregational support for similar activities in Britain, though some women religious in the 1960s and 1970s were individually involved in these larger protest movements.[18]

The wider discourse of '1968' emphasising participation and emancipatory ideals is germane to situating the tug of war within religious institutes over governance.[19] It also genders our knowledge of the global 1968 movements by exploring an emancipatory movement led, sustained, spread and sometimes obstructed by women. New ways of governing introduced fresh understandings of obedience alongside the post-conciliar vocabulary of 'pluriformity', 'subsidiarity', 'personal responsibility' and 'shared responsibility'. This religious world, as will be argued, moved from one that was hierarchically structured, to one that was consultative and participatory. As discussed in the first half of this chapter, this shift occurred first at the centre, through international collaborations and 'special' or *aggiornamento* chapters which occurred in 1968 (or thereabouts). The second half of the chapter explores local governance, examining the changing understandings of obedience, the lived experience of participation and the development of smaller communities.

International collaborations

International collaborations were encouraged by the processes of renewal that began in the 1950s with *Sponsa Christi*. The Poor Clares,

in 1960s Britain', *British Catholic History*, 32 (2015), 557–85; Alana Harris (ed.), *The Schism of '68: Catholicism, Contraception and Humanae Vitae in Europe, 1945–1975* (Houndmills: Palgrave Macmillan, 2018).

17 Amy L. Koehlinger, *The New Nuns: Racial Justice and Religious Reform in the 1960s* (Cambridge, MA: Harvard University Press, 2007); Mary Beth Fraser Connolly, *Women of Faith: The Chicago Sisters of Mercy and the Evolution of a Religious Community* (New York: Fordham University Press, 2014); Kathleen Sprows Cummings, Timothy Matovina, and Robert A. Orsi (eds), *Catholics in the Vatican II Era: Local Histories of a Global Event* (Cambridge: Cambridge University Press, 2017).

18 For lay activities in 1968 see Alana Harris, *Faith in the Family: A Lived Religious History of English Catholicism, 1945–1982* (Manchester: Manchester University Press, 2013), pp. 115–17.

19 One important exception is Sam Brewitt-Taylor, 'From Religion to Revolution: Theologies of Secularisation in the British Student Christian Movement, 1963–1973', *Journal of Ecclesiastical History*, 66 (2015), 792–811.

Figure 3.1 Poor Clare abbesses meeting at Baddesley Clinton, 1965

though residing in autonomous communities, interacted through epistolary relationships with communities outside Britain, and these interrelationships expanded during their renewal process with the development of the International Poor Clares Commission. Held in Rome, the Commission of twelve Poor Clares, including one nun from a Scottish community, contributed to the development of a Poor Clares common constitutions.[20] Figure 3.1 documents one of the first meetings of Poor Clare abbesses of England and Scotland, who came together to discuss renewal. Some autonomous communities created international federations. The Canonesses of the Holy Sepulchre in 1954 joined an international Confederation (later Association of Regular Canonesses of the Holy Sepulchre) with six other communities on the continent

---

20 Carmen M. Mangion, '"Shades of Difference": Poor Clares in Britain', in Christian Sorrel (ed.), *Le Concile Vatican II et le monde des religieux (Europe occidentale et Amérique du Nord, 1950–1980)* (Lyon: LARHRA, 2019), pp. 317–29.

(Belgium, the Netherlands and Spain), Brazil and in what was then Zaire. The Syon Bridgettines retained their autonomy, but travelled to discuss renewal matters with Bridgettine abbeys in Uden and Weert in the Netherlands and Altomunster in Germany.[21] Such transnational exchanges were opportunities to discuss the implications of and develop ideas on renewal, and often led to lifelong friendships and collaborations.

Aggiornamento chapters and devolution

International, centralised congregations such as the Society of the Sacred Heart and the Sisters of Charity of Our Lady, Mother of Mercy were instructed to organise an ordinary or extraordinary General Chapter, often referred to as an *aggiornamento* chapter, to implement the instructions of *Perfectae Caritatis*,[22] which encouraged women's religious institutes to radically rethink their way of living religious life, advising that:

> [T]he manner of living, praying and working should be suitably adapted everywhere, but especially in mission territories, to the modern physical and psychological circumstances of the members and also, as required by the nature of each institute, to the necessities of the apostolate, the demands of culture, and social and economic circumstances.[23]

The photograph of the 1968 chapter of the Institute of the Blessed Virgin Mary (Figure 3.2) shows that it included representatives from most of the countries where the Institute of the Blessed Virgin Mary was located: England, Germany, Austria, Italy, Spain, Hungary, Romania, Czechoslovakia, India, Brazil, Argentina, Chile and the United States. The General Chapters are a useful reminder that for religious institutes transnationalism was a time of physical border crossing, women religious met together to make decisions about the future of their religious congregation. In the process, they formed new networks, both formal and informal, and exchanged ideas about renewal and *aggiornamento*.

---

21   PDA: CMB 3.2, Letter from abbess to bishop, dated 19 May 1951; Letter from Abbess Magdalen [Nevin] to bishop, dated 13 June 1964.

22   Pope Paul VI, *Motu proprio Ecclesiae Sanctae: Establishing Norms for Carrying Out Certain Decrees of the Second Sacred Vatican Council*, trans. J. Leo Alston (London: Catholic Truth Society, 1967), II, part i, section I, no. 3. *Ecclesiae Sanctae* explained the implementation of several conciliar decrees; the second section in this work is related to *Perfectae Caritatis*.

23   *Perfectae Caritatis* (Decree on the Adaptation and Renewal of Religious Life), 28 October 1965, §3

Figure 3.2 General Chapter of the Institute of the Blessed Virgin Mary, 1968, Englburg, East Bavaria

Another important responsibility of the chapter was to change *ad experimentum* the norms contained in its Constitutions with the caveat that the 'aims, the nature and the character of the institute is not altered'.[24] This permission given by the Holy See to experiment was unprecedented; canon lawyer Elizabeth Cotter IBVM has noted that this 'far outweighed the authority previously experienced'.[25] The discussion below underscores

---

24   *Ecclesiae Sanctae*, part 1, no 4. Elizabeth M. Cotter, *The General Chapter in a Religious Institute: With Particular Reference to IBVM Loreto Branch* (Oxford: Peter Lang, 2008), p. 77.
25   *Ecclesiae Sanctae*, part 1, no 4. The Decree *Ad instituenda experimenta* (1970) granted faculties to religious institutes to make these decisions rather than ask for approval

the varied scope and speed of renewal inaugurated by the *aggiornamento* chapters of each institute.

Leaders of Catholic women's religious institutes managed the activities and internal affairs of their congregations and orders. Their governance structures had some parallels with the Holy See's hierarchical structures, with its centralised authority. Religious institutes were political cultures with much of the major decision-making in the hands of a small group, an often elected (sometimes for life) female leader and her four or five assistants. As political cultures, they were shaped by social class hierarchies and the practice of religious obedience.[26] For example, in 1950, the chapter of the autonomous Poor Clares of Scarthingwell, Yorkshire, elected Mother Veronica Ellison abbess for a three-year term. Though guided by her council, an elected vicaress and three councillors, she was the final arbiter in all decisions. The community's episcopal superior was the diocesan bishop of Leeds, who approved exceptions to their rule; he rarely involved himself with the daily affairs of the monastery. Centralised active congregations had a hierarchical structure that was more complex because they could operate numerous branch houses, sometimes spread around the world. Here too, like the Poor Clares, power and authority were centralised in a female leader and her council. In 1965, before the *aggiornamento* council, the more than 7,000 members of the Society of the Sacred Heart were led by Mother General Sabine de Valon. Though her council consisted of five assistants general (each responsible for a vicariate) who advised her, her decisions were final.[27] Each assistant general communicated decisions to the convents in their vicariate. Locally, each house was managed by a superior, with a small team of sisters handling administrative functions. While individual structures and leadership nomenclature may have varied between religious institutes, they were similarly structured, with authority over sometimes thousands of sisters vested in the women who comprised a council.[28]

---

of the Holy See. Cotter, *The General Chapter*, pp. 77–9. See also Barbara Lawler Thomas, 'Canon Law and the Constitutions of Religious Congregations', *The Way*, 50 (1984), 47–60.

26   Sarah Mulhall Adelman, 'Empowerment and Submission: The Political Culture of Catholic Women's Religious Communities in Nineteenth-Century America', *Journal of Women's History*, 23 (2011), 138.

27   SSH ENW: SHP UB/22, 'About the Society of the Sacred Heart' (1965), p. 11.

28   The authority of local bishops was defined by canon law. Diocesan communities and enclosed orders were often more reliant on episcopal approval as defined in their constitutions than were centralised congregations.

The regulations that defined the parameters of governance within a religious institute were based on its rule and constitutions. Such juridical documents outlined the 'object of the institute'; the meanings of the vows of poverty, chastity and obedience; rules on the reception of postulants, and their admission to the novitiate and their profession; and procedures for the system of governance including election of convent leadership.[29] Usually, the traditions of a community were codified in manuals and guides that were written by or considered to reflect the founder's directives. The detailed minutiae of this guidance regimented everyday life. Bridgettines were instructed in the *Syon Additions* (1425) on prayers and reading before, during and after meals. Three times during a meal, the nuns stopped to pray five Hail Marys.[30] According to their *Abridgement of a Guide for the Religious called Sisters of Mercy* (1866), a text used by some of the Mercy convents, the Sister of Mercy habit was black and 'neatly plaited from throat to waist'. The choir sister's habit had a train that measured three and a half fingers in length; the breadth of the habit was four to five yards according to the size of the wearer.[31] Manuals and guides, often dating from around the time of the foundation of the religious institute, were considered integral to the traditions of religious institutes despite their non-juridical status.

Hierarchies of authority within women's religious institutes were embedded in the concept of obedience and were intended to instil order in communities large and small where women of different characters, backgrounds and social class were expected to live as a cohesive group. This premise of subordinating one's will to one's superior was not out of place in the nineteenth to the mid-twentieth century, whether that superior was a schoolmaster, a matron or the *pater familias*.[32] Such obedience aided congregations in their missions to educate and nurse: they had a body of workers that were uniformly trained and easily relocated to where they were needed. It ordered the relationships between sisters and nuns in convent spaces. Infractions of rules of behaviour were easily recognised

---

29 For example, Mary Sullivan, *Catherine McAuley and the Tradition of Mercy* (Notre Dame, IN: University of Notre Dame Press, 1995), ch. 11.

30 Roger Ellis, *Syon Abbey: The Spirituality of the English Bridgettines* (Salzburg: Universität Salzburg, 1984), p. 113.

31 RSM Handsworth: [M. Francis Bridgeman RSM], *Guide for the Religious Called Sisters of Mercy. Amplified by Quotations, Instructions, &c. Part I. & II.* (London: Robson and Son, 1866), pp. 112–13.

32 For example, Carol Helmstadter, 'Building a New Nursing Service: Respectability and Efficiency in Victorian England', *Albion*, 35 (2004), 615; Richard Vinen, *National Service: Conscription in Britain, 1945–1963* (London: Allen Lane, 2014).

Figure 3.3 Refectory, Society of the Sacred Heart, Woldingham, 18 March 1957

and censured. Obedience was linked to the rules of governance; during their formation, postulants and novices studied the rule and constitution, with an emphasis on exactitude: 'It is impossible not be become great saints if we keep our rule exactly.'[33] Deference and rank were embedded within structures and practices: for example, sisters and nuns processed, voted and sat in refectory in order of their number of years in religious life. The photograph shown in Figure 3.3 (dated 1957) shows sisters and novices of the Society of the Sacred Heart in Woldingham, Surrey, silently eating their meal, watched over by their leadership at the top table. The great majority of sisters and nuns lived within this complex web of authority and obedience. No one escaped: even abbesses and mother generals rendered obedience and deference to their clerical superiors.[34]

Until the *aggiornamento* chapters, the governance structures of most religious institutes remained fairly static, with a narrow hierarchy of authority and decision-making. Like the students and workers of the '1968', the ordinary sisters were unrepresented in governance and had few opportunities to make their voices heard. Opportunities for self-determination existed, but were not equally shared. Social hierarchies within convent spaces identified distinctions in categories of women

---

33 Faithful Companions of Jesus, *Maxims of the Viscountess de Bonnault d'Houet* (London: the author, 1916), p. 21.
34 Deference will be discussed in more detail in Chapter 4.

religious and access to leadership roles could be based on age, social class, education or ethnicity. *Perfectae Caritatis*, however, urged consultation with the widest possible membership of the religious institute and the *aggiornamento* chapter was called to address this need for wider participation. For most religious institutes, this was new and uncharted territory. The subsections that follow, on questionnaires, provincial authority and delegates to the General Chapter, consider how participation was encouraged and lived (or not).

Questionnaires

For many religious institutes, the first step in preparing for the *aggiornamento* chapter, considering the call for wider participation, was the design and distribution of a questionnaire.[35] Such methods of surveying had become commonplace in wider society from 1945 as sociology and the 'creeping rise of the social science apparatus' established itself. This 'science of society' was being increasingly utilised to understand the nature of modern life.[36] Particularly significant from the 1950s was the literature reflecting the 'burgeoning sociology of women'.[37] Questionnaires were a means of discovering group attitudes to a host of topics. They also gave sisters and nuns the opportunity to have their say about the present and future of religious life. As will be discussed in Chapter 7, they became a form of consciousness raising – some sisters and nuns became more cognisant of and vocal about their own complicated feelings of both belonging and oppression. It led to a remaking of hierarchies of governance and a redrawing of power relations – eventually. But the process was also contested and challenged.

Women religious who had been taught during their formation periods not to question the rules of their religious institute were now being asked weighty questions about religious life. This was an unprecedented and a

---

35   *Ecclesiae Sanctae* proposed questionnaires as one means to preparing for the General Chapter. Pope Paul VI, 'Moto proprio "Ecclesiae Sanctae"', *The Furrow*, 17 (1966), 668–79, p. 669. Smaller religious communities, such as the Syon Bridgettines and the Canonesses of the Holy Sepulchre did not find it necessary to create questionnaires. When used, the questionnaires were typically designed by female religious but the analysis was sometimes done by consultants.

36   Michael Savage, *Identities and Social Change in Britain since 1940: The Politics of Method* (Oxford: Oxford University Press, 2010), pp. 7, 10, 68.

37   This includes the numerous publications of Pearl Jephcott, Alva Myrdal, Viola Klein and Judith Hubback. Helen McCarthy, 'Social Science and Married Women's Employment in Post-War Britain', *Past and Present*, 233 (2016), 269–305.

confusing adjustment for some. The breadth of the 1967 questionnaire distributed by the Institute of the Blessed Virgin Mary to its members (finally professed sisters and those who had renewed their vows for three years) was staggering: it contained fifty questions in eleven sections on such topics as: the religious state in general; rules and constitutions; solidarity; renewal and adaptations in the spirit of founder Mary Ward; training; interior life and the apostolate; the vows; relationships with God; ceremonies; and the government of the institute. The first two questions required sisters to question the future of religious life:

1   Do you believe that there is a future for religious institutes, contemplative and active, in their existing form? – Why?
2   Do you think that Secular Institutes and the lay apostolate will take the place of religious communities? – Why?[38]

Subsequent questions caused sisters to interrogate the very foundation and understanding of their vocation and perhaps too their institutional affiliation. This encouraged a rethinking of the way religious life was lived. Some women, who were already questioning the traditions of religious life, were equipped to respond to challenging questions, others were bewildered by the probing of what were to them the crucial tenets by which they lived religious life. When the responses were tabulated, the sisters were told that:

> The summary contains what the members wrote almost word for word, not changed or interpreted or touched up in any ways by the Generalate. Wherever possible we have left the original wording, and we have put the expressions of contrary opinions side by side.[39]

Transparency was important to building trust at this time of change and to encourage sisters to engage with the common goals of renewal. This excerpt suggests the need to impress upon the sisters that their opinions were acknowledged: 'contrary opinions' were acceptable and they were all valued members of the congregation.

Enclosed religious orders also employed questionnaires. The Poor Clares had an ambitious objective to theirs; the results were intended to inform a common constitution for use by all autonomous worldwide communities. Twenty British convents were part of the worldwide

---

38   ACJ/EP/C/32/b, Questionnaire circulated before General Chapter, 1968.
39   ACJ/EP/C/32/b, Letter from Mother Edelburga Solzabacher to Reverend Mother Provincial and sisters of the Commission, dated 19 December 1967.

Franciscan family of 615 Poor Clare monasteries and forty-three Poor Clare federations.[40] Their questionnaire consisted of fifty-five questions (many with numerous subsections) addressing a wide range of topics, including governance structures, categories of sisters, methods of enclosure and the rule of silence.[41] Each autonomous community was expected to discuss the questionnaire and send responses to the Poor Clare International Commission. Interviews with Poor Clares indicated the means of collecting responses varied by community.[42] One Poor Clare recalled deliberations on the questionnaire being dictatorial: 'I can remember her [the abbess] sitting at the top of the table', indicating, 'and this is what we will say to the answer to this question.'[43] Another Poor Clare from a different community recounted a more collaborative process: 'there was a discussion by everybody and then the general consensus, Mother would put down what it was'.[44] As will be explored in Chapter 7, the Poor Clare questionnaire disclosed a wide variance of responses, especially in relation to enclosure.[45]

Questionnaires were important to informing decision-making of the *aggiornamento* chapters and influenced changes that were made in the daily lives of the sisters.[46] Chapter outcomes, which in the past had come down simply as directives to be followed, were now discussed within the local communities. The Fenham, Newcastle upon Tyne, community of the Society of the Sacred Heart noted in their house journal in 1968 that 'Since Rev. Mother has returned from her meeting with Rev. Mother Provincial, she has been reading with us the decisions of the General Chapter and we have been discussing them.'[47] Decisions were not just being heard and obeyed, they were explained and deliberated. A hierarchy of decision-making was still in place, with decision-making flowing from the General Chapter to the Provincial to the leader of a

40 Francis Pullen Archives (henceforth FPA): Questionnaire Summary of Results.
41 *Ibid.*
42 Sixteen Poor Clares from five autonomous communities were interviewed.
43 Anonymised interview.
44 Anonymised interview.
45 This will be discussed in more detail in Chapter 7.
46 Other processes of participation existed. The Daughters of Charity met in local assemblies and made proposals that were sent to the provincial leadership: 2,000–3,000 proposals were analysed and communicated to the Extraordinary General Assembly held in June 1968. The Daughters also responded to questionnaires. Susan O'Brien, *Leaving God for God: The Daughters of Charity of St Vincent de Paul in Britain, 1847-2017* (London: Darton, Longman & Todd, 2017), pp. 322–3.
47 SSH ENW: Fenham House Journal, 9 February 1968.

community, but information from the centre filtered down not simply as directives. The transition from the old ways of decision-making to more participative ways was still in flux, but even the acts of personal explanation and discussion could be a profound and unsettling change.

Provincial authority

A key development at many *aggiornamento* chapters was the devolution of power to provincial bodies. The interrelated concepts of pluriformity and subsidiarity encouraged the delegation of authority. Pluriformity had developed out of friction between local churches and the Holy See's insistence on uniformity. The term's cautious unveiling in the 1960s reflected the awareness of religious plurality within local Catholic identities embedded in indigenous cultural traditions, customs and rituals.[48] It was interpreted within female religious institutes not simply as a means of embracing difference in cultural responses but also differences in generational reactions, as will be discussed in the next chapter. The concept of subsidiarity suggested that decisions would be made at the appropriate level.[49] In theory, local decisions would be made locally and decisions that impacted a province would be made by a provincial body. For individual sisters and nuns, individuals tasked with a job would be responsible for its implementation and completion. Provincial and local bodies were no longer simply conduits for decisions made by the central authority but decision-makers in their own right. In some congregations, like the Sisters of Charity of Our Lady, Mother of Mercy, this devolution

---

48   Pluriformity offered a *volte-face* after almost two centuries of centralising legislation emphasising uniformity as a means of reinforcing the universality of the Catholic Church. It suggested the 'unchangeable faith' that could be achieved through different cultural traditions and acknowledged national Catholicisms. In 1974, pluriformity was embedded in the apostolic exhortation *Evangelii Nuntiandi* and it became a duty. R. Scott Appleby, 'From State to Civil Society and Back Again: The Catholic Church as Transnational Actor, 1965–2005', in Abigail Green and Vincent Viaene (eds), *Religious Internationals in the Modern World: Globalization and Faith Communities since 1750* (Houndmills: Palgrave Macmillan, 2012), pp. 319–21; Walbert Bühlmann, 'Incarnating the Message of Christ in Different Cultures', in Padraig Flanagan (ed.), *A New Missionary Era* (Maryknoll, NY: Orbis Books, 1979), pp. 174–80; Carmen M. Mangion, 'A New Internationalism: Endeavouring to "Build from this Diversity, Unity", 1940–1990', *Journal of Contemporary History* (2019).

49   Gerald O'Collins, *Living Vatican II: The 21st Council for the 21st Century* (Mahwah, NJ: Paulist Press, 2006), p. 156. The development of the doctrine of subsidiarity derives from *Quadragesimo Anno* (1931). See Chapter 6 for more on Catholic social teaching and religious ministries.

process had begun in the 1950s with quasi-provinces.[50] The sister-authors of one congregation history explained that the 1961 full province structure was the

> climax to all the changes that were introduced, the houses of England and Wales became a province under the leadership of a Provincial Superior, Mother Ignatius and four councillors. This was in response to the adoption of the principles of pluriformity, collegiality, solidarity and internationalisation at the General Chapter in Rome. This development gave the possibility of freedom of decision in matters relating to local policy and to members of the British province themselves.[51]

In recalling this history in the 1980s, sister-authors emphasised local decision-making. Provincial teams were tasked to see to the execution of decisions of the General Chapters but also were given new responsibilities for provincial matters including the formation of postulants and novices, financial administration and governance of the British province. In 1968, Thérèse Mary Barnett, vicaress and acting superior general, announced:

> During the past years, since the division of the congregation into provinces, you have been learning what it means to be an independent unit, free to develop your religious life and your apostolate in your own particular English way, yet always within the unity of the whole congregation.[52]

Provincial governance was meant to acknowledge and accept national differences and customs. This emphasis on unity in diversity was difficult in practice. In 1961 the structure of the provincial team of England and Wales was similar to that of the generalate: it was hierarchical and organised under a provincial superior and her four councillors.[53] One member of the early council wrote a decade later that those early days were difficult: 'we were unsure of ourselves, lacking confidence' and indicated a 'certain hangover from the days of leaning on the Motherhouse and seeking our security there'.[54] In 1969, the provincial structure expanded and was advised by a consultative body whose delegates were elected by

---

50 SCMM-ENK: 2678, Thérèse Mary Barnet, 'Development of Autonomy in the Provinces 1961–1987' (January 1988).

51 SCMM-ENK: 2006, Bernadette Steele, Dolores Heys and Marie Wallbank, 'The History of the Sisters of Charity of Our Lady, Mother of Mercy in Britain and Ireland 1861 to 1982'.

52 SCMM-ENK: 1273, 'Report of the Provincial Chapter 1968'.

53 SCMM-ENK: 2006, Steele et al., 'The History', p. 109.

54 SCMM-ENK: 332a, 'English Province Chapter 1971–1972', written by Sister Anne Marie Newsham, Communication Person.

members of the province.[55] By 1971, one letter suggested the communities in England and Wales were in chaos: distrust, rumours, fears and suspicions caused by pressures 'for change' and 'against change'.[56] The tensions in some communities were open issues. Sisters in Pantasaph complained of indecision; they were 'looking for leadership – people who are not afraid to make a thrust in the direction of renewal'.[57] Some wanted the [Provincial] Council to resign. The Provincial Council responded that their suggestions were: 'judged as a destructive criticism and many things are taken personally; so much so that they can't discuss issues – it always ends up in personalities'.[58] Experimenting with different structures was simply a part of developing local ways of governing. In December 1971, the provincial government was restructured as less hierarchical according to a 'team concept'. They worked as a 'collegial body [with] no one person making decisions, all with equal rights, sharing the burden of responsibility and the work load and each member being responsible for a certain field of work'. Rather than one leader, the three members of the team would provide 'a thorough scrutiny' of requests, problems and suggestions and 'provide three different points of views ... before a decision was made'. The team concept was thought to allow for 'efficiency, initiative, adaptability and co-responsibility' but also eventually proved unworkable. The provincial team report acknowledged that:

> Team members are only human and initiative, capabilities and temperament vary a great deal and this has led to difficulties. Deep discussion was impossible, work load was not shared out, many sisters were inhibited from speaking when all three members were visiting a community.[59]

Despite best intensions, new systems of governance did not necessarily encourage freedom of expression. Perhaps intransigent differences of opinion or pressures from cliques led to silence as a form of protest or self-preservation. For many religious institutes, it took decades to develop governance structures that reflected a level of participation that was practical and effective.

55 SCMM-ENK: 2678, 'Development of Autonomy in the Provinces 1961–1987', Thérèse Mary Barnett, dated January 1988.
56 SCMM-ENK: 333a, Letter from Sister Bernadette Steele to Sister Thérèse Mary [Barnett], dated 29 June 1971.
57 SCMM-ENK: 98, 'Report on Visit to England – April 1 to 24, 1971 – Sr. Michael Marie'.
58 SCMM-ENK: 373, Letter from Anne-Marie Newsham to Michael Marie, dated [1971?].
59 SCMM-ENK, 332, 'Provincial Team Report', December 1971 to March 1976', dated 8 March 1976.

Delegates

The Society of the Sacred Heart initially opted for a more controlled approach to the devolution of authority within their congregation. They had operated under a vicariate structure since 1950; the vicars participated in the General Chapter and were tasked to disseminate the rulings from the General Chapter.[60] At the 1967 *aggiornamento* chapter, the vicariates were renamed provinces. Like the Sisters of Charity of Our Lady, Mother of Mercy discussed above, a new provincial leadership team was created with more autonomy on provincial matters. They spoke on behalf of the province to the General Chapter. A few years later, provinces elected delegates to chapter meetings. The first delegates to attend the 1970 General Chapter were tasked to communicate how experiments had strengthened or weakened religious life.[61] This shift from provincial leaders to delegates informing and reporting on the experiments was significant for the politics of governance. Responsibility and power were not simply in the hands of the provincial government, elected delegates also had a say in interpreting and relaying congregation developments.

Despite shifts towards more representation and participation in the highest level of governance, some complained of new hierarchies of knowledge and authority. One sister recalled: 'I do remember feeling somewhat resentful at the stage when only delegates went to Chapters: it seemed that yet another hierarchy was being established!!' She continued:

> In a Province like ours, it fairly soon became apparent that 'full' assemblies would be feasible. I found the swing from centralisation to a more Province-directed way of operating exciting. However, the ebb and flow of methods of consulting, nominating etc. for teams and committees irritated me.[62]

Representation and participation had a price: 'Full assembles' at the provincial level required that *all* sisters were involved in meeting and making decisions.[63] Though this sister welcomed more participation at

---

60 SSH ENW: DII/1bi, *Écho de la Maison Mère*, 5 September 1950, p. 1. The vicariate of England at this time included the houses at Newcastle, Oxford, Woldingham, Malta, India, Roehampton, West Hill, Hammersmith, Tunbridge Wells and Brighton.

61 SSH ENW: 1970 Provincial Chapter I, Batch 3, Opening of the Provincial Chapter by Mother Eyre, 28 December 1969, pp. 1–2.

62 SSH ENW: 'RSCJ and 1967', Remembrance 12.

63 The timing of this participatory movement varied by religious congregation. The English third-order Dominicans moved towards elected delegates and included non-voting observers to the 1983 General Chapter. The 1989 General Chapter led to 'open

the provincial level in theory, the new governance structures mandated that the ordinary sister was much more involved in decision-making. Committees and teams needed sisters as members who would participate, do research and debate potential decisions. This led, in the opinion of some, to a rather unending series of meeting.

New systems of representation and consultation coming out of the *aggiornamento* chapters replaced the traditional system where the general superior and her council made decisions for all members of the community. This dramatic governance restructure was mentioned by all participants as one of the most important features of the renewal of religious life.[64] It offered opportunities for more voices to be heard, whether via questionnaires or the creation of provincial bodies which made regional decisions, but the difficulty of pressure groups and the additional responsibilities of participation were also consequences of this democratising experience.

Local governance

Consultation and participation within local convents led to a rethinking of authority and obedience and sometimes a dismantling of local governance structures. As discussed above, governance documents provided a roadmap to ordered communal life in local convents configuring the activities and behaviours of a cohort of women sometimes with different cultural, class and national identities. They outlined the boundaries of authority held by the female leaders over a local community. The 1960s language of renewal encouraged openness to decentralisation and community decision-making. Conciliar documents introduced terms which historian John O'Malley called 'horizontal-reciprocity' and 'empowerment' words: pluriformity, subsidiarity, personal responsibility and shared responsibility.[65] Such terms were rife in the institutional documents and what later became a quasi-industry

chapter' where all perpetually professed members of the congregation had voting rights. Anselm Nye, *A Peculiar Kind of Mission: The English Dominican Sisters, 1845–2010* (Leominster: Gracewing, 2011), p. 203.

64   Forty-one of sixty-seven Daughters of Charity of St Vincent de Paul responding to Susan O'Brien's survey in 2005 also thought inclusive governance and consultation was the most important change in the British province. O'Brien, *Leaving God for God*, pp. 320–1.

65   John W. O'Malley, 'Vatican II: Did Anything Happen?', *Theological Studies*, 67 (2006), 28. For example, *Perfectae Caritatis*, §24; *Ecclesiae Sanctae* II, §7, §18.

of published works on the theology of religious life. Personal and shared responsibility were most often mentioned in interviews; they were crucial to many sisters' and nuns' understanding of renewal and had both relational and institutional implications. Institutionally, both personal and shared responsibility offered opportunities for more collaborative forms of governance within local communities. These concepts suggested an elasticity that had not existed before within governance structures. New freedoms were not without new responsibilities and logistical difficulties, as reflected in the three subsections below on the changing understandings of obedience, the lived experience of participation and the development of smaller communities.

Obedience and authority

The epitaph below the photograph of Sister Rudolph indicating she 'had all her life excelled in obedience' was not out of place in an otherwise modern history of the Congregation of Sisters of Charity of Our Lady, Mother of Mercy published in 1959.[66] Religious institutes as political cultures relied greatly on the vow of obedience for the efficient and smooth running of a convent. It was an unquestioned facet of religious life for sisters and nuns born in the 1930s and 1940s. One sister born in the 1930s explained her unquestioning obedience as commonplace for women of her time: 'The generation in which I grew up was one that was accustomed to a certain discipline in life, restrictions on your movements, and the idea of obedience was not something which was novel.'[67] Another nun of this same generation indicated that 'we used to be very, very literal in our obedience to the rules and things.'[68] Even those born in the 1940s opined: 'My generation, well me in my generation, I accepted ... and maybe that was my family background, you did what your parents told you to do, without question [laughs], that was it.'[69] Explaining the vow of obedience, one nun recalled:

> You kind of weren't able to think for yourself. You know, you do this like this, and that's how you did it. As I say, I'm not a quarrelsome sort of person, I would just accept the person and do what I'm doing, you know. Whereas somebody else might find that difficult, you see.

---

66 SCMM-ENK: 1770, *The Congregation of Sisters of Charity of Our Lady, Mother of Mercy* (Preston: the author, 1959), p. 21.
67 Anonymised interview.
68 Anonymised interview.
69 Anonymised interview.

Oh, I prefer another way, can do it an easier way. Because that was, I mean silly, I don't know if it was peeling apples or potatoes? No, it was potatoes. I was used to peeling with a knife at home, you know, I'd peel them with a knife, and that was one of my jobs as a postulant, peeling the spuds, I had to do it with a potato peeler. So I said, 'Can I not use the knife?' 'No, you use the potato peeler.' So, okay, well I'll use the potato peeler. It took me twice as long because I'd never used one of these things before. [laughs] But something like that, you see, just so mundane. And you have to ask if you could have a bath, wash your hair. You just didn't take that for granted.[70]

In defending her malleability, this nun revealed her acceptance of obedience as a normative feature of religious life. Born after the war, she benefited from a post-Butler education: she was educated at a Catholic secondary modern, then attended a further education college and enrolled in a nursing course. Yet, she was being taught in the mid-1960s novitiate about a blind obedience that meant being treated as a child even to the point of having to ask to take a bath.

Nuns and sisters were being introduced to new thinking on obedience. Even before the Second Vatican Council, Dominican Henry St John, speaking at a training workshop for novice mistresses at Spode House, Staffordshire in 1955, though 'commending authority to the young', declared that 'unreasonable' obedience 'because-I-tell-you' would 'bring the concept of obedience itself into disrepute'.[71] But it took future generations of religious to introduce the concepts of personal and shared responsibility to a 'co-operative project'.[72] Superior General Thérèse Mary Barnett, writing to the Sisters of Charity of Our Lady, Mother of Mercy in 1971, explained the relationship between obedience and personal and shared responsibility:

Sisters are acknowledged to be mature, intelligent women who can rightly be allowed to contribute to the making of important decisions concerning themselves, their communities and their province. By exercising their reason and judgment they can be of very great assistance to the authorities in arriving at a course of action which will be of great benefit to all concerned. In a sense it is much easier to say, 'I am here because my Superior put me here', thus implicitly relieving

70 Anonymised interview. There is a dark side to this blind obedience – see the Conclusion.
71 Henry St John, OP, 'Education of the Novice and Young Religious in the Life of Prayer' in Ambrose Farrell, Henry Saint John and F.B. Elkisch (eds), *The Education of the Novice* (London: Blackfriars Publications, 1956), p. 36.
72 Anonymised interview.

oneself of all responsibility than to join in the consultation needed to see just how and where the Lord plans to allow us to co-operate in what is, after all, His work.[73]

Barnett acknowledged that the sisters were adults, 'mature, intelligent women', who should be consulted about decisions. She appeared to be both reasoning with local leaders, justifying allowing sisters to make decisions, whilst reminding sisters that this 'right' was not without responsibilities. Both local leaders and sisters needed convincing of the attractiveness of collaborative decision-making. Barnett asserted that personal and shared responsibility did not allow for disobedience; the 'subjection of the will' remained imperative and this suggests that though obedience had become more collaborative, it had not disappeared from the religious lexicon.

This new style of obedience was not without dissent and confusion. One undated and unattributed list of points written in response to a report coming out of the Institute of the Blessed Virgin Mary's Chapter of 1968 insisted that 'Obedience in faith i.e. blind obedience (possibly a crucifixion) is still required.' The next point queried 'Obedience by consensus can hardly be the obedience asked by Jesus Christ.'[74] Both points reflected the historic understanding of obedience, the sacrificial quality of blind obedience, and both pilloried consensus decision-making. Some argued that the 'weakening' of obedience would lead to a 'breach in authority'.[75] Letters, discussions and workshops on obedience were a constant presence from the 1960s to the 1980s. Notes from the 1976 Provincial Chapter of the Sisters of Charity of Our Lady, Mother of Mercy plaintively asked 'why all this discussion?'. The reply reminded sisters that 'Formerly ideas of obedience were imposed from above without dialogue or consultation. Now obedience comes from each one in the group in a spirit of interdependence.'[76] In 1965, Cardinal John Carmel Heenan, Archbishop of Westminster, acknowledged at the Annual General Meeting of Superiors that 'at a time when the Church is undergoing a crisis of authority', convent leaders needed to

be very clever in order to avoid the extremes of either allowing people to do exactly what they like or refusing to acknowledge the changed

73 SCMM-ENK: 1728, 'Over the Atlantic', *Meeting Point* (May 1971), p. 1.
74 ACJ/EP/C/32/b, List of fourteen points.
75 SCMM–ENK: 52, 'Chapter 1964, Summary of the Reports of the Discussion of the Subjects offered for Discussion Oct.–Dec. 1963', pp. 17–18.
76 SCMM-ENK: 332, 'English Provincial Chapter', Woodhall Centre, 1–11 August 1976.

conditions. It is foolish for anyone in authority to expect subjects to have the same regard for authority as we had thirty or forty years ago. We have come into a new phase of the Church's life. We have to be very careful on the other hand not to court popularity by accepting uncritically the current views of authority or, indeed, of theology ... We need to be critical of the new versions of obedience which are gaining ground and causing trouble in certain great Religious Orders.[77]

Heenan's use of the term 'subjects' points to the continued emphasis on the significance of hierarchy, and his questioning the currency of this new obedience suggests his scepticism and perhaps his longing for a more unambiguous understanding of obedience.[78]

Religious communities weren't the only intentional communities struggling with non-hierarchical and non-authoritarian structures. Similar difficulties can be found in countercultural movements such as communes, which relied on collaborative decision-making and found themselves drowning in long, intense, sometimes emotive discussions and meetings. Strong leadership or rules and structures seemed a necessary feature of a successful intentional community.[79] Feminist Lynne Segal alludes to similar challenges in living collectively with other members of the Women's Liberation Movement in the 1970s: 'Notions of shared housework, childcare and commitments to the wellbeing of all existed in tension with ideas of personal independence, sexual autonomy and flexibility of lifestyle.'[80]

Within religious life, absolute obedience had been a key feature of the smooth running of a community. Personal and shared responsibility offered ways of developing new shared understanding of obedience

---

77 SCMM-ENK: 374, Letter from Thérèse Mary Barnett asking major religious superiors in England for 'present-day thinking about the Renewal of Religious Life in England'.

78 He was at this time also juggling the aftermath of *Sacrosanctum Concilium* (Constitution on the Sacred Liturgy, 1963), when liturgical experimentation and vernacular masses drew both the appreciation of the working classes and the ire of the very vociferous members of the Latin Mass Society. Alana Harris, 'A Fresh Stripping of the Altars? Liturgical Language and the Legacy of the Reformation in England, 1964–1984', in Kathleen Sprows Cummings, Timothy Matovina, and Robert A. Orsi (eds), *Catholics in the Vatican II Era: Local Histories of a Global Event* (Cambridge: Cambridge University Press, 2017), pp. 245–74.

79 Yaacov Oved, *Globalization of Communes: 1950–2010* (New Brunswick, NJ: Transaction, 2013), p. 88; Robert Houriet, *Getting Back Together* (New York: Coward, McCann & Geoghegan, 1971), p. 405.

80 Lynne Segal, *Out of Time: The Pleasures and Perils of Ageing* (London: Verso, 2012), pp. 141–2.

but were difficult concepts to put into practice, particularly when their meanings were not agreed upon.

Participation and consultation

Some women religious appeared to transition easily from obedience to consultation. One Poor Clare observed:

> I was amazed after the Council at how many people who had seemed totally unquestioning began to say things like, well I've always thought this was wrong, or we shouldn't do this, or it would be better if we did that. I was astonished at what came out.[81]

The speed of this vocalising of opinions suggests that some women had silently questioned authority; or, as other sisters have suggested, that such questioning was spoken of privately. She also reflected on the *zeitgeist* of the 1960s as relevant to religious life and the importance of consultation:

> [P]eople began to say things like 'they say we have to have community meetings', you were never clear who "they" were, but it was kind of in the air. Perhaps part of the cultural revolution. [laughs] It was kind of in the air that things needed to be more consultative, that it wouldn't continue to work just by saying 'do this and do that'. And once you start that ball rolling it can't be stopped actually, it takes on its own dynamic.[82]

A Poor Clare in another community remembered one particular emotionally charged meeting:

> We were so many at chapter we sat in two big circles on stools, the older people at the back and the younger people in the front, so the older Sisters had a chair and the younger people had a stool, like an inner ring, and the Abbess sat at a table in front on her own, and they were quite formidable chapters.

The configuration she described reflected the hierarchies of power within the monastery: older sisters on chairs, younger sisters on stools and the abbess in the centre. She continued:

> But one or two powerful characters, very courageous, would sometimes throw a spanner in the wheels in a very good way that when something was being proposed that was not right – I'll give one specific thing, and a Sister who's still with us, she's old now. Huge courage because it

---

81 Anonymised interview.
82 Anonymised interview.

was your whole world, so to oppose the Abbess in front of everybody when she had almost in those days like power of life and death ... And there was a planning permission notice at the bottom of the drive that the community hadn't been told about and it was going to affect us ... Most people wouldn't have dared say anything, but this Sister stood up and said, 'I believe there's a notice of planning permission for building a bungalow at the bottom of the drive and we have heard nothing about it, so please could you explain what this is all about?' I'd only been in the house about three months, I can remember sitting there, shaking, I was so frightened ... And the Abbess was outraged and she said the discreets have given permission for it – that was the council – and she persisted and she said well, what about the community, the community should know about it. We haven't been consulted. And the next week when the minutes were read, this wasn't mentioned, so she stood up again and she said, 'There's no mention of what I said, it should be recorded in the minutes' ... And afterwards people said to me, were you very shocked by what happened at chapter? I said, 'I thought it was marvellous.' I said, 'I thought it was absolutely wonderful. She's so brave', I said, 'I was so impressed.' So even in the best places it took courage, you know.[83]

The abbess and her council had initiated community meetings appearing to conform to consultation but used these forums to inform rather than to consult. They were operating in the authoritative ways they knew best. It took 'powerful characters' who stood their ground to insist on consultation. Despite a discourse of personal and shared responsibilities, leadership within the monastery or convent was not always ready to change; and when confrontation occurred, the frisson was palpable. This nun later remarked on the juridical nature of the changes.

> [T]he new constitutions went a long way to that because they gave very detailed lists of the things that a community must be consulted about or it would be invalid ... there were certain things that the Abbess must consult them and then she could, listen to them, and then presumably she could make her own decision. She had to hear what they had to say, but there were other things that the community had the say in, they must be settled by the chapter, the community chapter.

Shifts in governance became legalised in rewritten constitutions, which still gave the abbess some unilateral power but that power was shared (eventually) with the community chapter, which became according to this participant 'the main instrument of government'.[84]

83   Anonymised interview.
84   Anonymised interview.

New responsibilities that went along with consultation and participation required knowledge, interactions and decision-making. Sisters and nuns spoke of 'meetings upon meetings'[85] and being deluged by paperwork: questionnaires, circular letters, reports, newsletters and magazines. In order to communicate the importance of particular documents, the Sisters of Charity of Our Lady, Mother of Mercy received colour-coded documents. If a report was printed on pink paper, it must be read immediately; if on yellow paper, it was a chapter document.[86] Stanbrook's resident historian Dame Anne Field wrote of the 'dreaded Monday afternoon sessions' in her Worcestershire Benedictine monastery. She noted that 'Here for the first time many people learned to formulate their opinions on the nature of our life and … elected moderators learned a new skill in the art of summing up a meeting and presenting its findings to the Abbess and assembled community the next day.'[87] Discussions could become heated. In one offsite community meeting in 1972, Sisters of Charity of Our Lady, Mother of Mercy met in small groups to discuss 'Have the changes in community life made the individual sister's role easier or more difficult?' One group responded that life was easier when responsibilities were less shared, acknowledging the effortlessness of obedience.[88] The uncertainty and uncomfortableness of the changes in governance were reflected by those in the second group, who 'aimed at individual responsibility, yet felt guilty doing so, not being convinced that this was the right path to take'. This group was obedient to the precepts of 'personal responsibility' but acknowledged it felt contrary to their understanding of religious life. The third group was enthusiastic: they had

> felt that previously their difficulty had been in a life with restrictions imposed from outside themselves. Now, with the change of emphasis on personal responsibility these difficulties no longer existed, but now the responsibility for the depth of our commitment was our responsibility, and this did not make life easier – but they felt they were now truly living.

85 Anonymised interview.

86 SCMM-ENK: 332, Letter to All the Sisters of the English Province from Sister Marie, dated 15 June 1976.

87 Dame Anne Field, *A Year's Aggiornamento*, cited from Dame Scholastica Jacob, 'Stanbrook Abbey and the Reception of the Second Vatican Council'. Paper given at the English Benedictine History Commission Annual Symposium on 1 May 2014 and referenced here with the kind permission of Dame Scholastica Jacob.

88 SCMM-ENK: Stella Vigar, 'Communication process …', *Meeting Point* 6 (February 1973), pp. 23–5.

This diversity of opinion revealed the ruptures of convent living. Such discussions often led to 'difficult silences' and an atmosphere that was emotionally charged.[89] The strains and uncertainties of this time of flux remained a salient memory for many sisters and nuns: one sister acknowledged that though she 'relished and responded' to the 'new and stimulating attitudes', she became 'deeply anxious' as 'old and new norms were at war'.[90]

Relinquishing control and sharing decision-making was difficult. Some convent leaders needed to be coaxed and instructed on the new ways of managing convents. The general superior of the Institute of the Blessed Virgin Mary, Edelburga Solzabacher, wrote sympathetically to the Reverend Mother at York in 1969:

> I feel that the many new directives may cause you a little difficulty and that you may find the change in relations with the Sisters rather a problem: the right to discussion that must be allowed them and the right to information on house and school matters as far as discretion allows. Don't hesitate about all this, but try asking for the opinions and suggestions of your community and discussing things at recreation. Then you will find that you will hear many useful things that would not have occurred to you by yourself.

Such cajoling suggests that this local leader needed convincing of the benefits of participation. Fears that consultation and participation would lead to an uncomfortable 'change in relations' were very real for those who managed a convent or monastery. The local superior at York was encouraged to emphasise subsidiarity:

> Show the Sisters that you trust them. Give them freedom of action in the department under their charge. They should feel that they are responsible for it and can answer for it. All this will help to lighten your own burden a little. It is true that the way of governing a community nowadays calls on us to adapt ourselves more and show more consideration for persons and things, but still that very fact will give it more personal character and help to create kinder and happier relations between the Superior and the community.[91]

---

89   *Ibid.*
90   SSH ENW: 'RSCJ and 1967', Remembrance 7.
91   ACJ/EP/C/32/b, Letter from Mother Edelburga Solzabacher to 'Reverend Mother', dated 6 February 1969. Mother Edelburga Solzabacher was elected as General Superior of the Institute of the Blessed Virgin Mary Union in 1953 and remained in post until 1975.

The encouraging tone suggested that local superiors were not always invested in the process, and may have found it difficult to comply with this new way of managing.

Even those leaders who in theory supported consultation and participation found challenges to their own authority difficult to adjust to. One Poor Clare remarked:

> [O]n the level of the Abbess's personal power, that she didn't realise that that had to ... she'd made all these wise changes that she was very much, and rightly, esteemed for, but she didn't see at that point that her position was going to be untenable. You know, that she'd have to ... shared responsibility meant something different.[92]

One sister who entered in the 1940s admitted this was a difficult and slow process: 'But consciously, slowly, slowly ... we began to realise that things that came from above, that was one time, but in fact we were all responsible for the wellbeing, and so it all took on a completely different shape.'[93] The journey to achieve participation and consultation was full of roadblocks from both convent leadership who found it difficult to manage a community when they had to consult with the larger body of religious and from religious who found participation onerous and would rather be told what to do. Participation and consultation were critical to this change in governance within religious life, but they required a radical engagement that challenged entrenched feminine hierarchies and matriarchal structures.

Smaller communities

Experiments in community living were another aspect of the reshaping of religious life.[94] Some religious institutes, like the British Daughters of Charity of St Vincent de Paul, remained wedded to their local corporate structures with the Sister Servant managing the local community. Like so many religious institutes, they had historically founded both small and large communities.[95] Others, like the Dutch Sisters of Charity of Our Lady, Mother of Mercy and the Society of the Sacred Heart, held discussions on community size where advocates of small communities argued that large

---

92 Anonymised interview.
93 Anonymised interview.
94 By the 1990s, mixed communities with religious of other congregations or lay people were also a feature of the 'small community' movement.
95 O'Brien, *Leaving God for God*, pp. 340, 387–430. O'Brien's gazetteer of the houses of the Daughters of Charity of St Vincent de Paul records numerous small communities.

Table 3.1 Community size, Society of the Sacred Heart, 1969

	Less than 10	10–15	16–20	21–30	More than 30	unknown	Total
Worldwide	447	460	380	1,776	3,136	23	6,222
	7.2%	7.4%	6.1%	28.5%	50.4%	0.4%	100%
England and	18	29	1	51	225	1	325
Malta	5.5%	8.9%	0.3%	15.7%	69.2%	0.3%	100.0%

Source: RSCJ: KASKI (Katholiek Sociaal-Kerkelijk Instituut/Catholic Social Research Institute, Nijmegen), 'Questionnaire (novembre 1969). Resultats et interpretation', vol. 2, question 4.

convents were a deterrent to evangelisation and internal and external relationship-building. A study of the experiences of the Society of the Sacred Heart provides one detailed example of the re-engineering of the local governance structures of community life.

The majority of Sacred Heart sisters worldwide, 50.4 per cent, lived in communities of thirty or more.[96] The province of England and Malta had five large communities (Tunbridge Wells, Roehampton, Fenham and Woldingham in England and Tal Virtu in Malta) which serviced sizeable educational institutions that were staffed by large numbers of sisters who functioned as administrators, educators and domestic staff. Discussions on splitting up Fenham's 'over-large community' to experiment with living arrangements began in 1968.[97] In January 1970, the Provincial Assembly split the community into groups according to where sisters worked (in the grammar school, the college, etc.) but this division never really 'took' and by Easter it had 'petered out'.[98] Later that year, Fenham was redivided into three communities: a separate small community in Cedar Road and two communities within the Fenham complex (a community of ten members and another of the remaining thirty-one members).[99] The two

---

96   SSH ENW: KASKI (Katholiek Sociaal-Kerkelijk Instituut/Catholic Social Research Institute, Nijmegen), 'Questionnaire (novembre 1969). Resultats et interpretation', vol. 2, question 4. The questionnaire was sent to 6,639 members of the Society of the Religious of the Sacred Heart worldwide; 6,228 forms were returned (93.8 per cent). Of these members, 325 belonged to the Province of England and Malta. The first results were published in March 1970.
97   SSH ENW: Fenham House Journal, 28 June 1968.
98   SSH ENW: Fenham House Journal, January 1970. This entry was made retrospective as refers to April 1970.
99   SSH ENW: Fenham House Journal, September 1970.

Fenham communities residing in the same complex met for community meals at different times, prayed separately and recreated separately. In a 1970s survey of the province, many sisters remarked that smaller communities were a means of removing both unnecessary hierarchy and 'Victorian attitudes'.[100] One sister (aged forty at the time) noted 'there was an effort to realise that community life needs something more than just being twenty-five people together coming along [*sic*] for recreation'. She explained that the division into two communities allowed sisters 'to develop both our religious and our spiritual lives, as it were, together'.[101] Most interviewees, many of whom were considered 'younger' at the time, were enthusiastic about the move to smaller communities. Recollections acknowledged feelings of personal release, but also suggested the dissonance felt by others. Thinking back almost fifty years, one sister, recalling her early thirties, acknowledged that:

> Actually I didn't find that difficult at all because it actually was, for us it was a great thing … it was very hard for the other parts of the community and we had an experiment first of all, to divide into two communities along different lines and that for me was a disaster. I think for quite a lot of people it was a disaster. It just did not work because you were, it [was] a mixture of those who wanted to move and those who didn't. Or who were taking a long time to, so in the end that was abandoned and we did another hard thing which was to divide it along age lines really, and, and, um what our jobs were in the school … That was the big change to have two communities instead of one and to do it very specifically in terms of roles and ages, and it could have been an absolute disaster, and it was hard for the older ones but certainly for us the younger ones it was great.[102]

The fault lines, according to this sister and others, fell along generational divisions. The first division of the large communities disregarded age; the second was grouped by age. She suggests, as other narrators did, impatience with those 'taking a long time' and an older cohort who were resistant to change.

The shift to smaller, self-contained, new communities, such as the one in Cedar Road, seemed less contentious. Some welcomed it as an 'easing out the institutional structures'.[103] The Sisters of Charity of Our Lady, Mother of Mercy opened their first small experimental community of four sisters in England in 1968. The visitator praised this new style of living

---

100 SSH ENW: 10 Eng, 'KASKI Self-Survey', England–Malta Province, 1970.
101 Anonymised interview.
102 Anonymised interview.
103 Anonymised interview.

religious life: 'This small community, the first of its kind in the Province, illustrates especially the way in wich [sic] a community can be integrated into the life of the parish.' She commented on the genuine sharing of interests in small communities.[104] Such collegiality and camaraderie, though, was not guaranteed. After a visit to another community in 1987, visitators reported that after two years the community exhibited a lack of communication and uncertainty as to their purpose.[105]

Small community experiments occurred initially in the 1960s and 1970s for the Society of the Sacred Heart and the Sisters of Charity of Our Lady, Mother of Mercy. For some congregations, the shift to smaller communities occurred later. The development of small communities in the Institute of the Blessed Virgin Mary in the 1980s was part of a bigger move from managing large convent schools, to smaller parish-based ministries. The sisters who volunteered for an experimental community in Norwich in 1985 were in their fifties and seventies. In discussing the foundation of the new community, which met the diverse needs of a large Catholic parish in Norwich, one of the sisters recounted: 'Norwich was an opportunity to rethink community life. There was no "we always ..." and no school timetable; we were a small group, and the mission ... was to find out what needed to be done, and do it, according to our individual skills.'[106] For this sister, who had lived most of her religious life in the large communities in Cambridge and York, where she had primarily taught in and managed the congregation's schools, the Norwich community offered a new way of living religious life which allowed for more contact with ordinary Catholics and others in the local community.[107] The English Dominicans also rethought the structures of community life. One report discussed at the annual Easter Meeting in 1975 suggested that a new model of community life in smaller communities was possible. This initially caused some discord. By the 1990s, two forms of community life existed. Larger communities maintained much of what was traditional about religious life: an horarium that structured their day and timetabled meal times, prayer and recreation; the Divine Office was recited at prescribed hours as a community; hierarchical governance

104 SCMM-ENK: 98, Visitation Report – March 1968 'Kirkham; Our Lady of Lourdes Convent'.
105 SCMM-ENK: 342, 'Report of the Visit to Our Lady's Convent, Flint', 1–4 March 1987, by Sisters Thérèse Mary [Barnett] and Marie-Therese [Croke].
106 Sister Patricia Harriss, 'Looking Back on my Religious Life' (2014; in Sister Patricia's possession).
107 This form of evangelisation will be discussed in more detail in Chapter 6.

structures included traditional offices such as the prioress, chantress, infirmarian, librarian, etc. Smaller communities, which had more diverse missions, did away with the horarium, allowed for more flexibility in reciting the Divine Office and the work of managing the convent was done collaboratively.[108]

As the Dominican example above suggests, hierarchical ways of managing larger communities were not always suitable for smaller communities. Smaller communities, according to another sister, allowed sisters to 'to take more responsibility for the life of the group and not rely on the Superior'.[109] Some communities pushed this further and questioned the need for a local leader. One sister, after being appointed superior of a local community of five sisters in the 1970s, recalled being told 'I've got nothing against you personally … but I don't really think we need a Superior in this community'. She recounted the questioning within the Society of the Sacred Heart:

> Do we need a named person or do we just simply organise life among ourselves. And that was very much an issue and we did move into, the late seventies onwards, into most of the groups being, all of them were linked with a member of the provincial team who was Superior, if you like, but the community itself didn't have a named leader and the communities themselves worked out their own way of working and so on and um so that there was a transition from a named leader to a much more loosely knit structure where there was leadership in the province but there wasn't necessarily a named leader in the local group.

When asked about decision-making, she offered, 'we would just sit and talk about things and come to a consensus'.[110] This was a workable strategy for a small community of five, but for larger communities this would prove challenging.

Members of the women's movement also experimented with intentional communities and advocating anti-hierarchical, egalitarian, 'structureless' communities where decisions were made collaboratively. Radical feminist Jo Freeman in the early 1970s spoke of her experiences of the 'tyranny of structurelessness', arguing that such decision-making could easily be a way of 'masking power' maintained by an in-group who knew how decisions were made. She argued that some structure was necessary for 'getting things done' and

---

108 Nye, *A Peculiar Kind of Mission*, pp. 224–8.
109 Anonymised interview.
110 Anonymised interview.

advocated sharing information and resources and experimenting with delegation, distribution of authority and rotation/allocation of tasks.[111] Some communities of women religious did experiment in similar ways, removing some of the hierarchical features of religious life and experimenting with structurelessness.

Conclusion

Religious life had its own '1968'. It began with top-down directives coming out of the Second Vatican Council that insisted religious institutes develop cultures of participation and consultation. The female leaders of religious institutes rethought governance and replaced deeply embedded structures where the mother superior or abbess and her council made decisions for all members of the community. More women participated in governance, as delegates to General Chapters or as members of provincial structures. More voices were heard via questionnaires and consultative meetings. At the local level, changes in governance practices were experienced by each and every member of a community. Renewal released a social movement that gave voice to grievances and concerns about religious life and unleashed collective action that changed, in many communities, the lived experience of community life. And yet, this was in no way a straightforward story of progress. These changes polarised women religious in groups that were 'for change' and 'against change' and were highly contentious. The reactions to these changes were complicated and included feelings of liberation, confusion, regret and dismay. One cannot overstate the enormity of the shift in governance.

The challenges to governance and authority within convent spaces were analogous to the confrontations to authorities in the long 1960s. This gendered version of '1968' demonstrates an emancipatory movement led, sustained, spread and obstructed by women. The women religious who participated in this project rarely self-identified as feminist. Yet their actions, as documented in the archives and in their stories, were centred on creating what Sandra Schneiders calls 'alternative models of religious community'.[112] Sociologist Christine Gervais has highlighted in her work with Canadian women religious their commitment to governance in a

---

111 Jo Freeman, 'The Tyranny of Structurelessness', *Berkeley Journal of Sociology*, 17 (1972), 151–64.

112 Sandra M. Schneiders, *Beyond Patching: Faith and Feminism in the Catholic Church* (New York: Paulist Press, 1991), p. 102.

'circular model' that included processes of 'inclusive leadership, decision-making and action that involve the democratic distribution of tasks'.[113] Governance structures of religious communities continued to evolve into the twenty-first century. One nun explained the investment in consensus-building in her community:

> It's very easy to make a decision where you vote for something and there's so many 'yeses' and there's so many 'nos', but we don't do that in this community, because that's what can destroy and split a community. You've got to try and come to a consensus of opinion. We work very hard at that. We have outside facilitation in order to do that and we work on ourselves individually and we're trying to build something all the time. It's very hard, it's hard work.[114]

Experiences of governance and authority in individual convents could be stifling or liberating – they were often a product of the unique combination of leadership, community personalities and local circumstances. The next chapter moves us from governance of the community, to the lived experience within the community, especially the relational aspect of community living, traditionally linked to the common life.

---

113 Christine Gervais, 'Alternative Altars: Beyond Patriarchy and Priesthood and towards Inclusive Spirituality, Governance and Activism among Catholic Women Religious in Ontario', *Canadian Woman Studies*, 29 (2011), 11.
114 Anonymised interview.

4

Relationships, generational discourse and the 'turn to self'

Introduction

I knew when I was coming that I would only see my parents for four nights every year, I knew that I would have a habit that was cumbersome, a headdress that would be hot and sticky, that I'd have eventually a cloak in choir, a surplice, I knew that it would be strict. I didn't know all the funny things that we were asked to do. But at that stage we hadn't been taught to criticise, it was a very different education, it was much more a sort of, this is it, we're reasonably honest, so you accept it – do you know what I mean? But it was a big shock when after a couple of generations when they suddenly came in querying everything. Gracious me! [laughs] … the first big shock, joke, was that when they were going off to college they expected to have a new set of crayons. … but it was different to the way that one had learnt really, not just in the community. Because in the war you never expected anything new, you wore things out till the end, so it was a different way of thinking, you know?[1]

Born in the late 1920s, this sister entered religious life just after the war. She was aware religious life would be difficult, her relationship with her family curtailed and that her everyday life would be structured and strict. She identified herself as part of a 'we' that had been socialised to avoid proffering criticism, pointing to an automatic acceptance of traditions, customs and even 'funny things'. She recalled the 'shock' of encountering a cohort of women in the 1970s who began to question the status quo of religious life and who asked for (and received) 'a new set of crayons'. Then in her late forties, the religious life she knew and loved had begun to change. Some changes were structural and related to governance as

---

1   Anonymised interview.

discussed in the previous chapter; others were relational. In charting the shifts in relationships within the convent from the formal to the relational, this chapter turns to homosocial hierarchical and personal interactions that were a part of everyday life and identifies the conditions which shaped their formation, development and maintenance. It examines how post-war modernity impinged on these interactions and interrogates the meanings of the common life alongside the ways that generational discourse and lived experience shaped and complicated relationships. Such all-too-human interactions were linked to notions of authenticity, selfhood and identity that were part of the 'turn to self' that became identified with post-war modernity.[2] These notions also became integrated into the understandings of old and new Catholic religious practice within and without religious life.

Female homosocial communities have remained for scholars and contemporaries an enduring focal point of interrogation.[3] Nineteenth-century sororial networks enlarged women's sphere of action, not simply as church workers but as female-led communities.[4] Homosociality studies have considered the social bonds between same-sex persons, frequently emphasising sexuality and power.[5] Scholar Martha Vicinus has argued that well-run women's communities implied a female self-sufficiency, and an alternative to men's dominance;[6] others have emphasised the power of these women's worlds.[7] Lilian Faderman's work treats close friendship between women as 'romantic friendships' (though not sexual relationships), which she argues were central to women's lives until the early twentieth century. Homosocial networks within religious cultures

2   Nikolas Rose, *Governing the Soul: The Shaping of the Private Self* (London: Routledge, 1990).

3   Sharon L. Jansen, *Reading Women's Worlds from Christine de Pizan to Doris Lessing: A Guide to Six Centuries of Women Writers Imagining Rooms of Their Own* (New York: Palgrave Macmillan, 2011); Martha Vicinus, *Independent Women: Work and Community for Single Women, 1850–1920* (Chicago: University of Chicago Press, 1988); Pauline Nestor, *Female Friendships and Communities* (Oxford: Clarendon Press, 1985).

4   Sheila Wright, '"Every Good Woman Needs a Companion of Her Own Sex": Quaker Women and Spiritual Friendship, 1750–1850', in Sue Morgan (ed.), *Women, Religion and Feminism in Britain, 1750–1900* (Basingstoke: Palgrave Macmillan, 2002), p. 100.

5   Katherine Binhammer, 'Female Homosociality and the Exchange of Men: Mary Robinson's *Walsingham*', *Women's Studies*, 35 (2006), 221–40.

6   Vicinus, *Independent Women*, p. 46.

7   Carroll Smith-Rosenberg, 'The Female World of Love and Ritual: Relations between Women in Nineteenth-Century America', *Signs*, 1 (1975), 2, 14. See also Lilian Faderman, *Surpassing the Love of Men: Romantic Friendship and Love between Women from the Renaissance to the Present* (New York: William Morrow, 1981).

were noted places of deep friendship between women.[8] Scholars of women religious (including myself) have often focused on the forbidden practice of 'particular friendships'.[9] Close relationships within convent discourse were considered transgressive; they were seen as exclusionary and associated with the divisiveness of convent cliques. Academic scholarship has insisted that this transgression was more sexual, and implied that the prohibition of such rules against 'particular friendships' forbade sexual relationships.[10] Friendship (particular or otherwise), however, is only one form of homosocial interaction. This chapter turns to other forms of interactions including relationships that were companionate, collegial, deferential and adversarial to better understand the nature of the shift of convent interactions from formal to relational.

Twentieth-century historiography on female homosocial relationships is less robust than that of the nineteenth century. Sociologist Pearl Jephcott writing in the 1950s found that once young women began courting, their relationship with female friends waned.[11] Oral historian Elizabeth Roberts notes that homosocial relationships for working-class married women were often more about neighbourliness and communal sociability than about intimate friendship, especially after children were born. Female networks supported daily living through exchanges of goods and services but with a 'wary mutuality'.[12] Recent scholars suggest the demotion of women's friendships from their central location in women's lives upon marriage.[13] Perhaps this explains why Deborah M. Withers writing on the 1970s women's liberation movement suggests that there were 'few models for female homosocial relationships', finding

8   Linda Wilson, *Constrained by Zeal: Female Spirituality amongst Nonconformists, 1825–75* (Carlisle: Paternoster, 2000); Wright, ' "Every Good Woman" '.
9   Despite these efforts to structure and institutionalise relationships, some women found ways to develop and maintain friendships, even close friendships, in ways that did not appear to alert convent authorities to the potential of 'particular' friendship.
10 Rosemary Curb and Nancy Manahan, *Lesbian Nuns: Breaking Silence* (Tallahassee, FL: Naiad Press, 1985).
11 A. P. Jephcott, *Rising Twenty* (London: Faber and Faber, 1942), pp. 75–6.
12 Elizabeth Roberts, *Women and Families: An Oral History 1940–1970* (Oxford: Blackwell, 1995), pp. 199–207; Josephine Klein, *Samples from English Cultures*, 2 vols (London: Routledge & Kegan Paul, 1965), vol. 1, pp. 137–9; Ross McKibbin, *Classes and Cultures: England 1918–1951* (Oxford: Oxford University Press, 1998), p. 181.
13 Claire Langhamer, *Women's Leisure in England, 1920–1960* (Manchester: Manchester University Press, 2000), pp. 117, 128. Langhamer notes that pre-marriage relationships were centred on sociability.

that 'relational experiments were fraught with difficulty and sometimes became spaces of conflict'.[14] Like 1970s feminists, religious sisters and nuns found themselves in the midst of 'relationship experiments' as relationships shifted from the formal to the relational.

Post-war relationships have been studied as part of a growing body of literature on authenticity, selfhood and identity. Writer Jeremy Seabrook used his own experience of working-class life to scrutinise and explain post-war personal interactions, identifying a shift from 'role' to 'relationship'. He contrasted 'role' as 'familiar' but 'burdensome and intolerable' with an idyllic vision of 'relationship':

> The whole triumph of the various liberation movements lies in the extent to which they have helped people escape oppressive roles – felt to be unreal, constricting, inauthentic – in order to explore relationships, which, by contrast, attract words like rich, deep, exciting, lasting, developing. Everything that suggests dynamism, energy, is held in the word relationship.[15]

Authenticity was increasingly a post-war concern.[16] Marriage was reframed as a relationship, rather than an institution. Historian Claire Langhamer has demonstrated the centrality of authenticity and selfhood to the meanings of married love in this period.[17] Neil Armstrong has argued that the 'language of character and self-control was increasingly displaced by that of personality and interiority'.[18] Nikolas Rose identifies 'psy' professions as key to 'assembling' a selfhood reliant on 'choice, fulfilment, self-discovery, self-realization'.[19] The post-war generation is said to have developed a reflexive self, where young people recounted critically and personally their own history, demonstrating that the

---

14 Deborah M. Withers, 'Women's Liberation, Relationships and the "Vicinity of Trauma"', *Oral History*, 40 (2012), 85.

15 Jeremy Seabrook, *Working-Class Childhood* (London: Victor Gollancz, 1982), p. 140.

16 Charles Taylor, *The Ethics of Authenticity* (Cambridge, MA: Harvard University Press, 1991).

17 Claire Langhamer, 'Love, Selfhood and Authenticity in Post-War Britain', *Cultural and Social History*, 9 (2012), 277–97.

18 Neil Armstrong, '"I Insisted I Was Myself": Clergy Wives and Authentic Selfhood in England c. 1960–94', *Women's History Review*, 22:6 (2013), 996. A similar discourse shift occurred earlier in the United States: see Heather A. Warren, 'The Shift from Character to Personality in Mainline Protestant Thought, 1935–1945', *Church History*, 67 (1998), 537–55.

19 Nikolas Rose, 'Assembling the Modern Self', in Roy Porter (ed.), *Rewriting the Self: Histories from the Renaissance to the Present* (London: Routledge, 1997), p. 246.

'subaltern *could* speak'.[20] Philosopher Charles Taylor has argued the 'ethic of authenticity' identifies a post-war 'do your own thing' mentality that became expressivism.[21] This body of research has lent itself to the discourse of secularisation, but recent post-secular scholarship has linked authenticity to religious belief, and shifts (adoption or rejection) in new or old religious praxis.[22]

Religious beliefs, alongside praxis, have, of course, contributed to both private and public forms of selfhood.[23] Relationships within convent spaces both inhibited and encouraged forms of self-expression that shaped the self. The dominant accounts of relational change within the historiography of post-conciliar religious life addressed the shift from hierarchical relationships which were superior–subject-based to ones that became more collegial and egalitarian. Women religious, in both published memoirs and collections of interviews, often reflected back on the discipline and rigour of their pre-conciliar convent experience as impersonal and harsh. The North American literature, particularly memoirs, can be particularly uncompromising in the damning of the pre-conciliar impersonality of relationships. Without negating the legitimacy of these experiences, these narratives also reflect the concerns of the present, of validating the course of action taken after the Second Vatican Council for what has been touted as a more liberated, progressive version of religious life.[24] This recounting suggests a cultural script, often in the form of contrasting pre-conciliar harshness of convent rules and regulations with a post-conciliar enlightenment.

This chapter argues for a less stark pre-/post-conciliar dichotomy, and in turning towards the expansive landscape of homosocial

20 Carolyn Steedman, 'Writing the Self: The End of the Scholarship Girl', in Jim McGuigan (ed.), *Cultural Methodologies* (London: Sage, 1997), p. 114.
21 Charles Taylor, *A Secular Age* (Harvard, MA: Harvard University Press, 2007), p. 475.
22 Jane Garnett, Matthew Grimley, Alana Harris, William Whyte and Sarah Williams (eds), *Redefining Christian Britain: Post-1945 Perspectives* (London: SCM Press, 2006), pp. 12, 23–4. Armstrong, '"I Insisted I Was Myself"'.
23 Sue Morgan 'Introduction', in Sue Morgan (ed.), *Women, Religion and Feminism in Britain, 1750–1900* (Basingstoke: Palgrave Macmillan, 2002), p. 1.
24 Personal histories of both former and current female religious feature this cultural script. Richard Bennett, *The Truth Set Us Free: Twenty Former Nuns Tell Their Stories* (Mukilteo, WA: WinePress Publishing, 1997); Marie Therese Gass, *Unconventional Women: 73 Ex-Nuns Tell Their Stories* (Clackamas, OR: Sieben Hill, 2001); Mary Griffin, *The Courage to Choose: An American Nun's Story* (Boston: Little, Brown, 1975), pp. 66–9; Carole G. Rogers, *Habits of Change: An Oral History of American Nuns* (Oxford: Oxford University Press, 2011); Anne Patrick Ware (ed.), *Midwives of the Future: American Sisters Tell Their Story* (London: Sheed and Ward, 1985).

relationships adds to the developing scholarship of how authenticity, selfhood and identity were remade in the second half of the twentieth century. Participants, in discussing pre-/post-conciliar homosocial relationships, were overwhelming positive in commending the move to the relational. Yet they also recalled pre-conciliar life-giving relationship memories. The majority of the women interviewed for this project entered in the 1950s and 1960s, so while they experienced the shift to the relational, they were less embedded in the formalism of the past. Remembered memories have been mediated through subsequent life events, but also a canon of published theological and personal critique of religious life, and years of meetings and retreats often informed or convened by psychoanalysts and sociologists addressing the relational chaos in some communities. Few sisters and nuns emphasised convent tensions, though archive documents demonstrate they existed. A closer reading of the documents and analysis of the testimonies suggest that convent relationships were in flux from the 1940s to the 1980s. Material from the archives, in the form of reports, correspondence and inter-community newsletters, allow us to hear both institutional and personal concerns and enthusiasms about the changing nature of personal interactions, from the formal to the relational. Those in authority, sometimes unreservedly, sometimes in grudging obedience, encouraged less formal and more collegial interactions. Authenticity within the convent was much contested. It had been rooted in the fixed and unchanging rules and constitutions that had guided praxis in religious institutes for centuries. Renewal signalled a review of and reinterpretation of these and other traditional practices. Historian Marjet Derks in her research on religious life in the Netherlands suggests the silencing of oppositional narratives: in many religious institutes, the collective memory of the 1960s has been shaped into a discourse of renewal as progress, which omits or dismisses the voices of those who struggled with the changes in religious life. These oppositional voices were not silent in the archives. Considering narrative and memory, this chapter adopts a multivariate understanding of relational interactions, linking relationships and understandings of authenticity to religious identities during a time of conflict and change.

Relationships are enacted in a time, place and context.[25] Prescriptive and promotional convent literature portrayed community life as an

---

25   Steve Duck (ed.), *Social Context and Relationships* (London: Sage, 1993), p. xiv.

unchanging oasis of serenity grounded in fictive familial bonds.[26] In reality, homosocial relationships within the convent were more complicated, particularly during and after the structural changes of religious life discussed in the previous chapter. Women's experiences of religious life are analysed to understand how relationships were perceived and lived. The first section considers the common life, communal ways of inhabiting the social spaces of the convent that held religious life together. The formal structures of the common life provided a unity that was being questioned as relationships grounded in formerly rigid structures were being renegotiated. As the horarium which regulated the religious day was altered, the permission-centred model of religious life shifted to one that allowed for personal responsibility. The relational nature of these shifts resulted in tensions, and women religious self-identified and identified others as generational cohorts pitting 'old' against 'young'.[27] The second section uses this generational language to tease out the nature of the shifting relationships: it is through how sisters and nuns spoke about each other that we learn about their understandings of the authenticity of religious life. The convent, often imagined as a conservative site of religious piety, became a place of dissonance when a discourse of personal responsibility interpreted as individualism challenged feminine hierarchies and patriarchal structures.

Common life

The female world of conventual life provided an institutionalised social framework for relationships. In entering religious institutes, women engaged, individually and collectively, consciously and unconsciously, in the process of constructing themselves as women religious. Women who entered religious life in the 1940s had some awareness that being a 'nun', as discussed in Chapter 1, included 'dying to the world' and the sacrifice of familial and friendship relationships. The formation period, the postulancy and the novitiate, trained women to interact in convent spaces. Like other forms of professional training at the time, it was rigorous, structured and rooted in social-class-based ideals of deference that were

---

26 For example, *Bride of a King* (London: Daughters of Our Lady of Good Counsel, 1958). See Chapter 2.
27 I am aware of the conceptual differences between 'cohort' (a demographic term) and 'generation' (a structural term that typically implies a parent–child relationship). The women religious in this study use the term 'generation' to imply a structural, though non-kinship relationship within the convent.

an everyday part of private and public life.[28] Tutored and guided by a novice mistress, the formation process inculcated a hegemonic femininity that reflected ideals of Catholic religious womanhood and informed the tenor of relationships: emotional detachment, submissiveness and deference.[29] Commitment to these ideals required a self-discipline that was intrinsic to religious identity. Emotional detachment (withholding expressions of intimacy) was linked to the primary objective of entering religious life: the focus on the relationship with Christ. The identity of women religious was centred on this relationship, and presupposed (just as marriage did[30]) that other relationships were secondary. Such individual self-control, in theory, distanced family and friendship relationships and allowed the channelling of emotions to a higher cause, the spousal relationship with Christ. This love was spiritual rather than sexual, and indeed genital fulfilment would have led to a transgression against the vow of chastity. Emotional detachment was intended as sacrificial and suffering was a laudatory consequence. Submissiveness was not simply obedience to authority; it incorporated cooperation, a working together with women of (potentially) different cultures, social classes and ages, towards a greater good. The negation of individual desires reflected a unity in relation to the goals of the religious institute. Such cooperation also encouraged internal harmony and, on some levels, provided symmetry to personal relationships. Deference was linked to authority, but also age and experience; this reflected the rules that structured the social hierarchies within the convent. In many ways, this was a leveller: women of varying ages, experiences and social classes could have some power and authority within convent structures. Those in leadership positions such as the abbess, prioress, mother superior or novice mistress

28   Florence Sutcliffe-Braithwaite, *Class, Politics, and the Decline of Deference in England, 1968–2000* (Oxford: Oxford University Press, 2018); Richard Vinen, *National Service: A Generation in Uniform 1945–1963* (London: Allen Lane, 2014), pp. 136–61. Seabrook, *Working-Class Childhood*, pp. 202–8; Peter O'Brien, *Evacuation Stations: Memoir of a Boyhood in Wartime England* (the author, 2012), pp. 46, 264.

29   Hegemonic femininity is often discussed in relation to hegemonic masculinity, emphasising a complementarity that assumes the dominance of men and the subordination of women. In using the term hegemonic femininity I am emphasising that femininities are also structured and hierarchical separate from masculinities; this chapter points to a hegemonic femininity that is dominant within convent spaces. R. W. Connell, *Gender and Power* (Cambridge: Cambridge University Press, 1987), pp. 183–9; Mimi Schippers, 'Recovering the Feminine Other: Masculinity, Femininity and Gender Hegemony', *Theory and Society*, 36 (2007), 85–102, p. 94.

30   Claire Langhamer, 'Love and Courtship in Mid-Twentieth-Century England', *Historical Journal*, 50 (2007), 173–96.

expected absolute obedience. Those with less explicit power (and lower in the hierarchical pecking order), were due a respect linked to age and experience, such as the choir novice cutting potatoes obeying the older lay sister in the kitchen.[31] Deference was significant to maintaining these women-centred hierarchies of power and ordering relationships within convent spaces. Religious identities did not completely displace former relational identities: women religious were still daughters, sisters, cousins and friends though these relationships became secondary to their religious identity.[32]

Once women left the novitiate, the 'glue' of religious life was the common life, communal ways of inhabiting the social spaces of the convent. It reinforced a structured world made both rigid and secure, as discussed in the previous chapter, by governance documents such as the rule and constitutions. It also included traditions codified in customs books and reified and transmitted through the education in the postulancy and novitiate, as well as the lived example of present and previous generations of community members. Central to the common life were the material and spiritual practices linked to the horarium, the programme of religious life, which regulated community life; waking, praying, working, eating and sleeping were all timetabled and intended to be performed in tandem.[33] The horarium regimented time, but space was also strictly ordered. In chapel, during mealtimes and at recreation, sisters and nuns typically sat in order of their entry into religious life. This imposed a visible hierarchy of status based on length of service. The horarium was at the heart of community life, offering a known and consistent framework that provided stability as well as a unity in uniformity. It re-enforced a corporate identity linked to belonging to a particular religious institute and religious family. The horariums of enclosed contemplatives such as Poor Clares, Benedictines and Bridgettines centred on the Divine Office, a sequence of liturgical services performed in seven parts during the day and once in the night. The 1953 horarium for the Bridgettines of Syon Abbey (Table 4.1) demonstrates their ordered life, with the services of the Divine Office (prime, terce, sext, none, vespers, matins, lauds) at its heart. It scheduled times of prayer and convent labour, which included

---

31 There are some parallels with apprenticeship practices, for example those working in the trades, bricklayers, as well as within domestic service.

32 Carmen M. Mangion, 'Women Religious and Family Relationships', *Catholic Ancestor*, 16:2 (2016), 60–8.

33 Permissions for exceptions (for examples when someone was ill) were given by the abbess or local leader.

Table 4.1 Syon Abbey horarium, 1953

5.30 a.m.	Rise
6.00	Angelus – meditation
6.30	Prime
7.00	Mass
7.45	Terce
8.00	Breakfast
9.00	Sext and domestic work and offices
10.55	Inst[ruction] of novices
11.30	None
12.00	Dinner
1.00 p.m.	Recreation
1.30	Communion
2.00	Options
2.00	Vespers
3.00	Tea
3.30	Spiritual reading private
4.00	Work and offices
3.30	Recollection
4.45	Recreation
5.45	Great silence
6.00	Benediction
6.30	Silent prayer
7.00	Supper
8.00	Matins and Lauds
9.30	Retiring bell
10.00	Lights out

Source: Plymouth Diocesan Archives: CMB 3.1, Syon Abbey, Visitation of Syon Abbey, 4–5 February 1953.

producing and editing the *Poor Soul's Friend* and sharing in the domestic work of the monastery, acting in turn as cooks, cleaners and gardeners.[34] It was a full, regimented life that, as shown in Figures 4.1 and 4.2, included both *ora et labora*.

---

34   Carmen M. Mangion, 'Syon Abbey's "Second Summer", 1900–1950', in Elin Andersson, Claes Gejrot, E. A. Jones, and Mia Akestam (eds), *Continuity and Change: Papers from the Birgitta Conference at Dartington, 2015* (Stockholm: Kungl. Vitterhets historie och antikvitetsakademien, 2017), pp. 367–88. The two photographs shown in Figures 4.1 and 4.2 can also be found in Roger Ellis, *Syon Abbey: The Spirituality of the English Bridgettines* (Salzburg: Universität Salzburg, 1984).

Figure 4.1 Syon Bridgettines working in the garden, 1981, photographed by H. J. Deakin

Figure 4.2 Syon Bridgettines chanting the Divine Office, 1981, photographed by H. J. Deakin

The horariums of centralised religious institutes were often identical from one convent to another; they linked female religious across national borders. Sisters transferring or visiting another convent within their congregation would feel at home with the structure of the day. Such transnational praxis offered connection and coherence and a selfhood linked to their religious family. The British Daughters of Charity of St Vincent de Paul's adverse reaction to a suggested change in their horarium reflected its significance to their corporate identity. Daughters protested when Cardinal Herbert Vaughan, then President of the Conference of Bishops of England and Wales, suggested they move the 4 a.m. wake-up call to 5.30 a.m. to make it more convenient for clergy who said the first mass of the day. Susan O'Brien argues that belonging to the 'imagined community' of the international Daughters of Charity 'became part of every Daughter's identity'; they preferred to maintain unity (ignoring their own discomfort) with their motherhouse and other Daughters of Charity communities all over the world.'[35] With horariums, as with other matters, whether related to their religious habit, governance or ministerial work, sisters were expected to be and act in unity with their motherhouse. One sister of the Society of the Sacred Heart reflected, 'I think when I first entered [in the 1960s] you could have been in England or China or wherever and the customs would have been the same.'[36] The horarium was reified such that even changes that were in unity with the motherhouse brought concerns over the straying from tradition. In 1958, the Augustinians at Hayward's Heath followed the lead of their motherhouse in Bruges in shifting the beginning of their day from 4.45 a.m. to 5.30 a.m. (with lights-out moving from 10.00 p.m. to 10.30 p.m.). Prioress Mary Patrick noted the nuns' dismay over the change despite it being 'on the cards for some time':

> As was to be expected, it has been hard for the older people, but they have been splendid, & I hope they will soon feel less strange. We all feel very strange so far & sometimes I think 'What have I done? Why did I ever embark on this new regime?' But on the whole, I think people are pleased & that it will work out well.[37]

35 O'Brien, *Leaving God for God*, pp. 116–17, 139–40.
36 Anonymised interview.
37 DUL CHS: E, Letter from Mother Mary Patrick to Reverend Mother, dated 6 August 1958.

Pre-conciliar changes to the horarium or any entrenched practices were often small in scope, but loomed large in communities which valorised tradition and the unchanging nature of religious life.

Prayer was integral to religious life as a support to both inner spirituality and the ministerial work of a religious institute. The times of prayer were clearly demarcated in the horarium; community and silent prayer were allocated to particular times of the day and linked to the common life of a community. For enclosed, contemplative orders, the performance of the Divine Office at specific times throughout the day and night was essential to their identities as religious. Religious congregations with active ministries such as teaching and nursing were not bound to pray the Divine Office, and many prayed the less physically and temporally onerous Little Office of Our Lady.[38] As a form of liturgical prayer, the Office was not simply the spoken or sung prayer of the Psalms and other readings, but also an act of community which reflected the conscious embodiment of prayer, through the unison of thoughts, movement, breath and time.[39] Prayer throughout the day became more difficult for sisters in active ministries as state requirements for education and health care came to impinge on the horarium.[40] One sister who entered the Canonesses of the Holy Sepulchre in the 1950s described the emphasis on prayer, but also the resulting need to become more flexible:

> I think the life of prayer has always been the basis of our life from the very beginning. Susan Hawley made it absolutely plain that the Divine Office and our prayer life, our contemplative life, was paramount. And so you just automatically attended all the Office and things were arranged so the community could get to the Office. That was before the huge pressure of education, because the time came when that wasn't

---

38 This is also a liturgical office and structured as Major Hours (matins, lauds and vespers), Minor Hours (prime, terce, sext, none) and compline (evening prayer), but it is shorter and less vocally complex.

39 Anne Bagnall Yardley, *Performing Piety: Musical Culture in Medieval English Nunneries* (London: Palgrave Macmillan, 2006), p. 8. Divine office consists of eight offices (or hours) matins (or vigils) at midnight; lauds at daybreak; prime, terce, sext and none at 6 a.m., 9 a. m., noon and 3 p.m.; vespers before dark and compline at bedtime. Each of these hours has fixed liturgical structure with matins the most elaborate of the day; prime, terce, sext and none the simplest. Also known as the Liturgy of Hours and *opus dei*.

40 Sean Whittle, *Vatican II and New Thinking about Catholic Education: The Impact and Legacy of Gravissimum Educationis* (Abingdon: Taylor & Francis, 2016).

possible. And so there were some people, house mistresses very often didn't attend choir.[41]

Founder Susan Hawley had in the 1640s bound the Canonesses to the recitation of the Divine Office at a time when education was unregulated and religious controlled the content and timetable of the convent school. The horarium of the Canonesses was altered to meet the secular requirements of the teaching day as required by the Education Act of 1944 and subsequent education legislation.[42] Similar scheduling alterations took place in the Society of the Sacred Heart; in 1961, the hours of the Office were aggregated.[43]

It was not only the structure of the horarium that was changing, but also the practices that were entrenched in structured life. Daily life for contemplative nuns and active sisters included times of silence intended as periods for contemplation and being present to their heavenly spouse. Ethnographer Francesca Sbardella interprets this silence as an 'active quietness with a communicative function', where 'silence is interpreted and experienced as a means to activate a communicative sharing' with God and the community.[44] It was a component of the common life: spaces and times of silence were learned and silence was given meaning in ways that were shared and that enhanced relationships. Personal struggles to maintain silence could become a shared struggle. In contradictory ways, silence enhanced togetherness within separateness. Sbardella posits sharing silence as a means for women religious to 'express their desire to belong to that particular group'.[45] Silence was also experienced as an enforced absence from others; it could be a means of avoiding relationships and internal

---

41   Anonymised interview. Typically, exemptions to the horarium required specific permission of the mother superior or mother abbess.

42   Changes to the horarium specifically tied to the Divine Office were made in 1947 (DUL CHS: D4, Sister Mary Peter, 'Archive Records of Community History in the Twentieth Century', p. 30), 1958 and 1961 (DUL CHS: F3, Minutes of Council Meetings, 1 April 1958, 27 November 1960, 26–27 December 1961; A3a, *Simul in Unum* (1961), p. 34).

43   'Reverend Mother has had instructions from the Mother House that the Hours of the office will be changed – 7pm Matins & Compline Before Mass Lauds & Prime; Terce, Sext, None & Vespers at 2pm. Both these changes will begin this week.' SSH ENW: Fenham House Journal, 22 January 1961.

44   Francesca Sbardella, 'Inhabited Silence: Sound Constructions of Monastic Spatiality', *Etnográfica*, 17 (2013), 520.

45   *Ibid.*, p. 523.

conflict.[46] Women religious were expected to converse sparingly and to only speak when necessary.

Conversation was acceptable in some spaces and times, such as recreation, but even here, speech could be restrained by convent etiquette and conventions. Recreation was expected to be a time of structured relaxation when women religious could converse. One Syon Bridgettine who entered in the 1950s recounted:

> [Y]ou would sit beside somebody wherever the place was, and you could talk to your neighbours on either side and if the Abbess began to speak or the Prioress, whatever, everybody stopped and you listened ... people would talk about if they'd had visitors they would tell you how the little children looked and how much they'd grown and that sort of thing. You may talk about something you'd read with your neighbour if the conversation was general.[47]

The crux here was that conversation was general and limited by one's location in the room; spatial practices and a level of emotional detachment circumscribed conversations. Deference to authority was enacted in the attention paid to the conversation of the abbess and prioress. Like many other narrators, she also described the enforced productivity of recreations: '[Y]ou always had something to do, you were either knitting or whatever, you couldn't have idle hands.'[48] One former Poor Clare recalled recreation as a busy time, with nuns perched on low rush-seated stools, knitting, sewing, pasting recycled Christmas cards or contrasting coloured silks for embroidery; the soundscape included sharing news from family letters or reading aloud.[49] The photograph in Figure 4.3 shows Bristol Sisters of Mercy novices during their recreation in 1951, with sisters positioned around the table, likely with the novice mistress at the head of the table; they appear to be mending and doing needlework as they recreated. The photograph of the Shaftesbury community of the Institute of the Blessed Virgin Mary taken a decade later (Figure 4.4) suggests a less structured and more relaxed recreation. Recreations could be joyful

46 This could be particularly important within convents that contained both English- and Irish-born sisters. Sisters in McKenna's oral histories spoke of their discomfort during the Provisional IRA's bombing campaigns in England in the 1970s. See Yvonne McKenna, *Made Holy: Irish Women Religious at Home and Abroad* (Dublin: Irish Academic Press, 2006), pp. 99–107.

47 Anonymised interview.

48 Anonymised interview.

49 Sister Giles, *The End and the Beginning* (Stanhope: The Memoir Club, 2007), pp. 14, 23.

Figure 4.3 Bristol Sisters of Mercy novices at recreation, 1951

Figure 4.4 Recreation in the garden, Shaftesbury, *c.* 1960s

and energetic. Sister Francis Pullen, writing in 1968 to her community in Liberton near Edinburgh, recounted: 'Last night at recreation I told them the story about the boy God made and they thought it absolutely killing.'[50] Alan Whicker's documentary series 'Within a Woman's World' (1972) included one scene with young, lively Poor Clares at Baddesley Clinton playing football during recreation.[51] That same year, a Darlington Poor Clare recorded in the annals a memorable recreation on St Patrick's Day that included an Irish concert accompanied with 'three hand red' danced by the mother abbess, mother vicaress and Sister Mary Carmel all dressed in Irish costume and the singing of Irish songs, such as 'The Dear Little Shamrock', 'Mother Machree', etc.[52]

Experimentation

As the previous section suggests, small changes were made before the Second Vatican Council that altered the common life but the precepts undergirding it remained unchanged. The common life relied on a unity grounded in uniformity. It was based on material and spiritual practices of religious life performed in unison, and for many, these practices were invested with deep meanings embedded in tradition and unity with an international community of sisters.[53] The discourse of renewal and personal responsibility that developed out of the Second Vatican Council challenged the precepts and practice of the common life in extraordinary ways. As understandings of the common life shifted, this religious world moved from one that was permission-centred to one that allowed more personal responsibility. *Perfectae Caritatis* (Adaptation and Renewal of Religious Life, 1965), suggested a distancing from the uniformity of the common life, proposing that the

> manner of living, praying and working should be suitably adapted everywhere, but especially in mission territories, to the modern physical and psychological circumstances of the members and also, as required by the nature of each institute, to the necessities of the apostolate, the demands of culture, and social and economic circumstances.[54]

50 FPA: Letter from Francis Pullen to community, 31 August 1968.
51 BFI: Tx 2.8.1972, *A Girl Gets Temptations – But I Wanted to Give Myself to God* ('Whicker, Within a Woman's World' series) (1972).
52 OSC Much Birch: Darlington Chronicles, 1972, p. 57.
53 See for example Monique Luirard, *The Society of the Sacred Heart in the World of Its Times 1865–2000* (Saint Louis, MO: iUniverse, 2016), pp. 240–1.
54 *Perfectae Caritatis*, §3.

This instruction was approached in myriad ways by religious institutes; the extent, timing and enthusiasm for experimentation cannot be summed up in one overarching narrative. The one constant was that experimentation influenced personal relationships amongst members of religious institutes. Alterations to forms of prayer and the tradition of silence (as well as other changes) brought both emotional distress and elation and caused many nuns and sisters to question the meaning of the common life.

The *Aggiornamento* Chapter of 1967 directed the sisters of the Society of the Sacred Heart to reconsider their prayer life. Sisters were allowed to experiment and moved away from the 'very regulated' prayer life timetabled by the horarium, which included the communal Office, daily mass, prayer of the rosary, private time for examination of conscience, spiritual readings and prayer before the Blessed Sacrament.[55] One sister found her spiritual life 'floating' for a year or two as she involved herself with various modes of spirituality, including the charismatic movement and John Main spirituality.[56] Another sister, recounted the trialling of new ways of prayer explained: 'so we devolved a kind of meeting every evening to pray over the gospel or to have prayer prepared rather than saying Office'. She explained: 'Because if we were centred on the Gospel then our life should be informed by the Gospel.'[57] 'Gospel living' became a prominent leitmotif of authentic Christian living that influenced personal and communal prayer as well as the shifts in ministry that will be discussed in the Chapter 6. The praxis of prayer transitioned from religious exercises almost exclusively based on interiority (linked to the personal search for and encounter with God) to one that referenced and acknowledged world events and crises. Throughout this time of change, an emphasis on 'personal responsibility' made women religious individually responsible for reauthenticating their own prayer life.

Experimenting with different timing and forms of prayer jarred with the emphasis on the common life. One member of the Sisters of Charity Our Lady, Mother of Mercy stressed the importance of prayer whilst dismissing the value of community prayer in unison:

---

55 Anonymised interview; Luirard, *The Society of the Sacred Heart*, pp. 606–20.
56 Anonymised interview.
57 Anonymised interview.

To me, as a young sister, it does not seem important that we, as a congregation say the same prayers daily at the same time, but it does seem very important that we PRAY always and at all times. It isn't important that we spend 15 mins. in spiritual reading and 15 mins. in [a] visit to the Blessed Sacrament.[58]

She implied that though prayer was important, the minute details of the horarium – '15 mins. in spiritual reading and 15 mins. in [a] visit to the Blessed Sacrament' – were not valuable to her. Others felt devolving prayer threatened the common life. Sister Elizabeth van den Ven found common prayer essential: 'It is the summit and centre of our community living.'[59] Another sister from the same congregation questioned the prescriptive nature of prayer but insisted on the value of the common life: 'Our common life together sharing in the Eucharist, our prayer life, our joys sorrows, work etc., are links in the chain of solidarity. All our gifts whether of nature or grace are gifts from God to bring to our common life.'[60] The common life was often characterised as the glue that held religious life together: 'the breakdown of that common life will be seen as the breakdown of community life.'[61]

Silence was also enshrined in the practice of everyday life and its function in convent spaces was being questioned in active congregations. The Hammersmith community of the Society of the Sacred Heart held a local assembly in January 1969 to discuss silence. The meeting included deliberations on the 'greater silence' and 'speaking in a low voice'.[62] The times and places allocated to speaking and the volume of speech was in flux. The difficulty in getting the 'right balance between silence and speech' was addressed in a report on 'The State of the Province':

[S]everal groups stress the need for us to realise the spiritual and sociological value of silence for the individual, as well as the community need for peace and quiet, and that this silence should help our speech to be positive and creative. With the lessening of structures, our speech tends at times to unconstructive criticism, to lack of discretion, and to emotional out-pourings. No one wants to go back to the rigid structure; some think that more defined norms would help, many are trying to take as their principle Consideration for Others which would include control and quietness of word and action.[63]

58 SCMM-ENK: 1728, Sister Marie Therese Southworth, 'On Religious Renewal', *Meeting Point* (May 1971).
59 SCMM-ENK: 1728, *Meeting Point* (June 1972), p. 8.
60 SCMM-ENK: 1728, *English Province Newsletter* 6 (March 1970), p. 6.
61 SCMM-ENK: 349, *Meeting Point* 4 (October 1974), p. 22.
62 SSH ENW: 12/01/12 Hammersmith House Journal, 24 January 1969.
63 SSH ENW: 1970 Provincial Chapter II, Batch 3, 'The State of the Province' (1970), p. 2.

One sister acknowledged the difficulty of the transition:

> [W]hen the lid came off, you know, and people began to share and exchange it was very ... People, well violence is the wrong word but aggressive and yes, we were very unskilled at differing from other people and things, and some people were angry and sort of disorientated and lost ... So it took us a long time and a lot of re-education really to get people to be able to decently disagree with one another and, you know work things through.[64]

Those who valued silence found the cacophony of voices disruptive and jarring.[65] The disappearance of a structured life was linked to an emotiveness of speech that was in sharp contrast to the emotional detachment, submissiveness and deference that had previously been convent protocol. Communication skills needed to be relearned.

Not all religious institutes experimented with silence in the 1960s and 1970s. One sister explained the discomfiting consequences in the mid-1970s of transgressing convent silence not by speaking, but by introducing sound:

> I can remember, in the holidays we had to scrub the school from top to bottom ... And I switched the radio on, so I had the radio going as I was scrubbing some stone stairs. I mean it wasn't anything sort of wild and sort of ... you know, it was just music ... And another nun, finally professed nun came over ... she said, 'Oh, oh, do you need the radio on?' Right. And I thought, I wonder how long it'll be before I'm summoned, you know. I went, you know, we finished at, I think, five o'clock or whatever it was to get cleaned up, and there was a note under my door, would I call on [deleted]. Oh. I hadn't asked permission, we don't do that, it's a time for recollection, duh-duh-duh-duh-duh-duh-duh.[66]

For this young sister, then in her late twenties, switching on the radio was a commonplace means of alleviating the grimness of a tiresome task. The older sister and the leader of the congregation interpreted the young sister's behaviour as a transgression of convent rules. Religious, especially novices and young professed sisters, routinely performed manual labour not simply because the convent or monastery needed to be cleaned, but also because manual tasks were thought to encourage humility and aid

---

64 Anonymised interview.
65 Karen Armstrong in her after-convent memoir writes of how jarring everyday sounds were after being trained to create as little noise as possible in walking, closing doors and speaking. Karen Armstrong, *The Spiral Staircase* (London: HarperCollins, 2004), p. 21.
66 Anonymised interview.

spiritual recollection. The sister had transgressed in numerous ways: she was avoiding recollection in silence; she had not asked permission; and it seems likely her humility was questioned. This example reminds us that the introduction of experimentation and personal responsibility was not embraced in the same way or at the same time in all religious institutes; many religious institutes remained permission-centred environments.

Communication

The restructuring of communities and social spaces along with the reframing of the common life disrupted community life and required new ways of communicating. In this new environment, communication skills had to be relearned. Two issues were at the forefront of problems of communication. The first was communication of experimental ways of living; the second was intercommunication between members of a community.

The Society of the Sacred Heart, like many other international congregations, addressed the issue of communication through additional reporting. The newly created Sacred Heart Office of Communication (SHOC) published a weekly journal – *SHOC Tactics* – to keep in touch with 'scattered brethren' and functioned as an 'exchange and mart' for liturgical and ecumenical news, book recommendations, spiritual and educational work, births and deaths, etc. The term 'tactics' was intended to relay that the newsletter was a means of 'personal contact and, also, that things are alive and moving'.[67] Members of the Society of the Sacred Heart's province of England and Malta were aware that 'Communications need careful study to become efficient and satisfying'.[68] This magazine responded to complaints about the lack of communication or miscommunication of important changes coming from the motherhouse or provincial leaders with its reporting of these matters.

Community relationships also became a theme for retreats and workshops that women religious attended. The Fenham community of the sisters of the Sacred Heart, which had split into three communities (named Fenham United, Galilee and Lindisfarne), attended 'community-building' exercises in August 1971.[69] Other congregations such as the Sisters of Charity of Our Lady, Mother of Mercy attended seminars and courses at the Catholic retreat centre at Spode House, which offered

---

67   SHCJ: *SHOC Tactics*, 1 (18 December 1969).
68   SSH ENW: 1969 Vision Self-Surveys, 'Vision of the Society England–Malta', dated December 1969.
69   The Galilee community, which was the largest, was later divided into five communities.

week-long courses on subjects such as 'Community relationships'. Seminar topics included prayer and spiritual life, co-responsibility and authority of a superior, living in mixed religious communities and sociological perspectives of community and emotional independence.[70] Sisters who returned from these courses distilled what they learned and instigated further discussions within individual communities, sometimes writing up their experiences in community magazines like *SHOC Tactics*.

Many groups introduced sociologists and psychologists to help sisters understand and help process the experience of renewal. One sister argued that sisters lacked the 'training in relationships and the group process' and were 'unable to communicate their thoughts in an acceptable manner'.[71] Another group found that 'Nearly all agreed that help was needed in order that we could relate to each other on a deeper level and come to understand each other that little bit more.' The Fenham House Journal, after one meeting on the difficulties with challenges of experimenting with greater freedom noted that:

> We, as a Society, have had no training for this changed life that the Church asks of us, so that we must co-operate experiment, risk & learn from our mistakes.[72]

The changes being contemplated were without precedent and sisters and nuns had no experience to help guide implementation.

Redefining common life and community

Changing praxis of prayer and silence and the emphasis on new communication methods highlights the shifting understandings of the common life and recognises varying understandings of the authenticity of religious life. Some sisters and nuns were invested in the common life as unity in uniformity; others insisted on the value of personal responsibility and the significance of the self for an authentic religious life. Balancing these two views was difficult: many feared a 'do-it yourself' approach to religious life that ran counter to the common life.[73] Concerns about 'sisters becoming isolationists' and of 'the danger of losing sight

---

70   SCMM-ENK: 1728, 'Discussion Topic: Community', *Newsletter* 8 (February 1971).
71   SCMM-ENK: 98, 'Report on Visit to England – April 1 to 24, 1971 – Sr. Michael Marie Keyes'.
72   SSH ENW: Fenham House Journal, 25 April 1969.
73   SCMM-ENK: 1730, *English Province Newsletter* 23 (October 1976).

of one's commitment to the community' were voiced.[74] Others sought to redefine the common life giving it a Christological emphasis. One sister writing on the common life in the 1970s explained it as 'total dependence and service to one another. This bond is solidarity. Nobody is allowed to live for himself … Christ transformed the shaping force of history by his solidarity.'[75] Her understanding of the common life was as solidarity rather than uniformity. Some saw these changes as a new form of relationships: '[W]e are beginning to understand what community living is all about.' She argued that community was not about physical togetherness but it required a connectedness 'which can only be achieved if the members of a community are prepared to sit down and spend time with each other in a mutual exchange of ideas'. Another explained: 'Community will be manifested and maintained by intensively meaningful moments rather than by a state of cohabitation.' She asserted she was not questioning the nature of religious life: 'On the contrary it ensures its vigour by delivering it from the weight and formalism of earlier days.'[76]

A uniform common life was constructed as the central means of achieving Danièle Hervieu-Léger's 'chain of memory':

> [The] normativity of collective memory is reinforced by the fact of the group's defining itself, objectively and subjectively, as a lineage of belief. And so its formation and reproductiveness spring entirely from the efforts of memory feeding this self-definition. … there is belief in the continuity of the lineage of believers … It is affirmed and manifested in the essentially religious act of recalling a past which gives meaning to the present and contains the future.[77]

Religious institutes identified themselves through a lineage of belief that recognised the common life as formalised in the horarium and uniform social practices. The transmission of beliefs, traditions and identities was linked rigidly to the horarium and the enculturation it represented. The meaning given to uniformity was integral to a religious identity and selfhood that was linked not only to a way of being a religious but also a community's corporate identity. Pre-conciliar changes to the structure

---

74 SCMM-ENK: 332, 'Provincial Team Report, December 1971 to March 1976', dated 8 March 1976.
75 SCMM-ENK: 1730, *English Province Newsletter* 6 (March 1970).
76 SCMM-ENK: 1730, Sister Agnes McAdam, 'On Small Communities', *English Province Newsletter* (Easter 1975).
77 Danièle Hervieu-Léger, *Religion as a Chain of Memory* (Cambridge: Cambridge University Press, 2000), p. 125.

of the common life were imposed from above with little (if any) local input or discussion. The post-conciliar experimentation initiated a collaborative approach linked to personal and shared responsibility and that required community discussions and negotiation. Those embracing experimentation interpreted it as a means of authenticating their prayer life and making it more meaningful. They defined the common life more expansively through 'meaningful moments' rather than unity and unison and offered an alternative means of achieving a 'chain of memory'. Nuns and sisters were 'unskilled' at this type of interaction and one result, as we'll see in the next section, was a generational discourse that was grounded in what philosopher Charles Taylor has identified as an 'ethic of authenticity' with differing opinions on what was 'authentic' religious life.[78]

Generational discourse

Religious life has always relied on social categories to demarcate difference (between religious life and 'the world'; between professed and non-professed religious; between choir and lay sisters) so perhaps it is not unexpected that in the 1960s degrees of agedness appear as a social category resulting in a pronounced discourse emphasising a 'generation gap'. Generations, in sociological thinking, are cohorts born in different time periods that share experiences that unite them and give them similar perspectives on life.[79] Sociologist Robert Wuthnow defines them as a 'social unit bound together by a common structural location, a common cultural system, self-consciousness as a social unit, and social interaction and solidarity among its members'.[80] Sociologist Karl Mannheim's 'identity location' coheres generations as those 'submitted to the same determining influence', thus identifying with a particular historical event and context.[81] In large congregations and orders, novitiate groups often self-identified as a cohort, bonding as a result of their common novitiate experience.[82] It is not surprising, therefore, that the language of 'generations', with an

78 Taylor, *A Secular Age*, p. 475.
79 Karl Mannheim, 'The Problem of Generations', in *Karl Mannheim: Essays*, ed. Paul Kecskemeti (New York: Routledge, 1972), pp. 276–322; Jane Pilcher, *Age and Generation in Modern Britain* (Oxford: Oxford University Press, 1995).
80 Robert Wuthnow, 'Recent Pattern of Secularization: A Problem of Generations?', *American Sociological Review*, 41 (1976) 851.
81 Mannheim, 'The Problem of Generations'.
82 In large congregations, novices were often of similar ages.

emphasis on attributes of 'older sisters' and 'young sisters', was notable in both archival material and oral testimonies. Discursively, narratives often closely followed sociologist Karl Mannheim's 'positivist' and 'romantic-historical' models, demonstrating the tension between those that embraced the progress seemingly inherent in post-conciliar Catholicism and those who wept for the demise of traditional ways of living religious life.[83]

The generational trope is well rooted in popular culture and often deployed to convey intergenerational conflict. The media version of the 'radical sixties' displays the 1960s movements as driven by the young. Design historian Hilary Fawcett's argument that 'youthful femininity' became 'consistently represented across popular culture' identifies the centrality of fashion as a visual reference of the 1960s.[84] 'Baby boomers', those born between 1946 and 1964, are seen as shapers of the 1960s social movements and their social, cultural, economic and political afterlives. Sociologist S. N. Eisenstadt, writing in 1971, sees the expansion of youth culture in terms of personal autonomy, social life, higher education, work and leisure activity and, significant to this chapter, interpersonal relations.[85] Looking specifically at religious belief, Hugh McLeod sees affluent youth as key to encounters across sectarian divides and as among the most religiously active groups in the population.[86] Callum Brown associates the 1960s generation (and particularly the decline of 'pious women') with the 'death of Christian Britain'.[87] But others like Arthur Marwick have suggested that historical actors participating in social change had a more intergenerational complexion.[88] Anna von der Goltz's critique of generational belonging and its subjective use argues for multiple 'generation-units' within the 1968 generation.[89] One recent study of intergenerational transmission

83   Mannheim, 'The Problem of Generations'.
84   Hilary Fawcett, 'Fashioning the Second Wave: Issues across Generations', *Studies in the Literary Imagination*, 39:2 (2006), 96.
85   S. N. Eisenstadt, *From Generation to Generation: Age Groups and Social Structure* (London: Collier Macmillan, 1971; originally published in 1956), p. xxviii
86   Hugh McLeod, *The Religious Crisis of the 1960s* (Oxford: Oxford University Press, 2007), pp. 106, 115.
87   Callum G. Brown, *The Death of Christian Britain: Understanding Secularisation, 1800–2000* (London: Routledge, 2001), pp. 190–2.
88   Arthur Marwick, 'The Cultural Revolution of the Long Sixties: Voices of Reaction, Protest, and Permeation', *International History Review*, 27 (2005), 799.
89   Anna von der Goltz, 'Generations of 68ers', *Cultural and Social History*, 8 (2011), 473–91.

and generational transformation encouraged the recognition of multiple voices and diverse experiences.[90]

Many scholars insist that such reductive linking of generational discourse with social change is unhelpful and obfuscates more than it reveals.[91] This section examines the 'generation gap', suggesting that the discourse was conditioned by both a secular public discourse and the ways in which the renewal process was structured to emphasise agedness. The situation in the convent or monastery was more complicated than a simple binary of 'older' and 'younger' suggests, by individual attitudes, by specificities of the changes in religious life and by the 'middle group', in their forties in the 1960s, who in some communities were champions of modernisation.

'Generation gap'

The language of a 'generation gap' was emphasised again and again in interviews and convent documents characterising 'older' sisters and nuns as unwilling to accept renewal. This discourse was a world away from a past deference centred on agedness, wisdom and veneration; 'older' in some congregations and orders came to reflect outmoded and out-of-touch thinking. Much of the narrative that addressed the 'older sister' was written by those insistent on renewal. In the 1960s and 1970s, leaders writing about the older sisters of the Sisters of Charity Our Lady, Mother of Mercy constantly stressed: 'There is a fear among some sisters that the object of the exercise is to try and change them. When they have reached their twilight years they do not want to change.' The reasons for opposing change attributed to the older sisters were varied. 'Older sisters' were said to be 'very afraid of becoming inactive and of houses closing'.[92] They felt isolated and separated from active sisters.[93] For some, the 'changes have

---

90   Jane Garnett, Matthew Grimley, Alana Harris, William Whyte and Sarah Williams (eds), *Redefining Christian Britain: Post-1945 Perspectives* (London: SCM Press, 2006), p. 124.

91   *Ibid.*, pp. 115–26. For more on the obfuscation in lumping women into generational cohorts see Astrid Henry, *Not My Mother's Sister: Generational Conflict and Third-Wave Feminism* (Bloomington: Indiana University Press, 2004), p. 6.

92   SCMM-ENK: 339, 'Report of the Province Days held on October 31st & November 1st 1978'. For a modern analysis of ministry and ageing see Catherine Sexton, 'Theologies of Ministry among Older Roman Catholic Sisters in the UK', unpublished PhD dissertation, Anglia Ruskin University, 2018.

93   SCMM-ENK: 98, 'Visit to England – Sr. Thérèse Mary [Barnett] Sr. Michael Marie [Keyes] – August 1971'.

been too sudden' and the 'older sisters do not want to be disturbed'.[94] One 'very old sister' made clear she thought 'change is a modern evil'.[95] Sisters found it 'difficult to understand why there needs [to] be renewal, they have a fear of what the bishop and clergy might think or react'.[96] Many older sisters were said to be comfortable with allowing convent superiors to make all decisions.[97]

In some communities, older sisters did form pressure groups that rejected renewal. One enclosed nun spoke of the difficulties she and another nun encountered after attending a meeting about renewal for enclosed communities. She recounted how the abbess had prepared the community for their arrival and their report back of the meeting:

> So when we got back the Abbess had organised everybody, she'd cooked them a nice supper and they'd said compline early so that when we came back we could eat together and we could tell them the news, and every single Sister had gone to bed, not stayed up. Well, that didn't surprise me because if you went away you were kind of punished, there was a kind of a common disapproval, because people had been so deprived that they did that then to the next generation. 'It was done to me so I'll do it to you.'[98]

One visitor corroborated the deep conflict within the monastery, noting that the abbess and the two youngest sisters were open to renewal but that the majority of 'older nuns' wanted nothing to do with the outcomes of the Second Vatican Council, reflecting that 'Some of them were incapable of dialogue without becoming irate and showing personal dislike of others'.[99] This community remained deeply divided on renewal and closed in 1981.[100]

---

94 SCMM-ENK: 332a, 'Report of the Meeting held with Mr. V. I. Pitstick and the Provincial Council, Advisory Body and Superiors'.

95 SCMM-ENK: 373, 'Annual Report of the House', January 1970, Convent of St Francis Xavier, Preston.

96 SCMM-ENK: 333a, 'Annual Report of the Bryn Mair Community', 1969, written by Marie Wallbank, Superior.

97 SCMM-ENK: 98, 'Visit to England – Sr. Thérèse Mary [Barnett] Sr. Michael Marie [Keyes] – August 1971'.

98 Anonymised interview.

99 PDA: CMP2, 'Observations written after living with Poor Clare community at Sclerder 12 Feb–11 Mar 1975'.

100 'Taking Stock, Catholic Churches of England and Wales'. http://taking-stock.org. uk/Home/Dioceses/Diocese-of-Plymouth/Sclerder-Our-Lady-of-Light, accessed 8 December 2018.

Young sisters were not all in favour of renewal. In some communities, reports mentioned alliances between some of the 'young sisters' and the older ones who 'like themselves, don't accept some of the changes brought about by the renewal chapter of '69. It was obvious here that the older sisters <u>do have</u> an influence on the thinking of the young.'[101] Such statements muddy the binary which suggested that only 'older sisters' were unhappy with renewal.

Pro-renewal sisters often self-identified as 'younger' sisters and also formed, in some communities, pressure groups. Perhaps not unexpectedly, most of the oral testimony suggests that 'younger' sisters were willing to experiment, whilst the 'older' community followed a 'more conventual life'.[102] When talking about the changes in religious life, one sister born in the 1940s noted that 'most of us were delighted and they were overdue and um I think it was a difficult time because there were some particularly older people who were unprepared and unhappy with the changes and we as a younger group were very much pushing for them'.[103]

Another, born in the 1920s noted:

I think the older religious mostly found the changes difficult but for us younger religious I think there was a sense of greater freedom.[104]

The 'self' encountered here was one that welcomed experimentation and a 'greater freedom'. The age range for identifying 'younger' sisters frequently included sisters in their twenties into their forties. Two sisters in their mid-forties attended a meeting of older sisters and reported that:

As Senior Religious, work diminishes but witness must grow more profound, – in prayer, charity, resignation, understanding. ... They identify themselves as 'Mary' rather then [sic] 'Martha' ... There is a real need when doing the Province planning to present to them some plan which will help them feel secure.[105]

'Younger sister' Marie Therese Southworth writing 'On Religious Renewal' in her province's monthly magazine *Meeting Point* noted that the term 'renewal has different meaning for younger sisters and older sisters'. She

101 SCMM-ENK: 98, 'Visit to England – Sr. Thérèse Mary [Barnett] Sr. Michael Marie [Keyes] – August 1971'.
102 Anonymised interview.
103 Anonymised interview.
104 SSH ENW: 'RSCJ and 1967', Luirard survey, Remembrance 16.
105 SCMM-ENK: 1731, 'Our Identity as Senior Religious', *The Beam English Magazine* (Christmas 1978), p. 10.

addressed the 'generation gap' optimistically: 'It is only by understanding each other's point of view that the "age-gap" can be bridged and a better understanding exist between all members of the Congregation.'[106] There were attempts to understand and explain the behaviour of the older sisters. Sociologists and psychologists were brought in to the convent to explore and explain changing convent relationships. Younger sisters were encouraged not to push the older sisters aside. A report from one sociologist advised:

> It is necessary to meet them as a group to get data from them. Involve each member of the group, find out what she does and why she does it. The individual sisters are aware of their tasks and we must become aware of what they do. Older sisters have the greatest visibility as senior sisters. They have been singled out for something they do not wish to be singled out for: it is more negative than positive.[107]

The generational trope was encouraged by the sociological tools of the renewal process. Questionnaires and surveys commissioned by religious institutes included analysis of responses based on age groupings; these often highlighted cohort differences and emphasised the older sisters' and nuns' discomfort with many of the changes in religious life. This emphasis on age also influenced the way meetings were structured. Small-group meetings which discussed experiments in religious life often segregated participants into age groupings. In 1969, the Society of the Sacred Heart's 'Young professed' (professed for three to ten years) formed meeting groups to discuss education, formation and community life.[108] Six months later, they met for a retreat and weeklong discussion of renewal.[109] Such segregation featured in other congregations also. From the 1960s, the sisters of the British province of the Sisters of Charity of Our Lady, Mother of Mercy had 'contact days' in Pantasaph by age groups; separate meetings continued on into the 1980s.[110] Sometimes agendas were set to appeal to particular to age groups. One such meeting was organised for

---

106 SCMM-ENK: 1728, Marie Therese Southworth, 'On Religious Renewal'. *Meeting Point* (May 1971), p. 9.
107 SCMM-ENK: 332a, 'Report of the Meeting held with Mr. V. I. Pitstick and the Provincial Council, Advisory Body and Superiors'.
108 SSH ENW: 1969 Provincial Assembly, Batch 1, 'Junior Professed at its Assembly', 1–6 January 1969.
109 SSH ENW: DII/1bi, *Écho*, 15 July to 31 July 1969, p. 1.
110 SCMM-ENK: 340, Circular dated 24 May 1969 from Anne-Marie Newsham; SCMM-ENK, 340, Circular to 'Dear Sisters' from Sister Marie, dated 6 July 1982. The meetings were arranged for the following age groups: 25–45; 46–60; 61–75; 76–90.

the forty-five- to seventy-year-old group to discuss 'future living', with an emphasis on retirement.[111] The boundaries of age groupings were contested, suggesting a perceived self incongruent with the groupings:

> It seems that some sisters 60+ feel they do not belong to the older age group and have more in common with the 45–60 group. It was explained that the younger group asked for a meeting together and since the first one was such a success the group has stayed together. To allow more sisters into this group would make it too large and unmanageable.[112]

This report justified the need for group meetings by age by suggesting common interests. Segregated reporting and meetings isolated the older sisters from the younger, and perhaps created more barriers than bridges to communication and relationship-building.

'Middle group'

The question of who was considered 'older' and 'younger' was, as can see above, problematic. Reports and interview narratives rarely assigned ages to these descriptors. One report published in 1970 attempted to explain divisions between sisters, linking them to various cohorts: the 'young', who entered in the 1960s and were likely in their twenties; the post-war generation, who would presumably be in their thirties and forties; and those who entered during the war years, who were likely in their fifties and older.

> We are none of us, unaware of the sociological ipheaval [*sic*] that has overtaken us in waves since the last war. Those who joined our ranks in the war years, in the post war yeara [*sic*] and in the 60's have all entered from different social baselines. Is it any wonder that we, ALL OF US, have to revise our THINKING. This will probably be easier to the over 40's for they have experienced being young, whereas the under 40's have not had the chance of knowing what it is like to be old! To the young the world is NOT CHANGING. It is just 'the world we know' whereas to the older members of the community the world they knew and loved is crumbling round them and they often cannot help feeling that some are deliberately hastening on the destruction of much that they hold very dear.[113]

---

111   SCMM-ENK: 339, 'Report of the Meeting held on November 2nd'.
112   SCMM-ENK: 340, 'Report of the Advisory Body Group', dated 22 December 1978 from the Provincial Board Recent meeting of the Advisory Body Group.
113   SSH ENW: 1970 Provincial Chapter II, Batch 3, Sister Honor Basset, 'Summary of the Assessments of Experiments Made in This Province' (March 1970), p. 2.

Age cohorts were identified as having different ways of understanding the changes in religious life. The young were depicted as being presentist and more adaptable to the modern age; the old, negative and resistant to change. The over-forties, a 'middle group', were thought to have the easiest time in revising their thinking because they had experienced both the old ways of living religious life and were willing to experiment with new ways. There is no clear sense of who were the 'older members of the community', though they were likely over forty. As discussed earlier, the social and cultural experiences of those who entered religious life before the Second World War, just after the Second World War and in the 1960s varied; these were women bringing diverse life experiences into the convent.

The 'middle group' deserves some attention. Gender scholars have posited that the post-war generation of young women (in their twenties in the 1940s) developed a sense of 'independent selfhood' and prioritised 'individual choices, fulfilment of potential, self-development in place of sacrifice, self-denial'.[114] They were often more educated than other members of their family, and historian Lynn Abrams suggests their mothers represented 'constraining values and attitudes which had little relevance in new times'. Abrams has called this generation of mothers the 'transitional' or 'breakthrough generation',[115] indicating that they envied their daughters' abilities to avoid the narrow confines of 'good womanhood', with its associated moral codes of respectability.[116] By the late 1960s, Abrams proposes that these women, in their forties, found little reason to be involved with the women's movement, though they benefited from feminism.[117] Some members of this transitional generation later suggested ageist attitudes within the women's movement. Meg Stacey ends her vignette about her experience in the Women's Liberation Movement with 'ageism must go!'. As a professional woman in academia in her fifties in the 1970s, she felt slighted by the women's movement

---

114 Lynn Abrams, 'Mothers and Daughters: Negotiating the Discourse on the "Good Woman" in 1950s and 1960s Britain', in Nancy Christie and Michael Gavreau (eds), *The Sixties and Beyond: Dechristianisation in North America and Western Europe, 1945–2000* (Toronto: University of Toronto Press, 2013), pp. 69–70.

115 Betty Jerman, *The Lively-Minded Women: The First Twenty Years of the National Housewives Register* (London: Heinemann, 1981); Mary Ingham, *Now We Are Thirty: Women of the Breakthrough Generation* (London: Eyre Methuen, 1981); Lynn Abrams, 'Liberating the Female Self: Epiphanies, Conflict and Coherence in the Life Stories of Post-War British Women', *Social History*, 39 (2014), 14–35.

116 Henry, *Not My Mother's Sister*, p. 5.

117 Abrams, 'Mothers and Daughters'.

and excluded from consciousness-raising groups due to her age and her position in academia. She felt labelled as part of the 'traitor generation' who had after the Second World War married and raised a family.[118]

The convent 'middle group' entered after the war years. By the 1960s, they would have been in their forties. Many had been conscripted during the war and had experiences of work. One former female conscript, explaining the post-war cohort, her own generation of entrants, noted:

> Deprivations and low expectations they saw as normal, but many entered with a wider experience of life than had previous generations. Many had already learned to take responsibility and to act on their own initiative. In an educational Congregation many of them were sent to University after their novitiate, and there they were encouraged to accept no statement without question; they tried to keep this separate from their religious training which had expected that they accept without question all that was handed out, even the apparently illogical.[119]

The suggestion here is that women of her generation, the 'middle group' who had spent the war years employed in responsible jobs, were conflicted by two very different messages. This was a selfhood expected to respond differently to two worlds. Her university education encouraged critical thinking; yet within convent communities, she was expected to accept traditional practices, no matter how outlandish they appeared, without comment. In another congregation the 'middle group' was thought supportive of a more radical renewal: 'They are open and see many of the difficulties. They would like to see the leadership really attack some of the problems and act towards a solution.'[120]

Some of the 'middle group' were critical of what they construed as 'indecision' and the lack of leadership of the Provincial Council. They wanted 'people who are not afraid to make a thrust in the direction of renewal'. One member of the Council, also in the 'middle group', expressed her hurt: 'She could not understand why that group did not give the Council the benefit of the doubt.' This same report discussed factions within the British province, questioning the influence of professed sisters who spoke to younger sisters criticising their novice mistress, who was hesitant about renewal. The report writer acknowledged: 'She is not sure

---

118 Meg Stacey, 'Older Women and Feminism: A Note about My Experience of the WLM', *Feminist Review*, 31 (1989), 140–2. This is by necessity anecdotal but suggests a very fruitful area of research.

119 SSH ENW: 'RSCJ and 1967', Luirard survey, Remembrance 14.

120 SCMM-ENK: 98, 'Visit to England – Sr. Thérèse Mary [Barnett] Sr Michael Marie [Keyes] – August 1971'.

herself of some renewal aspects as to their soundness etc.' This 'middle group', according to one observer, 'frightens the more conservative element and puts the Council on the defensive'.[121] The 'middle group' was deemed vocal, sure of themselves and critical. Yet there was also a sense that it was also overburdened, its members often in positions of responsibility and perhaps unable to take advantage of the additional training or further education offered to younger sisters. In another congregation, the middle-aged religious who

> found the demands of religious life very difficult and have heroically accepted them, now sometimes feel a certain bitterness: is it all worth it? Those who seem to have set themselves up as guardians of the past with a kind of missionary zeal, clinging to old structures and opposing change.[122]

Interview narratives and documents demonstrate the reliance on a generational language and a consciousness that religious life and the self was influenced by the social and cultural experiences of each cohort. Members of the older cohort spoke of their experience of 'restrictions' and a structured life along with deference to elders that pre-dated their entry into religious life. The younger cohort identified themselves, and were identified as, 'independent women' who expected to participate in decision-making.[123] Interviews were devoid of the emotion and angst of much of the material from primary sources written at the time. They reflect an understanding of generational difference informed by the growing literature of religious life as well as workshops and seminars held for women religious that addressed renewal.[124] This, alongside the introspective nature of religious life and the encouragement to address the authenticity and disruption of religious life (with the help, in some communities, of sociological and/or psychoanalytical specialists) within the community, has led to a cohort awareness that encouraged today an understanding that went beyond generational stereotypes.

121 SCMM-ENK: 98, 'Report on Visit to England – April 1 to 24, 1971 – Sr. Michael Marie'.
122 SSH ENW: Chap/03, 'Society of the Sacred Heart of Jesus. Study of the Provinces', May 1970, England–Malta, p. 6.
123 Carmen M. Mangion, 'Community Voices and "Community Scripts"', *Studies*, 107:427 (2018), 302–13.
124 Many of the theologically, spiritually or sociologically infused works focused on the disruption of religious life and new opportunities for religious life. For example, James Sweeney, *The New Religious Order: A Study of the Passionists in Britain and Ireland, 1945–1990 and the Option for the Poor* (London: Bellew, 1994); Gerald A. Arbuckle, *Strategies for Growth in Religious Life* (Middlegreen, Slough: St Paul Publications, 1986). For more on how feminist theologians influenced female religious life see Chapter 7.

These stances representing the politics of renewal were often linked to age groupings. Convent relationships studied through the generational discourse highlight the emphasis of the generational tropes, including the 'generation gap', but also suggest its contradictions and the trope's self-referential qualities. What is certain, was that generational language united as well as divided, both encouraging and hindering relationships, in ways that divided communities but also brought some sisters together.

Conclusion

The common life, often symbolised by the horarium, formalised the daily life in the convent and the ways nuns and sisters inhabited the social spaces of convents and monasteries. It both helped and hindered the development of homosocial relationships. Formal structures provided a means to which women religious of different social classes, ages and interests could live together. These had been effective ways of defining community and the self, demonstrating belonging. When the ritual and practices which structured religious life and relationships were dismantled and/ or disrupted, the initial responses results were nebulous and uncertain. Experimentation of a less formalised common life led to difficulties in relationships. Generational discourse muddied the process. Problems of interpersonal relationships were not always identified as age-related; one 1970 survey reported that the 'so-called generation gap' was being over-emphasised and 'individuals [were] basically fearful or feeling themselves unaccepted', suggesting that internal divisions about experimentation were more individual.[125] The journey from 'role' to 'relationship' that suggests relationship as a positivist definition was very difficult to live up to. One sister acknowledged the lengthiness of this process:

> We are now slowly recovering from our own form of 'ageism' and becoming more and more aware that we are part of a 21st century that has lost its bearings.[126]

Some women found it difficult to relate to each other in this non-formal way. For others, this shift to the relational was welcomed and more congruent with their previous life in the world and their sense of self, though, even for them, the process was fractious.

The next chapter moves us from women religious engaging with each other, to engaging with the modern world.

---

125 SSH ENW: 10 Eng, 'KASKI Self-Survey', England–Malta Province 1970, p. 15.
126 SSH ENW: 'RSCJ and 1967', Luirard survey, Remembrance 5.

5

The world in the cloister and the
nun in the world

Introduction

In 1972 Alan Whicker, a British journalist and presenter of the widely watched *Whicker's World*, together with his television crew, entered the silent and hidden world of the cloister.[1] As part of a series entitled 'Whicker, Within a Woman's World' he had secured permission to film for a twenty-six-minute programme about the Poor Clares, an enclosed Catholic community of nuns, whom he introduced as 'the most unliberated women in the world'. Pruriently entitled *A Girl Gets Temptations*, the programme opened evocatively with barefoot young nuns skimming lightly along a shiny wooden floor. Covered from head to toe in their brown Franciscan robes, with only their faces, hands and bare feet showing, the nuns were filmed going about their daily activities: cooking, cleaning and, of course, praying the Divine Office. During a particularly lively recreation young nuns laughed and played football, with older nuns clearly enjoying the spectacle. The abbess, Paula Smallwood, spoke to Whicker about the challenges, the sacrifices and the purpose of their life 'to give everything for God, to God, for the world'.[2] What was broadcast to small screens in family homes across Britain was a world seemingly untouched by modernity. Whicker, his crew

---

1   A cloister (from Latin *clausura* meaning enclosure) is a covered walkway. In this chapter, it is used to refer to the seclusion of monastic and convent spaces. Nuns taking solemn vows were bound by papal cloister, a strict form of seclusion with an obligation to remain within enclosure. Sisters taking simple vows were bound by a common cloister (episcopal or pontifical), thus set and enforced by either the bishop or the rule and constitutions of a religious institute.
2   BFI: Tx 2.8.1972, *A Girl Gets Temptations – But I Wanted to Give Myself to God* ('Whicker, Within a Woman's World' series) (1972). The book cover photo is a still from this programme.

and then the television audience crossed the threshold into a hidden monastic world while the nuns, or at least their virtual presence, entered the modern world beyond their cloister. A crossing of the spatial and conceptual boundaries of the cloister is the subject of this chapter, along with an exploration of the manner in which sisters and nuns increasingly engaged in an embodied turn towards modern and secular society.

In Catholic thought, particularly before the Second Vatican Council, the world was perceived to be tainted by opportunities for sinfulness. Religious life was seen to embody the sacred ideal of a 'higher calling' that sanctified suffering, valorised sacrifice and rejected modernity. The ideal of many in the Catholic hierarchy was of a 'fortress church' that preserved a Catholic subculture and encouraged all Catholics to remain within Catholic institutions and structures for the preservation of their souls.[3] Such separateness often demonised the 'modern world' and encouraged the 'otherworldliness' emphasised by the Archbishop of Liverpool, George Andrew Beck, in a 1950 collection of essays published to celebrate the centenary of the restoration of the Catholic hierarchy.[4] Others revelled in the idea that Catholicism was a 'cultural force: a powerful critique of the modern world and all its errant ways'.[5] This credo appeared to be effective, given the demographic growth and cohesiveness of the English Catholic community during the 1950s and 1960s: it was not diminishing in the way that other religious denominations were at this time.[6] This same insular worldview was evident in the report sent by the bishops of England and Wales for the preparatory stage of the Second Vatican Council, which, according to Kesper Aspden, was concerned with internal Church matters and ignored the 'role of the Church in the surrounding world'.[7]

At the same time studies of Catholic lived histories suggest that there were more interactions between Catholics and the modern world than

3   Kester Aspden, *Fortress Church: The English Roman Catholic Bishops and Politics 1903–1963* (London: Gracewing, 2002), p. 264. See also Peter Coman, *Catholics and the Welfare State* (London: Longman, 1977).

4   George Andrew Beck, 'To-day and Tomorrow', in George Andrew Beck, ed., *The English Catholics, 1850–1950* (London: Burns, Oates, 1950), p. 604. Hornsby-Smith has argued that the 'fortress church' was more aspiration than lived experience. See Michael P. Hornsby-Smith, *Roman Catholics in England: Studies in Social Structure since the Second World War* (Cambridge: Cambridge University Press, 1987), p. 91.

5   Dennis Sewell, *Catholics: Britain's Largest Minority* (London: Penguin Books, 2001), p. 48.

6   Adrian Hastings, *A History of English Christianity 1920–1990*, 3rd edn (London: SCM Press, 1991), pp. 475–6.

7   Aspden, *Fortress Church*, p. 290.

this high clerical discourse suggests. Alana Harris contends that Catholic identity formation and decision-making in the pre-war period was less reliant on religious authority than the 'fortress church' argument assumes.[8] David Geiringer has argued that both religious and worldly factors were influencing Catholic sexual attitudes in the 1950s and 1960s.[9] Corrin writes of 'new breed' of Catholic intellectual working outside the fortress church mentalities and informing the curriculum in English seminaries that prepared the clergy in the 1960s.[10] Similarly, for women religious the two worlds of the sacred and the secular were not hermetically sealed one from the other, despite the centuries-long discourse propagated by promoters of Catholic religious life for women, which lauded the nun's separation from the world as a good in itself. Scholars of women religious, whether writing on medieval nuns or modern sisters, have identified how the theoretical boundaries were permeated or transgressed in different times and places.[11] Over the six chapters to this point we have already seen how these boundaries were assailed by Catholic women religious 'becoming modern' from the middle of the twentieth century, beginning with applications from modern girls to enter the convent or monastery and advanced through the introduction of more participatory governance and less formal relationships.

The full or partial cloister that had separated women religious from family, friends and the people they served underwent change in a movement from separateness to engagement. Embodied and physical spatial boundaries that had served to define female religious life were rethought and redefined in the decades after 1950. Though the divide

8   Alana Harris, *Faith in the Family: A Lived Religious History of English Catholicism, 1945–1982* (Manchester: Manchester University Press, 2013), pp. 48–9.
9   David Geiringer, 'Catholic Understandings of Female Sexuality in 1960s Britain', *Twentieth Century British History*, 28 (2017), 209–38.
10 Jay P. Corrin, *Catholic Progressives in England after Vatican II* (Notre Dame, IN: University of Notre Dame Press, 2013), pp. 46, 60.
11 Caroline Bowden, 'The English Convents in Exile and Questions of National Identity, *c.* 1600–1688', in David Worthington (ed.), *British and Irish Emigrants and Exiles in Europe, 1603–1688* (Leiden: Brill, 2010), pp. 297–314; Barbara Diefendorf, 'Rethinking the Catholic Reformation: The Role of Women', in Daniella Kostroun and Lisa Vollendorf (eds), *Women, Religion, and the Atlantic World, 1600–1800* (Toronto: University of Toronto Press, 2009), p. 31; Marilyn Dunn, 'Spaces Shaped for Spiritual Perfection: Convent Architecture and Nuns in Early Modern Rome' in Helen Hills (ed.), *Architecture and the Politics of Gender in Early Modern Europe* (Aldershot: Ashgate, 2003), pp. 151–76; Anne M. Little, 'Cloistered Bodies: Convents in the Anglo-American Imagination in the British Conquest of Canada', *Eighteenth Century Studies*, 39 (2006), 187–200.

between the cloister and the world was always to some degree permeable, the post-war re-evaluation of the conditions of that cloister implied a new direction. Institutions and social structures maintained relationships and behaviours in a sort of equilibrium of understood norms, values and beliefs. In religious life space and place were critical to the production of social relations, norms and values, reproducing the idea that the internal spaces of the convent were sacred and requiring the regulation of travel outside the convent or monastery in order to reduce contamination from the world. As the social ordering of religious life shifted with the engagement with modernity, so the use of space was un- (or sometimes re-) regulated.[12]

Like every shift in religious life already discussed, the extent of change in spatial reordering varied by religious institute, and sometimes even between communities within the same religious congregation. The timing of changes differed too, but early shifts in the practice of cloister faintly visible in archival sources from the 1940s quickened with the publication of Council documents *Perfectae Caritatis* (Adaptation and Renewal of Religious Life, 1965) and *Lumen Gentium* (Dogmatic Constitution on the Church, 1964), with their emphases on engagement with the world. Likewise, the reasons for change were not uniform or straightforward: the impact of wartime conditions; pre- and post-war shifts in ecclesiology; *nouvelle théologie*; interwar and post-war female youth cultures; the Second Vatican Council itself; and the activist movements of the long 1960s all played a part. Several of these factors are examined below.

But first, in considering how women religious engaged with the 'modern world', attention has to be paid to the difficulties inherent in the concept of 'modernity', with its diverse disciplinary meanings and varying interpretations in economic, political and cultural spheres.[13] The definition of modernity used by the contributors to *Modern Times* – 'the practical negotiation of one's life and one's identity within a complex and fast-changing world' – is apposite for considering modernity with respect to the changes in religious life.[14] Yet, such a definition is perhaps

12   See for example Kevin Hetherington, *The Badlands of Modernity: Heterotopia and Social Ordering* (London: Routledge, 1997), p. 20.

13   Marshall Berman, *All That Is Solid Melts into Air: The Experience of Modernity* (New York: Simon & Schuster, 1982). Berman draws on a well-established narrative of modernity that encompasses capitalism, materialistic greed and loss of communities as a price of progress.

14   Alan O'Shea, 'English Subjects of Modernity', in Mica Nava and Alan O'Shea (eds), *Modern Times: Reflections on a Century of English Modernity* (London: Routledge, 1996), p. 11.

too individuated to be adopted wholesale: the convent and the monastery were negotiating this new world, not simply the individual sister and the nun. A further relevant complication is reflected in the assumption that the emergence of modernity was associated with the public sphere and concomitantly with masculinity. Some scholars have even suggested that modernity was antithetical to femininity.[15] But the challenges of modernity were definitely encountered by women, as this chapter will demonstrate, and manifested themselves in patterns of utilisation of material goods and media, in further education and professionalisation and in familial relationships.

The language of modernity was emphasised in post-war Britain as a 'key signifier and a general referent'.[16] David Kynaston addressed the significance of 'Modernity Britain' in its becoming a

> dominant (albeit top-down) zeitgeist – a spirit of the age epitomised by the desire in relation to the built environment to dump the past, get up to date and embrace a gleaming, functional, progressive future.[17]

This future appeared to be in the hands of 'experts'; the advancement of professional expertise became one of the 'torch-bearers' of modernity.[18] Despite a sparkling rendition of progress which suggested the significance of capitalism, consumption and individualism, stability, family and comfort had their place in Britain's ideal of modernity.[19] And, of course, ambiguity and uncertainty were also the hallmarks of modernity.[20] It is something of a truism to claim that the transition to modernity was also a transition to secularisation. But scholars are challenging this dominant perspective. Charles Taylor has refuted the 'subtraction model' of modernity, instead explaining modernity as 'a movement from one constellation of background understanding to another'.[21] The authors of

---

15 Rita Felski, *The Gender of Modernity* (London: Harvard University Press, 1995), pp. 16–17; Mica Nava, 'Modernity's Disavowal: Women, the City and the Department Store', in Mica Nava and Alan O'Shea (eds), *Modern Times: Reflections on a Century of English Modernity* (London: Routledge, 1996;), p. 39.

16 Becky Conekin, Frank Mort, and Chris Waters (eds), *Moments of Modernity: Reconstructing Britain 1945–1964* (London: Rivers Oram Press, 1999), p. 10.

17 David Kynaston, *Modernity Britain: Opening the Box, 1957–1959* (London: A&C Black, 2013), p. 46.

18 Conekin *et al.* (eds), *Moments of Modernity*, p. 14.

19 O'Shea, 'English Subjects of Modernity', p. 18.

20 Berman, *All That Is Solid Melts into Air*, p. 15.

21 Charles Taylor, 'Two Theories of Modernity', *Hastings Centre Report*, 25 (1995), 24.

Redefining Christian Britain: Post-1945 Perspectives illustrate this changed constellation of Christian belonging through emphasising the diversity of Christian practices rather than church statistics.[22]

The cloister or enclosure was a significant spatial marker of religious life for all sisters and nuns. For contemplative orders enclosure was visibly demarcated by the grille, which acted to separate private monastic space from the modern world. Nuns taking solemn vows were bound by papal cloister; they did not leave monastic spaces without special permission. Religious congregations of sisters, episcopal or pontifical, did not have the same rigid rules of enclosure; the simple vows of religious sisters bound them to a common cloister or space that was often defined in the rule and constitution of their congregation. Even without a visible grille, enclosed places within the convent were sacrosanct and demarcated as sister-only spaces. One sister recalled saying goodbye to her family at the age of twenty-three in the early 1950s when she entered the Society of the Sacred Heart as a postulant:

> [A]nd then I had to say goodbye to them and I remember being taken to a door … the Novice Mistress said 'You are now going into enclosure.' Well. So I raised my body, straightened my back and thought 'This is it' … and in I went but I can't remember feeling happy, not even sad, I wasn't homesick or anything um because you know this, I was coming home, home.[23]

But, of course, the ministries of teaching, nursing and parish work usually required sisters to leave their convent spaces. When outside the convent, enclosure was consciously performed in embodied ways: through distance and detachment from those they served, through the proscription against taking food or drink with others, in religious dress and in the norm of being accompanied by another sister. In interviews many active religious sisters referred to living a partially cloistered or semi-enclosed life. One sister from the Society of the Sacred Heart, a teaching congregation whose schools and colleges were often located in convent grounds, remarked:

> We were semi-enclosed religious, we never went out unless it was for a very special purpose. We went to the dentist but the rest, the doctor, came to the house. You had everything. In the old days apparently you didn't even go out for that.[24]

22 Jane Garnett, Matthew Grimley, Alana Harris, William Whyte and Sarah Williams (eds), *Redefining Christian Britain: Post-1945 Perspectives* (London: SCM Press, 2006).
23 Anonymised interview.
24 Anonymised interview.

By the 1950s permissions to leave the convent were being sought and granted more frequently. Sisters required permission even for routine activities, such as voting at polling stations; doctors' visits and hospitalisation; or to study for higher degrees and qualifications. Even in the semi-enclosed Society of the Sacred Heart, where enclosure had always been rigidly defined, the extent of enclosure was now questioned and it was brought up for discussion at the General Council in 1952. At this time, Mother General Marie-Thérèse de Lescure (1884–1957), fearful that a more flexible enclosure would signal the weakening of the spirit of prayer and recollection, refused to consider any changes to the parameters of enclosure.[25] Although enclosure can be seen simply as a tool of social control to structure, monitor and contain relationships and activities, it was not (and is not) always experienced in this way. Reflecting on her life, Sister Prue Wilson, a member of the Society of the Sacred Heart since the mid-1940s who had experienced its strict enclosure, saw it as a means of contemplation. She described it as creating an artificial 'city of God', freed from pressures of the world, where prayer, quietness, order and charity favoured an 'other-worldly' life.[26]

The world in the cloister

Questioning of enclosure by some members of the Society of the Sacred Heart in the 1950s reveals that the modern world was already infiltrating the world of the cloister. In Britain the circumstances of the Second World War, the permeation of mass media and the advent of modern conveniences served to necessitate the accepting of some aspects of modernity which, in turn, modified the nature of convent spaces. As a consequence cloistered spaces were opened up in unprecedented ways to new social interactions and to the sounds, visual sights and material culture of the modern world.

War years: destabilisation

Religious life was influenced in unforeseen ways by the Home Front conditions of the Second World War. War-time experiences of evacuation or sharing of accommodation, of thundering air raids and of interrupted

25   Mary H. Quinlan, *The Society of the Sacred Heart, 1914-1964* (the author, 1995), pp. 31, 155.
26   Prue Wilson, *My Father Took Me to the Circus* (London: Darton, Longman & Todd, 1984), pp. 63–4.

communications between mother or sister houses destabilised the established norms and patterns of religious life, providing nuns and sisters with new experiences and encouraging interactions with others.[27]

The nature and practice of childhood evacuation in Britain during the Second World War was a significant part of the story of the Home Front experience.[28] Since a large number of Catholic sisters ran schools and orphanages, evacuation was significant to their experience also. New Hall School, located in Essex and run by the Canonesses of the Holy Sepulchre, was one of the many schools in the path of German bombers. In 1940, sisters and students were evacuated to Newnham Paddox in Warwickshire, where they remained for six years.[29] The evacuation was unsettling for everyone, but especially some of the older sisters who had not left the enclosure since their entry into New Hall. Travelling in a motor car speeding northward along the carriageway was frightening for those whose last journey down the mile-long 'Avenue' to New Hall had been in a horse and carriage. The Canonesses strict requirements of enclosure dictated a separation between the residence of the sisters and the school and this was not possible in their temporary accommodation in the rundown stately home they were evacuated to at Newnham Paddox.[30] Students, however, revelled in new-found freedoms. Melissa Metcalf, then in her pre-teens, recounted the 'great adventure' of the evacuation, with mattresses sliding down New Hall School stairs before being packed onto vehicles.[31] She and others recounted the excitement of roaming the extensive grounds with fields, lakes and all manner of flora and fauna.[32] Relationships were altered by these close quarters, which could not replicate the formal surroundings of New Hall School

27 The influence of the war years on religious life is a rich topic needing far more attention than can be given in this short section. O'Brien in her gazetteer of the houses and works of the Daughters of Charity of St Vincent de Paul records houses that were closed, evacuated and requisitioned during the war. Susan O'Brien, *Leaving God for God: The Daughters of Charity of St Vincent de Paul in Britain, 1847–2017* (London: Darton, Longman & Todd, 2017), pp. 387–430.

28 John Welshman, *Churchill's Children: The Evacuee Experience in Wartime Britain* (Oxford: Oxford University Press, 2010).

29 DUL CHS: A3a, Sister Emanuel, 'Some Experiences of the New Hall Community in World War II', *Simil in Unum* (1948), pp. 16–19; *Fishy Tales: Living Memories of New Hall 1930–2012* (Colchester, Essex: Canonesses of the Holy Sepulchre, 2012), p. 72.

30 DUL CHS: D4, Sister Mary Peter, 'Archive Records of Community History in the Twentieth Century', pp. 16–18; Sister Anthony Magdalene, 'Recollection of a Nonagenarian (1880–1970)', p. 44; see also *Fishy Tales*, p. 79.

31 *Fishy Tales*, pp. 79, 84.

32 *Ibid.*, pp. 72–111.

with its clearly demarcated cloistered and school spaces. More than one student recalled being 'in close contact with all the nuns' in ways which encouraged less formal relationships.[33] One student who entered religious life shortly after the war emphasised the spatial division at New Hall by referring to the Canonesses' cloister as 'the other side':

> [We were] completely free and the nuns we got to know really well, because whereas if I'd gone at New Hall they'd been very much the other side (that was the sort of term for it) and here they were out logging and we went logging with them, or we went playing in the woods, you know, everything. It was great.[34]

Other convent school pupils recounted similar experiences. One former evacuated pupil recalled 'the nuns were our best friends and we used to ask, will you take me for a walk, and that meant you had one nun privately to yourself for the duration of that walk'.[35] Of course, as the historiography of the over 3,000,000 child evacuees makes clear, experiences were not all benign or pleasant, some were of neglect, others of trauma and abuse.[36] But in these recounted stories, close bonds were a feature of the evacuation experience.

Some communities with extensive convent grounds shared their premises with evacuated schoolchildren, soldiers and prisoners of war. The fields of Syon Abbey were requisitioned by the wartime government and became the US Army Marshalling Area Camp K7 just before D-Day. The Syon Bridgettines were joined in their convent chapel by Catholic members of the 29th Infantry Regiment.[37] One nun recalled that their 'whole-hearted participation and singing will never be forgotten', nor would the more raucous tunes from *Annie Get Your Gun* played on camp loudspeaker systems within earshot of Syon Abbey.[38] The Roehampton convent school of the Society of the Sacred Heart was evacuated to Stanford Hall, near Rugby, in 1943, and talented artist Sister Catherine Blood documented the gift of eighteen figs received by the sisters from the

---

33 *Ibid.*, pp. 79, 86.
34 Anonymised interview.
35 Anonymised interview.
36 Julie Summers, *When the Children Came Home: Stories of Wartime Evacuees* (New York: Simon & Schuster, 2011), p. xi; Welshman, *Churchill's Children*. For a personal story of wartime evacuation, see Peter O'Brien, *Evacuation Stations: Memoir of a Boyhood in Wartime England* (the author, 2012).
37 E. A. Jones, *Syon Abbey 1415–2015: England's Last Medieval Monastery* (London: Gracewing, 2015), p. 121.
38 'Syon Notes', *Poor Soul's Friend*, 16:6 (1968), p. 140.

Figure 5.1 Sister receiving figs from an Italian prisoner of war. Drawing by
Catherine Blood, RSCJ

Italian prisoners of war who attended mass in their chapel (Figure 5.1).
The Canonesses in Newnham Paddox, too, were joined at Sunday mass
by Italian prisoners of war interned nearby.[39] These were unprecedented
interactions that demonstrate how the modern world interrupted the
usual separateness of monastic spaces.

Like all Britons, nuns and sisters were galvanised in support of
those on the front lines as well as those on the Home Front. Enclosed
contemplatives participated by knitting garments for the troops[40] and
planting victory gardens,[41] but they saw their most urgent 'war work'
as praying for the end of the war. The Poor Clares of Arundel, only
four miles from the vulnerable English Channel,[42] had their fair share

39   DUL CHS: D4, Sister Mary Peter, 'The Twentieth Century. Records of the History of
the Community New Hall', p. 26.
40   Arundel and Brighton Diocesan Archives (henceforth ABDA): Poor Clares folder,
Canonical Visitation of the Convent, 1941.
41   The Syon Bridgettines were required to plant their pastureland with potatoes and root
vegetables. Jones, *Syon Abbey*, p. 121.
42   The Poor Clares of Arundel did not want to leave their enclosure so they did not
relocate to a site that was safer. ABDA: Poor Clares folder, Letter from Sister M. Clare

of sleepless nights, with almost continual air raid sirens and enemy planes 'passing over the Convent day and night', some dropping bombs nearby.[43] During the war years, they were isolated from the family and friendship networks who would normally provide information about local and world events. The usual visitors were occupied with war work, at home or in active service, and this along with petrol rationing and Arundel's location as a defence area near the Sussex coast kept them away. At a time when many feared the invasion of England was imminent, they, like many Britons, listened to the wireless for the news of the war. The Bishop of Arundel and Brighton, Peter Amigo, writing in 1941, questioned this practice. Abbess M. Clare Campbell's impassioned defence of their use of the wireless, written one week after the bombing of Pearl Harbor by the Japanese, feels raw with frustration. She forcefully reminded the bishop:

> [T]he world passes us by – we rarely see people; and, if our Sisters are to maintain unflagging fervour in prayer for the peace so ardently desired, the majority at least need to have some knowledge of what is happening in regard to the ghastly struggle now raging. With the burden of so many extra prayers, their war work and the ever present anxiety concerning those dear to them now on active service, it would be unwise and unkind to deprive them of hearing <u>once</u> a day, for twenty or twenty-five minutes, the war news as given on the Wireless. Not only that – but on the outbreak of war, being in a defence Area, we were particularly requested by the authorities to keep our Wireless in working order and even to take it to the 'shelter' during an air raid because important instructions would be broadcast should a crisis arise.[44]

The wireless, the abbess insisted, was critical for the nuns' 'fervour in prayer' and their emotional resilience. She highlighted not only the patriotism of the sisters but the significance of their connections to those 'dear to them' on the front lines. Amigo elicited advice from Franciscan Capuchin Father Alphonsus, who concurred that in these conditions listening to the wireless was necessary, but counselled that the wireless 'so easily afford[s] a means of introducing a worldly and distracting spirit

---

to bishop, dated 11 September 1940. 'We want to carry on our work for God and the world <u>here</u> as long a God Wills it.'

43 ABDA: Poor Clares folder, Letter from Sister M. Clare to archbishop, dated 15 August 1940.

44 ABDA: Poor Clares folder, Letter from Sister M. Clare to archbishop, dated 14 December 1941.

which utterly ruins the spirit of recollection and prayer'.[45] His response reflects the ideals of the architecture of enclosure designed to foster spiritual perfection. He seems infuriatingly oblivious to the Poor Clares' own emotional trauma; concern for the 'distracting spirit' of air raids and enemy bombing would have seemed more apt than a focus on the worldly spirit of listening to the wireless.[46] It was the unsolicited interaction with the world at war through the cacophony and violence of enemy action that resulted in the unwelcomed mitigation of the rules of enclosure.

Disruptions were faced in Europe too, especially in countries that had been bombed or invaded.[47] International congregations with motherhouses in Europe sometimes faced obstacles to communication. Decision-making had devolved to local superiors of the Sisters of Charity of Our Lady, Mother of Mercy and a temporary novitiate had opened in Pantasaph during the war years because of irregular communication with their Dutch motherhouse.[48] Sister-historian Alix von Molengraft hints at the after-effects of the war, when she suggests that the Dutch General Council found it difficult to reinstate the uniform observance of customs and rules in some international houses after the war.[49] In her memoir, Sister Prue Wilson wrote about how the stability of religious life in her own congregation 'had been badly shaken by the war situation, by the bombing of two of the London convents, and by the mitigation of the rules of enclosure during evacuation'.[50] Wartime experiences led to an often unwelcome as well as unexpected intrusion into the pattern of religious life in Britain. Some women religious welcomed the stability as well as the safety of the return to the cloister after the war, but others had seen the possibilities of a less enclosed form of religious life.

45   ABDA: Poor Clares folder, Letter from Father Alphonsus OFM Cap to Bishop Peter Amigo, dated 17 December 1941.
46   Sandra M. Schneiders, *New Wineskins: Re-Imagining Religious Life Today* (New York: Paulist Press, 1986), p. 2. Schneiders argues that such focus on the framework of canonical religious life over the practicalities of lived experience were characteristic of what preoccupied men religious.
47   For a European perspective see Georgio Vecchio (ed.), *Le suore e la Resistenza* (Milan: Ambrosianeum, 2010); Flora Derounian, 'Representations and Oral Histories of Working Women in Post-World War Two Italy (1945–1965)', unpublished PhD dissertation, University of Bristol, 2018. From the perspective of an international religious congregation see Monique Luirard, *The Society of the Sacred Heart in the World of Its Times 1865–2000* (St Louis, MO: iUniverse, 2016), pp. 365–440.
48   Wrexham Diocesan Archives: SCMM Files, Letter from William Godfrey, Apostolic Delegate, to Daniel Joseph Hannon, Bishop of Menevia, dated 6 November 1941.
49   Sister Alix van de Molengraft, *It All Began with Three Beguines: History of Ten Thousand Sisters of Charity* (Preston: Nemco Press, 1992), pp. 157–8.
50   Wilson, *My Father Took Me to the Circus*, p. 50.

News of the world

As noted above, the rules of enclosure also normally prohibited forms of media within convent spaces on the grounds that they were likely to introduce a 'worldly and distracting spirit'. Restrictions on old and new forms of 'instruments of social communication', newspapers, radio and later television, were commonplace in most religious communities. One nun who entered an enclosed monastery in the late 1950s spoke of not having access to newspapers or radio, though she was aware that 'one old sister' had permission to read the local paper. She indicated that 'all you got really was what you heard from family, friends, when they visited'.[51] Another Poor Clare spoke in a similar vein: 'We had no newspaper, no television, no radio and we were in the back of beyond'.[52] Often it was up to the mother abbess or mother superior to decide whether and when to inform their community of newsworthy events. Active congregations faced similar proscriptions. Yet, attitudes differed amongst congregation leaders. The prioress of the Augustinian Canonesses surprised her sisters in June 1953 with a rented television set so that the community could watch Queen Elizabeth II's coronation day together.[53]

By the late 1950s, young women entering religious life after the war were accustomed to access to news and entertainment via newspapers, radio, cinema and cine newsreels. Television was fast becoming Britain's most important leisure activity and as a mass medium was becoming a part of everyday culture.[54] The communal experience of gathering around the television with neighbours or at a local pub to watch the unfolding of state events, such as the 1953 coronation of Queen Elizabeth II, was becoming commonplace. It brought a shared awareness of public and international affairs. Television was linked to national cultural identity and public information.[55] Once in the home, it became its centre as families watched

51   Anonymised interview.
52   Anonymised interview.
53   DUL CHS: D2a, Chantress Book, vol. 15, 1 June 1953.
54   Arthur Marwick, *British Society since 1945* (London: Allen Lane, 1982), p. 121.
55   Fifty-six per cent of the adult population of Great Britain watched the coronation; half of the 20 million viewers watched it at homes of friends. John Corner (ed.), *Popular Television in Britain: Studies in Cultural History* (London: BFI Publishing, 1991), p. 4. In 1955, 40 per cent of the population had a television, by 1959, this had jumped to 75 per cent and by 1969, to 93 per cent. Tim O'Sullivan, 'Television Memories and Cultures of Viewing, 1950–65', in John Corner (ed.), *Popular Television in Britain: Studies in Cultural History* (London: BFI Publishing, 1991), p. 161.

television together; this was significant to the privatisation of leisure and by the 1970s the television was a symbol of affluence.[56]

Some Catholics saw mass media as an unwelcome tool of the secular world. Catholic journalist Michael de la Bedoyere reflected scathingly on media in 1953:

> Radio and television are calculated in the long run to undermine our defences ... Nevertheless the fact remains that for many hours of each day the very citadel of Catholic society, the home, is invaded from outside by minds which taken as a whole are actuated by solely secularist principles and outlook.[57]

Pope Pius XII offered a more nuanced view in 1957 with *Miranda Prorsus* ('Wonderful Indeed'), an encyclical letter on modern media: motion pictures, radio and television.[58] As its introductory words infer, it celebrated mass media as a means of spreading the Catholic faith but also sternly warned it could be a 'source of countless evils' when it was 'opposed to right moral principles'.[59] In common with Michael de la Bedoyere, sisters who trained novices in England reiterated the encyclical's concerns that 'Television leads to worldliness' and possibly endangered chastity by 'awaken[ing] a desire for life in the world ... portrayed in such glowing colours in plays, features and advertisements'.[60]

Religious communities took these concerns seriously. At Syon Abbey, Abbess M. Peter Wallace wrote to her bishop that she put a stop to the nuns watching the news during evening recreation as instructions from the Holy See stipulated that television must be of a 'religious nature'. She indicated with some regret that some sisters felt 'lost' at knowing so little of what was going on in the world.[61] The bishop's reply in 1969 was markedly similar to Father Alphonsus's response in the 1940s:

> The contemplative life seeks to leave the world outside and to bring it inside again through radio and television would seem to contradict

56 Harold Perkin, *The Rise of Professional Society: England since 1880* (London: Routledge, 1989), p. 421; Elizabeth Roberts, *Women and Families: An Oral History 1940–1970* (Oxford: Blackwell, 1995), pp. 103–4. Corner (ed.), *Popular Television in Britain*, p. 12. Jeffrey Hill, *Sport, Leisure and Culture in Twentieth-Century Britain* (Basingstoke: Palgrave Macmillan, 2002), p. 104.
57 Michael de la Bedoyere, 'The Problem of Radio and Television', *Clergy Review* (December 1953), p. 719.
58 *Vigilanti Cura* (1936).
59 *Miranda Prosus* (1957).
60 SCMM-ENK: 374, 'Training to be Given in the Noviciate to Prepare Sisters to Meet Present Day Problems', p. 3.
61 EUL: CMB 3.2. Sister M. Peter [Wallace] to bishop, dated 16 October 1969.

that spirit. The newspaper brings in quite sufficient news of the World for which you are praying and dedicating your lives, and it does so without disturbing the peace and recreation of those who may not want to hear the sounds of the radio or television. Any particular items of news that call for special thought and prayer can be mentioned by your good self or one of the other Sisters.[62]

Written warnings of the perils of 'indiscriminate use of television' from bishops and women religious abound in convent documents in the 1960s and 1970s, but television, and the world, slowly, though with many restrictions, entered religious communities. Mother M. Ignatius in her 1963 circular letter to the British convents of the Sisters of Charity of Our Lady, Mother of Mercy grudgingly permitted television for 'educational purposes and for the news; but only occasionally as a means of recreation, not as a regular practice. The Sisters may never stay up late solely to watch television, or to listen to the radio, unless it is something of ecclesiastical or national importance.'[63] The instructions from the Mother General of the Institute of the Blessed Virgin Mary, a teaching congregation, sent in 1969 to superiors offered more latitude: 'All members are free to listen to the news on radio or T.V., and also to what is useful for their general and professional education, and to religious programmes. The Light Programme can sometimes be allowed for the sake of relaxation.' She felt the need, though, to add: 'As a matter of principle Sisters should not unhesitatingly stay on watching T.V. and let other duties suffer.'[64] One sister from this congregation recalled watching television in the 1960s, indicating that 'we did watch a bit, but it was monitored and occasionally – you've probably heard this already – the newspaper was put across the television, bits that we shouldn't watch. Upstairs Downstairs. I mean it was very much, it was definitely Mother and the children.'[65] Numerous narrators recounting their memories were often critical of how the rules of enclosure infantilised them.

Newspapers, radio and television brought the world into convent spaces. They opened up horizons to what was happening locally, nationally and internationally. The secular world entered the sacred space of the convent through its sounds and sights. For the Church and some convent leadership, 'instruments of social communication' were necessary, but

---

62 EUL: CMB 3.2. Letter from A. Bede Davis, bishop's secretary, to Mother Abbess, dated 18 October 1969.

63 SCMM-ENK: 342, 'Report of Visitation by Mother Provincial', Dartford, 28 April 1961.

64 ACJ/EP/C/32/b, Letter from Mother Edelburga Solzabacher to Reverend Mother, dated 6 February 1969, with attachment entitled 'Practical Notes on the Decrees of the General Congregations 1968', p. 5.

65 Anonymised interview.

were to be controlled and monitored by those in authority, who were concerned about inappropriate content, 'worldliness' and the potential attractiveness of the modern world. They were seen as disrupting the sacrality of convent spaces.

Modern conveniences

Internal convent spaces were changing, too, with the introduction of domestic modern conveniences.[66] Many sisters and nuns lived in dormitories divided by curtains for privacy.[67] In 1958, walls and doors replaced curtains that divided cubicles in the cells of the Sisters of Charity of Our Lady, Mother of Mercy. Washbasins with both hot and cold water and electric lights were added to private cells. Mother M. Ignatius Stirzaker 'wished to give some comfort and space' and provided the sisters with small tables and comfortable chairs for their cells.[68] Similar changes were occurring in other congregations too. One narrator recalled the building works happening in the motherhouse in London:

> [T]he house was turned upside down because, the motherhouse, because they were putting basins in every room instead of having to lug cans of water down the corridor [laughs] and so things like that were happening.[69]

The Canonesses of the Holy Sepulchre documented their modernity with photographs of their modern laundry and kitchen (Figures 5.2 and 5.3). In 1965, the weekly *Catholic Pictorial* touted the modernity of the Sisters of Notre Dame de Namur of Wigan by featuring photographs of 'Britain's Most Modern House'. The new convent included 'modern conveniences' such as a lift, and sisters were residing in their own bedrooms with hot and cold running water, a mirror and a wardrobe cupboard. The article concluded by suggesting that 'Picture windows and oil-fired central heating destroy forever the dark, cold and cheerless convent image.'[70] Catholic critique of convent austerity reflected some of the public attitudes to the rigours of religious life.

---

66 See Claire Langhamer, 'The Meanings of Home in Postwar Britain', *Journal of Contemporary History*, 40 (2005), 349.

67 For example, see O'Brien, *Leaving God for God*, p. 171.

68 SCMM-ENK: 2006, Bernadette Steele, Dolores Heys and Marie Wallbank, 'The History of the Sisters of Charity of our Lady, Mother of Mercy in Britain and Ireland 1861 to 1982', pp. 30, 68, 109. Molengraft, *It All Began with Three Beguines*, pp. 174–5.

69 Anonymised interview.

70 'Britain's Most Modern House', *Catholic Pictorial* (5 September 1965), pp. 14–15.

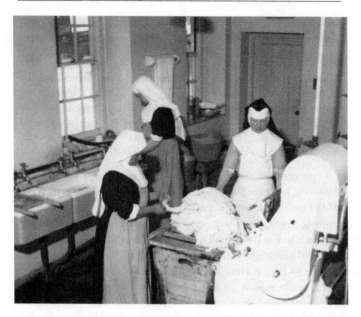

Figure 5.2 Canonesses of the Holy Sepulchre working in the laundry

Figure 5.3 Canonesses of the Holy Sepulchre employed in the kitchen

Even those who embraced relaxing some austerity had concerns. One Augustinian prioress voiced her anxiety about the alterations she had introduced in the late 1950s:

> So many changes have taken place, even in the material arrangements – but they seemed really necessary, or inevitable, so that I hope I will not have to burn in Purgatory for my share in making the life less austere than in the past. Sometimes it quite worries me, but I <u>certainly</u> would not have chosen it … Now, however, we have electric light in the cells, instead of candles & this last winter, heating has also been put in.[71]

Some communities were slow to propose the use of modern conveniences, believing they were contrary to the vow of poverty and would lead to a diminishment of asceticism. In the late 1970s, the Syon nuns, whose average age was sixty-eight, were still doing laundry and other domestic work manually. Jesuit Lachlan M. Hughes wrote after his canonical visitation of the community that 'Among the older Sisters there seems to be a certain literalism in relation to the rules (and this very often really means former custom) whereby such matters as the use of television and the understanding of enclosure, &c., seems to be marked with fear rather than due accuracy.' On Hughes's insistence, the Syon community purchased washing machines, tumble dryers, vacuum cleaners and floor polishers.[72] The introduction of modern conveniences into convent spaces reflected the physical modernisation of conventual life, but with the ushering in of hot and cold running water and electric light came disquiet about reducing asceticism. Many religious welcomed the privacy, convenience and comfort of these changes, and public discourse heralded this shift as a removal of a 'cheerless convent image'.

Nuns in the world

Traditionally, excursions outside the convent were few and confined to what was strictly necessary. Leaving the convent even on convent business or for medical reasons required a series of permissions and approvals. Interactions with 'seculars' were controlled by customs that mandated a physical and emotional distance and detachment from family,

---

71 DUL CHS: E, Letter from Mother Mary Patrick to 'dearest Mother', dated 16 December 1961.
72 PDA: 'Canonical Visitation', 23 March 1979; Anonymised interview.

friends and the people they served.[73] As the world entered the cloister, women religious became more visibly present outside the convent and monastery. Mother Mary Andrew, novice mistress of the Franciscan Missionaries of the Divine Motherhood, reported in her lecture to other novice mistresses: 'I counted six different pairs of Nuns coming and going at London Airport, in the space of 20-minutes.'[74] This travelling to and fro was a function of changing parameters of governance, the need for professional training and relationships which led to a more visible presence of women religious in the world.

'Trotting about'

Leaders of centralised congregations had always travelled for annual visitations of convents and provinces, but decentralised governance, discussed in Chapter 3, led to ordinary sisters travelling more frequently to attend committee consultations, provincial assemblies and to act as delegates at chapter conferences. These interactions encouraged exchanges of ideas on renewal practices, pointing to the connectedness of transnational encounters even while moving away from a common life and uniformity. One newly appointed novice mistress explained her journey to the motherhouse thus: 'I was in Holland in '63 for a short time to get some ideas … to understand something of what was happening.'[75] The Second Vatican Council mandated new regimes for the training of novices and the novice mistress was expected to be familiar with new Church teachings and the psychologies of the Modern Girl.[76]

Even enclosed nuns, such as Prioress Mary Patrick of the Priory of Our Lady of Good Counsel in Haywards Heath, found themselves travelling more frequently. Writing to another prioress in 1958, after a bout of journeys to sister communities in Hoddesdon and Bruges to discuss adjustments 'to the needs of modern times', she noted that:

---

73   'Seculars' was the term used commonly to refer to men and women who were not members of religious institutes or clergy.

74   SCMM-ENK: 374, 'Training to be Given in the Noviciate to Prepare Sisters to Meet Present Day Problems'.

75   SCMM-Tilburg: SCMM 009 interviewed by Annemiek van der Veen (2003).

76   Joachim Schmiedl, 'Reception and Implementation of the Second Vatican Council Religious Institutes', in Leo Kenis, Jaak Billiet and Patrick Pasture (eds), *The Transformation of the Christian Churches in Western Europe (1945–2000)* (Leuven: Leuven University Press, 2010), p. 305.

[T]he dear older part of the Community here are inclined to feel that I have done enough 'trotting about' for the present & want to feel that we are settling down to a quiet & regular spell. I have also had to go 'out of enclosure' in these last weeks to visit one of the Community who is in hospital.[77]

Some congregations, for instance the Sisters of Charity of Our Lady, Mother of Mercy, identified personal contact as an important form of building communication and unity in what was a large international congregation. Sisters encouraged transnational encounters through correspondence with sisters of other provinces and invitations to visit. Congregation leadership articulated the need to break down barriers which hindered unity, encouraging 'true communication', to remove 'negative attitudes' and encounter 'diverse mentalities'.[78] The move to provincial novitiates in 1960 was welcomed, but the link with the motherhouse weakened. One solution was that 'brides' (newly professed sisters) travelled to the Netherlands 'in order to make acquaintance of the Motherhouse and the different works of the Congregation'.[79] Visits from older sisters were encouraged in order to renew the 'bond of unity' through 'links with the Motherhouse and memories of their early years in the Congregation'.[80]

Catholic sisters were entering the modern world in other ways also. The *Catholic Pictorial* included numerous photographs of sisters on bicycles and motorbikes with captions such as 'Little Sisters go all modern'.[81] One article titled 'The Mercy Squad' included a photograph of four Little Sisters of the Assumption on scooters, ready to travel to the bedsides of their patients.[82] The article assured their readers they were 'highly competent riders'. An inset photograph reinforced the tradition of their ministry: it was of a nursing sister, in full habit, nursing at the bedside of an elderly woman in her home. The traditional and modern were visually displayed side by side to assure Catholic readers that the 'essentials', the traditional caring work of sisters, would not be forgotten despite modernisation (Figure 5.4). On a more mundane level, day-to-day activities no longer needed intermediaries. One sister recalled, 'as

77   DUL CHS: E, Letter from Mother Mary Patrick to Mother Prioress, dated 1 May 1958.
78   SCMM-ENK: 1273, 'Sisters of Charity Now and in the Future', 1986.
79   SCMM-ENK: 332a, 'Notes on "Report of the General Chapter 1964"'.
80   SCMM-ENK, 2708, 'Report on the Three Months April to June 1989' for the General Council from the English Province, written by Thérèse Mary Barnett, July 1989.
81   'Received with Thanks', *Catholic Pictorial* (18 March 1962), p. 3; 'The Nuns Get a Brake', *Catholic Pictorial* (1 July 1962), p. 4.
82   'The Mercy Squad', *Catholic Pictorial* (7 January 1962), p. 15.

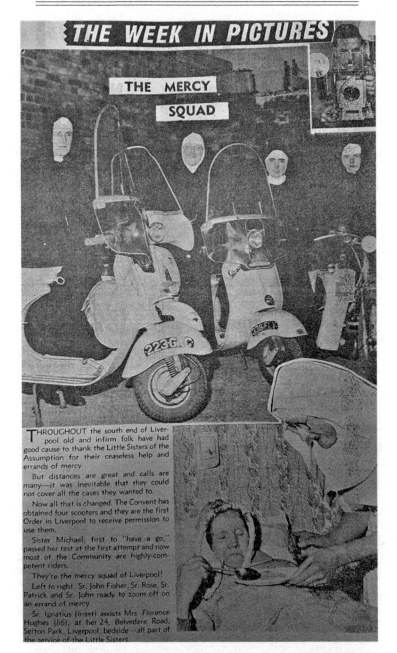

Figure 5.4 'The Mercy Squad', *Catholic Pictorial* (7 January 1962), p. 15

I was bursar, it made such a difference to be able to go out and go to the bank and to do things myself instead of people doing things for me. I always used to have a commissionaire to buy things people wanted.'[83] Women religious travelling to and through secular spaces of the world on convent business was both a novelty and a source of tension.

Education/professionalisation

From the 1930s, the Holy See pressed women religious to obtain academic credentials to attain professional competency on par with their secular colleagues.[84] In 1951, Pius XII urged further training at the First International Congress of Teaching Sisters:

> See to it, therefore, that they are well trained and that their education corresponds in quality and academic degrees to that demanded by the State.[85]

Professional training was reiterated again at the Congress of Superiors General in 1952. One sister's handwritten notes of Pope Pius XII's speech reported his instructions:

> Be broad-minded and liberal here, and admit of no stinginess. Whether it be for teaching, the sick, the study of art or anything else, the Sister should be able to say to herself, 'My Superior is giving me a training that will put me on an equality with my secular colleagues.' Give them also the opportunity and the means to keep their professional knowledge up to date. Of this, too, we spoke last year. We repeat it, to emphasize its importance for your Sisters' peace of soul and for their work.[86]

This was all, of course, reinforced by *Perfectae Caritatis*, published in 1965, which linked obtaining academic degrees to renewal:

> Adaptation and renewal depend greatly on the education of religious. Consequently neither non-clerical religious nor religious women should

---

83 Anonymised interview.
84 Abbé Gaston Courtois (ed.), *The States of Perfection* (Dublin: Gill, 1961), p. 218. The *Catholic Nurse* reported on the first Congress of Catholic Nurses in 1935, noting that the 'Holy Father's wishes that the training of nursing nuns should be increased, to render their services equal on the scientific side to the lay nurses.' 'Nuns and Maternity Work', *Catholic Nurse* (April 1936), p. 6. The 1936 decree *Constans ac Sedula* allowed women religious to perform surgical and obstetric work but also encouraged women religious to obtain medical and nursing degrees.
85 Papal Encyclicals Online, 'Council to Teaching Sisters', 15 September 1951.
86 ACJ/EP/C/17/26, 'Address by the Holy Father', 15 September 1952, p. 2.

be assigned to apostolic works immediately after the novitiate. Rather, their religious and apostolic formation, joined with instruction in arts and science directed toward obtaining appropriate degrees, must be continued as needs require in houses established for those purposes.[87]

Continued emphasis relays the significance of professional education and academic degrees but suggests too that some religious institutes may have been slow to educate sisters, perhaps because of the difficulty of managing institutional staffing needs.

Congregations were proud of the training made available to their sisters. The Canonesses of the Holy Sepulchre reported in their federation magazine that seven sisters had obtained various degrees and qualifications from 1968 to 1971. They earned university degrees in biology and German; diplomas in education and matron-housekeeping; and one sister became a registered nurse. Five Canonesses were listed as attending courses in 1972: at the Eastbourne Council for Further Education, at Oxford Technical College, at Sussex University, at Chelmsford Technical College and at the University of Kent.[88] This was a substantial investment for a congregation with forty-odd members and attests to the seriousness with which they addressed educating the Canonesses. Photographs of the Sisters of Mercy at their desks (Figure 5.5) were included in vocation brochures published by the congregation re-enforcing the significance of educated sisters.

Teaching and nursing congregations sent sisters, often after their novitiate, to teacher training colleges or nursing schools. Some, especially if they were to teach in secondary schools, were sent to university.[89] The women on the receiving end of this educational thrust welcomed these opportunities. In interviews, sisters recounted a renewed emphasis on obtaining university degrees. One spoke of her congregation realising that 'people needed degrees and they couldn't just, you know, it had been a bit amateurish before. So a bevy of us went and did our degrees there [at Oxford]'.[90] The 1950s educational experience was remembered as intellectually stimulating, but many also recalled the rules and regulations that restricted their personal interactions and activities: they were chaperoned back and forth to tutorials and were discouraged from

---

87 *Perfectae Caritatis*, §18.
88 DUL CHS: A3a, 'New Hall', *Simul in Unum* (1972), p. 7.
89 Currently, there is no extant data that quantifies the training of sister-nuns who taught in primary and secondary schools in Britain in the twentieth century. This is yet another research topic that needs serious attention.
90 Anonymised interview.

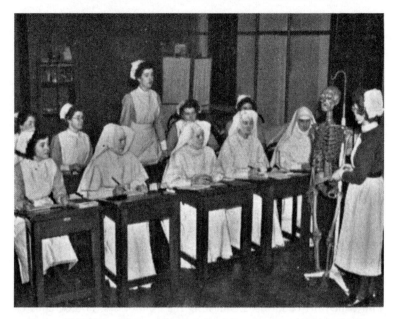

Figure 5.5 Sisters of Mercy and nurses studying in the lecture hall, vocation brochure 'Sisters of Mercy', c. 1957

mingling with other students.[91] Some of these same sisters returned to university two decades later, retraining for new ministries. Often in their late thirties and forties, they acknowledged a very different experience. One sister compared her time at Oxford in the late 1940s to that two decades later, when:

> [W]e all the more relished the freedom to cycle to daily mass at the Dominican Priory, to join an archaeological society, attending lectures and going out on general expeditions. Within community there was more informality, spontaneity and relaxation, which gave support to the different branches of our study and our serious reading and study. We still wore the habit, and veil. But we also were enabled to make and cement lasting friendships with Dons from our college and others in ways that had not been possible previously.[92]

Another sister recalled 'It was there that I matured, that I was treated as an intelligent adult, able to think, study and express my opinions with

---

91   SSH ENW: 'RSCJ and 1967', Luirard survey, Remembrance 6.
92   *Ibid.*, Remembrance 7.

my tutors.'[93] Academic interactions became a part of the educational experience.

Women religious were also encouraged to acquire theological knowledge. Pope Pius XII's 'Motu Proprio', *Nihil Ecclesiae* (1956) approved the Pontifical Institute Regina Mundi which provided theological education for women religious in Rome.[94] It was founded in 1952, and there women religious took courses in theology (fundamental, dogmatic, ascetical and mystical), Holy Scripture, Canon Law, Church history, archaeology, sacred art, liturgy, missiology, catechetical methods, and the social teachings of the Church. The three-year diploma course enabled sisters to teach religion in any school in their diocese or archdiocese.[95] Closer to home, Corpus Christi College, a London-based catechetical college opened in 1965, aimed at updating Catholic educators on the message of the Second Vatican Council. Religious and laity attended courses and the popular evening seminar series.[96] The consistent message that women religious must be adequately trained was matched with the development of opportunities for further professional and theological education.

Contemplative communities also offered more learning opportunities to their nuns. Franciscan President of the Central Commission for Nuns in the General Curia Ignatius Omaechevarria suggested to Poor Clares in 1968 that nuns should 'not bury their talent in the ground but must diligently cultivate, develop and perfect it for the service of their neighbour, so that they can work faithfully and devotedly'.[97] Some Poor Clare communities took this seriously. Poor Clare Gabriel Taggert wrote to Abbot Christopher Butler apprising him that her Liberton community kept themselves 'informed and instructed'; they had joined 'tape Libraries from where we get very good tapes on Theology, Scripture, and

93   *Ibid.*, Remembrance 6.
94   The first students enrolled in 1954.
95   'News, Notes and Texts', *The Tablet* (25 September 1954), p. 20.
96   Soon after it opened, Cardinal John Heenan heard complaints of a 'speculative theology'. In 1968, Heenan asked the Council of Major Religious Superiors to send only mature religious and priests for training. By 1975 Corpus Christi had closed. McClelland noted: 'The Corpus Christi affair did more than anything else to ensure that the English penchant for caution prevailed.' V. Alan McClelland, 'Great Britain and Ireland', in Adrian Hastings (ed.), *Modern Catholicism: Vatican II and After* (New York: Oxford University Press, 1991), p. 373. Vincent Alan McClelland, 'John Carmel Heenan, the Second Vatican Council and the Rise and Fall of an English Lumen Vitae', in Aidan Seery (ed.), *Essays in Tribute to J. Valentine Rice, 1935–2006* (Dublin: Lilliput Press, 2010), pp. 69–97.
97   AAW: BU E.39, Poor Clares Notting Hill and Barnet (1968–1975), Letter from Sister Gabriel Taggert to Christopher Butler, dated 2 April 1967.

the Council Decrees. Also we have good books, and do quite a good deal of reading, and quite frequently have days of recollection given by Priests and other conferences.'[98]

But, on occasion, nuns wanted more than what was on offer. Abbess M. Paula Smallwood wrote in frustration to Father J. V. Healey, the ecclesiastical superior of nuns in the archdiocese of Birmingham:

> I am rather taken back by Sister Francis Clare's behaviour since the Novice Mistresses Conference. She is full of the charismatic renewal and very starry eyed by Dame Maria Boulding of Stanbrook and has had contact with her. She came to me full of enthusiasm asking could she do some study of Holy Scripture or theology etc. ... I told her that the old 'A' levels that Diane had, were available. Then she said that she would like to take exams and maybe a 'B.A.' I said that this was out. We did not need exams. All we needed was to study with an end of incorporating it into our life. She then said that if she could not take exams, she didn't want to do it. Within an hour, she had been to Sister Ruth to say that I did not want her to study. She mentioned to others outside the community, that I am anti intellectual. So, I have been putting this right.[99]

Not everyone received the education they requested. Some sisters were left behind in this education drive. Archive sources are incomplete in regard to this, but narrators have suggested that those at the end of their teaching or nursing ministries, or retired, or responsible for domestic duties were not always given opportunities for further education. Additionally, some sisters opted out, feeling unequal to further studies, and this created its own tensions.

Critics of this education drive warned against 'career-itis': the potential that sisters would become more interested in professionalisation and a 'career' than their religious ministry.[100] Others linked further education with individualism. One community historian warned that 'religious who live in the world want to sacrifice the monastic community to the individual, material elements in the world. We must try to steer clear of personal selfishness.'[101] The Church of England was facing similar issues. Hugh McLeod has argued that in the 1960s the push towards

---

98 FPA: Letter to the nuns from Father Ignatius Omaechevarria, dated 12 August 1968.

99 BAA: CC/B/1/L/3, Correspondence, Letter from Sister Paula to J. V. Healey, dated 5 November 1973.

100 SCMM-ENK: 374, 'Training to be Given in the Noviciate to Prepare Sisters to Meet Present Day Problems', p. 4.

101 SCMM-ENK: 1780, 'History of the Congregation of the Sisters of Charity of Our Lady, Mother of Mercy', Sister Thérèse Quant, SCMM (1972?), p. 30.

professional training, especially in those areas where churches were often involved (education, youth work, social work, 'caring' professions), led to the neutralisation of religion.[102]

Family

Perhaps the most profound shift in the notion of cloister for women religious was that which took place in their relationships with their own families. The discourse of 'dying to the world' was intrinsic to the vocation story told by women who entered in the 1940s and 1950s in particular. They entered religious life knowing the sacrifice asked of them and their parents. Women were expected to disconnect physically and emotionally from their past lives, their family and their friendships. Such detachment was lauded in convent rules, regulations and obituaries. Practically, it allowed more time to devote to their spiritual life and their role as spouse of Christ.

Most communities allowed both personal visits and correspondence between women religious and their family, but often within very stringent parameters. Maintaining close family relationships, according to pre-conciliar understandings of religious life, was thought to lead to a 'weakening [of] the religious spirit'.[103] Family visits were typically limited in number, and allowed only during certain times of the year. In many convents and monasteries, it was required that another member of the community be present during these visits. Sisters and nuns were aware before entering religious life they would rarely see their families, and at the time accepted this as a sacrifice that was a necessary component of religious life. But for women religious and family members, it could be difficult and full of strains. One sister who entered a teaching congregation the early 1960s remembered:

> I think it was put into quite an artificial context at the beginning, but they sort of were the rules of the game, which as an 18 year old I sort of swallowed whole really. I know my family found those visits very, very difficult. You could have, I think it was five days in the year, and they used to come for a day at Christmas, after Christmas, a day at Easter and three days in the summer ... But we sort of were with them for limited periods during the day and then we went away to eat and they

102 Hugh McLeod, *The Religious Crisis of the 1960s* (Oxford: Oxford University Press, 2007), p. 115.
103 Institute of Our Lady of Mercy Archives (henceforth RSM Institute), Bermondsey: IOLM/BER, Bermondsey Annals, 1854, pp. 204–7.

went away to eat and I suppose I was more conscious of this is just the way it is, rather than finding all that terribly difficult at the time.[104]

Exceptions to these regulations were frowned upon. One report of the visitation of the Poor Clares in Arundel emphasised that 'essential' rules should be enforced:

> It is not always possible to arrange for a Sister to remain in the parlour during visits to the grille, but I urge great prudence in allowing visits without this supervision. In some cases – e.g. the visit of a parent – it may be quite alright to allow a sister to have a private interview with the visitor, but there are some occasions where it is essential that the rule be strictly kept.[105]

Written correspondence was limited to a certain number of letters a year sent at certain time periods, and all correspondence leaving and entering the convent could be opened by the novice mistress or the abbess or superior. This surveillance of correspondence was a typical feature of religious life and may have added further strain to familial relationships. A sister who entered a teaching congregation in the 1940s explained:

> Oh, in the beginning we had hardly any contact with our families. Our letters were opened and read. I told my family, because I thought they'd better know, and people were quite cross that I'd said, you know, I'd told them. But I said, if my letters are being read they have a right to know. So that meant inhibited conversation.[106]

Some participants found that family relationships 'didn't continue to develop'. Sibling interactions suffered also. One sister who entered in the late 1960s was instructed to tell her eleven-year-old sister who was sending daily letters to stop writing during Lent. Her sister's reaction was abrupt: 'and she never wrote to me again after that'. One enclosed nun admitted: 'My brothers, I've discovered since, think that I just deserted them. And it's taken a very long time to rebuild that relationship.'[107] Unsurprisingly, women religious found it most difficult to miss family events like a sibling's wedding or, more distressingly, the illness or death of a parent. Some religious institutes allowed sisters to visit dying family

---

104 Anonymised interview.
105 ABDA: Poor Clares folder, Canonical Visitation of the convent, dated 30 March 1950.
106 Anonymised interview.
107 Anonymised interview.

members for 'the salvation of a soul, or some other most important reason'.[108]

Other communities appeared less prescriptive about family visits. The house diaries of one enclosed community were replete with the names of family members who were visiting their daughters, sisters, aunts and cousins. One sister who entered the same order as her maternal aunt stated that her parents, who lived locally,

> knew the place well, they had been involved in it, because whenever there was a big celebration where there would be a meal afterwards, my mother waited table. Always she would be there, and her friends, because she would cajole them to do it as well, you see. So my mother was quite involved.[109]

Her relationship with her parents was less inhibited than those recounted above. This same community, in 1948, celebrated one novice's twenty-first birthday with a 'gay party' attended by the family and the community (separated by the grille) and a birthday cake with twenty-one candles.[110]

Both *Sponsa Christi* (1950) and Pope Pius XII's discourse to delegates to the First International Congress of Religious Orders in 1950 at Rome encouraged religious institutes to adapt 'to the changes of the times'.[111] Religious institutes rethought the circumscribing of familial communications. One superior general's New Year's letter of 1957 announced that sisters could leave the convent to visit their family one day each year; by 1964, this leave had been extended to three days. The year before, permission had been given to sisters passing by the house of a family member to visit for fifteen to twenty minutes, but only with advance permission of the superior. By 1972, the British provincial team approved visits to immediate family in case of serious illness, though the sister was required to return home the day after the funeral. If the family member had a sudden illness, the sister was allowed three full days' leave.[112]

The transition towards allowing family visits was complicated by new rules and regulations, as these examples illustrate. One sister recalled:

---

108 [Francis M. Bridgeman], *Abridgment of a Guide for the Religious Called Sisters of Mercy* (London: Robson and Son, 1866), p. 12.

109 Anonymised interview.

110 'Syon Notes', *Poor Souls Friend*, 54:10 (1948), p. 163.

111 As quoted in Sister Mary Laurence, OP, *They Live the Life* (London: Blackfriars Publications 1954), p. 14.

112 SCMM-ENK: 2006, Bernadette Steele, Dolores Heys and Marie Wallbank, 'The History of the Sisters of Charity of Our Lady, Mother of Mercy in Britain and Ireland

'I was told I might go with my mother and she could show me the house where they were living from the outside but I couldn't go inside, you know, that is barmy' [laughs].[113] Another sister from the same congregation recollected 'So at that time we started to go out and we were allowed to go home, but not to have a meal to begin with, and then they gradually said you could have tea or something like that but then it grew.'[114]

After the Second Vatican Council, family visits became more commonplace but the strain of stunted relationships took years to remedy. One sister recollected:

> But we were really cut off and it took a long time for the relationship to grow again, because my parents had sort of got used to my not coming home then and it took a little while to get right, and then of course it was wonderful ... But it was one of the very hardest things about our way of life.[115]

Not all women religious welcomed these changes. One enclosed nun on being given permission in 1969 to visit her octogenarian parents appeared apologetic in explaining to the bishop her reasons for visiting parents she had not seen in seventeen years: 'I don't care to leave the enclosure for my own sake' but there were 'not many who visit them'.[116] One teaching sister recollected her initial opposition to the abolition of this rule of enclosure:

> I was at first very against going 'home' i.e. to my parents' house! I felt very strongly that 'home' was a big gift I had given to God on entering and I did not want to rescind it.

She confessed afterwards

> I began to see how blindly I had accepted the 'package' of entering ... focussed on my gift of self ... What it cost my parents I didn't apprehend ... how inhuman that old system was, and how amazing that my parents accepted it so willingly.[117]

Catholic socialisation and the social norms of religious life that emphasised the 'gift of self' and the separateness of the life of enclosure had taken on sacral dimensions. But post-war modernity gave rise to a

1861 to 1982', p. 68; 2712, Circular dated 22 January 1963 by Mother M. Ignatius [Stirzaker]; 340, Circular dated 7 February 1972 from provincial team.
113   Anonymised interview.
114   Anonymised interview.
115   Anonymised interview.
116   PDA: Syon files, Correspondence 1953–1960 and newsletters 1958–1978, Letter from Sister Veronica to bishop, dated 5 January 1969.
117   SSH ENW: 'RSCJ and 1967', Luirard survey, Remembrance 12.

new concept in direct competition with such ideas. As Pat Thane has argued, new constructions of the family placed it more firmly as the means and the symbol of both personal stability and national wellbeing.[118] In this context, Church thinking about the value of enclosure and the separateness of religious women, so deeply embedded as a characteristic of religious life, became increasingly out of sync with contemporary understandings about family.

Conclusion

In the preface to *She Takes the Veil* (1952) written by Dominican Prior Provincial Hilary J. Carpenter, he writes that the author, Dominican Sister Mary Laurence, had a 'keen appreciation' of the modern world and wrote 'in the language of the outside world of today'.[119] His acceptance of her engagement with the modern world on its own terms, in its own language exemplifies this new relationship with modernity. In accepting the modernity of the world, and their own place in it, women religious addressed the secularity of the world. In 1970, the international report from the Society of the Sacred Heart did not demonise secularisation, but acknowledged its existence and sought to address its influence:

> In the process of secularisation which has already begun and which will continue, new ways of making contact with God (prayer) and living according to the Gospel must be found or created: the same summons, which, coming from God and from men inspired eminent men and women in the past to found new religious congregations, is making itself felt today. It is tirelessly existential and is a challenge to renew religious life.

The Society of the Sacred Heart and other religious institutes began to see themselves as religious in a secularised world.[120] For many active sisters, their movement into a secular world was justified by the life of Jesus of Nazareth. Sacred Heart sister Prue Wilson related that:

118 Pat Thane, 'Family Life and "Normality" in Postwar British Culture', in Richard Bessel and Dirk Schumann (eds), *Life after Death: Approaches to a Cultural and Social History of Europe during the 1940s and 1950s* (Cambridge: Cambridge University Press, 2003), p. 198.
119 Sister Mary Laurence, OP, *She Takes the Veil* (London: Blackfriars Publications, 1952), p. vii.
120 For example, in 1973, 200 sisters (alongside 200 'seculars') attended a 'Convention on Secularization' organised at Roehampton. See SSH ENW: Fenham House Journal, 24 August 1973.

[M]any found it good, expressing the Christian belief that the risen Jesus belongs to this time and this world. Many of us saw more clearly than ever before that the work of the Church we mirror is to be the good news that what is secular waits to be made holy by His presence, and that we Christians are that presence.[121]

Believing that the secular had the potential for being 'made holy', women religious emphasised an incarnational theology, linked to the ministry of Jesus of Nazareth. This is, as we will discuss in the next chapter on ministry, what led some women religious to move out of strictly Catholic environment, convents, schools, hospitals, to ministries that were more engaged with the wider secular world.

For much of its history, the cloister represented a separateness that was purposeful; it mirrored an otherness that was integral to the understandings of religious life and to personal, corporate and ecclesial identities. It bound sisters together as a corporate body, also separating them from their personal history (family and friends) and the people they served. Women who entered religious life in the 1940s and 1950s expected and even valued enclosure for the freedom it offered for a centredness on prayer. Uninvited, the world entered the cloister in myriad ways. Wartime disrupted the patterns of religious life, in some cases changing the tenor of relationships or creating opportunities for interactions. The modernity of mass media arrived with the new recruits to religious life. Women religious moved into the world through changes in governance and the development of professional and technical skills. Becoming part of the world was a response to both religious and secular change. Increased personal mobility reduced some of the strict divisions between the secular and the religious world. Travelling to and through secular spaces of the world offered both a novelty and a source of tension. For many sisters and nuns, it was not a sudden thrust into the world, but a gradual shift, not always welcomed when it disrupted patterns of living and beliefs about the sacred/secular divide. The next chapter introduces other developments and charts further interactions with the world via changing religious ministries, where the local and global were integrated as sisters and nuns began to identify themselves as 'citizens of the world'.

121   Wilson, *My Father Took Me to the Circus*, pp. 68–9.

6

Local and global: changing ministries

Seeing ourselves as citizens of the world helps us to relatavise [*sic*] our own situation, since it is part of a much bigger whole.[1]

Sister M. Philip (née Elizabeth) Rendall's worldview changed sometime in the late 1960s. She began transitioning from her local, teaching-centred ministry to a global ministry ignited by her passion for justice. Born in London in 1924, she attended St Angela's Ursuline Convent School at Forest Gate. She entered the Ursulines, aged eighteen, a few years before the Second World War began. After her novitiate training, she took simple vows and was sent to Queen Mary University of London, where she read medieval history. She took perpetual vows in 1948, and then qualified as a teacher; by 1959 she was head teacher of the Ursuline Convent School in Wimbledon. Then, in 1968, she joined the staff of Christ's College of Education in Liverpool as a lecturer in divinity and was thrust into a Catholic and secular world of radical thinking. This newly established Catholic teacher training college, the first to admit men and women, opened in 1964 and welcomed, questioned and engaged with the documents coming out of the Second Vatican Council.[2] She became acquainted here with a new way to 'be Church' and began the journey that propelled her into a world of social justice; grounded in the local, but influenced by the global. She 'plunged into fresh new experiences' that

---

1   SCMM-ENK, 79, 'Reflections on the Meeting between the General Board and the Provincial Board of the Netherlands, Rome, March 11th–15th 1974'.
2   Bernard Longden, 'Widening Participation in Higher Education', in R. John Elford (ed.), *The Foundation of Hope: Turning Dreams into Reality* (Liverpool: Liverpool University Press, 2003), p. 56. 'Nottingham Loss is Liverpool Gain', *Catholic Herald* (1 December 1961), p. 15. I have been unable to locate the archives of Christ's College and I am grateful to Susan O'Brien, who was employed by its successor, Liverpool Hope University, for explaining its significance in Catholic circles.

encouraged a globalised politicisation: teaching on liberation theology and world development issues; witnessing student demonstrations and debates on race relations. During her twelve years in Liverpool her engagement with justice issues was local, ecumenical and national; she served on the Education Committee of the National Justice and Peace Commission, the Churches' World Development Committee and on the diocesan Justice and Peace Commission.[3] When the decision to withdraw the Ursuline community from Christ's College was made in 1980, she took the opportunity to join a small community of Ursulines located in the town of Shotton, North Wales, where steel closures, unemployment and uncertainty were part of the inhabitants' daily lives. She was ready for this new opportunity, which she wrote 'offered a way forward' and she saw herself meeting 'a desire for ways in which education in its broadest sense could be extended to others embedded in the inner city'. The values of justice and peace coming out of the Second Vatican Council and putting Gospel values at the heart of the mission of the Church were at the centre of her community's mission. Rendall was involved with Pax Christi, the CAFOD campaign 'Just Food', the launch of the deanery Justice and Peace group and the World Food Assembly in Rome.[4] She was also a parish sister, organising the parish newsletter, setting up a parish council and facilitating a group of young wives. She continued to inform herself on global matters. Her correspondence revealed her delight at visits to London to hear political activist and social scientist Susan George talk about *How the Other Half Dies: The Real Reasons for World Hunger* (1976) and hearing Jesuit J. Luis Alegre who worked with peasant groups in Bolivia on rural development.[5]

These activities, in Rendall's words, 'inevitably introduced questions into the fabric of religious life'.[6] After forty years as an Ursuline she decided to leave the congregation; it was a decision that was both painful and freeing. She wrote poignantly: 'Personally, I experience my going as the beginning of a second vocation, grown out of – not rejecting – the first. More and more the gospel imperative challenges me.'[7] Her correspondence suggests that her personal passions were not attuned

3   Pope Paul VI inaugurated the Holy See's Justice and Peace Commission in 1967 'to demonstrate the Holy See's concern for developing nations'. National, deanery and parish Justice and Peace groups were set up afterwards all over the world.
4   CAFOD, the Catholic Agency for Overseas Development, was founded in 1962.
5   Elizabeth Rendall Archives, in private hands (henceforth ERA): Letter from Mary Philip to Sister Ignatius, dated 17 February 1984.
6   ERA: 'Narrative about Shotton community'.
7   ERA: Letter to Sister Bonaventure from Elizabeth Rendall, dated 16 March 1984.

to the common life of her religious congregation. She felt 'A painful sense of being out-of-step with many', although her correspondence also acknowledges some Ursuline support of her journey. In her self-reflexive 'statement of my position: my own act of faith', she identifies within herself the emergence of a 'new age'.[8] She became a consecrated virgin in order to devote herself exclusively to working for justice and peace then spent the next twenty-seven years committed to global social issues.[9] She worked for CAFOD for a short time, grounding her support of liberation theology in her 'commitment to the world, especially the world of the poor'. Her obituaries in the local press celebrated her influence. She joined Peace and Justice groups in East London which supported people unfairly detained without trial.[10] Her passion for the environment came to the fore as a 'Green nun' involved in the Renewing the Earth Campaign, Christian Ecology Link and Operation Noah.[11]

Sister M. Philip Rendall's experience is perhaps not typical, but it is one of many that demonstrate a personal shift in religious ministries, where the local and global were integrated as sisters and nuns began to identify themselves as 'citizens of the world'. This process, of course, was not without personal and community tensions. Rendall's story began with the personal. First, her ministry came from an individual desire of 'being Church' motivated by the teachings of the Second Vatican Council.[12] There was a difficult 'letting go'; she belonged to a congregation whose identity was firmly embedded in education very traditionally defined and her new activities were, for some, beyond the pale. At the time, her social activism 'inevitably introduced questions into the fabric of religious life'. Second, this case study addresses the influence of the world outside the convent on her worldview and activism. Third, though Sister M. Philip's ministry remained firmly in the local, her activism was informed by

---

8   ERA: 'A statement of my position: my own act of faith'.

9   According to Canon Law 604, a consecrated virgin is 'consecrated to God, mystically espoused to Christ and dedicated to the service of the Church, when the diocesan bishop consecrates [her] according to the approved liturgical rite'. She attends mass daily, prays the Divine Office and spends much time in private prayer. She often has specific active ministries.

10   ERA: Rebecca Bird, 'Green Nun Was an Inspiration', press clipping, no date or newspaper.

11   Operation Noah is an ecumenical Christian charity, based in the UK, that campaigns exclusively on global climate change.

12   For more on 'being Church', see Sandra Schneiders, *Finding the Treasure: Locating Catholic Religious Life in a New Ecclesial and Cultural Context* (New York: Paulist Press, 2000), p. 349.

global concerns and global activism. Fourth, her religious motivation imbricated as it was with the ideals of social justice became a form of 'sacralized work'.[13]

This chapter addresses these four points to highlight the ways in which religious ministries diversified, reworking nineteenth-century models of charity linked with salvation to embrace a post-war emphasis on social activism. The histories of religious congregations had traditionally recounted institution-building: orphanages, schools and hospitals were highlighted as tools of the Church, used to propagate teachings and train the faithful. The Catholic Church, as a minority religion within a protestant British state, and as a poor church, growing through immigration, relied on religious institutes to educate the Catholic poor in parish schools and the middle and upper classes in their convent schools. As women's religious institutes were influenced by the social movements of the post-war world they began questioning social structures, gender relations and the dynamics of power and authority. This was not always a linear transition of moving from one form of religious ministry to another. Rather, what will be explored in the sections below are the diverse ways women religious engaged in social activism, transitioning from charity towards social justice by incorporating into their ministries the Gospel imperative centred on the option for the poor and marginalised. The aims of social justice initiatives are to provide social and economic equality to those on the margins of society, often through advocacy of their rights to material goods including housing, employment or medical care, or pressuring for structural reforms that result in social and economic inequalities.[14]

Much of the North American historiography emphasises a major shift in the work of women religious, charting the movement from traditional 'works of mercy' to more progressive social justice.[15] Scholars

13 Lisa Moses Leff, *Sacred Bonds of Solidarity: The Rise of Jewish Internationalism in Nineteenth-Century France* (Stanford, CA: Stanford University Press, 2006).

14 Ian Linden, 'Social Justice in Historical Perspective', in Michael P. Hornsby-Smith (ed.), *Catholics in England 1950–2000: Historical and Sociological Perspectives* (London: Cassell, 1999), p. 140.

15 Jo Ann McNamara, *Sisters in Arms: Catholic Nuns through Two Millennia* (London: Harvard University Press, 1996), pp. 639–41; Amy L. Koehlinger, *The New Nuns: Racial Justice and Religious Reform in the 1960s* (Cambridge, MA: Harvard University Press, 2007); Mary Beth Fraser Connolly, *Women of Faith: The Chicago Sisters of Mercy and the Evolution of a Religious Community* (New York: Fordham University Press, 2014); Rosa Bruno-Jofré, 'The Process of Renewal of the Missionary Oblate Sisters, 1963–1989', in Elizabeth M. Smyth (ed.), *Changing Habits: Women's Religious*

of Dutch women religious have argued a similar reorientation towards work with the poor and marginalised but have suggested Dutch women religious distanced themselves from the charitable ethos and institutional nature of their past work.[16] This chapter suggests a more gentle trajectory in the British context, incorporating both continuity and change from the mid-1970s to the end of the 1980s as religious communities attempted both to maintain current ministries and accommodate the desires of individual sisters and nuns who experimented with new ministries that offered a 'preferential option for the poor'. Susan O'Brien's close, textured study of the Daughters of Charity of St Vincent de Paul notes their formal re-evaluation of ministries in the late 1980s, pointing to a 'degree of continuity in life and mission'. Significant new missions developed in partnership with other agencies and included a sharing of the Vincentian charism with co-workers.[17] Anselm Nye in his history of the English Dominicans also points to continuity and change. The Dominicans continued their apostolate to tertiary education through a new theological training centre but also approved individual ministries with Pax Christi and the Campaign for Nuclear Disarmament.[18] Much of the social justice work done by religious institutes was initially ad hoc; by the late 1980s and 1990s, after a few decades of experimentation, many religious institutes developed more strategic ministerial visions.

Catholics during the long 1960s were actively involved in secular protest movements. In some countries, Catholic activism

played a vital role within the wider cycle of protest that unfolded in and around 1968. Not only did it provide a training ground for activists in the student, labour, women's and other movements, but it also

---

Orders in Canada (Ottawa: Novalis, 2007), pp. 247–73; Carole G. Rogers, Habits of Change: An Oral History of American Nuns (Oxford: Oxford University Press, 2011).

16   Marit Monteiro, Marjet Derks and Annelies van Heijst, 'The Stories the Religious Have Lived by since the 1960's', in R. Ruard Ganzevoort, Maaike de Haardt and Michael Scherer-Rath (eds), Religious Stories We Live by: Narrative Approaches in Theology and Religious Studies (Leiden: Brill, 2014), p. 230. Van Heijst argues that sisters in the 1970s and 1980s distanced themselves from their charitable ethos. Annelies van Heijst, Models of Charitable Care: Catholic Nuns and Children in their Care in Amsterdam, 1852–2002 (Leiden: Brill, 2008), pp. 357–61.

17   Susan O'Brien, Leaving God for God: The Daughters of Charity of St Vincent de Paul in Britain, 1847–2017 (London: Darton, Longman & Todd, 2017), 338–9. The fruits of their strategic thinking can be seen in Noah Luton and the Depaul Trust.

18   Anselm Nye, A Peculiar Kind of Mission: The English Dominican Sisters, 1845–2010 (Leominster: Gracewing, 2011), pp. 263–82.

constituted a redoubtable source of protest and mobilization in its own right.[19]

Gerd Ranier-Horn's research demonstrates that Catholics in Europe were an integrated part of the larger movements, pointing, for example, to the 'hidden Christianity' of some of the leading student radicals. There were also exclusively Catholic movements of associations of radical parish priests and basic ecclesial communities (also called base communities), where ecclesial study and action reflected social concerns or political action.[20] In Britain, Catholic lay activism was less visible. Some have accounted for this by pointing to a Catholic recusant mind-set[21] and the leadership of a conservative and ultramontane episcopal hierarchy that has been described by one historian as 'insular, apolitical or at least politically conformist, highly authoritative, and out of touch with what was transpiring among Catholic theologians'.[22] Despite this, Catholics were active in existing protest movements. Bruce Kent's leadership in the Campaign for Nuclear Disarmament from the 1960s began when he was a young priest.[23] Catholic lawyer Peter Benenson established the campaigning human rights organisation Amnesty International in 1961, incorporating political action with 'bearing witness'.[24] The development work of Catholic Aid for Overseas Development began with the National Board of Catholic Women in 1961 hosting a Family Fast Day for a mother and baby health care scheme in the Caribbean Island of Dominica.[25] Progressive Catholic theologians including Dominicans Laurence Bright

19 Rebecca Clifford and Nigel Townson, 'The Church in Crisis: Catholic Activism and "1968"', *Cultural and Social History*, 8 (2011), 531.
20 Gerd-Rainer Horn, *The Spirit of Vatican II: Western European Progressive Catholicism in the Long Sixties* (Oxford: Oxford University Press, 2015), pp. 61–109, 111–63, 173–4.
21 Harris pointed to the aversion to 'innovation' in regard to liturgical changes in Alana Harris, 'A Fresh Stripping of the Altars? Liturgical Language and the Legacy of the Reformation in England, 1964–1984' in Kathleen Sprows Cummings, Timothy Matovina and Robert A. Orsi (eds), *Catholics in the Vatican II Era: Local Histories of a Global Event* (Cambridge: Cambridge University Press, 2017).
22 Jay P. Corrin, *Catholic Progressives in England after Vatican II* (Notre Dame, IN: University of Notre Dame Press, 2013), p. 19.
23 Eric O. Hanson, *The Catholic Church in World Politics* (Princeton, NJ: Princeton University Press, 1987), pp. 306–8. His leadership of the group in the 1980s and other political activities were seen as controversial and he left the priesthood in 1987. For more on Catholics involved in the Campaign for Nuclear Disarmament see Corrin, *Catholic Progressives*, pp. 187–90.
24 Stephen Hopgood, *Keepers of the Flame: Understanding Amnesty International* (London: Cornell University Press, 2006), pp. 60, 65.
25 http://kidzzone.cafod.org.uk/about-cafod/history-of-cafod/, accessed 30 July 2018.

and Herbert McCabe encouraged a dialogue with Marxism.[26] Though censured by ecclesiastical authorities and the Holy See, they remained influential in their writings on the social implications of the Gospel. Anglicans and other Christians were facing a similar impetus to social action fuelled by new theologies. Hugh McLeod suggests that the drop in ordinations in 1967 may have been related to the call of social action and the practical Christianity that could be found outside the Church. He suggests many privileged 'love thy neighbour' through social welfare work rather than the priesthood.[27]

Influenced by Catholic conservativism, it is perhaps unsurprising that women religious entered new ministries slowly and cautiously. Experiments were initially developed 'from below' by sisters and nuns like Sister M. Philip Rendall. It is these early experiments of the 1970s and 1980s that this chapter primarily addresses. Rather than exploring institutional strategies, this chapter examines individual efforts of women religious. The determination of women religious to stand with the poor and marginalised was intrinsic to experimental ministries and undergirded a humanitarianism that would be political, without being overtly activist or protest-oriented.[28]

Change took place within a particular context, four aspects of which can be singled out as significant. First was a Catholic theological dimension that emanated from the *nouvelle théologie* of the 1930s, a theological, spiritual and pastoral renewal that aimed at making the Catholic faith more relevant to Catholics' lived experience in the modern world through liturgical reforms; an underscoring of Scripture and patristics; emphasis on Christ's humanity rather than divinity; and advancing of ecumenical relations.[29] It is difficult to ascertain whether ordinary Catholics were acquainted with these new theologians, especially given historian Jay Corrin's suggestion that the Second Vatican Council

---

26 Also see Jay Corrin on the '*Slant* movement'. Corrin, *Catholic Progressives*, pp. 216–50.

27 Hugh McLeod, *The Religious Crisis of the 1960s* (Oxford: Oxford University Press, 2007), pp. 84–92. For more on the transition to secular movements see also Sam Brewitt-Taylor, 'From Religion to Revolution: Theologies of Secularisation in the British Student Christian Movement, 1963–1973', *Journal of Ecclesiastical History*, 66 (2015), 792–811.

28 McLeod, *The Religious Crisis of the 1960s*, p. 89; Matthew Hilton, 'Politics is Ordinary: Non-Governmental Organizations and Political Participation in Contemporary Britain', *Twentieth Century British History*, 22 (2011), 230–68.

29 Erik Sengers, '"Although We Are Catholic, We Are Dutch": The Transition of the Dutch Catholic Church from Sect to Church as an Explanation for Its Growth and Decline', *Journal for the Scientific Study of Religion*, 43 (2004), 136–7. Corrin, *Catholic Progressives*, pp. 70, 73–4, 155.

documents were ill-received by the episcopal hierarchy in England and Wales. That said, some of these ideas filtered down to the laity. Alana Harris has demonstrated how a 'newer, social-justice orientated and eschatological spirituality' was being lived by lay Catholics in the 1950s; this was considered more necessary than a 'devout pietism' to 'arm workers against the allure of Marxism'.[30] This lived experience suggests that the influence of the *nouvelle théologie* percolated to at least some of the Catholic faithful.

Second, the Second Vatican Council urged women religious to re-examine religious life and to relocate it from the narrow confines of a Catholic world to a more prominent place in civil society and the global world stage. Three documents were particularly significant. *Gaudium et Spes* (Pastoral Constitution on the Church and the Modern World, 1965) suggested a two-way relationship between the Church and the modern world which linked to a global vision and, for some, a radical egalitarianism.[31] One enclosed nun recalled the potential of *Gaudium et Spes* to change directions, to move away from the religious ideal of *fuga mundi* (flight from the world):

> [B]ut I think there was an awareness that things weren't going to be the same, that actually, especially as it began to develop, once you began to read things like *Gaudium et spes*, you could see that there'd been a whole turnaround of the way we looked at the world, and the world was now God's kingdom, rather [than] the thing to run away from. And in a sense you could see how that could change everything, though I don't think we had any … I don't think we had an unshakeable confidence that it would happen, only that it opened up doors where it could happen.[32]

For this nun, the walls that divided the cloister from the world began metaphorically tumbling down. *Lumen Gentium* (Dogmatic Constitution on the Church, 1964) redefined church, not as the hierarchy and clergy or as leaders and followers but as the 'people of God'; the laity shared

---

30 Corrin, *Catholic Progressives*, p. 155. Alana Harris, *Faith in the Family: A Lived Religious History of English Catholicism, 1945–1982* (Manchester: Manchester University Press, 2013), p. 115.

31 John W. O'Malley, 'Vatican II: Did Anything Happen?', *Theological Studies*, 67 (2006), 12; Lisa L. Ferrari, 'The Vatican as a Transnational Actor' in Paul Christopher Manuel, Lawrence C. Reardon and Clyde Wilcox (eds), *The Catholic Church and the Nation-State: Comparative Perspectives* (Washington, DC: Georgetown University Press, 2006), p. 37.

32 Anonymised interview.

in the 'salvific mission of the church'.[33] Female religious interpreted this
as an impetus to remove barriers between themselves and the people,
especially as they found themselves identified, not with a higher calling,
but as laity. *Perfectae Caritatis* (Adaptation and Renewal of Religious Life,
1965) called for the renewal of religious life. Renewal included, amongst
many things, ministerial renewal. Religious communities were instructed
'to maintain and fulfil the ministries proper to them' and

> after considering the needs of the Universal Church and individual
> dioceses, they should adapt them to the requirements of time and place,
> employing appropriate and even new programs and abandoning those
> works which today are less relevant to the spirit and authentic nature of
> the community. The missionary spirit must under all circumstances be
> preserved in religious communities.[34]

The third factor which straddled the religious and the secular worlds
was the emergence of liberation theology.[35] The Second Conference of
Latin American Bishops (CELAM) held in Medellín, Colombia in 1968,
and the later one in Puebla, Mexico in 1979, articulated a particular
response to poverty and oppression through the 'preferential option
for the poor'. Base communities were one manifestation of liberation
theology: they not only educated the poor, but also empowered them
as agents by encouraging them to challenge the political and economic
structures that created their poverty.[36] The social teachings of the Catholic
Church came to the fore at the 1971 Synod of Bishops, where the theme
'Justice in the World' emphasised the Gospel imperative: 'Action on
behalf of justice and participation in the transformation of the world fully
appear to us as a constitutive dimension of the preaching of the Gospel.'[37]

---

33   *Lumen Gentium*, §33.
34   *Perfectae Caritatis*, §20.
35   Liberation theology was a radical movement that emerged in Latin America in the
      1960s as a reaction to the poverty and oppression of the poor. Timothy Gorringe,
      'Liberation Theology', in Akira Iriye and Pierre-Yves Saunier (eds), *Palgrave Dictionary
      of Transnational History* (Basingstoke: Palgrave Macmillan, 2009), pp. 588–9.
36   The bishops at this meeting decided that the greatest challenge in Latin America was not
      one of faith, but one of poverty. The emphasis on social justice derived in part from the
      work of Peruvian Dominican theologian and diocesan priest Gustavo Gutiérrez, who
      published *A Theology of Liberation* (1973). By the 1980s, liberation theology was out of
      favour, and blamed for violence and revolution in Latin America. Timothy G. McCarthy,
      The Catholic Tradition: Before and After Vatican II 1878–1993 (Chicago: Loyola
      University Press, 1994), pp. 253–9; Horn, *The Spirit of Vatican II*, pp. 111–24.
37   This third international ecclesiastic synod was attended by Cardinal John Carmel
      Heenan of Westminster and Bishop Michael Bowen of Arundel and Brighton as
      representatives of the hierarchy of England and Wales. Kevin Muir, 'Open Synod

This liberation language becomes significant to the development of Catholic missions from the 1960s.

And the fourth context was the secular world: Church teachings appeared congruent with some of the ideologies that informed the 1960s social movements. The 1960s were not exclusively about personal freedoms or challenging authorities; they also engaged and acted on questions of social and economic justice for those living with socially constructed inequities: the poor, the homeless, the aged, the physically or cognitively impaired, the imprisoned and other marginalised persons.[38] Secular movements also de-emphasised charity to address social problems that were local, such as inadequate housing for single women, unliveable rates of pay, limited job opportunities, occupationally compromised health, limits to educational opportunities and industrial conditions, and global: ecological matters, anti-war movements and civil rights.

Activism 'from below'

Discussions about leaving institutional ministries to take on smaller new ministries pushed many sisters out of their comfort zone. At the 1969 three-day retreat for religious, fifty-two sisters from twelve congregations met at the Leeds Diocesan Pastoral and Ecumenical Centre and wrangled about the 'value of change' and the alterations to the common life. They paid particular attention to experiments in religious ministries, including sisters working in small groups addressing an assortment of social needs. In discussing the future of religious life, some suggested the future included a transition from large institutions to smaller works where religious met local needs with sisters trained in parish visiting, social work and nursing, underpinned with a knowledge of theology and catechetics. The nod to catechetics, the theology of religious instruction, reflects the continued significance of salvation. But the 'possibility' of fewer sisters, 'quality not quantity', and a larger range of apostolic works was a difficult change to absorb.[39] One attendee, after hearing a La Sagesse

Ahead', *Catholic Herald* (23 July 1971), p. 4. The synod report can be found at: www1.villanova.edu/content/dam/villanova/mission/JusticeIntheWorld1971.pdf, accessed 24 March 2019.

38 Arthur Marwick, 'The Cultural Revolution of the Long Sixties: Voices of Reaction, Protest, and Permeation', *International History Review*, 27 (2005), 791.

39 SCMM-ENK: 352, Notes of the 15–22 April [1969] Retreat for Religious held at the Leeds Diocesan Pastoral and Ecumenical Centre, Wood Hall Wetherby.

sister lecture on her experience of living in a small community, remarked that 'this was received by her audience with a great deal of protest and real opposition'. She and the five sisters of her community left the retreat feeling 'very uncertain and confused'.[40]

The traditional emphasis of the Church on charity was being challenged by an understanding of social justice that pushed for structural change. In the 1970s, the Conference of Major Religious Superiors of England and Wales commissioned the Liverpool Institute of Socio-Religious Studies at Christ's College (which Sister M. Philip joined in 1968) to write a piece on the Church and Social Work. The foreword by the Reverend Michael Gaine, its director, underscored that charity was not enough. Church critics demanded that:

> [T]he Church should strive actively to abolish suffering, not simply to make it more bearable. They charge that the Church connives in the continuation of injustice and inequality, by helping the victims to cope with the consequences of our imperfect society. Charity may not only dull the resentment of the victims of an unjust system, but it may also blunt the consciences of those church members with power and wealth.

The report's author, social scientist Una Cormack, insisted that the Church should move into the field of social work and that social reform was 'a matter of social justice, a task for formal social organisation which the Church at its peril has frequently neglected'.[41]

Individual sisters moved by the Gospel imperative centred on the option for the poor and marginalised often led the way to ministerial change with their requests to be moved out of institutional ministries. They sought permission to experiment, often interpreting their founder's spirit and aims more widely than was comfortable for their leadership. Teaching congregations with convent schools faced additional challenges. New ministries had no means of ensuring the conformity to the rules and regulations of religious life; they proposed an uncomfortable unknown. Institutional ministries centred on educational establishments could easily integrate work life and prayer life. Many sisters thrived on a corporate identity, where a community lived and worked together. There was a regularity and routine to religious life that offered a known and explicit way of being a religious. Some sisters were anxious to take on

---

40 SCMM-ENK: 373, Letter from Anne-Marie Newsham to Thérèse Mary [Barnett], dated 18 October 1969.

41 Una Cormack, *The Church and Social Work* (Liverpool: Liverpool Institute of Socio-Religious Studies [for] the Conference of Major Religious Superiors of England and Wales, 1977), p. 7.

board the challenge of news ministries. One teaching sister recalled a meeting in the 1970s:

> [A]ll of us who were not yet finally professed but young and a certain age and the question was 'Where do you see yourselves in five years' time?' And when we shared that there wasn't anyone in the room who saw themselves in a [school]. So it was at that time, that movement really away from that kind of privileged education and ... more to, how do we go out and share in the lives of the people and find God there.[42]

This desire to share 'in the lives of the people' was grounded in incarnational theology, linked to a Gospel imperative that saw Jesus of Nazareth's ministry on earth among the poor and marginalised as a ministry to emulate.

Not everyone recalled wanting to leave established institutional ministries and there were differing definitions of the 'poor'. Another sister from a teaching congregation recollected:

> Sisters coming out of school saying they didn't want to do this work any more, why should they teach the elite of the land. Now, that to me, I have never had a problem because they're all children, in my sight, whether they're rich or poor. They're poor in different ways. They're poor because they have no, you know, they may come from mixed homes, broken homes.[43]

In some congregations, these differing positions were politicised. One group of sisters meeting before a provincial chapter in 1972 responded to the question 'How do you see religious life within the society in which the sisters are living?' by identifying two factions within their congregation:

> We see it in two distinct divisions: – One group doing their utmost to implement renewal and the other group either going backwards or stationary – this situation is not helped by having an hierarchy who are ultra conservative and don't help to co-ordinate any renewal movement whatsoever.[44]

The conservative influence of the ecclesiastical hierarchy was spoken of with disparagement. The explicit judgement in this response

---

42 Anonymised interview.
43 Anonymised interview.
44 SCMM-ENK: 341, Letter from Sister Marie Wallbank to Sister Thérèse Mary [Barnett], dated 28 June 1972. This is a reply to a letter dated 10 March 1972.

identified renewal as 'progress' and any disagreement as 'backwards' and characterised the political and contentious debates that were occurring in many communities in the 1970s and 1980s.

Some sisters argued that there was room for continuity as well as change in congregation ministries. One Sacred Heart Sister writing in 1969 reflected that both those who wished to experiment and those who wanted to remain teaching in large institutions could be accommodated. She advised:

> I don't suppose for a moment that anyone here wants to deny that the vocation of the Society as a whole, is the education of youth. It was in the context of our fourth vow concerning the education of youth that all of us made our religious profession. As a result of an increased social awareness there may be individual vocations turning towards social work among the deprived, but unless the Society has been on the wrong track since the year 1800, I cannot imagine that the Society as a whole is under any obligation to change its direction, away from Education properly so-called … We must consider whether we ought to engage more closely and more deliberately with the underprivileged world than we have done in the past.[45]

The implications of this hybrid alternative were not explored in this document, but its implementation was becoming less likely given an ageing population, a decline in postulants and the departures of professed sisters.[46] Each congregation's journey towards new ministries was different, but in the 1970s and 1980s the move out of institutional work in schools and hospitals was dictated far more by the decline in numbers of religious than the actual desire of the minority of sisters who were attracted to new ministries.[47]

---

45   SSH ENW: 1970 Provincial Chapter I, Batch 2, Sister J. Scott 'Education, Our Apostolate', December 1969, p. 1.

46   To be discussed in more detail in the Conclusion.

47   Susan O'Brien, 'Religious Life for Women', in V. Alan McClelland and Michael Hodgetts (eds), *From without the Flaminian Gate: 150 Years of Roman Catholicism in England and Wales, 1850–2000* (London: Darton, Longman & Todd, 1999), pp. 108–41; Nye, *A Peculiar Kind of Mission*, pp. 268–79. James Sweeney suggests a similar trajectory for the Passionists, whose numerical decline was 'statistically inevitable' in 1960 and who established the 'option of the poor' as their congregation's focus in 1988. James Sweeney, *The New Religious Order: A Study of the Passionists in Britain and Ireland, 1945–1990 and the Option for the Poor* (London: Bellew, 1994), pp. 8, 54–7.

Engaging with the secular world

William Beveridge's post-war manifesto with its tackling of the five 'giant' problems (Want, Ignorance, Disease, Squalor and Idleness) through state welfare provision was the antidote to what was considered by some as 'yesterday's solution' to poverty: patronising and ineffective charitable provision.[48] Despite lofty aims to eradicate poverty, it was 'rediscovered' and the voluntary sector was reinvigorated by a social and cultural world that valued protest, participation and structural change.[49] From the 1950s, new organisations joined the voluntary sector: campaigning bodies whose focus was to critique and improve public policies, entities that aided constituents navigating the statutory sector, groups supporting those overlooked by government services and overseas development organisations. Older philanthropies rethought their processes and objectives.[50] The informal sector saw a resurgence of self-help and community activity.[51] Conservative government (1979–1990) cuts to welfare programmes also bolstered the activities of the voluntary sector. The call for 'Active Citizenship' encouraged volunteers to make up for the shortfall in social services. By the 1980s, some constituents of the voluntary sector were partnering with state and local authorities for funding.[52]

Just as the voluntary sector was altered by a new post-war social world, women religious also engaged with or became a part of this

48   For discussions of the negative reputation of charity see Barry Knight, *Voluntary Action* (London: CENTRIS, 1993), p. 22. Interestingly, Beveridge was less chary of charity. He saw the state providing a national minimum which left room for 'supplementary' provision by what he considered a more socially conscious voluntary sector. William Beveridge, *Voluntary Action: A Report on Methods of Social Advance* (London: George Allen & Unwin, 1948), pp. 7–10.

49   Nicholas Deakin, 'The Perils of Partnership: The Voluntary Sector and the State, 1945–1992', in Justin Davis Smith, Colin Rochester and Rodney Hedley (eds), *An Introduction to the Voluntary Sector* (London: Routledge, 1995), pp. 49–50; Rodney Lowe, *The Welfare State in Britain since 1945* (Houndmills: Macmillan, 1998), p. 148; Geoffrey Finlayson, *Citizen, State, and Social Welfare in Britain 1830–1990* (Oxford: Clarendon Press, 1994), p. 313.

50   Marilyn Taylor, 'Voluntary Action and the State', in David Gladstone (ed.), *British Social Welfare: Past, present and future* (London: UCL Press, 1995), pp. 222–3.

51   Maria Brenton, *The Voluntary Sector in British Social Services* (London: Longman, 1985), pp. 36–9; The language of 'sectors' had become important to identify welfare provision from four sectors: the public sector (governmental agencies), the private sector (commercial suppliers), the voluntary sector and the informal sector (mutual aid).

52   F. K. Prochaska, *Philanthropy and the Hospitals of London: The King's Fund, 1897–1990* (Oxford: Clarendon Press, 1992); Taylor, 'Voluntary Action and the State', pp. 216–18.

revivified voluntary sector. New ministries in the 1970s and 1980s took many forms – individual ministries, parish communities, inserted communities and international missions. Some communities continued in traditional institutional ministries interpreting the 'signs of the times' by making adjustments to address justice and peace issues. In what follows, one case study examines how one community integrated the understanding of justice into their school curriculum; another examines how one institutional ministry, Providence Row, was rethought and integrated into the voluntary sector. In the 1970s and 1980s, new ministries and old were influenced by global issues but often remained embedded in the local environment. The final example demonstrates how international missions took on the mantle of liberation theology. Both continuity and change were threaded into these ministerial shifts, and convent discussions reflected both uncertainty and enthusiasm.

Case study: individual ministries

The language of the margins was used frequently in the recollections of individual sisters and in convent documents. Sisters often found themselves torn between their responsibilities to their congregation and what they saw as a call to work with those on the margins of society. One sister recalled how in the 1980s she told the leader of her congregation she wanted to 'go out into the margins'

> I realised that I could no longer honestly teach middle-class children in a middle-class environment and that I needed to really go out into the margins for a bit. And when I put this to [deleted] she wasn't too thrilled with the idea, because I'd got quite a responsible position in the school and was quite key there, so she said go back there. And actually that was a very, very demanding two years, because I felt with all my being that actually I didn't need to be there, but [in] our congregation, obedience is a key element of it and it was a critical time for me, because I've got a very strong will and plenty of ideas of my own and even I could see that actually to go back there and give my all and to trust that what was needed would happen was a necessary state of affairs.[53]

Her obedience was rewarded. After two years, she was given *carte blanche* to look for a new ministry. Her choice of working in the voluntary sector, outside a Catholic environment, was radical for her congregation.

53 Anonymised interview. City Roads was a residential detox, crisis intervention and stabilisation service in London opened in 1969. It now operates as Cranstoun.

Influenced by the plight of homeless youth, she joined Centrepoint, a charity begun in the 1970s by the self-styled community theologian the Reverend Ken Leech, an Anglican who married prayer with political action. By the 1980s, Centrepoint was a thoroughly secular organisation. After a difficult few months where she seriously questioned having left a busy, influential life of 'doing' for a role of simply listening, she found her feet. She described her experience as 'transformative':

> I learnt so much from them ... I did notice that people were sidling along to talk about fairly serious things under the cover of whatever we were doing, going to the cinema or whatever. ... And what was more interesting was often they would talk about their own faith, which usually was, I mean very often appalling negative experiences of schools or nuns or priests, not necessarily sexual, but of repression, of feeling not understood or they were often difficult children so they'd not felt accepted. But so often they wanted to talk, not necessarily about faith specifically, not about God, but about values, about what they were doing.[54]

She experienced a relationship of exchange: of giving and receiving. Her response was not one of preaching, but of presence and a listening ear.[55] She obtained an understanding of the concerns of those on the margins of society. She received 'practical' help also. She recalled the 'extraordinary kindness of these two blokes who were genuinely worried about my welfare'. Having explained her vow of poverty to these two young men, they insisted on teaching her how to shoplift. She smiled at me as she explained: 'And they showed me the coat, both of them had coats made with special pockets inside, and they told me all the techniques of shoplifting.'[56]

Individual ministries varied, and could be a source of tension within the convent. Some were more overtly political: Sister Catherine worked with refugees.[57] Others were linked with those marginalised by disability: Sister Patricia took a post as charge nurse in a 'centre for the handicapped'. Others were more wedded to Catholic teaching, such as Sister Eileen's catechetical ministry to the deaf and hard of hearing.[58] The congregation these three sisters belonged to, the Sisters of Charity of Our

54 Anonymised interview.
55 On the significance of presence see Catherine Sexton, 'Theologies of Ministry among Older Roman Catholic Sisters in the UK', unpublished PhD dissertation, Anglia Ruskin University, 2018.
56 Anonymised interview.
57 SCMM-Tilburg: SCMM 007 interviewed by Annemiek van der Veen (2003).
58 SCMM-ENK: 340, Circular to 'Dear Sisters' from Sister Marie 4, dated 6 July 1982

Lady, Mother of Mercy, welcomed sisters being 'inserted into works run by the State or other responsible bodies in order that their influence may be more widely felt.'[59] Writing in 1964, the provincial superior noted: 'Our approach of apostolate should be directed to the outside world even towards the working together with other groups and organisations such as Amnesty International, Cafod, etc.; these opportunities were not there in the past.'[60]

Though these sisters were supported by their congregation leadership, some sisters in their community questioned these ministries: 'Our sisters seem to be functioning as unpaid district nurses and home helps ... but isn't this the role of local authorities?'[61] These tensions did not disappear, and a decade later the British provincial leadership explained:

> Many sisters cannot understand why some sisters have sought work outside the existing works of the Province, but if we are to allow sisters to develop their own potential then we have to allow them the means of doing so. The world is evolving continuously and people are advancing into an ever increasing technological age and if we are to serve the needs of the society in which we live, then we ourselves must be educated and prepared in a proper manner to meet these challenges in a world which God has created. If sisters are willing to take risks and branch out into other fields of apostolic labour, then we must grant them this and give them our fullest support.[62]

Her response suggests that both the needs of society and self-realisation of the individual were important linking to Catholic teaching on human flourishing.[63]

Individual ministries were not necessarily new to religious institutes, but they became more commonplace from the 1960s.[64] For many female religious these were political acts, linking their faith with a 'preferential option for the poor', suggesting that the current socio-economic structures were not meeting basic human needs. In supporting those on the margins, they attempted to ameliorate injustices

---

59 SCMM-ENK: 340, Letter from Sister Thérèse Mary [Barnett] to Sisters of the English Province, dated 11 Jan 1977.

60 SCMM-ENK: 2782, Letter from Mother Ignatius [Stirzaker] to Mother Agnes, dated 15 January 1964

61 SCMM-ENK: 1273, 'Report of the Provincial Chapter 1966', Paper 12: Sister Michael Leeming, social work, p. 39.

62 SCMM-ENK: 332, 'Provincial Team Report, December 1971 to March 1976'.

63 Sexton argues the significance of this in her study. Sexton, 'Theologies of Ministry', p. 175.

64 Nye, *A Peculiar Kind of Mission*, pp. 225–7, 309.

faced by individuals by accompanying those on the margins navigating government bureaucracy. In working with global organisations such as Amnesty International or groups that supported refugees they were aligning themselves with entities with political aims of structural change. On a personal level, women religious were addressing their own self-realisation by participating in social movements that engaged with those marginalised by society.

Case study: parish sisters

The introduction of small communities discussed in Chapters 3 and 4 was not only related to governance and relationship; it was also a response to sisters' desire to connect more personally with the 'people of God', sharing the everyday lives and worries of those on the margins. Small communities, like Sister M. Philip's Shotton community, were designated as parish communities and linked to the parish, often in areas of high unemployment or impoverishment and were typically invited by its priest, who requested their support. There is a long, disregarded history of women religious as parish sisters. Some religious institutes such as the Daughters of Charity of St Vincent de Paul were well known for their parish visiting from their arrival in Salford in 1847 into the 1970s; they built 'strong networks, being known across family generations and by all parts of the community'. O'Brien notes that their 'Evangelisation and sacramental intervention sat comfortably with the provision of practical care and assistance'.[65]

The role of parish sister was revitalised in the 1970s. One sister writing in 1973 identified it as a new 'trend': 'Yes the trend here, with regard to the Religious, is to take a more active part in Parish work, and Sisters must recognise their membership in the People of God. As yet, all these new ideas are at an experimental stage.'[66] Parish sisters in small communities had varied responsibilities and the latitude to react to the needs of the parish. In one small community in Flint, sisters catechised and organised parish RCIA programmes, rosary groups and

---

65   O'Brien, *Leaving God for God*, p. 195. Many congregations had a long history of visiting Catholic homes as well as workhouses, hospitals and infirmaries. For example, Edna Hamer, *Elizabeth Prout, 1820–1864: A Religious Life for Industrial England* (Oxford: Gracewing, 1994), p. 71.

66   SCMM-ENK: 374, Letter from Margaret to Sister Thérèse Mary [Barnett], dated 12 March 1973.

play schools.[67] Many organised justice and peace groups and developed lay participation in Church ministries. Sisters organised outreach to the 'unchurched' or 'partly churched'; one parish community held services in a working-men's clubroom open to those not comfortable in a Catholic church. Ecumenical interactions were also significant. In one community pastoral concerns were shared with female Anglican deacons and a Methodist woman minister at regular lunch meetings.[68]

Parish sisters who spent most of their lives in large congregation ministries found the role life-changing. One sister who became a parish sister in 1971 recalled:

> It was a very, you know, it was transforming, it changed us all really. We were all suddenly in a different situation … What I mean to say was, you know, local people would just call in. We just weren't used to it, it was totally … we were no longer in an institution and that was quite something.[69]

She was a long way from the semi-cloistered religious life where religious were emotionally and physically distant from those they ministered to. Another sister remarked: 'And so really it's a listening process here, people come with their stories and their worries and some come to pray with us in the chapel.'[70] A third sister described her own fulfilment in the personal interaction with parishioners.

> All in all, our community was open to the parish, and the parish was open to us. For me, it was the fulfilment of a vision of what religious life might be, with no separation between 'life' and mission – but also with full respect for each member's personal space.[71]

Convent spaces were no longer separate and sacrosanct. These were reciprocal relationships, where women religious received as well as gave support.

These parish communities were also a form of inserted communities, participating in the work of the Catholic parish, but also concerned with the lives of their neighbours. Sisters visited and worked in day centres

---

67 Rite of Christian Initiation of Adults (RCIA) is a process where prospective converts are introduced to aspects of Catholic beliefs and practices.
68 Sister Patricia Harriss, 'Looking Back on my Religious Life' (2014; in Sister Patricia's possession). A history of the post-war ecumenical work of women religious needs to be written.
69 Anonymised interview.
70 Anonymised interview.
71 Harriss, 'Looking Back'.

for the elderly and women's refuges.[72] They attended to marginalised groups like drug addicts, alcoholics, travellers, the unemployed, young people and single parents, setting up support groups and liaising with voluntary and statutory agencies to make sure their needs were met. One sister explained: 'Lots of people just need to be referred, if they're younger and they've had family problems they just need to be referred to somewhere, you know, to help them. And I know lots of Sisters help with filling forms and various things like that.'[73] This type of advocacy work addressed inequalities by ensuring that the demands of the excluded and marginalised were heard by those in government distributing welfare.

Some sisters questioned whether parish involvement was really work for those on the margins, arguing the role of the parish sister was 'obscure'. Parish sisters who 'run the parish' were criticised. One sister remarked: 'We had one of the old nuns did everything all in the church; flowers, funerals, you name it. And we fought it and fought it that we should separate ourselves, we're not the parish.' The parish priest, she asserted, 'shines in his own glory for everything, because everything is done for him.'[74] Even parish sisters were not beyond critique.

Case study: Providence Row

Cathy Come Home, Ken Loach's BBC documentary of a young woman and her two children's journey to homelessness, provoked widespread outrage when it was aired in 1966. Its portrayal of 1960s London was a far cry from the hedonistic headlines of swinging London. Housing charities Shelter (1966), Crisis (1967) and St Mungo Community Housing Association (1969) started out in the aftermath of the uproar that *Cathy Come Home* elicited. Homelessness was not news to the Sisters of Mercy. They had been running Providence Row, the small Catholic night refuge opened by Father Daniel Gilbert, since 1860. Shocked by the destitution he witnessed on the streets of the East End of London, he fundraised to build the purpose-built premises on Crispin Street that provided beds for 200 men and women. The Sisters of Mercy, as was common in the nineteenth century, provided lodging and meals; taught practical skills such as sewing and reading; and prepared resident Catholics for the sacraments.[75]

---

72   SCMM-ENK, 342, 'Report of the visit to Our Lady's Convent, Flint', 1–4 March 1987.
73   Anonymised interview.
74   Anonymised interview.
75   [Mary Teresa Austin Carroll], *Leaves from the Annals of the Sisters of Mercy* (New York: Catholic Publication Society Company, 1883), vol. 2, p. 296.

They were a vital component of the nineteenth-century philanthropic marketplace. Over the years, Providence Row continued to develop to meet expanding needs. By 1912, the complex included accommodations for 262 occupants, as well as a training home for twenty-four servants, a hostel for thirty young women, a laundry and a soup kitchen. In the 1950s, the Sisters added a domestic training schools for girls and hostels for 'business girls', many of whom were part of the great wave of Irish economic migrants.

Despite the vast array of services offered by the welfare state, the Sisters saw no abatement in the need for Providence Row's services. They were becoming acutely aware of how few public services met the needs of homeless families. One former child resident recalled the day in 1958 when her mother, fleeing an abusive husband, took her and her three siblings to London. They arrived at Victoria station with no place to go, and travelled across London on that long day, searching for family accommodation in convents and churches, going from 'pillar to post', until they were directed to Providence Row. Once there, Vicky Moses, then ten years old, recalled 'we were safe'. She recounted the plain but healthy food and the basic but clean dormitory where she, her mother and her three siblings resided for several months with other homeless women.[76] A decade later, the Sisters of Mercy regularly provided housing for homeless families. They turned Gilbert House into eight flats where families could stay together.[77] In 1972, when the adjacent St Joseph's School closed, it also became flats for families. Services by the 1980s had expanded to provide not only beds and meals but drop-in-centres, medical care, counselling, rehabilitation and referral services. Providence Row provided immediate, short-term care alongside long-term assistance addressing the root cause of an individual's homelessness. As the number of sisters declined, new strategies and collaborations were necessary. In the 1980s, Providence Row Night Refuge and Home had gained a sister organisation, Providence Row Housing Association, which addressed provision of housing management.[78] Sisters of Mercy received professional training and worked side by side with employees,

---

76   Bishopsgate Institute: Bishopsgate Voices, Vicky Moses interviewed by Lynda Finn on 21 September 2012. http://spitalfieldslife.com/2012/06/26/the-return-of-vicky-moses/, accessed 24 March 2019. I am grateful to Mica Schloesser for discussing her postgraduate research on Providence Row with me.

77   RSM Union: GB1858/10/200/6/3, Report of the Providence (Row) Night Refuge and Home for 1964, p. 3.

78   Bishopsgate Institute, *Providence Row Annual Review 1991/2*, p. 8.

volunteer workers and eventually professional management. Expansion was funded from benefactions and traditional fundraising efforts alongside partnerships with the charity and housing association and local government funding.[79] This model, of religious and lay expertise and collaborations with local and state funders, became the prototype for other Mercy Centres.[80] Annual reports chart the evolution of the shifting understanding of homelessness. Sister Margaret Mary Kennedy wrote to Providence Row supporters: 'The homeless people who come to Crispin Street, and who will come to Gunthorpe Street, are not begging for charity. They are claiming their rights.'[81] Providence Row furthered social justice aims by ensuring the rights to state social welfare such as housing or medical care were obtained by those in need.

Case study: schools

In 1978, the Canonesses of the Holy Sepulchre who ran New Hall School, an independent school for girls in Chelmsford since 1799, initiated with lay staff and parents, a voluntary service programme which encouraged student awareness and activism on local and global justice and peace issues.[82] They were part of broader developments in student volunteering, which by the 1970s was an increasingly popular form of social action.[83] By the 1980s, voluntary service was a requirement for Year 9 (age thirteen) New Hall students.[84] They provided companionship to those in their local community marginalised by age, illness, poverty and impairment. They

---

79 The last two Sisters of Mercy employed at Providence Row left in 1983 and Providence Row transitioned from a charity to a housing association. The Sisters of Mercy remain involved with Providence Row and one sits on the board of trustees. See 'Nuns Pull Out of Providence Row Hostel', *Catholic Herald* (12 August 1983), p. 1. I am grateful to trustee Dan Regan, who kindly agreed to be interviewed on Providence Row.

80 For example, Bodmin Convent in Cornwall supported people living with HIV/Aids in Bethany Centre (1988–1993) and St Catherine's Mercy Centre for the homeless in Edinburgh opened in 1992 (https://mercycentre.org.uk/the-homeless-project, accessed 14 July 2019).

81 Bishopsgate Institute, *Providence Row Annual Review 1991/2*, p. 5.

82 *History of the New Hall Community of the Canonesses Regular of the Holy Sepulchre* (Roehampton: Manresa Press, 1899), p. viii.

83 Georgina Brewis, *A Social History of Student Volunteering: Britain and Beyond, 1880–1980* (New York: Palgrave Macmillan, 2014), pp. 186–8, 199. Brewis demonstrates that 'the educative function of voluntary action for students has often been seen as more important than its impacts on communities or causes'.

84 This later became an option for all students attending the upper school and 90 per cent opted for voluntary service.

played games, served and shared meals and exchanged life experiences. Students developed and participated in fundraising campaigns to meet local needs. They could also join a Justice and Peace group that fostered awareness of social justice issues through education, prayer and action. One sister remembered:

> [I]t was being involved, it was really making them understand what issues were. There was a fast day every Friday and money was collected for South Africa. When there was a particular need, whether it was political, humanitarian, things would happen immediately, there'd be a prayer vigil and then there'd be: what are we going to do? how are we going to support this?

The 'fast day'[85] was not only related to penitence but created an awareness of the physical presence of hunger, building solidarity with those who fasted involuntarily. It was a sacrifice complementing the work for justice by a sharing of resources: consuming less so that others could consume more. Justice and peace issues were also added into the school curriculum. This Canoness recalled writing a curriculum that combined religious education (RE) and general studies

> So I know when I started there I did a whole thing on South Africa, but it was linked in with the RE programme as well, so we took issues and the school prioritised that as something that they wanted the students to go out with and a social/political awareness.[86]

Another Canoness recalled: 'we were working with a school in South Africa, we had CAFOD fast days once a week to get money for this school. So we really had an outward dimension, our outward dimension that filtered through into the life of the school.'[87] Students were expected to engage with the social, cultural, economic and political issues related to current events. Civic responsibility and influencing lawmakers at Westminster was also part of the politics of social justice:

> I remember once, I can't remember what issue it was, but it was one where you petitioned Parliament about something, and I was one of the people that were getting the girls going to petition, and they rang

85   In Catholic teaching, fasting is the reduction of one's intake of food, while abstinence refers to refraining from meat. The apostolic constitution *Paenitemini* (On Fast and Penitence, 1966) by Pope Paul VI recognised the continued important of penance as 'a religious, personal act which has as its aim love and surrender to God' but suggested the penitence of fasting and abstinence could be replaced by prayer and works of charity.

86   Anonymised interview.

87   Anonymised interview.

up from Downing Street and said, please stop. [laughs] It's just wasting our time, we're getting so many hundreds of letters from your school.[88]

These issues were not isolated in the school, the entire community, even those not involved with teaching at New Hall School, became involved: 'So for instance, if the school were having really good speakers, then all of that would overlap with what we were doing in the community.'[89]

The Canonesses sought to inform their students' understanding of local and global inequalities through the voluntary service programme. Students interacted with those marginalised in society in order to counteract misinformation and humanise living with stigma and discrimination. They were taught to organise, to raise funds and to engage with powerful decision-makers as active and informed citizens.[90] The Canonesses not only encouraged 'good works' but examined with students the wider structural issues of poverty. Catholic social teachings were integrated into the student experience and embedded into the curriculum so that the values of social justice would become rooted in the daily lives of students.

Case study: inserted community

One Canoness commenting on voluntary service and the measured rate of change in her community offered: 'So it was responding, I think that's what the community have always been very good at, is actually responding to change, taking their time, but being ready for the next thing'. She recollected another proposal brought to the community: 'saying we actually need to have some experience of a poorer area and let's try looking at that'. At the time, the suggestion was too controversial: 'I think that probably, I hadn't realised how scary that would be for people, and so I put it back in my drawer.'[91] Over the next two decades, the Canonesses discussed off and on creating a new type of community. Sister Magdalen John, in her eighties, recounted (perhaps wearily) discussions of the future: 'we talk and we talk and we talk and we talk ...'[92] By the noughties,

---

88 Anonymised interview.
89 Anonymised interview.
90 Peter Gatrell, *Free World? The Campaign to Save the World's Refugees, 1956–1963* (Cambridge: Cambridge University Press, 2011), p. 42. Throughout his monograph, Gatrell discusses how charitable work 'would enable volunteers to become socially active in ways that prepared them for active citizenship'.
91 Anonymised interview.
92 DUL CHS: CD, *New Hall Voices* (Sound Archive).

talk became action. As a community, they agreed to transition New Hall School into lay hands and create several small community houses 'inserted' in deprived areas. In Leyton, East London, two members of the community cooperated in running a drop-in centre for asylum seekers.[93] In Chelmsford, four Canonesses moved into a housing estate, offering a range of services for the local community and parish:

> We run something for the elderly, we run a couple of homework clubs, a toddler group, cookery, a fun week in the summer, cooking for children in the holidays and … a variety of things with lots of volunteers, many of whom are connections from our New Hall days who have … stayed in contact. In our minds we're a church on the street. We belong to the parish church and we participate in things, but the parish church doesn't touch the estate. I mean the majority of the people on the estate wouldn't touch the church either. But we feel we … bring the church to the estate, we don't talk church unless people indicate to us that they want to talk church, but we do – we hope – live and behave in a way that speaks of the gospel and Christianity. And I think people recognise that when we've known them, sometimes ask questions.[94]

This is both a new ministry and an old one. It contains elements of traditional parish work, but also includes community-building and a wider outreach beyond the Catholic community. Another Canoness reflected on her own experience of ministry:

> [T]here's been a huge freedom … I work with the homeless, I work with some small children, I do stuff on the streets, things I could never, never have done while I was at New Hall. … the Gospel is actually crying out for people to do things for those on the margins and the only way you're going to do things for those on the margins is to actually live a bit on the margins.

The significance of the ministerial work of the Canonesses was their focus on the marginalised. Sometimes Canonesses worked together in ministries, at other times they worked individually. Even those with individual ministries working sometimes in insalubrious places and at insalubrious times remain connected to their community. One Canoness remarked:

> And I do those things, most of those things on my own, but I feel part of a community … [deleted name] is my prayer partner and I know every time I go out she's my guardian angel, she's going to make sure I don't get stabbed. [laughs] … the greater freedom has given us a greater

---

93 Anonymised interview.
94 Anonymised interview.

sense of community, and I don't just mean community in living, but community prayer, because I think that is, because our prayer actually is coming out of a need. And I'm not saying that the Office wasn't the needs of the world, but this comes from a raw need sometimes of where you are in the space you're in.[95]

Her recollection sheds light on how the community found ways to share individual ministries through prayer and mutual support.

These inner-city foundations were also attractive to enclosed, contemplative orders. In the early 1990s, the Poor Clares began contemplating a new kind of religious community. By 2001, the decision was made to form a Franciscan inserted community, and in 2003 one was opened in East Sussex in the midst of a housing estate with Poor Clares at its contemplative heart, but with Franciscan friars and sisters doing apostolic outreach.[96] Passionist and sociologist James Sweeney wrote of inserted communities as a means by which religious followed a 'prophetic way', close to ordinary people in local neighbourhoods. He saw their 'credibility' embedded in 'the relationships and friendships they strike up; they are seen to value individuals, families and communities who on a routine basis are socially disregarded and used to being discarded. Their mission is to witness to hope in the midst of what seems like hopelessness.'[97]

Like small communities in parishes, inserted communities became for women religious an important means of addressing the needs of the poor and marginalised by putting Gospel values at the heart of the mission of the Church.

Case study: Peru

Prior to the encyclical letter *Evangelii Praecones* (1951) the impetus of Catholic missionary work had been centred on the salvation of souls and expanding the influence of the Catholic Church. *Evangelii Praecones* encouraged a renewed focus on Catholic foreign missions. In criticising both communism and capitalism and emphasising social justice, it proposed that charity was not enough: social reform was necessary.[98]

95 Anonymised interview.
96 'The Poor Clares, Arundel'. www.poorclaresarundel.org/communityArundel, accessed 12 December 2018.
97 James Sweeney, 'Prophets and Parables: A Future for Religious Orders', *Informationes Theologiae Europae*, 4 (2001), 284.
98 Joe Holland, *Modern Catholic Social Teaching: The Popes Confront the Industrial Age, 1740–1958* (New York: Paulist Press, 2003), pp. 282–3.

Pius XII's encyclical to Catholic bishops, *Fidei Donum* (On the Present Condition of the Catholic Missions, 1957), called for a 'keener interest in the missionary apostolate among your priests' and for bishops to make priests available for missionary activities, especially to Africa.[99] Pope Paul VI's encyclical *Populorum Progressio* (1967) highlighted the injustice of poverty. The apostolic exhortation *Evangelii Nuntiandi* (1975) connected proclaiming and witnessing the Gospel with social justice, underscoring that it was integral to evangelisation. The Latin American episcopal conferences, particularly those in Medellín (1968) and Puebla (1979), added another dimension to missiology. Latin American bishops emphasised the 'church of the poor', linking together the poverty caused by injustice.[100] They suggested that evangelisation would not occur without transformation of the structures of society. They encouraged conscientisation – helping people understand that remaining impassive made them responsible for injustice.

In 1961, the Bishop of Leeds, George Dwyer (1908–1985), responded to *Fidei Donum*'s appeal by sending diocesan priests to work with the Columban Fathers in Peru. In 1969, he approached the Sisters of Mercy, who sent a multi-community team of four sisters (three educators and one nurse), to Tupac Amaru, a barrio of 40,000 on the fringes of Lima, Peru.[101] These four sisters, and the sisters that replaced them afterwards (the community was rarely larger than four sisters), were inspired by the call of the poor and marginalised. In 1984, another group of Sisters of Mercy founded a separate mission at Villa Sol in Lima Peru (Figure 6.1). Both groups began their ministries as they did in their founder Catherine McAuley's time by visiting the sick poor, keeping in mind Catherine McAuley's admonition regarding visitations: 'act with great tenderness … relieve distress … promote cleanliness, ease and comfort … since we are always better disposed to receive advice and instruction from those who show compassion for us'.[102] They educated children and adults and taught catechism. In continuity with how ministries had operated throughout their history, evangelisation was still a core feature of the missionary

---

99 *Fidei Donum*, §4. For more on women religious and medical missionary work in Africa see Barbra Mann Wall, *Into Africa: A Transnational History of Catholic Medical Missions and Social Change* (London: Rutgers University Press, 2015).

100 McCarthy, *The Catholic Tradition*, pp. 253–4.

101 Institute of Our Lady of Mercy Archives (Bermondsey, London) (henceforth RSM Institute): IOLM/PERU/1/3, 'The Peru Mission'; IOLM/PERU/3/1, 'Peru Mission'.

102 RSM Institute: IOLM/PERU/3/1, 'Mercy Response to the Cry of the Poor', photocopied typescript, no author, no date but ends 1992, p. 19.

enterprise.[103] These missions, however, did some things differently: they avoided the institutionalised emphasis that had been characteristic of Catholic foreign missions in the past.[104] What underpinned this ministerial response of the 'option for the poor' was the desire to be 'present' to the poor, by redistributing resources and personnel to the poor of Lima, sharing with the people of the barrios in which they worked their 'anxieties and hopes', encouraging the independence of the peoples of Tupac Amaru and Lima in all things practical and allowing them to minister to their own people for their own journey of much hoped-for 'liberation'.[105]

The Sisters of Mercy in Tupac Amaru immediately set up a clinic in the convent; by 1984 this was a stand-alone brick structure, a *posta medica* that was managed by local administrators.[106] When they arrived in 1969, improving health (tuberculosis was rife at this time) was a priority. As well as providing knowledge of standards of hygiene and medical practices, the training of barrio residents created employment opportunities; one sister wrote of 'getting some of our girls into the local hospital to be trained'.[107] Other health initiatives were more rudimentary and included organising kitchens (*comedores*) throughout the barrio where local women cooked and provided meals at a nominal charge to the 70 per cent of the barrio inhabitants who were un- or under-employed. Tupac Amaru women created income-generating native crafts that were later sold by Mercy communities throughout England.[108] This income gave women independent access to funds to help run their home and educate their children. One sister wrote describing her daily work:

103 RSM Union: MISS/1, Papers re. Peru mission, 1980s–2000s, 'Villa Sol, Lima, Peru, 1983–1992'.
104 Not all Catholic foreign missions chose this route – the Irish Sisters of Mercy ran schools in Peru. See M. Angela Bolster, *Mercy in Cork 1837–1987: A Sesquicentennial Commemoration* (Cork: Tower Books, 1987), pp. 59–63; Phyl Clancy, *A Journey of Mercy: From Birth to Rebirth* (Achonry, Co. Sligo: Congregation of the Sisters of Mercy, 1994), pp. 153–61. Many thanks to Marianne Cosgrave, archivist of the Mercy Congregational Archives in Dublin, for directing me to these works.
105 RSM Union: MISS/1, Papers re. Peru mission, 1980s–2000s, 'Villa Sol, Lima, Peru, 1983–1992', p. 5.
106 RSM Institute: IOLM/PERU/3/1, 'Mercy Response to the Cry of the Poor', Letter from Mother Imelda Keena to sisters re: February to March 1985.
107 RSM Institute: IOLM/PERU/3/1, 'Mercy Response to the Cry of the Poor', photocopied typescript, no author, no date but ends 1992, p. 12.
108 RSM Institute: IOLM/PERU/1/3, Circular letter from Sister M. Mildred McNamara to sisters, dated 1985, p. 5.

We help the sick; we help in the *comedores* or communal kitchens; we help with crafts; in fact we try to help the women move out of the isolation of their homes, often little more than a shack, so that they can learn to organise, share their concerns & find the support of friendship. For the women it is the food, medicines or money earned, that matter most. That is what makes the difference between life & death for them & their families. But we hope they see us as people who represent the God of life, interested in helping them & their families to live.[109]

Written in the 1980s, this excerpt demonstrates the Sisters of Mercy's embrace of the traditional 'caring' work of the corporal works of mercy. Yet the language suggests a difference from the past: sisters were 'helping' rather than managing. Barrio women were expected to take the lead in these enterprises and to 'learn to organise'. The traditional work of the Sisters of Mercy – 'visiting the sick' – was being organised by members of a women's group. Another group was organising a new *comedor*. One sister wrote that 'Having already acquired the cooking utensils they must now provide a secure roof to safeguard this equipment.'[110] The priority of the barrio women was the practical work of survival: 'food, medicines or money earned'. But it seems important too that these women 'share their concerns & find the support of friendship', suggesting consciousness-raising in relation to the larger social structures that were complicit in the poverty that oppressed them. Throughout the correspondence readers were told 'out of respect for their human dignity, the poor were encouraged to be actively involved in every effort being made to improve their lot – spiritually, physically and materially'.[111]

The mission to Peru brought together sisters from several communities in England and also introduced them to other groups of Sisters of Mercy missioned to Peru from Ireland, the United States, Canada, Australia and New Zealand.[112] These autonomous groups became more interconnected from the late 1970s. North American groups of Mercies in Latin American united under the umbrella 'Mercy

109 *Ibid.*
110 *Ibid.*
111 RSM Institute: IOLM/PERU/3/1: 'Mercy Response to the Cry of the Poor', photocopied typescript, no author, no date but ends 1992, p. 4.
112 Mary Beth Fraser Connolly briefly discusses the 1961 Chicago Sisters of Mercy Sicuani mission to Peru to establish school and health care with a focus on pre-conciliar evangelisation. Connolly, *Women of Faith*, pp. 162–3. For more on the United States missions see Angelyn Dries, *The Missionary Movement in American Catholic History* (Maryknoll, NY: Orbis Books, 1998), pp. 179–246.

Union General of the United States'.[113] The Sisters of Mercy then expanded this grouping internationally, deciding it would be fruitful to connect as one body in Latin America, though links to home countries remained in place. They were united in a Mercy identity that became stronger as they became 'more conscious of being part of Mercy – on all levels: local, Latin America, International'.[114] They operated transnationally, sharing and exchanging views and praxis at national and regional conferences. The Latin American and Caribbean conference of 1989 had as one of its aims to 'grow towards greater unity'.[115] Together they drew up the 'Common Criteria for Formation Programs in L.A. [Latin America]'. Many were also wedded to an understanding of mission which incorporated social-justice language such as the desire to 'insert oneself among the poor (house, work, Heart)'; 'allow the poor to evangelize us'; and 'accompany the people in their struggles to defend life (justice initiative, co-ops, workshops, etc.)'.[116]

Sisters did not shy away from politicisation of poverty. They arranged for speakers to explain to barrio residents 'more fully their position in a fast declining economy, as well as the various ways in which they may try to overcome exploitation'.[117] They organised human rights groups and 'building, furnishing & organising a workshop for the Craft Group which will also provide an overnight refuge for battered women to be named "Casa de Misericordia"'.[118] They promoted native culture by organising Peruvian folk groups that were 'essential', according to one sister, 'because many of the children born in the barrio have lost their 'roots' be it religious/musical/dance, etc.' Barrio women were encouraged to organise, facilitate groups, raise funds; ultimately taking responsibility for their own communities and organising in collaborative, non-hierarchical ways. The Sisters of Mercy acknowledged the political ramifications of what they did.

---

113 RSM Union: MISS/1, 'Villa Sol Lima Peru 1983–1992', 'Policy Regarding the Peru Mission', p. 5.

114 RSM Union: MISS/1, 'Villa Sol Lima Peru 1983–1992', 'Common Criteria for Formation Programs in L.A. [Latin America]'.

115 RSM Union: MISS/1, 'Villa Sol Lima Peru 1983–1992', anonymous undated typescript.

116 RSM Union: MISS/1, 'Villa Sol Lima Peru 1983–1992', 'Common Criteria for Formation Programs in L.A. [Latin America]', undated.

117 RSM Institute: IOLM/PERU/1/3, Letter from Mother Imelda Keena to sisters re: February to March 1985, p. 54.

118 RSM Institute: IOLM/PERU/1/3, Circular letter from Sister M. Mildred McNamara to sisters, dated 1985.

Figure 6.1 Sisters of Mercy and helpers in Peru, *c.* 1980s

One sister admitted: 'In such a complex scene, it is not easy to steer a middle course, in giving witness to Christian values of social justice and human rights, with sufficient sensitivity not to provide an excuse to someone in a power-position to retaliate against the very people our Sisters are trying to serve.'[119] In a position paper dated 1987, the Union sisters reported on 'signs of life' among the barrio members. These included barrio members organising to put in basic services of water, sewerage and electricity but also recording the struggles to maintain democratic processes within the barrio structures. Their position paper acknowledged that their intent, to create an active, Catholic populace with networks, confidence, skills and knowledge to address their own oppression, was not complete. It was only beginning.[120]

119 RSM Institute: IOLM/PERU/3/1: 'Mercy Response to the Cry of the Poor', photocopied typescript, no author, no date but ends 1992, p. 67.
120 RSM Union: MISS/1, 'Villa Sol Lima Peru 1983–1992', 'Position Paper – Peru November 1987'.

The Sisters of Mercy's work was a mix of old and new. It was undergirded by their faith and an evangelisation that promoted European ideas of orthodox Catholicism linked to the Universal Church: 'The general opinion is that our people were baptised but never evangelised. To awaken them spiritually means first of all the eradication of superstition.'[121] There was little radical in this thinking. But they also encouraged the development of base communities and in this they were emboldening a Catholicism that would be Peruvian, not European.[122] Base communities were often created by the poor and marginalised and were a church *of* the poor rather than a church *for* the poor.[123] These groups were still connected to their local parish; community activities included weekly formation meetings, prayer groups and youth groups who prepared the liturgy.[124] The Sisters of Mercy instructed catechists, barrio residents who in turn taught Catholic doctrine and catechism and prepared their co-religionists for the sacraments of communion and confirmation. Barrio catechists became the primary agents of evangelisation in their communities.

The educational remit of the Sisters of Mercy extended beyond the barrio. Their regular letters to their home communities were a means of fundraising as well as 'bearing witness', thus making their eyewitness accounts of political and economic injustices and structural inequities faced by barrio residents visible to a larger British audience. 'Bearing witness', according to theorist Fuyuki Kurasawa, encompasses a 'web of cosmopolitan testimonial practices structured around five dialectically related tasks and perils': voice against silence; interpretation against incomprehension; empathy against indifference; remembrance against forgetting; and prevention against repetition.[125] Epistolary exchanges in

---

121 RSM Institute: IOLM/PERU/3/1: 'Mercy Response to the Cry of the Poor', photocopied typescript, no author, no date but ends 1992, p. 12.
122 Basic ecclesial communities grew rapidly in Latin America in the 1950s and 1960s. They were small, non-hierarchical church communities. Some were connected to a local Catholic parish, others were stridently anti-institutional. They developed also in Italy, France and Spain, where they were known for their 'radical' Catholicism peopled by those who were unhappy with the Church hierarchy and sought a space to discuss and question Church teachings and actively develop social justice and political initiatives, not all of which would have been congruent with Church teaching. Clifford and Townson, 'The Church in Crisis'.
123 Ellen M. Leonard, 'Ecclesial Religious Communities Old and New', *The Way Supplement* (2001), 123.
124 RSM Institute: IOLM/PERU/1/3, Circular letter from Sister M. Mildred McNamara to sisters, dated 1985.
125 Fuyuki Kurasawa, 'A Message in a Bottle: Bearing Witness as a Mode of Transnational Practice', *Theory, Culture & Society*, 26 (2009), 92.

the 1970s and 1980s were important means of communication in the early days of the transnational 'era of the witness', when media coverage was less instantaneous and relentless.[126] Bearing witness did not 'cure' or even alleviate injustice, but it was, as Kurasawa argued, an 'act of resistance' that potentially enabled participation, empathy and knowledge to cross national borders.[127] 'Bearing witness' had a remarkable similarity to one of the 1979 Puebla commitments: to give public witness for the Church's solidarity with the poor.[128] In these subtle ways, Sisters of Mercy criticised the injustices lived daily by barrio residents and expressed solidarity with the poor whilst conscientising Catholics in Britain.

Sacralised work

The case studies examined in the previous section explored a small range of the post-war ministries women religious engaged with. They were disparate in many ways, but in regard to their religious underpinning they had two factors in common. First, they represented a form of 'sacralized work'.[129] Women religious were guided by a Catholic ethos that provided the religious motivation to engage with modern ideas of social justice. Jaclyn Granick in her work on sacralised humanitarianism examined faith-based organisations and argued that they drew on their faith 'for motivation, for justification, for empathy and combined it with the liberal ideas of the times … They interpreted the world in light of their particular beliefs and adapted their organizations to navigate the balance of an ever-changing world and religious tradition.'[130] Like Granick's humanitarian organisations, Providence Row was reconfigured professionally and financially, appropriating a 'modern infrastructure' through its volunteers and permanent staffing and partnerships with local government. Liberation theology with its 'preferential option for the poor' allied with the idealism and activism of the long 1960s and informed the works of women religious whether they were instructing students or employed in the voluntary sector, or working as a community in parishes, deprived neighbourhoods or in foreign missions.

126 Annette Wieviorka, L'ère du témoin (Paris: Plon, 1998).
127 Kurasawa, 'A Message in a Bottle', p. 106.
128 McCarthy, The Catholic Tradition, p. 255.
129 Leff, Sacred Bonds of Solidarity, pp. 168–74.
130 Jaclyn Granick, 'Sacralized Humanitarianism: A Comparison of Three Faith-Based Private Associations', 2011. www.swiss-quakers.ch/ge/library/e-documents/7971-Granick2011.pdf, accessed 26 February 2016.

Second, these case studies required sisters and students to be 'present'. Theologian Catherine Sexton's work on 'presence' has identified it as a form of ministry 'in terms of accompanying and being present to, and a way of being', recognising it as both 'incarnational and sacramental, in making God's presence a reality, through their ministry to others and their relationships'.[131] Whether listening to those with drug addictions, visiting the elderly, finding homes for the homeless, acting in solidarity with those on a housing estate or serving in the barrio, women religious interpreted their 'presence' as social action: a means to rebalance inequitable structures and relationships. Sacralised work and presence may seem contradictory to an instrumentalising, activity-driven world which sees protest and politics as the only means for social justice, but many women religious understood their work for social justice in these terms.

The sacred was personal, as well as political. Individual ministries came out of the individuated needs of sisters and nuns to engage in ministries that were centred on the option for the poor and marginalised. The women interviewed were guided throughout their ministerial work by their relationship with God; many found the new connections and relationships with the 'people of God' transformational. Their decision to move outside of traditional convent ministries, or to stay within convent ministries, was not lightly taken – it was informed by a discourse of social justice that emanated from pontifical letters and encyclicals and their interpretation of the needs of the world. For religious life, these shifts in the 1970s and 1980s were a radical response at a time of transition. Admittedly, such radicalness does not translate well in a secular world that identifies 'radical' with 'radical politics'. Ethnographer Marla F. Frederick suggested from her study of black women and faith that 'women's refashioning of their world may not always coincide with traditional interpretations of radical politics; nevertheless, the communities they create and the life changes they inspire speak to the agentive possibilities of their faith'.[132] It is this agentive possibility that is critical to the radical nature of the early adopters of experimental religious ministries. For many women, working with the poor was inherently political as it critiqued the inequities faced by the marginalised.

American Dominican theologian Anneliese Sinnott proposes that after the Second Vatican Council 'the meaning of ministry changed from

131 Sexton, 'Theologies of Ministry', p. 5.
132 Marla F. Frederick, *Between Sundays: Black Women and Everyday Struggles of Faith* (Berkeley: University of California Press, 2003), p. 12.

church work to the work of the church.[133] Both types of work were valued. In Britain, the 'work of the church' was relevant to women who remained in Catholic institutional ministries (schools and parishes); others, like the sister who worked at Centrepoint or inserted communities, took their Catholicism into the secular world. They interpreted the work of the Church through a broader lens. There was continuity in the continued emphasis on 'care'.[134] Whether working in a parish or in a barrio, women religious were embedded into indigenous people's lives through their work in health, education and religious catechesis but were consequently less visible than when they had managed large-scale institutions.[135] In the process they went from conversion and salvation to creating active, informed citizens; and whether in foreign missions like Peru or in Catholic schoolrooms, they sought to build 'social capital': networks, confidence, skills and knowledge.

Conclusion

Journalist George Scott, in his 1967 report on 'R.C.s' explained that 'Roman Catholics, as a community, are only just starting to catch up with the idea of social action'.[136] By the 1970s and 1980s, despite diminishing numbers women religious were involved in social action. They became innovative in ministry, and new ministries and old emphasised the marginalised, both at home and abroad. Whether working as parish sisters or in the barrios of Peru, sisters and nuns held on to global objectives that were not narrowed to geography. This encompassed a move from the spiritual and corporal works of mercy, to more politicised ministries. The politics of social justice and liberation theology introduced a vocabulary that became relevant whether addressing local or global initiatives. The scope of their service was transnational and global, not simply because they went on missions, but because they connected local problems to global

---

133   Anneliese Sinnott, 'Mission and Ministry: The Task of Discipleship', in Nadine Foley (ed.), *Journey in Faith and Fidelity: Women Shaping Religious Life for a Renewed Church* (New York: Continuum, 1999), p. 99.
134   For more on the ethics and theory of care see Ann Bradshaw, *Lighting the Lamp: The Spiritual Dimension of Nursing Care* (Harrow: Scutari, 1994) and van Heijst, *Models of Charitable Care*.
135   Susan Fitzpatrick-Behrens, 'From Symbols of the Sacred to Symbols of Subversion to Simply Obscure: Maryknoll Women Religious in Guatemala, 1953 to 1967', *The Americas*, 61 (2004), 204.
136   George Scott, *The R.C.s: A Report on Roman Catholics in Britain Today* (London: Hutchinson, 1967), p. 88.

movements. As individuals, they joined the voluntary sector to practise their 'caring' ministry and the ministry of presence. They engaged with the new direction of voluntary action by identifying deficiencies in existing services for the marginalised: provision for homeless, institutional care of elderly or cognitively impaired, services for disabled. Women's religious institutes remained active participants in the voluntary sector that met unmet needs in the social welfare state. They adapted their ministries to meet current needs. This was not an inevitable and smooth trajectory for each congregation and order, and declining numbers were significant to this shift in ministries; new ministries often resulted in a letting-go of old ministries that were sometimes enmeshed in the core identities of congregations. Some communities travelled on this road in the 1960s, others towards the end of the century. And others remained focused on their institutional work, though altering educational curricula to emphasise elements of social justice. More research is needed to elaborate more fully on their interpretations of social justice and ways of living it. However, what this chapter proposes is that new ministries, and even old ones, were influenced by the discourse of social justice and an interplay with the secular world. The interaction of the sacred with the secular continues in Chapter 7, which addresses how both religious and secular ideas shaped nuns' and sisters' awareness of their womanhood.

7

Becoming a woman

[W]ith apologies to Mrs. Pankhurst, the '<u>Emancipation of Religious Women</u>' – that is the question of the world in the cloister, and the Nuns (I use the word in the popular sense) in the world; and the critical eyes of the world which are turned on the Nuns whether she is in her Convent or out of it.[1]

Introduction

In making reference to Emmeline Pankhurst, the leader of the suffragette movement of the early twentieth century, Mother Mary Andrew, a member of the Franciscan Missionaries of the Divine Motherhood, was suggesting that the changes in religious life were leading to the 'emancipation' of women religious. But did she consider that a good thing? Speaking to novice mistresses on a training day in the early 1960s, she underscored the difficulties that women religious faced, inside and outside the convent and in the 'critical eyes of the world'. Disparaging female religious who were ignorant of world problems, she instead expected them to be aware of the major 'crisis of their times': atomic weapons, strike mentality, 'atheistic communism' and the break-up of family life. At the same time she regretted the development of 'career-it-is' and a loss of authority within religious life, worrying out loud that movement into the world would lead to sisters becoming restless, desiring change and returning to the convent 'soaked to saturation point with the news and views of the world'. Mother Mary Andrew did not suggest turning the clock back by creating new rules and regulations (a typical pre-conciliar response to

---

1   SCMM-ENK: 374, 'Training to be Given in the Noviciate to Prepare Sisters to Meet Present Day Problems' [no date].

challenges of the world). Her solution to the 'potential' problems of the 'emancipation' of women religious was renewal-centred: it addressed the formation of novices and grounded it in the renewed spiritual, intellectual and apostolic understanding of religious life.

Television presenter Alan Whicker was less convinced of the emancipation of women religious. In his series 'Whicker, Within a Woman's World' he introduced a community of Poor Clares as 'the most unliberated women in the world'.[2] But were they? Many scholars of nineteenth-century women religious have argued that women religious had agency, some even controversially suggesting their proto-feminism.[3] However, decision-making power among women religious was limited to the small number in leadership positions; their agency and authority was always circumscribed to some extent by male prelates. Throughout the post-war changes in religious life in Britain, the relationship between women's religious institutes and the episcopal hierarchy remained relatively cordial, despite occasional criticism of the slow, or hasty, pace of renewal.[4] Interviews and archival documents record few significant altercations. Renewal was initially inward-facing. The changes in governance within a religious institute or the relational turn within a community were not always obvious to outsiders. It was the outward-facing changes that garnered more public attention, the shift in ministries, the movement into the world and – one of the shifts that will be discussed in this chapter – the changes to religious dress. The Women's Liberation Movement was an important social movement of the long 1960s and it is through its methods and goals that we will chart a nascent female consciousness and the growing awareness of a feminine self within religious sisters and nuns. Few British women religious from 1945 to 1990 would have claimed a feminist identity but in their words and deeds, and in their efforts to live an authentic religious life, they merged their Catholic faith with a more 'emancipated' religious life.

Jacqueline deVries has noted that feminist scholars' (many of them participants of second-wave feminism) insistence on religion as 'a monolithic site of antifeminist resistance and a potent source of patriarchal

2 BFI: Tx 2.8.1972, *A Girl Gets Temptations – But I Wanted to Give Myself to God* ('Whicker, Within a Woman's World' series) (1972).

3 Kathleen A. Brosnan, 'Public Presence, Public Silence: Nuns, Bishops, and the Gendered Space of Early Chicago', *Catholic Historical Review*, 90:3 (2004), 473–96.

4 This is in marked contrast to some US experiences. See Susan M. Maloney, 'Obedience, Responsibility, and Freedom: Anita M. Caspary, IHM, and the Post-Conciliar Renewal of Catholic Women Religious', *US Catholic Historian*, 32 (2014), 121–49.

oppression' had shut the door on the nuances of alternative feminisms that were reflected in the first suffrage movement. What she and others maintain was that many of the suffrage campaigners of the early twentieth century were women whose religious faith was integral to their identities, and who used religious language and ideas to legitimate the political suffrage of women.[5] Recent revisionist scholarship reconsiders twentieth-century religious and conservative groups to analyse their relationship with emancipation and women's movements.[6] Caitríona Beaumont's work involving six such groups examines their efforts at securing social and economic rights for working women after they received the vote in 1928, using the language of citizenship, rather than feminism. On some political issues, they worked side by side with explicitly feminist organisations. She argues that the 'women's movement', as an umbrella term that highlights those who wanted to improve the position and status of women in society, needs to be delinked from an exclusively feminist agenda.[7] Taking us into the 1960s, Callum Brown has persistently argued that the social movements of the long 1960s, especially the women's movement, was deeply implicated in the decline of religious affiliation of young women, with Hugh McLeod countering that any rejection of Christianity occurred before the women's movement.[8] Historian Sarah Browne concluded from her interviews with 'second-wave' feminists that the Women's Liberation

5   Jacqueline deVries, 'More than Paradoxes to Offer: Feminism, History and Religious Cultures', in Sue Morgan and Jacqueline deVries (eds), *Women, Gender and Religious Cultures in Britain, 1800–1940* (London: Routledge, 2010), p. 190. See also Anne Summers, *Christian and Jewish Women in Britain, 1880–1940: Living with Difference* (New York: Palgrave Macmillan, 2017); Brian Heeney, *The Women's Movement in the Church of England, 1850–1930* (Oxford: Clarendon Press, 1988).

6   Maggie Andrews, *The Acceptable Face of Feminism: The Women's Institute as a Social Movement* (London: Lawrence and Wishart, 1997); Carmen M. Mangion, 'Religious Suffrage Societies', in Krista Cowman (ed.), *Women's Suffrage* (Abingdon: Routledge, forthcoming).

7   Caitríona Beaumont, *Housewives and Citizens: Domesticity and the Women's Movement in England, 1928–64* (Manchester: Manchester University Press, 2013), p. 3; Caitríona Beaumont, 'Citizens Not Feminists: The Boundary Negotiated between Citizenship and Feminism by Mainstream Women's Organisations in England, 1928–39', *Women's History Review*, 9 (2000), 411–29; Caitríona Beaumont, 'Moral Dilemmas and Women's Rights: The Attitude of the Mothers' Union and Catholic Women's League to Divorce, Birth Control and Abortion in England, 1928–1939', *Women's History Review*, 16 (2007), 463–85.

8   Callum Brown, 'Women and Religion in Britain: The Autobiographical View of the Fifties and Sixties', in Callum G. Brown and Michael Snape (eds), *Secularisation in the Christian World* (Farnham: Ashgate, 2010), pp. 159–74; Hugh McLeod, *The Religious Crisis of the 1960s* (Oxford: Oxford University Press, 2007), p. 182.

Movement in Scotland was informed by religious discourse. She has also linked women's Catholicism with their feminism, identifying feminists who credited their convent education as an impetus for their engagement with feminism.[9] Neil Armstrong's research on clergymen's wives in the 1960s, to take another example of this reassessment, attributes their use of a liberal secular discourse of individualism framed in a Christian understanding to an implicit feminism.[10] Using religion as a category of analysis, this chapter examines how 'becoming a woman' manifested itself in women religious, linking it to the methods and aims of the Women's Movement.[11] Women religious, like feminists, claimed for themselves the right to define their own place in both secular society and the Catholic world as women.[12] Rather than posit these changes as secularisation, the chapter aims to demonstrate how religious and secular ideas shaped these women's awareness of their womanhood.

It is with much trepidation that I use the 'f' word: feminism or even feminist consciousness in regard to women religious.[13] In writing of contemporary feminism in religious life, feminist theologian and Cenacle sister Kate Stogdon acknowledges the incongruity between 'feminist commitments to freedom and self-determination' with the making of the religious vows of poverty, chastity and obedience.[14] Women religious in their obedience and their support of teachings of women's traditional role in the family historically embraced and

9   Sarah F. Browne, 'Women, Religion, and the Turn to Feminism: Experiences of Women's Liberation Activists in Britain in the Seventies', in Nancy Christie and Michael Gavreau (eds), *The Sixties and Beyond: Dechristianisation in North America and Western Europe, 1945–2000* (Toronto: University of Toronto Press, 2013), pp. 84–97. An American version of this is: Liesl Schwabe, 'Everything I Know about Feminism I Learned from Nuns', *New York Times* (16 February 2019). www.nytimes.com/2019/02/16/opinion/sunday/catholic-school-nuns-feminism.html, accessed 17 February 2019.

10   Neil Armstrong, '"I Insisted I Was Myself": Clergy Wives and Authentic Selfhood in England c. 1960–94', *Women's History Review*, 22 (2013), 995–1013.

11   Timothy W. Jones, 'Postsecular Sex? Secularisation and Religious Change in the History of Sexuality in Britain', *History Compass*, 11 (2013), 92.

12   Jane Rendall, *The Origins of Modern Feminism: Women in Britain, France and the United States, 1780–1860* (London: Macmillan, 1985), p. 13.

13   See Karen Offen's valiant attempt at a cross-cultural and cross-temporal definition of feminism. Karen M. Offen, 'Defining Feminism: A Comparative Historical Approach', *Signs*, 14 (1988), 119–57. As Offen's article (and the responses to it) make clear, feminism is a contested concept. In this chapter, I am not attempting to interrogate how women religious defined feminism; nor am I saying all religious were feminists though some were.

14   Kate Stogdon, '"Nothing Was Taken from Me: Everything Was Given": Religious Life and Second Wave Feminism', in Gemma Simmonds, CJ (ed.), *A Future Full of Hope?* (Dublin: The Columba Press, 2012), p. 71.

propagated a patriarchal Catholicism. They supported and collaborated with the male institutional power of the Holy See, and their own local ecclesiastical hierarchy. Historian Phil Kilroy writes of the institutional church 'colonizing' women religious: religious communities were 'offered security on condition of submission and cooperation. If women religious complied they were rewarded, given status, and they were expected to execute all the policies of the colonizer. If they objected they were silenced or cast out, certainly side-lined.'[15] Women religious were simultaneously marginalised and assigned a high status. Yet, there was a degree of agency within religious life, especially for those who held positions of authority, managing sometimes large congregations and educational or charitable institutions. Some women religious did, of course, identify themselves as feminist. Christian feminist women imbibed a feminism that sat with their faith, not outside it. According to theologian Ursula King faith-filled feminism was influenced by secular feminisms:

> [T]he rise of the women's movement with its new spiritual insights, its strong potential for empowerment and transformation, as well as its necessary critique in search for renewal and reconstruction, are not only of the greatest importance for contemporary women and men, but herald a promising horizon of hope for Christianity in today's world.[16]

Catholic feminist theologian Sandra Schneiders suggests a 'gospel feminism' where women of faith were 'claiming as their own the agenda of Jesus in the gospel … and insisting that feminist commitment is not just compatible with but is integral to commitment to the gospel'.[17]

In the United States, historian Mary Henold has identified a rich and robust history of Catholic women and women religious embracing the feminist movement.[18] American historian Elizabeth Kolmer noted 'the feminist movement, in varying degrees, has been a common experience for the Catholic sisters'.[19] North American women explicitly

15 Phil Kilroy, 'Coming to an Edge in History: Writing the History of Women Religious and the Critique of Feminism', in Deirdre Raftery and Elizabeth M. Smyth (eds), *Education, Identity and Women Religious, 1800–1950: Convents, Classrooms and Colleges* (London: Routledge, 2015), p. 26.

16 Ursula King, 'Women's Contribution to Contemporary Spirituality', *The Way Supplement*, 84 (1994), 36.

17 Sandra M. Schneiders, *Beyond Patching: Faith and Feminism in the Catholic Church* (New York: Paulist Press, 1991), pp. xv–xvi.

18 Mary J. Henold, *Catholic and Feminist: The Surprising History of the American Catholic Feminist Movement* (Durham, NC: University of North Carolina Press, 2012).

19 Elizabeth Kolmer, 'Catholic Women Religious and Women's History: A Survey of the Literature', *American Quarterly*, 30 (1978), 645; Helen Rose Ebaugh, *Women in the*

identified themselves as feminists; some, like Sisters Mary Joel Read and Mary Austen Doherty, sat on the board of the National Organisation for Women.[20] In Britain, Catholic women participated in wider social movements of the 1960s, including the Women's Liberation Movement, but researchers have yet to substantively analyse their participation.[21] The Movement for the Ordination of Women brought together women of various religious denominations, but publications, often authored by participants, rarely contextualise its activities within the movements of the long 1960s. In part, this may be because, as Susan Mumm suggests, it is a 'crude oversimplification to depict all advocates for women's ordination as feminist, let alone radically feminist; many were theologically and socially conservative, especially among the group seeking ordination themselves'.[22] Catholics wanting fuller participation in the Church were inspired by *Lumen Gentium* (1964), the Dogmatic Constitution on the Church, that insisted laity, and this category included women religious, as the 'people of God' were

> by baptism made one body with Christ and are constituted among the People of God; they are in their own way made sharers in the priestly, prophetical, and kingly functions of Christ; and they carry out for their own part the mission of the whole Christian people in the Church and in the world.[23]

Vanishing Cloister: Organizational Decline in Catholic Religious Orders in the United States (New Brunswick, NJ: Rutgers University Press, 1993), pp. 133–48.

20 Henold, *Catholic and Feminist*, p. 17; Rebecca Sullivan, *Visual Habits: Nuns, Feminism, and American Postwar Popular Culture* (Toronto: University of Toronto Press, 2005), p. 48.

21 There is little research on women (Catholic or otherwise) within movements other than the Women's Liberation Movement. Lynne Segal, 'She's Leaving Home: Women's Sixties Renaissance', in Gurminder K. Bhambra and Ipek Demir (eds), *1968 in Retrospect: History, Theory, Alterity* (Houndmills: Palgrave Macmillan, 2009), p. 31. Sarah F. Browne, 'Women, Religion, and the Turn to Feminism: Experiences of Women's Liberation Activists in Britain in the Seventies', in Nancy Christie and Michael Gavreau (eds), *The Sixties and Beyond: Dechristianisation in North America and Western Europe, 1945–2000* (Toronto: University of Toronto Press, 2013), pp. 84–97.

22 Susan Mumm, 'Women, Priesthood, and the Ordained Ministry in the Christian Tradition', in John Wolffe (ed.), *Religion in History: Conflict, Conversion and Coexistence* (Manchester: Manchester University Press in association with The Open University, 2004), pp. 203, 207.

23 *Lumen Gentium*, §31. Also, *Apostolicam Actuositatem* (1965), the Decree on the Apostolate of the Laity, insisted that the laity should influence their surroundings with Christ's teachings.

The laity was intended, however, to 'support and extend the action of the priest', so the long arm of the institutional church was always meant to be present.[24] Women belonging to St Joan's International Alliance, founded in 1911, were in the forefront of the attempts to improve Catholic women's participation in Church matters. In the early 1960s the Alliance made official requests to the Holy See that women be trained as deacons, for lay men and women to be Vatican Council observers and, more radically, for the admission of women to the priesthood.[25] Several groups were set up in the 1970s, including Roman Catholics Feminists (1977) and the Alliance of Women Religious (1977), to explore and study more deeply the theological and social issues related to the ordination of women.[26] In 1993 the Catholic Women's Ordination movement was formed. Catholic feminists, including women religious, were not quiescent in the 1960s, but they remained a small movement.[27]

Feminist French philosopher Simone de Beauvoir's (1908–1986) book *Le Deuxième Sexe* (1949), published in English as *The Second Sex* in 1953 and then published in paperback in 1961, raised the feminist consciousness of generations of women in Britain.[28] It was a powerful, widely read book that introduced a constructed womanhood where 'One is not born, but rather becomes a woman'. Becoming a 'woman', de Beauvoir attested, led to a life as 'object and prey' for man, never a 'sovereign subject', never a 'free and autonomous' being.[29] Two decades after its publication, these words still motivated women of all ages who would become a part of the Women's Liberation Movement.[30] Arthur

---

24 Cardinal Leon Joseph Suenens, *The Nun in the World: New Dimensions in the Modern Apostolate* (Westminster, MD: Newman Press, 1963), p. 172. For more on the visibility of the laity in the Church see Alana Harris, *Faith in the Family: A Lived Religious History of English Catholicism, 1945–1982* (Manchester: Manchester University Press, 2013).

25 Nancy Stewart Parnell, *A Venture in Faith. A History of St. Joan's Social and Political Alliance, Formerly the Catholic Women's Suffrage Society, 1911–1961* (London: St Joan's Alliance, 1961); Anne Marie Pelzer, 'St Joan's International Alliance' (1977). www.womenpriests.org/interact/pelzer.asp, accessed 8 November 2018.

26 Lorna Brockett, *The Ordination of Women: A Roman Catholic Viewpoint* (London: MOW, 1982), pp. 12–13.

27 Harris, *Faith in the Family*, pp. 110–14.

28 David Bouchier, *The Feminist Challenge: The Movement for Women's Liberation in Britain and the USA* (London: MacMillan Press, 1983), p. 35. Lynne Segal calls it the 'founding text' of the Women's Liberation Movement. Segal, 'She's Leaving Home'. This 800-page tome sold 22,000 copies a week in 1949 and is still being purchased and debated today.

29 Bouchier, *The Feminist Challenge*, p. 35.

30 Sheila Rowbotham, *Woman's Consciousness, Man's World* (Harmondsworth: Penguin Books, 1973), pp. 10–11, 21

Marwick argued that this awakening of feminist consciousness reflected the 'gentler, more traditional' feminism of the 1960s in contrast to the radical activism of the 1970s.[31] Activist Amanda Sebestyen, writing in the early 1980s, recalled the early years of the movement, with its 'truly British reticence', being told by some feminists that 'it doesn't do to get angry'.[32] The early protests in the late 1960s by angry and certainly not reticent working women in Hull and Dagenham to rectify unequal wages and unsafe working conditions seem to have become a minor footnote in the historiography.[33] Some argue they were overtaken by university students and middle-class women whose political goals and activism appeared more ambitious.[34] Their experience in the leftist student movements, anti-war protests and direct action groups was their education in political activism. They were integral to these movements, though some complained they found themselves relegated to serving tea and sex. Not all radical activist men spouting militant political discourses embraced sexual equality. The 'permissive moment' in those early days seemed more about women's sexual availability to men, than women's pleasure. The 'conflict of gender' or the 'revolution within a revolution' in the social movements of the long 1960s led to a separate women's movement.[35] The Women's Liberation Movement, through consciousness raising groups, political activism and direct action, worked to overturn the ways in which women's lives rendered them subordinate to men, in both personal and public life. They identified the personal, particularly the structure of the family, as significant to women's oppression.[36] Radical

31 Arthur Marwick, *The Sixties: Cultural Revolution in Britain, France, Italy, and the United States, c.1958–c.1974* (Oxford: Oxford University Press, 1998), p. 615.
32 Amanda Sebestyen, 'Britain', in Robin Morgan (ed.), *Sisterhood Is Global: The International Women's Movement Anthology* (Harmondsworth: Penguin Books, 1984), pp. 95–6.
33 George Stevenson, 'The Women's Movement and "Class Struggle": Gender, Class Formation and Political Identity in Women's Strikes, 1968–78', *Women's History Review*, 25 (2016), 741–55. The film and play *Made in Dagenham* and its exploration of equal pay struggles in the 1960s has put that strike firmly into the public discourse.
34 Bouchier, *The Feminist Challenge*, p. 57.
35 Marwick, *The Sixties*, pp. 616–17. From Bracke's review of Wolfgang Kraushaar, *Acht und Sechzig: Eine Bilanz* (Berlin: Propyläen), in Maud Anne Bracke, 'One-Dimensional Conflict? Recent Scholarship on 1968 and the Limitations of the Generation Concept', *Journal of Contemporary History*, 47 (2012), 641. Sheila Rowbotham, *Promise of a Dream: Remembering the Sixties* (London: Allen Lane, 2000), p. 188. Peter Stansill and David Zane Mairowitz (eds), *BAMN (By Any Means Necessary): Outlaw Manifestos and Ephemera, 1965–70* (Harmondsworth: Penguin Books, 1971), pp. 199–206.
36 Diana Gittins, *The Family in Question: Changing Households and Familiar Ideologies* (London: Macmillan, 1985).

feminist groups became more visible in the late 1970s and added layers of militancy to feminist politics. The Women's Liberation Movement's lack of formal structures or registered membership reflected its anti-authority and anti-hierarchy principles. It developed and expanded through consciousness-raising, converting many women to the cause by making them aware of their own subordination. Despite varied methods and emphases among feminists, there was a degree of solidarity and purpose to these disparate groups that were united by the seven demands: equal pay; equal education and employment opportunities; free contraception and abortion on demand; free twenty-four-hour nurseries; financial and legal independence; an end to all discrimination against lesbians; and freedom from intimidation by threat or use of violence or sexual coercion.[37]

The practice and ideologies of the Women's Liberation Movement may appear a world away from the renewal of religious life within British convents and monasteries. Very few of the over eighty participants I spoke to alluded explicitly to the women's movements of the long 1960s, but then again, the majority of participants had entered their convents by 1970. In addition, I rarely asked directly about feminism, choosing to frame my questions more broadly in order to elicit what was important to the participants in terms of changes in religious life. Most would have been aware of feminist activism of the 1970s and 1980s through newspapers and television, and discussions with their students and visitors. English sister Prue Wilson opened her 1980s published memoir with: 'The convergence in the 1960s of the insights of the women's movements with those of women religious was an important part of our growing self-awareness.'[38] But not all sisters would have agreed with her. One sister who entered in the late 1950s told me emphatically that the women's movement of the 1970s had little impact on her congregation:

> In fact, I suppose many of them [the sisters in her congregation] would have thought the feminists were upstarts, and so if you were that way inclined you kind of kept it quiet, you didn't say very much about it. I read a lot and I would have been aware of mostly American writers on feminist issues and there were some hard heads and kind of nutcases and you kind of felt, you know, they're not doing any service, you know. This great movement among some women, Theologians for Ordination of Women, you see, and that was enough to turn off so many people.

---

37   Bouchier, *The Feminist Challenge*, p. 60.
38   Prue Wilson, *My Father Took Me to the Circus* (London: Darton, Longman & Todd, 1984), p. 4.

It wasn't the first thing that needed to happen. It would have been the consequence of a liberation of women, but it wasn't the first thing.[39]

Her response does not register an anti-feminist stance, but was practical: 'It wasn't the first thing that needed to happen.' She was cognisant of feminism through her reading of American theologians, even recognising 'the great movement' for the ordination of women. She acknowledges the transnational nature of the Catholic feminist movement; this was a literature that crossed national borders, was read and debated amongst some British sisters. What was it that needed to happen first? Just as feminists critiqued the family as the site of their oppression, women religious critiqued the convent. The hierarchies of power within religious life were stifling for many, with power held by very few women. The sphere of influence of the individual sister and nun to participate and make changes in her community and in the direction of her own vocation was narrow. Previous chapters have demonstrated the developments that were a part of the renewal of religious life. In defining their own place in society, women religious first addressed the private sphere of the convent. The decentralisation of the management of religious life discussed in Chapter 3 invited sisters and nuns to express their opinions and to participate in the governance of their convents and monasteries. Chapter 4 introduced how relationships altered in religious life; the common life became less codified and rigid and allowed more personal agency and acknowledged the importance of relationships. Chapter 5 explored the entry of women religious into the modern world, where they embraced more prominently and publicly their role in the project of modernisation of the Church: this included being trained professionally and theologically. Female religious life still remained linked to self-sacrifice, service and obedience, but Chapter 6 on ministries revealed how some women religious claimed for themselves the right to define their own apostolate, influenced by the ideals of social justice and liberation theology.

The remainder of the present chapter addresses how women religious engaged with 'becoming a woman', claiming for themselves the right to define their own place in the Church. The four sections that follow are mapped to developments within the women's movement of the long 1960s, taking up historian Nancy A. Hewitt's suggestion that feminist ideas were '"in the air" even when people are not actively listening.'[40]

---

39 Anonymised interview.
40 Nancy A. Hewitt (ed.), *No Permanent Waves: Recasting Histories of U.S. Feminism* (New Brunswick, NJ: Rutgers University Press, 2010), p. 8.

The women's movement, like many of the social movements of the long 1960s, was a transnational movement with ideas flowing back and forth via individual connections, but also a body of published material. The first section examines both the Church's role in redefining expectations of women religious and the developing theology that influenced the self-understanding of women religious. Next, we examine consciousness-raising, convent-style, as a means of disseminating understandings of renewal but also building an awareness of women's oppression within Church structures. The third section examines how the personal became political in debates about one of the most 'charged symbols' of enclosed religious life, the grille, and acknowledges the differences in definitions of womanhood. The final section examines the sister and nun physically 'becoming a woman' through the changes in the religious habit. Throughout these examples, the fruits of consciousness-raising become apparent: renewal encouraged women religious to rethink their place in society, both as female religious and as women. Not all women found it necessary to change, but many used their voices and felt empowered not only to see themselves as women but to critique female and male authority and power and challenge women's subordination to an ideal of religious womanhood that to some, appeared antiquated.

It began with a book

In 1957, the charismatic Cardinal Leo Jozef Suenens, Archbishop of Brussels-Malines, spoke at the Congress of States of Perfection[41] emphasising that religious sisters were significant auxiliaries to clergy (as were all laity) in evangelisation. He voiced concern, though, that they were out of sync with modern womanhood and this hindered their effectiveness and discouraged vocations.[42] This was the basic premise of *The Nun in the World*, published in 1963 and translated into seven languages, reaching a worldwide readership.[43] Suenens was, at the time, one of the most important promoters of Church renewal at the Second Vatican Council. His book was exciting, challenging and controversial. It

---

41 The International Congresses of the States of Perfection were held from 1950, addressing the perfecting of religious and clerical vocations.

42 Leon-Joseph Suenens, trans. Father Austin Flannery, OP, 'Nuns and the Lay-Apostolate', *Doctrine and Life*, 8:3 (1958), pp. 115–19. This was the paper read by Suenens at the Congress of the States of Perfection in Rome.

43 It was originally published in French as *La Promotion Apostolique de la Religieuse*. Elizabeth Hamilton, *Cardinal Suenens: A Portrait* (London: Hodder and Stoughton, 1975), p. 79.

began by acknowledging the history of the Church in silencing women as part of a long pattern of institutionalisation that centralised the power of the Holy See. Suenens apologised for the 'masculinist mentality' and 'anti-feminist tradition' embedded in Canon Law.[44] The tradition in the Church was one of strict hierarchies, with the Holy See at the apex, followed by bishops and clergy, with the laity as servants and followers. Non-clerical male and female religious were liminally placed.[45] Their role and function, whether enclosed or active, gave them a 'special place' in the Church, but always at the behest of the local clergy or bishop. Women religious were expected to support and serve the Church with humility, submission and invisibility.[46] The rules and regulation of religious life had become more reified and intrusive after the publication of the Code of Canon Law in 1917, which formalised religious life within a rigid framework.[47] Historian Phil Kilroy has powerfully argued that when 'feminism was gaining ground, women religious were travelling in another direction'.[48]

The Nun in the World was revolutionary in some ways, but in others it was of its time. Suenens was wedded to a gendered construction of womanhood, which would have been invisible and unproblematic for most of his Catholic readership.[49] It was, as scholar Rebecca Sullivan explains, his 'explicit embrace of feminism and encouragement of women's independence both in the Catholic Church and in society' that was astounding.[50] Markedly, he spoke *to* women religious, rather than *about* them. Religious communities, he told women religious, should be 'centres of evangelisation'.[51] The active sister must be a 'modern woman' who 'takes charge', and does not 'passively accept her fate'.[52] He paints

44 Suenens, *The Nun in the World*, p. 47.
45 Vincent Viaene, 'International History, Religious History, Catholic History: Perspectives for Cross-Fertilization (1830–1914)', *European History Quarterly*, 38:4 (2008), 578–607.
46 Kilroy, 'Coming to an Edge in History', pp. 6–30; Brosnan, 'Public Presence, Public Silence', pp. 474, 496. Brosnan argues that women religious inhabited a gendered public space that demanded a prominent presence and a substantial silence.
47 Most religious institutes spent years updating their rules and constitutions to comply with the new Code of Canon Law.
48 Kilroy, 'Coming to an Edge in History', p. 21.
49 He remained convinced women's role was one where she 'ennobles and raises man up by her presence, by creating a climate of beauty and human mobility'. Suenens, *The Nun in the World*, p. 15.
50 Sullivan, *Visual Habits*, pp. 36–7.
51 Suenens, 'Nuns and the Lay-Apostolate', pp. 115–16, 118.
52 Suenens, *The Nun in the World*, pp. v, 10.

a contemporary world where women were a part of the workforce and the advancement of women was 'a *fait accompli*'.[53] He envisioned female religious life that was in 'harmony with the evolutionary state of the world and womankind', retaining from the past what was of 'lasting value'.[54] He controversially argued that active women religious were 'out of touch' and an anachronism, linking this to 'the lack of vocations'. What was once 'pioneer work' had become 'functionary', with women religious identified as 'just a teacher' or simply a 'ward sister'. Suenens insisted they become 'modern women', acknowledging 'the positive contribution of feminism'.[55]

This was a controversial but widely distributed and well-read book. In introducing the book in 1963, the *Catholic Pictorial* proclaimed a 'new era for nuns', suggesting his work was an antidote to what already was well known: 'fewer and fewer modern girls feel the call to the convent'. Convent life was dated, which was 'why good Catholic girls say with a shudder: "I would never be a nun"'. The article enthused that female religious life should 'reflect the new status of women', attesting that the Cardinal was 'frank, even revolutionary', encouraging women's congregations to adapt to the world though without engaging with 'worldliness'.[56] The *Catholic Herald* considered the book significant enough to review it twice, after its initial publication and then a year later, when the revised edition was published. The favourable reviews emphasised that female religious life needed updating, with the replacement of rote and 'arid' religious exercises and more access to news media so that religious were aware of world events. Religious congregations were encouraged to shift their ministries to 'discovering and stimulating lay apostles'. *Catholic Herald* readers were told that this book was 'no subversive manifesto seeking to cause disastrous upheavals, to undermine authority and to be responsible for the destruction of much that is good', which suggests these concerns did in fact exist.[57] In the United States, some scholars claim the work was enthusiastically 'read by virtually every American nun'.[58] The evidence

53 *Ibid.*, pp. 13–14. He addressed this work specifically to active women religious in 'developed countries'.
54 *Ibid.*, p. 35.
55 *Ibid.*, pp. 21–2.
56 'A New Era for Nuns', *Catholic Pictorial* (3 March 1963), p. 15.
57 Father Vincent Rochford, 'The Nun's Place in the Modern World', *Catholic Herald* (16 January 1963), pp. 3; 'The Nun in the World of Today', *Catholic Herald* (17 January 1964), p. 6.
58 Renée D. Bondy, 'Roman Catholic Women Religious and Organizational Reform in English Canada: The Ursuline and Holy Names Sisters in the Diocese of London, Ontario, 1950–1970', unpublished PhD dissertation, University of Waterloo, 2007.

is less absolute in British convents.[59] In 1962, Father Daniel Shanahan, a canon lawyer and chancellor of the diocese of Brentwood, informed Mother Prioress Mary Veronica Boland of the Canonesses of the Holy Sepulchre that 'an important book by Cardinal Suenens on the religious life is to appear shortly: it may presage the changes that may be effected by Vatican II'.[60] Though the book was written for active apostolic sisters, its reach extended to enclosed convents. One reader of *The Nun in the World*, a forty-six-year-old Syon Bridgettine, wrote to Bishop Cyril Edward Restieaux of Plymouth in 1969 that 'many of the proposals some of us would wish to see taken up'.[61] It is equally evident that some congregation leaders were threatened by Suenens's book.[62] Former sister Karen Armstrong notes that it was forbidden reading in her convent, suggesting that in Britain there was a caution about the modernisation that Suenens was proposing.

Even before the Women's Liberation Movement formed, it was becoming patently difficult for the Holy See to ignore women's changing role in the modern world. Pope John XXIII in his encyclical *Pacem in Terris* (Peace on Earth, 1963) acknowledged:

> [I]t is obvious to everyone that women are now taking a part in public life. This is happening more rapidly perhaps in nations of Christian civilisation and more slowly but broadly among peoples who have inherited other traditions or cultures … Since women are becoming ever more conscious of their human dignity, they will not tolerate being treated as mere material instruments, but demand rights befitting a human person both in domestic and in public life.[63]

And yet it was not so obvious to John XXIII that women should be invited to participate in the Second Vatican Council. Two years after the

Bondy indicates that each of her interviewees read Suenens work; Philip Gleason, 'A Browser's Guide to American Catholicism, 1950–1980', *Theology Today*, 38:3 (1981), 378–88; Elizabeth Kolmer, ASC, *Religious Women in the United States: A Survey of the Influential Literature from 1950 to 1983* (Wilmington, NC: Michael Glazier, 1984), pp. 45–6.

59 None of my over eighty participants mentioned *The Nun in the World* and it is rarely mentioned in archival documents.

60 DUL CHS: Letter dated 29 November 1962 from D. Shanahan, Vicar-General for Religious, to Mother Prioress.

61 PDA: Syon files, Correspondence 1953–1960 and newsletters 1958–1978, Letter from Sister Sebastian [Smith] to bishop, dated 23 May 1969.

62 Karen Armstrong, *Through the Narrow Gate: A Nun's Story* (London: Flamingo, 1981), p. 161.

63 *Pacem in Terris*, §§18–19.

opening of the Council, at the intervention of Suenens, who reminded the Pope that 'Women too should be invited as auditors, unless I am mistaken, they make up half of the human race', twenty-three women became auditors and were included as participants on the Theological Commissions.[64] Theologian Mary Ellen Sheehan emphasises 'something *new* happened':

> [W]omen were *there*, present and participating, in the universal church gathered in Council. *Precisely as women*, they become symbols, visible signs of the presence and participation of women in the church as institution. In effect, the normative practice of the exclusion of women from church deliberations was overcome.

Though the significance of this gesture cannot be understated, Sheehan, unfortunately, was being overly optimistic. Fifty years on, few Catholic women have been included in recent synods.[65]

There is little evidence that Simone de Beauvoir, Betty Frieden or Germaine Greer were being read in British convents, but many, as suggested above, were reading American Catholic feminist theologians such as Mary Daly, Elisabeth Schüssler Fiorenza and Rosemary Radford Ruether, who were advocating correcting the injustices of sexist theology and praxis within the Church.[66] Later, Sisters Joan Chittister and Sandra

---

64 Carmel McEnroy, *Guests in Their Own House: The Women of Vatican II* (New York: Crossroad, 1996), pp. 3, 35. Eight of the women were leaders of women's religious congregations (though three were not Roman Catholic rite). Also Mary Luke Tobin, 'Women in the Church since Vatican II', *America*, 155 (1 November 1986), p. 243.

65 Mary Ellen Sheehan, 'Vatican II and the Ministry of Women in the Church: Selected North American Episcopal Statements and Diocesan Practice', in M. Lamberigts and L. Kenis (eds), *Vatican II and Its Legacy* (Leuven: Leuven University Press, 2002), pp. 470–1. Karen Kuruvilla, *HuffPost* (16 October 2018). www.huffingtonpost.co.uk/entry/catholic-activists-demand-womens-voting-rights-at-major-vatican-meeting_us_5bc4e943e4b03ef92497e4ba, accessed 4 November 2018.

66 British theologian Maria Grey noted the significance of these three in the 1960s. Mary Grey, '"Expelled Again from Eden": Facing Difference through Connection', *Feminist Theology*, 21 (1999), 10. Rosemary Radford Ruether, *Sexism and God-Talk: Toward a Feminist Theology* (London: SCM Press, 1983); Mary Daly, *The Church and the Second Sex* (Washington, DC: Catholic University of America Press, 1968); Elisabeth Schüssler Fiorenza, *In Memory of Her: A Feminist Theological Reconstruction of Christian Origins* (New York: Crossroad, 1983); Amy L. Koehlinger, *The New Nuns: Racial Justice and Religious Reform in the 1960s* (Cambridge, MA: Harvard University Press, 2007). On the significance of the Second Vatican Council to the laity's study of theology see Elizabeth A. Johnson, 'Jesus and Women: "You are Set Free"', in Catholic Women Speak Network (ed.), *Catholic Women Speak: Bringing Our Gifts to the Table* (New York: Paulist Press, 2015), pp. 19–22, and Ursula King, 'The Catholic

Schneiders would bring a distinctly feminist Catholic theology to their experience of religious life. Britain had its own constellation of Catholic feminist theologians, such as Benedictine Maria Boulding, Dominican Cecily Boulding,[67] Maria Grey, Ursula King, Notre Dame sister Myra Poole and Janet Soskice, who were not as internationally known as the American cohort, but offered new theological thinking not only through their published work, but also through lectures at the many seminars and workshops that were attended by women religious. Many of their talks and seminars were recorded, and archives still hold a vast number of tapes that were listened to and discussed by women's communities. One sister from a teaching congregation spoke of community discussion groups:

> We had quite an awareness of some of the big, you know, Sandra Schneiders and Co., writers, and [*The*] *Fire in these Ashes* [1995] and Joan Chittister, and various people would say, let's have some meetings to look at this article .... And that came from possibly a handful of individuals, probably on the younger side of it, but we always tried to be inclusive. And so all these, they were never a break-off group, we'd have meetings for everybody, we'd have the same meeting at different times to accommodate whatever anyone was doing, to try and get everyone in the sort of thinking together.[68]

This was consciousness-raising convent style.[69]

The *Nun in the World* directed women religious to modernise and adapt to the needs of society. It was a response to women's growing role and responsibilities in the secular world. Feminist theologians using a developing feminist body of scholarship translated feminist secular thinking into a religious framework. Their publications crossed international borders and were shared and discussed by women religious and linked to their own growing understanding of council documents that emphasised equality and justice.

Intellectual Tradition and Women Theologians', in Catholic Women Speak Network (ed.), *Catholic Women Speak: Bringing Our Gifts to the Table* (New York: Paulist Press, 2015), pp. 11–14.

67 For more on her work see Anselm Nye, *A Peculiar Kind of Mission: The English Dominican Sisters, 1845–2010* (Leominster: Gracewing, 2011), pp. 269–70.

68 Anonymised interview.

69 This book doesn't address the feminist content of such work – another research topic that urgently needs attention.

Consciousness-raising: Poor Clare constitutions

Consciousness-raising was central to disseminating understandings of women's oppression for the Women's Liberation Movement. Small groups were formed where each member shared their individual experiences of liberation and oppression. Their aim was mutual support and a self-knowledge that could lead to collective action.[70] Consciousness-raising convent-style happened locally in small groups as mentioned above, but also, as we shall see below, through transnational exchanges being communicated through epistolary correspondence.

Though the Poor Clares were an international religious order, each community was autonomous. Unlike religious congregations, there was no centralised structure through which reactions to the council documents could be discussed.[71] The renewal process was expected to be guided by the community's abbess under the jurisdiction of the local bishop. But in 1965, the Sacred Congregation of Religious appointed the Order of Friars Minor to oversee the process of renewal of the Poor Clares alongside the revision of their constitutions.[72] The renewal letter sent by the Vicar General of the Friars to 615 Poor Clare monasteries and forty-three Poor Clare federations worldwide asked them to discuss and respond to a questionnaire with fifty-five questions ranging from querying the traditions of the Poor Clares to critiquing features of governance and the formation of novices.[73] The Friars obtained permission (with much difficulty) from the Congregation of Religious for the formation of the International Commission of Poor Clares.[74] In 1968, twelve representatives from the Poor Clares gathered in Rome and formed a temporary community commissioned to tabulate the questionnaire results.[75] They were also charged specifically with informing the development of a common constitution in light of their understandings of *aggiornamento* and adaptation; their set aims were to 'return to the sources of your monasteries' and 'clarify them [the sources], understand them better' and 'put them into the context of reality as a whole, to find the middle path'.

---

70 June Hannam, *Feminism* (Harlow, Pearson Education, 2012), p. 81.
71 Anonymised interview.
72 ABDA: Poor Clares folder, Letter from Paul Philippe to Constantine Koser, dated 29 November 1965. In 1965, the Sacred Congregation was responsible for issues which concerned religious and secular institutes and Societies of Apostolic Life.
73 FPA: Questionnaire Summary of Results.
74 FPA: Letter from Francis Pullen to Liberton community, dated [13 June 1968].
75 FPA: Questionnaire Summary of Results, p. 87.

Their ambition was to create a Poor Clares constitution 'wide enough to allow these various ways'.[76] These 'various ways' could appear in additional legislation developed by each monastery. The General Constitutions were to be developed and approved through a rather circuitous process which began with the International Commission deconstructing and then reconstructing the responses of the questionnaire in conversation with their national community. This analysis was forwarded to the Friars Minor, who wrote the General Constitutions that were returned to the Poor Clare communities to be lived for a period of time, and then reported on. Any revisions, based on the reports from the Poor Clares, would be made by the Friars Minor. And finally, the *Officium pro Monialibus* was to be the final authority before the text was sent to the Congregation for Religious for final approbation.[77]

The Holy See's decision to deputise the Order of Friars Minor to aid their renewal was not enthusiastically welcomed by all Poor Clares. Sister Gabriel Taggert of the Scottish community at Liberton wrote to Benedictine abbot Christopher Butler, then acting as auxiliary bishop of the Westminster diocese, in 1967:

> You see we are in no way connected with or under the Minister General of the Friars – they of course are handling the Constitutions simply because men have always done these things – why shouldn't we do our own?? But they have no authority over us at all.[78]

Her letter criticised the decision of the Holy See, which had, she implies, unjustifiably assigned the Friars to write their constitutions. 'Men have always done these things' was no longer a reasonable rationale. She rebelled against a thinking which assumed that women were incapable of dealing with matters of their own governance. Other abbesses seemed to be of the same opinion. Abbess Mary Veronica of Arkley, writing to Abbess Paula Smallwood of Baddesley Clinton in 1974, also questioned the authority of the Friars: 'We have no quarrel with the Friars, Minor or Capuchin, but I do not think they should legislate for us.'[79] Poor Clare abbesses had a great deal of power within their own monasteries, though their final authority was the local bishop. The Holy See appeared to replace one male authority, the bishop, with another, the Friars. They believed the

76 FPA: 'Discourse of Very Rev. Father General, Fr. Constantine Koser', 8 June 1968.
77 Email conversation with Joseph Chinnici, dated 26 September 2014.
78 AAW: BU E.39, Poor Clares Notting Hill and Barnet (1968–1975), Letter from Gabriel Taggert to Christopher Butler, dated 11 October 1967.
79 Birmingham Archdiocesan Archives: Letter from Mary Veronica PCC of Arkley to Mother Abbess [Paula], dated 7 January 1974, p. 3.

'common constitution' being encouraged by the Friars would limit their authority within their community and thus not be 'authentic' to their understandings of Poor Clare life.[80] Their bishops, less enthusiastic about renewal than the friars, were likely to support them in their efforts to maintain the status quo.

On the surface, the tasks of the International Poor Clares Commission appear quite functional and mundane. Sister Francis Pullen of the Liberton (near Edinburgh) community, who had been chosen as the British member of the Commission, collected ancillary documents including statistics, histories of each British and Irish monastery and spiritual texts.[81] She also collated, summarised and analysed the responses from the questionnaire by making a card index of all the responses. These cards were pooled together to create a British/Irish summary, and then she worked alongside eleven other Poor Clares to create a worldwide summary.[82] The Commission's work was not simply a set of mundane administrative tasks. First, it was a collaborative effort amongst women who had different perspectives on Poor Clare life. Such collaboration and collegiality between sisters of different Poor Clare traditions was unprecedented. The Vatican Council's call for collegiality was interpreted as decision-making based on consensus and collaboration rather than authoritative structures often linked to hierarchical or clerical relationships. Historian John O'Malley calls this collegiality the 'lightening rod issue' at the Council.[83] The processes of the Poor Clares Commission enabled a culture of collaboration, shared responsibility and collegiality between women of different understandings of Poor Clare life. This was in stark contrast to the hierarchical structure that remained in place in many Poor Clare monasteries through to the 1970s and 1980s.

The International Poor Clare Commission was intended to set the direction for the final form that the constitutions would take. The Franciscan Friars Minor were tasked to write the first draft of the new constitutions but they did not take the sole authority and power in creating this document. The International Commission was doing the thinking, the collating and

80 Carmen M. Mangion, "'Shades of Difference": Poor Clares in Britain', in Christian Sorrel (ed.), *Le Concile Vatican II et le monde des religieux (Europe occidentale et Amérique du Nord, 1950–1980)* (Lyon: LARHRA, 2019), pp. 317–29.
81 FPA: Questionnaire Summary of Results, p. 9.
82 FPA: Letter from Francis Pullen to Liberton community, dated 30 May 1968.
83 John W. O'Malley, *What Happened at Vatican II* (Cambridge, MA: Harvard University Press, 2008), p. 163. O'Malley was discussing episcopal collegiality but the term and this meaning can be used in the discussion of the developing relationships between women religious.

the summarising of this material that was to influence the final form the constitutions would take. The nuns' knowledge of the day-to-day Poor Clare life and local customs was essential to the development of the constitutions. Father General Koser stated in his initial letter to the monasteries that the Commission's 'important work' was 'the study of the documents to see what the nuns think'.[84] Pullen re-emphasised this Poor Clare contribution in her circular letter to the Poor Clares in Britain and Ireland. She explained Koser's advice:

> What he said about the work was not to give us any particular direction but to encourage us to think for ourselves, and to keep a middle course between slavish adherence to tradition and the tendency to discard the past entirely ... He also mentioned a healthy spirit of criticism – not to be 'yes women' even as regards the Franciscans. Not many people need to be told this nowadays, but he did say that here again there is such a thing as a happy medium.[85]

She alludes here to the independence that was embedded in her own critical thinking process, and, she suggests, those of her fellow Poor Clares. She also acknowledges, though lightly, women's responsibility and agency in the reinterpretation of the Poor Clare vocation. These Poor Clares were creating the framework for their constitutions for the Friars Minor, who would perform the legal and administrative work of assembling them.

Sister Francis constantly reminded the sisters in her letters that they controlled the development of the constitutions. Their responses to her queries were pivotal to the shaping of the document that would govern their lives and she advised them to think more expansively: 'The tendency nowadays is to leave more to the discretion and less to the letter of the law; but, of course now it is not my job to tell anyone what to say. It might just save special permissions later on, though.'[86]

She regularly emphasised the intended breadth and non-prescriptive nature of the constitutions: 'I got the impression that he [Koser] wants the constitutions to give very broad outlines which will allow for development according to the spirit of each nation.' Pullen's epistolary communication provides an important means of not only conveying the process of the development of the constitutions, but also sharing

84 FPA: 'Discourse of Very Rev. Father General, Fr. Constantine Koser', dated 8 June 1968.
85 FPA: Letter from Francis Pullen to Liberton community, dated [13 June 1968].
86 FPA: Letter from Francis Pullen to Liberton community, dated 16 July 1968.

interpretations of *aggiornamento* and renewal. She commented that Father General Koser was

> keen that we (i.e. I take it all P.C.s) should be well informed about the concerns of the Church, and the things of God and the traditions of the Order, but he did not make any suggestions about how we were to obtain the information. Reading, of course he did mention, but I know that the English and Irish houses are aware of the need of a good library.[87]

The members of the International Commission of Poor Clares were expected to be immersed in the documents coming out of the Council. Their knowledge informed their analysis of the questionnaires and was shared with the communities that read Sister Francis Pullen's correspondence. Shared knowledge was, in turn, critical to Pullen taking an active part in the debates about the constitutions.

The agency of the Poor Clares was, of course, circumscribed. The Friars controlled the process and Koser's aims for broad constitutions were influential. However, the International Poor Clares Commission did not simply gather and collate the data; Pullen and the other members of the Commission shaped the questionnaire results with their analysis of the responses which were informed by their understandings of *aggiornamento* and renewal. Pullen communicated that they were not to be 'yes women' and were expected to offer input and critique the process. The consciousness-raising process, the back and forth of ideas between the twelve nuns in Rome to and from their own home communities was transnational. Pullen was sharing knowledge gained from her international sisters and others in Rome, the centre of new ideas and praxis on renewal and *aggiornamento*, with the sisters of her community in Scotland, England, Wales and Ireland.

The personal is political: the convent grille

Consciousness-raising occurred at the local level in discussions of the fifty-five questions of the questionnaire. One of the most emotive questions was related to the grille. In this section, we hear the voices of 'ordinary' sisters that participated in the process of consciousness-raising, and more critically we learn how the personal was political and 'freedom behind the grille' had different meanings for women as they took the dramatic step of airing their views publicly.

---

87   FPA: Letter from Francis Pullen to Liberton community, dated [13 June 1968].

The convent grille, an opening with horizontal and/or vertical bars side by side, was a ubiquitous feature of cloistered religious life; it was supposed to ensure and protect enclosure.[88] Some grilles were fixed and unmovable, others had cords which allowed them to be opened on certain occasions. Some had bars that were far apart, some were narrow; some had openings within the grille itself where items could be passed through. Grilles were located in parlours where nuns met their visitors, as is represented in Figure 7.1, taken in 1962. Mother Mary Peter, a Poor Clare from the Baddesley Clinton monastery, sits in the parlour speaking to visitors and separated from them by a double grate. In monastic chapels and churches, the grille also separated the nuns from the mass attendees; in Figure 7.2 the Poor Clares watch the mass behind a grate with a large opening to better view the celebrant. The size, shape and dimensions of the grilles were usually a function of a community's rules and constitutions, or community tradition.

The grille had a practical functionality in providing a physical barrier between a nun and her visitor, thus regulating interactions. As a 'charged symbol' of enclosed religious life, it represented the division between a tainted world and the sacred monastic space. Historian Joseph Chinnici in examining the symbolic activities of religious practices has identified a 'language' of religious life existing 'at the intersection between theological or religious meaning, institutional allegiance, and personal commitment'.[89] The grille was a material representation of the 'symbolic world of the cloister' and an emotive symbol of tradition and belonging. Renewal led to the questioning of its role in enclosed religious life, and the often vociferous debates offered women both private and, in one rare case, public opportunities to voice contradictory gendered understanding of womanhood.

Poor Clares

Question 46 of the Poor Clare renewal questionnaire addressed enclosure and asked what precepts should be 'revised, adapted, or abrogated as obsolete'. A minority, forty monasteries and one federation (of 615 Poor Clare monasteries and forty-three Poor Clare federations worldwide), argued that 'papal enclosure be maintained in all its rigour and that the same be strengthened', with some suggesting

88   Some nuns even wore an enclosure veil (over the face) when speaking at the grille.
89   Joseph P. Chinnici, 'Religious Life in the Twentieth Century: Interpreting the Languages', *US Catholic Historian*, 22 (2004), 41.

Figure 7.1 Poor Clare Mother Abbess at the grille, *c.* 1962

Figure 7.2 Poor Clares behind the grille, Baddesley Clinton, *c.* 1963

accentuating 'the positive side' of enclosure: 'the motive of love, of openness to the Holy Spirit who inspires separation from the world for the sake of a more perfect union with Himself'. The majority of the Poor Clares felt some revision of the rules of enclosure was necessary but their recommendations ranged from the need to suppress 'minute prescriptions and details' to 'Everything should be changed: All the present prescriptions concerning enclosure are out of date; they should be completely abolished and replaced by others which express an adult commitment.'[90] Diverse opinions existed locally also. In Arundel, one Poor Clare revealed: 'I agree with the idea of opening up the grille, and I think it would be a good thing. I do not like the grille and never have done.' Another responded: 'Don't take away the grille. It will be the ruin of the community. Taking away the grille will do no good, and will do a lot of harm.'[91] One Poor Clare who had collated the responses to the questionnaire in her local English convent recalled: 'we ploughed our way through piles of totally contradictory answers. Some people were saying if you don't do away with the grille I shall leave, and other people saying it's essential to my spiritual life to have a grille.'[92]

These varied responses to the grille reflect individual perceptions of their terms of enclosure and the place of the grille as a corporeal symbol of their separation from the world. The discourse of tradition and progress was reflected in many arguments. The emotionality of these comments can be felt through the language used: the grille was a charged symbol of enclosed religious life and all that was associated with it: tradition, authenticity and status. These divisions reflect not simply the physical architecture of the grille, but theological differences and in some cases a resistance or enthusiasm for the spirit of the Council. Enclosed nuns gave positive and negative reasons to keep the grille: the link to tradition, the threat to relationships and its necessity to giving oneself wholeheartedly to God. Embedded in this also was a distinct repositioning of the meaning of the grille from keeping outsiders out to the positive side of enclosure, the motive of love and union with God. Some Poor Clares saw the grille as a hindrance to a relationship with the 'people of God'. Others wanted to be treated like adults and resented the many rules of enclosure. In these responses, some Poor Clares

---

90   FPA: Questionnaire Summary of Results, p. 56.
91   ABDA: Poor Clares folder, 'Convent of the Poor Clares: Arundel'.
92   Anonymised interview.

suggested an understanding of the philosophical concept of personalism that emphasised the role of the individual and self-determination in responding to circumstances but also encouraged co-responsibility.[93] This would seem contrary to the collective nature of religious life which de-emphasised the individual. Each community made its own decision regarding the grille. Some retained the grille and made it more open by widening the slats, others took it down completely. Others tried to cater to the varied opinions in the monastery by offering a movable grille; larger communities were able to offer the option of a grille and a no-grille parlour.

Consciousness-raising is evident throughout these debates. In completing the questionnaires women were rethinking what they understood and experienced about enclosed religious life, making their voices heard by responding to the questionnaire sometimes in anonymous ways and other times within the community.[94] One nun who entered in the late 1950s summarised the contradictions of the grille:

> I always spoke out against it, I never saw the point of it. But then my Novice Mistress said to me when I entered, she said, 'You're one of the new breed.' I came in at that time. The Sisters who had entered before me, before I did, were … came in at the end of the war, right? Now, that was when changes were happening for women. I was that much further on, at the end of the war I was still a child and I'd grown up with the changes for women. And she said probably I had a good family, I had a good relationship with my family, my parents, I don't know, I would speak out my opinion in the family discussions, you know.[95]

In distinguishing herself from those nuns who were of the pre-war generation she was addressing the intergenerational tensions that were part of her community's discussions. In some communities, there was pressure to conform.[96] In others, as some nuns recounted, opportunities were taken to discuss amongst themselves the future of the convent grille.

93 Personalism is an eclectic and diverse movement that emphasises the sacred dignity of the individual. James J. Farrell, *The Spirit of the Sixties: Making Postwar Radicalism* (London: Routledge, 1997).
94 Patricia Wittberg, *The Rise and Fall of Catholic Religious Orders: A Social Movement Perspective* (New York: SUNY Press, 1994).
95 Anonymised interview.
96 As discussed in Chapter 2 some questionnaires were completely collectively and nuns felt pressure to conform or defer to the opinions of the abbess.

Benedictines

Most discussions regarding the grille occurred in the private spaces of the convent or monastery. More exceptional was the public debate about the grille that occurred in the Catholic press in 1966. 'A Benedictine from Stanbrook Abbey' wrote an impassioned editorial letter to *The Tablet* championing the grille as integral to the cloistered way of life. Her defence speaks volumes for the emotiveness of the topic, and of the difficult debates taking place in her monastery and others. Her autonomous community were in the midst of renewal, and the many customs and regulations of enclosed religious life, including the grille, were being scrutinised. Her argument for retaining the grille reflected both its functionality and its symbolic importance, which are underpinned by her understandings of womanhood and her community's history of exile.

Her editorial letter began by contrasting active with contemplative religious life, explaining that active sisters who taught in schools, nursed in hospitals and interacted regularly with 'seculars' were 'conditioned to cope with the contemporary world'. The worldly interaction of active sisters implied they were skilled at addressing 'the complexities of human relationships as inevitably encountered outside'. These were relationships, she implied, that disrupted the 'spiritual singleness of purpose' and a nun's 'wholehearted concentration on God'.[97] Enclosed nuns, who were separated from the world once they entered an enclosed monastery, were more 'vulnerable', naïve and fragile than their active sisters. She proposed the grille functioned as a means of separating and protecting the nun from the complexities of a secular world. The cloister with its grille was intended as a social space of safety, where nuns could be 'safe-guarded from intrusion by seculars'.[98] In positing the grille's functionality, she insisted it allowed for 'freedom behind the grille'.[99] Her gendered understanding of womanhood was firmly wedded to 'vulnerable' enclosed women who needed to be watched and monitored.

---

97 I would be curious to hear this Benedictine from Stanbrook's thoughts on Rumer Godden's portrayal of enclosed religious life in *In This House of Brede*. Godden spent several months with the Benedictines of Stanbrook doing research for the book. Published in 1969, it depicted very clearly some of the 'the complexities of human relationships' within the monastery.

98 AAW: BU E.39, Letter from Abbess Sister Mary Veronica PCC to Christopher Butler, dated 3 August 1968.

99 This sentiment appears in *In a Great Tradition: Tribute to Dame Laurentia McLachlan, Abbess of Stanbrook* (London: John Murray, 1956), p. 242.

The grille had an added layer of symbolic meaning relating to her Benedictine community's turbulent history of exile. The Stanbrook Benedictines had been founded in 1623 in Cambrai, Flanders (now Belgium) at a time when religious life was illegal in England. During the anti-clerical years of the French Revolution, religious life was seen to be an enemy of state-sponsored *liberté, égalité, fraternité*; they were arrested and imprisoned in Compiègne for eighteen months before they were allowed to escape to England.[100] In 1795, they arrived in London destitute and shaken from their experiences and facing the prospect of residing in a Protestant England that did not welcome their form of religious life. Many of the privileges of enclosed life were denied to them; they were initially forbidden to wear their religious habit, and rather than recite the full Divine Office, they 'obediently bent themselves to the highly uncongenial task of educating young ladies'.[101] Their history, written in 1956, only ten years before *The Tablet* editorial was published, recounted their sorrow at their inability to establish enclosure – 'All they could do was to erect a wooden grille – symbol of their hopes – to divide the sanctuary from the nuns' chapel' – and their joy at the reinstatement of the iron double grille when in 1880 'The Cambrai grates were restored at last.' Our Benedictine nun worried that renewal debates suggested 'superficial notions of evolution, which becomes, in the popular mind, a means of disowning the past'.[102] For her, the past was relevant and alive, not simply because of the long tradition of the grille in enclosed religious life but because of her foremothers' history of struggle, of loss, of exile and of sacrifice. Having been taken away and proscribed, the grille, like the religious habit and praying the Divine Office, were sacred privileges of her authentic experience of religious life. Importantly, she identifies herself not simply as a Benedictine, but as a Benedictine of Stanbrook Abbey. Her community's history in exile in Cambrai and their dramatic return to England would have been well

---

100 Some women religious were executed during the French Revolution. Mita Choudhury, *Convents and Nuns in Eighteenth-Century French Politics and Culture* (Ithaca, NY: Cornell University Press, 2018), pp. 178–81.

101 They made a 'heroic and pathetic attempt' to recite the Divine Office. *In a Great Tradition*, pp. 42–4, 58, 242. See also Jane E. Hollinshead, 'From Cambrai to Woolton: Lancashire's First Female Religious House', *Recusant History*, 25 (2001), 461–86; Tonya J. Moutray, *Refugee Nuns, the French Revolution, and British Literature and Culture* (London: Routledge, 2016).

102 A Benedictine from Stanbrook, 'Freedom behind the Grille', *The Tablet* (11 June 1966), p. 7.

known in Catholic circles and she was reminding readers of *The Tablet* of her foremothers' sacrifice.[103]

Curiously, she did not mention at all the Second Vatican Council and *aggiornamento*. Her community was in the throes of discussing renewal and the changes that would need to be made in how enclosed religious life was lived. Instead, she proposed that the anti-grille sentiment was a 'reaction against the excessive tightening-up and regimentation of recent years'. She blamed male clerics 'who never would or could have done what they demanded of us' for the 'petty' regulations in place. She seems not to have realised that such self-assured and direct criticism was in stark contrast with her depiction of the vulnerable, naïve and fragile contemplative nun who needed to be safeguarded and monitored. The removal of the grille, she believed, would lead to tedious rules and regulations supposed to control nuns' behaviour when with visitors. She implies no sea change in attitude towards the actual reason for the grille: detachment and surveillance. Proponents of the grille, like the secular priest she mentioned at the opening of her letter, often argued that the grille was a 'strong sign' to the world that youth were 'ready to turn their backs completely upon it to give their whole lives to God'.[104] She suggests that the youth of 1966 were not so different from the youth of earlier times.

The following week, *The Tablet* published the self-assured response from another enclosed nun, a Discalced Carmelite, Sister Teresa Margaret, who was equally assertive and direct, and sounded distinctly feminist. Expounding on modern girls of the 1960s she reported: 'young single girls enjoy freedom of movement, emancipation from parental control, and autonomy in the management of their affairs'; they were 'conditioned by independence, self-determination and immunity from cramping restrictions imposed by former social conventions'. She also, like our Poor Clare earlier, linked the present with the past by contrasting pre-war from post-war womanhood in order to argue the grille's functionality was redundant: 'Fifty years ago it was unthinkable for a girl who valued her good name to remain for long periods in male company unchaperoned.' She suggested encounters in the parlour should be 'conducted sensibly, in a dignified manner, and in line with normal contemporary usages governing the drawing room or business interview'.

103 Their story could be found in the *Laity's Directory* ('The Narrative of the Sufferings of the English Communities under the dominion of the French Republicans' (1796), pp. 6–31) and also in *In a Great Tradition*.
104 A Benedictine, 'Freedom behind the Grille', p. 7.

She explicitly rejected the grille's symbolism, linking it, again, to a past age: 'The grille is only an external sign that was relevant in a previous age when it was consistent with the existing norms governing women in secular spheres as well. It does not do the work for us, and never did.'[105] Her argument against the grille centred on a depiction of 1960s young women who appeared neither vulnerable, naïve nor fragile. She agreed that detachment was necessary but that the grille was redundant as young women knew how to behave.

The public nature of this dialogue was remarkable. It suggests that women religious of all ages felt aggrieved enough to publicly debate this contentious topic on a national stage. Respected theologian and Stanbrook Benedictine Maria Boulding, writing two years after the grilles were removed from Stanbrook Abbey, noted a revised understanding of the grille that offered latitude for 'cultural conditions'.

> Enclosure has to some extent characterised the life of nuns from earliest times. It is a sign and guarantee of their renunciation of aspects of life that are merely this worldly, and it helps to keep them free for the work they are called to do. Since the Council of Trent, it has often been symbolised by grilles, but grilles are not essential to enclosure and recent directives of the Church have paid more attention to local cultural conditions.[106]

Our anonymous Stanbrook Benedictine must have felt a deep sense of disappointment with the removal of the grille, though, no doubt, obedience triumphed and she accepted the personal sacrifice that this would have entailed.

Becoming a woman

Debates over another charged symbol of religious life, the religious habit, were significant to sisters and nuns as they came to understand their own womanhood. Religious dress was worn by most enclosed and active women religious and remained a static reminder of the religious institute's early history and a sister's and a nun's corporate identity. From the 1950s, congregations and orders began to make modest modifications of the religious habit to simplify it and make it more modern and amenable

---

105 Sister Teresa Margaret, DC, 'Signs of the Times: Another View of Grilles', *The Tablet* (25 June 1966), p. 10.
106 Mary Boulding, *Contemplative Nuns: Are They Wasting Their Lives?* (London: Catholic Truth Society, 1973).

to their ministries. Some, by the 1970s, had relinquished the religious habit and instead wore a symbol of their consecration. Phil Kilroy has commented that the time-consuming debates within the convent over the modifications of the religious habit eclipsed the more substantive issues of renewal.[107] Media attention (then and now) continued to be fixated on religious dress.[108]

The religious habit was not the only visible change linked to religious identity. Many religious institutes required women religious take on a religious name.[109] Sisters and nuns mentioned the loss of personal identity when they were given a religious name, particularly when given a male name. One sister remarked that it was as though she had become 'another identical person'.[110] When religious institutes in the 1960s gave sisters and nuns the opportunity to return to their baptismal name, some did. One former sister recalled how it became much more egalitarian to call each other by their birth names.[111] But others kept their religious name, signaling an identity attached to their religious name. One sister explained: 'I went back to my baptismal name when we stopped wearing our religious habits, because it was rather awkward to have a man's name wearing women's clothes, so I went back to being Mary, so I've always been called Sister Mary.'[112]

The religious dress of nuns and sisters derived from medieval clothing[113] and according to Cardinal Suenens owed its origin to a legalistic Church obliging female religious to accept *clausura*.[114] The religious habit became reified, sanctified and seen as intrinsic to religious life though in some countries and in some situations, the habit was

---

107 Kilroy, 'Coming to an Edge in History', p. 22.
108 Margaret Susan Thompson, 'Of Nuns, Habits, Chainsaws, and Why the Combination Is Less Than "Nuntastic"', *Global Sisters Report* (26 September 2017). www.globalsistersreport.org/blog/gsr-today/trends/nuns-habits-chainsaws-and-why-combination-less-nuntastic-49416, accessed 16 October 2018 and Carmen M. Mangion, 'Bad Habits? France's "Burkini Ban" in Historical Perspective', *History Workshop Online* (4 October 2016). www.historyworkshop.org.uk/bad-habits-frances-burkini-ban-in-historical-perspective/, accessed 4 November 2018.
109 Danielle Rives, 'Taking the Veil: Clothing and the Transformation of Identity', *Proceedings of the Western Society for French History*, 33 (2005), 465–86.
110 SCMM-Tilburg: SCMM 008 interviewed by Annemiek van der Veen (2003).
111 Anonymised interview.
112 Anonymised interview.
113 Elizabeth Kuhns, *The Habit: A History of the Clothing of Catholic Nuns* (New York: Doubleday, 2003).
114 Suenens, *The Nun in the World*, pp. 39–41.

banned.[115] From the 1950s, the Holy See encouraged a simplification of the religious habit. Superiors were told at the First International Congress of Superiors General of Orders and Congregations of Women that 'The religious habit should always express the consecration to Christ; that is expected and desired by all. In other respects the habit should be appropriate and in keeping with the demands of hygiene.'[116] *Perfectae Caritatis* (Adaptation and Renewal of Religious Life, 1965) emphasised again that religious dress 'should be simple and modest, poor and at the same time becoming. In addition it must meet the requirements of health and be suited to the circumstances of time and place and to the needs of the ministry involved.'[117]

The repetitive nature of this request suggests that many women religious in the 1950s ignored this directive or perhaps that changes were so subtle that as to be unnoticeable.[118] The religious habit appeared increasingly incongruous in the twentieth century as fashions for women changed. In Britain, the fashion trends from the 1950s were moving towards casual dress and simplicity.[119] Many religious habits used volumes of heavy fabric, and were often fiddly, cumbersome and difficult to keep clean, leading to concerns about hygiene.[120] Professional requirements (for example in nursing) could be incompatible with some types of religious habit. It was also increasingly a potential health and safety hazard; peripheral vision was reduced by veils, especially when driving. Suenens argues that 'the layman' considers the religious habit 'archaic and inconvenient' and warns of the nun on her moped 'flapping through the streets ... with her habit and veil streaming behind her to the imminent danger of herself and other traffic'.[121] Some suggested the religious habit inhibited vocations. In 1955, Mother Josephino van

115 For example, Kathleen Holscher, 'Contesting the Veil in America: Catholic Habits and the Controversy over Religious Clothing in the United States', *Journal of Church and State*, 54 (2012), 57–81.
116 Kuhns, *The Habit*, p. 140.
117 *Perfectae Caritatis*, §17.
118 Sally Dwyer-McNulty, *Common Threads: A Cultural History of Clothing in American Catholicism* (Chapel Hill, NC: University of North Carolina Press, 2014), p. 162; Mary Griffin, *The Courage to Choose: An American Nun's Story* (Boston: Little, Brown, 1975), p. 84.
119 Brian Harrison, *Seeking a Role: The United Kingdom, 1951–1970* (Oxford: Clarendon Press, 2009), p. 492.
120 Kuhns, *The Habit*, p. 36.
121 Suenens, *The Nun in the World*, p. 20.

Dinter wrote: 'We are considering changing our habit. Perhaps that is preventing girls from entering.'[122]

Historians, sociologists, theologians, ethnographers and scholars of dress have scrutinised the religious habit. Of all the changes in religious life, the 'change in habit' continues to elicit the most scholarly, popular and media comment, far in excess (as many interview participants emphasised) of its significance in terms of religious change. Journalist Elizabeth Kuhns's popular book on the religious habit identifies the various tropes of religious dress in its chapter titles: 'enigma', 'tradition', 'holiness', 'conformity', 'emblem', 'charity' and 'courage'. More recent books like *Looking Good: A Visual Guide to The Nun's Habit* (2016) decode and highlight the significance of the 'distinguishing identifiers' of forty 'types' of sisters and nuns. It features modish graphic design images of disembodied religious habits and a homogenised and somewhat sanitised vision of religious life.[123]

The religious habit trumpeted a separateness from the secular world; it was a recognisable sign of institutional forms of religious identity. It was a symbol of allegiance to the Roman Catholic Church and a particular religious institute, conveying a religiosity expressed in public. The habit as a visual code used colour, form and symbol to communicate a distinctive belonging to a particular religious institute.[124] As a visible symbol, it publicly ritualised conformity.[125]

The religious habit was functional. Benedictine Macaria Neussendorfer has written of the habit as a 'walking cloister', a form of protection from secular influences but also a means of evangelising, teaching and nursing in places normally considered insalubrious for women.[126] It referenced an identity that was clearly separate and could encourage distance or attract unwanted (or wanted) attention. It symbolised a commitment to the evangelical vows of poverty, chastity and obedience. It linked women religious to the sacred through its perfection and purity. It could also represent professionalisation, responsibility and power.[127]

122 AZG, 1.1.g.3,25.3.1955, cited in Sister Alix van de Molengraft, *It All Began with Three Beguines: History of Ten Thousand Sisters of Charity* (Preston: Nemco Press, 1992), p. 159.

123 Veronica Bennett, *Looking Good: A Visual Guide to the Nun's Habit* (London: GraphicDesign&, 2016)

124 www.wallpaper.com/art/sister-act-religion-fashion-and-semiotics-collide-in-new-guide-to-the-nuns-habit, accessed 8 December 2018.

125 Dwyer-McNulty, *Common Threads*, p. 83.

126 M. Neussendorfer, 'Modernizing the Religious Habit', *Sponsa Regis*, 36 (1964), 72.

127 Yvonne McKenna, 'A Gendered Revolution: Vatican II and Irish Women Religious', *Irish Feminist Review*, 1 (2005), 78.

Religious dress has also been seen as a symbol of Catholic tyranny. In the name of anti-clericalism or anti-Catholicism it has long been recognised as a sign of the 'other'.[128] Kathleen Holscher argues that the veil in the United States represented oppression: in some counties women religious were forbidden to wear the religious habit if teaching in state-run schools.[129] Elsewhere, the religious habit was illegal.[130]

Much of this symbolism behind the religious habit has been constructed in different times and places. Sally Dwyer-McNulty has argued that Catholic clothing as a symbol was 'naturalised by those in power, and while they hold sacramental meaning, they are also freighted with social and political significance'.[131] Sociologist Marta Trzebiatowska's work emphasises this ambiguity in the indeterminacy of religious dress in the eye of the beholder in Catholic Poland.[132] Catholic apparel operates 'as a battleground where Catholics work out issues of power, identity, and sacredness in their everyday lives'.[133]

Modernising the religious habit brought complications. Ethnographers have emphasised the complexity of the transformation of identities after the Second Vatican Council in religious life through religious dress.[134] Susanne Michelman argued that dress 'has been critical not only in reflecting, but also in helping to construct social change for women religious'.[135] New forms of dress introduced the personal identity of women religious in visible ways that could be interpreted as worldliness. Wearing the religious habit, like wearing any uniform, avoided issues that related to fashion and appearance that were associated

---

128 Then and now. Carmen M. Mangion, 'Bad Habits? France's "Burkini Ban" in Historical Perspective', *History Workshop Online* (4 October 2016). www.historyworkshop.org. uk/bad-habits-frances-burkini-ban-in-historical-perspective/, accessed 25 October 2018.

129 Holscher, 'Contesting the Veil in America'.

130 For example, Vincent P. Tinerella, 'Secret Sisters: Women Religious under European Communism Collection at the Catholic Theological Union', *Theological Librarianship*, 3 (2010), 8–15; Gemma M. Betros, 'The Female Religious Communities of Paris during the French Revolution and First Empire, 1789–1815', unpublished PhD dissertation, University of Cambridge, 2007, ch. 4.

131 Dwyer-McNulty, *Common Threads*, p. 1.

132 Marta Trzebiatowska, 'Habit Does Not a Nun Make? Religious Dress in the Everyday Lives of Polish Catholic Nuns', *Journal of Contemporary Religion*, 25 (2010), 51–65.

133 Dwyer-McNulty, *Common Threads*, p. 1.

134 Danielle Rives, 'Taking the Veil: Clothing and the Transformation of Identity', *Proceedings of the Western Society for French History*, 33 (2005), 465–86.

135 Susan Michelman, 'Breaking Habits: Fashion and Identity of Women Religious', *Fashion Theory: The Journal of Dress, Body and Culture*, 2 (1998), 167.

with the secular world: 'women religious found themselves visibly re-entering the secular world from the perspective of appearance'.[136] Michelman's research pointed to the conflict of the religious habit with the vow of poverty.[137] More controversially, Yvonne McKenna proposes that in removing the habit, women religious left behind a countercultural position of identifiable Catholicity and became invisible, merging into mass culture, thus allowing themselves to be silenced by secularism.[138] Theologian Sister Gemma Simmonds suggests the need to discern an 'alternative conception of visibility' that makes clear a public articulation of the distinctiveness and particularity of religious life.[139] The issue of visibility remains contentious within the Church.[140]

As discussed in Chapter 4, religious life up until the 1950s and 1960s suppressed personal identities in order to retain a focus on a corporate identity. National identity was a key target for suppression, as this example from the 1957 short history of the Poor Clares in Notting Hill implies: 'There are also Sisters of many nationalities and once the Sister enters the Community, she leaves her country behind, inasmuch as she is neither French, English or Irish etc., but simply Franciscan'.[141] It was a revelation when other identities, including that of 'woman', were publicly acknowledged and encouraged. In 1966, Mother M. Andrew speaking to juniorate mistresses explained that future sisters must realise that they were 'human, women, Christian' even before they were religious or sisters of a particular religious congregation.[142] Sister Prue Wilson acknowledged the same in her memoir: the 'call to renewal included a recognition by the Church that they were not only religious, but women'.[143] Many of my

---

136 Susan O. Michelman, 'Changing Old Habits: Dress of Women Religious and Its Relationship to Personal and Social Identity', *Sociological Inquiry*, 67 (1997), 350.

137 Michelman, 'Breaking Habits', p. 169.

138 McKenna, 'A Gendered Revolution', p. 8.

139 Gemma Simmonds, CJ, 'Religious Life: A Question of Visibility', in Gemma Simmonds, CJ (ed.), *A Future Full of Hope?* (Dublin: The Columba Press, 2012), pp. 117, 125.

140 Richard John Neuhaus, *The Catholic Moment: The Paradox of the Church in the Postmodern World* (San Francisco: Harper & Row, 1987), p. 61. See also Joseph P. Chinnici, 'An Historian's Creed and the Emergence of Postconciliar Culture Wars', *Catholic Historical Review*, 94 (2008) 219–44.

141 BAA: CC/B/1/G/5, 'A Brief Account of the Community of the Poor Clares Colettines, Notting Hill, London' (1957), p. 9. Numerous examples of this can be found in similar prescriptive and descriptive texts of religious life.

142 SCMM-ENK: 350, 'Training in Liturgy', paper read by Mother M. Andrew at the conference for Juniorate Mistresses held at East Finchley, 19 April 1966.

143 Prue Wilson, *My Father Took Me to the Circus* (London: Darton, Longman & Todd, 1984), p. 3.

participants illustrated their own experience of becoming a woman. One sister who entered in the 1950s explained, 'Well, I often say, I grew up as a person, as a woman, and as a nun, basically. I grew up. I went as a child, I suppose, because that was what religious life did to you.' She acknowledged that though she held a professional role as head teacher, inside the convent decisions were made for her.[144] Another sister recalled 'becoming a woman':

> Extraordinary, because you had to start deciding what sort of woman you were. And what did you wear, you know, you suddenly were able … who were you as a woman. And I think it is a, I mean that is really critical, because it demands a growing-up that one has not had to address before and what was my sexuality. I think I'd had to struggle with my sexuality earlier anyway, but what was my femininity, what sort of woman, how was I going to present, who was I rather than how was I going to present, and that took quite a lot of working out. It was also hugely liberating and a vast relief.[145]

Though she speaks of liberation, she also identifies the difficulty, the decision-making and the discernment. This was not an intuitive process for women who had lived much of their adult lives in convents. Lived femininity was complex, especially for those women who had suppressed their femininity for decades.

Prior to the 1960s, the vow of chastity was rarely discussed in the convent. When it was mentioned, it reflected a narrow understanding of the chasteness of physical purity that prohibited sexual relationships and encouraged a distance that inhibited other relationships. That distance was reflected in a literature that encouraged an avoidance of eye contact, physical touching or emotional connectedness. Women religious were told that their relationship to Christ, their spouse, was exclusive and they must renounce affection towards and from all others. Sisters and nuns came to see themselves and to be seen as asexual beings and the religious habit that 'repressed the female form' emphasised this asexual identity.[146] Female religious revisited the vow of chastity again and again after the Second Vatican Council. In one congregation chastity was reframed into a 'complete oneness to Christ' that 'liberates us for a greater love of

144 Anonymised interview.
145 Anonymised interview.
146 McKenna, 'A Gendered Revolution', p. 78; Yvonne McKenna, *Made Holy: Irish Women Religious at Home and Abroad* (Dublin: Irish Academic Press, 2006), pp. 80–1.

God and all men'.[147] This wider definition retained its sexual chasteness but embraced rather than rejected relationships with family, friends and those who were ministered to. Where once personal sexuality was ignored, it was now discussed in novitiates and some reflected on their own sexuality with more candidness and honesty. Sexuality for some was natural and not something to be ignored in religious life. One Poor Clare explained in her candid interview with journalist Mary Loudon that in the beginning of her religious life twenty-four years earlier: 'I began to be aware of a sort of physical *restlessness* inside me. It was a pain: it was a real ache. My body at times screamed out for satisfaction.' In explaining her continued commitment to religious life, she reasoned that 'And I think the very fact that I don't express my love through my body highlights my ability to express it in other ways.'[148] For some women, especially those who entered as young women, acknowledging their sexual and their female identity led to a discernment that led to their departure from religious life. Others, after years of sublimating these identities, were less comfortable with acknowledging this personal dimension of life.

Conclusion

Simone de Beauvoir in writing of 'becoming a woman' identified womanhood as constructed. Two decades later, women were remaking themselves from 'home-making to self-making'.[149] The 'late modern project of the self' despite allowing post-war women to embrace 'individual worth, entitlement, self-propulsion and independence' remains a 'fragile project'.[150] Religion and self-making, as this chapter suggests, could coexist, though sometimes problematically. Through the *Nun in the World* and feminist theologians, women religious experienced a more thorough grounding in theology that acknowledged their womanhood and sexuality and linked it to a deeper understanding of their faith. Heated discussions on alterations to or abolition of the grille and the religious habit centred on their function and significance as

147 SSH ENW: 1970 Provincial Chapter I, Batch 3, 'Affirmations of the England–Malta Province, Provincial Chapter 1970'.
148 Mary Loudon, *Unveiled: Nuns Talking* (London: Chatto & Windus, 1992), p. 114.
149 Penny Long Marler, 'Religious Change in the West: Watch the Women', in Kristin Aune, Sonya Sharma and Giselle Vincett (eds), *Women and Religion in the West: Challenging Secularization* (Aldershot: Ashgate, 2008), pp. 47–9.
150 Linda Woodhead, '"Because I'm Worth It": Religion and Women's Changing Lives in the West', in Kristin Aune, Sonya Sharma and Giselle Vincett (eds), *Women and Religion in the West: Challenging Secularization* (Aldershot: Ashgate, 2008), pp. 148–9.

markers of identity and their relationship to ministry. For some, these unchanging symbols of religious life signified tradition, security and the authenticity of religious life. For others, the need for modernity, to meet the modern world in different ways, offered a 'renewed' way to be an authentic religious. The changing meanings of the grille and the religious habit were disturbing because they also altered long-standing gendered female identities within religious life. The debates on these two markers of identity and of the authenticity of religious life spilled into the public sphere. The discernible partial or full enclosure that had separated women religious from family, friends and the people they served slowly changed in form and function. Women religious may or may not have been feminists but, like feminists, they claimed for themselves the right to define their own place in both secular society and the Catholic world. This chapter has demonstrated that both religious and secular ideas shaped these women's awareness of their womanhood.

Conclusion

One sister's prayer has been with me throughout this research. It was published in the meeting minutes of the 1976 General Board of the Sisters of Charity Our Lady, Mother of Mercy:

Pain of Change
Sometimes I feel, Lord, if only I could just
Stop and switch off and not go on and on.
Everything is always changing.
No sooner am I used to one way, than another comes along.
Lord, is your world going too fast now?
It hurts to pull up roots all the time.
Even ideas about you change so rapidly.
Is there no security, or peace, or time to stop and think?
Yes, it's your world and you gave it to us to bring into fullness.
This I know deep down, so I ask you now for the courage to move on, the patience to accept people digging me up with new ideas, the love to love them and their keen movements even when I revolt from change.[1]

Its author was rooted in a form of religious life that brought her security, peace and stability. She was taught not to criticise, and in her silence and deference she also kept quiet about the 'funny things' of religious life. She may have felt pressured to change. She does not speak like a sister who welcomed the Modern Girl, who embraced the changes in governance where she attended meetings and debated decisions. She may have enjoyed the known quality of formal relationships that were deferential and distant. She likely saw justice in teaching or nursing or perhaps did not want additional theological training and felt out of touch with this

---

1   SCMM-ENK: 80, 'Meeting of the General Board 6th–18th September 1976 in Rome'.

new language of the Second Vatican Council. And perhaps 'becoming a woman' was just a series of difficult decisions about what clothes to wear or how to style her hair that seemed irrelevant to her life as a bride of Christ. She had probably experienced the possibilities and traumas of becoming modern proposed by philosopher Marshall Berman:

> To be modern is to find ourselves in an environment that promises us adventure, power, joy, growth, transformation of ourselves and the world – and, at the same time, that threatens to destroy everything we have, everything we know, everything we are.[2]

The 'pain of change' was less emotively noted in the narratives of the nuns and sisters I interviewed though many experienced the tensions and the pain of everyday life in the midst of changing structures. The majority had entered in the 1950s and 1960s, and have now spent the greater part of their religious lives in a renewed Church. They participated in and negotiated with the modernity of religious life of the post-war secular age. Their life stories, too, have been crucial to my understanding of religious life. Many participants, fifty or sixty years on from their entry into religious life, recalled their early years with its spiritual joy and feelings of stability alongside discomfort about convent traditions which emphasised an asceticism and deference that seemed at odds with their life experiences. Though they may have experienced the 'pain of change' in the past, they were more eager to express their appreciation of religious life becoming more participatory, relational and engaged with the world. I hope I have told both of these seemingly contrasting stories; they both represent the desire for an authentically lived religious life in a world that was changing.

This Conclusion returns to the original remit of this work, to consider how the changing dimensions in women's religious life were influenced by the wider social movements of the long 1960s; the role of transnationalism alongside the factors that make this a British story; and the struggles of competing and contradictory ideas of collective, institutional identities. It then connects the past with the present, to address diminishment and the abuse scandals that have rocked religious life and the Catholic world.

---

2   Marshall Berman, *All That Is Solid Melts into Air: The Experience of Modernity* (New York: Simon & Schuster, 1982), p. 15.

Social movements

Catholic Nuns and Sisters in a Secular Age has charted forty-five years of continuity and change within female religious life influenced by religious and social movements. The post-war Modern Girl who entered religious life had life experiences that widened her horizons: she participated in diverse forms of war work, likely had increased financial independence and greater occasion for relationships with men and women within and outside her own social class. Pope Pius XII's awareness of women's changing role in a modernising world and a decline in vocations led to the apostolic constitution *Sponsa Christi* (1950) and subsequent international congresses encouraging the 'adaptation' and 'modernisation' of religious life.[3] The Second Vatican Council and its sixteen documents, particularly *Perfectae Caritatis* and *Gaudium et Spes*, were accelerators of change welcomed by female religious though perhaps not uniformly interpreted.[4] An emancipatory movement led, sustained, spread and obstructed by women religious demonstrated a gendered version of '1968', with hierarchical structures slowly replaced by more participatory governance of the 1970s and 1980s. Relationships were changing too: the common life, in some communities, became less rigid, and relationships between sisters shifted from the formal to the relational, though not without personal and generational tensions. As the nun entered the world and the world entered the cloister, the sacred world of the convent and monastery became more in sync with the modern world and women religious, as religious in a secularising world in their turn sacralised modernity. The emphasis on social justice and liberation theology of the 1970s (along with declining numbers) encouraged new ministries and altered old ministries, often through experimentation by individual sisters. Becoming a woman was not only found through dress; nuns and sisters sought a more thorough grounding in theology that acknowledged their womanhood, linking it to a deeper understanding of their faith. Over the forty-five years covered by this study, changes in religious life were authenticated in the understanding of the continuity of the spirit of their religious institute and informed by self-reflection and theological education. Women enacted these changes as part of, not separate from, a modern world. Religious life, like 'religion in general' as historian Jeffrey

3   João Miguel Almeida, 'Progressive Catholicism in Portugal: Considerations on Political Activism (1958–1974)', *Histoire @Politique*, 30 (2016), 1–15.
4   Many scholars explain that women religious took on renewal with the greater vigour. Sandra M. Schneiders, *New Wineskins: Re-Imagining Religious Life Today* (New York: Paulist Press, 1986), p. 1.

Cox argues, had become 'not only compatible with modernity, but as in some contexts a species of modernity'.[5]

Scholars of social and cultural histories of the long 1960s have failed to recognise the significance of the cultural shifts within the Catholic Church in the second half of the twentieth century in relation to wider social movements. If at all acknowledged, the emphasis has often been placed on how the ideals and values of Christian denominations were challenged by shifting moral standards resulting in declining church attendance. A new religious history has begun to acknowledge the social movements within denominational Christianity, reflecting the tensions between those who favoured holding on to the traditions of their Church and others who were anxious to make 'progressive' changes.[6] Historian Hugh McLeod has outlined the complexities of the 'religious crisis' of the 1960s within the secularisation debates that have garnered more historical attention than the changes in the practices of institutional church life.[7] The post-secular view of *Catholic Nuns and Sisters in a Secular Age* acknowledges secularisation, but examines the influence of religious and social change in the destructuring and restructuring of Catholic female religious life.

Women's Catholic religious institutes participated in Arthur Marwick's 'tapestry of interweaving movements challenging existing authorities and conventions'.[8] As part of their own social movement, female religious used their collective power in united (though not unanimous) action to implement systemic changes as a means of addressing grievances regarding convent life.[9] We can see this happening in the development of new governance structures that shared authority

---

5   Jeffrey Cox, 'Provincializing Christendom: The Case of Great Britain', *Church History*, 75:1 (2006), 123.

6   Sam Brewitt-Taylor, *Christian Radicalism in the Church of England and the Invention of the British Sixties, 1957–1970: The Hope of a World Transformed* (Oxford: Oxford University Press, 2018); Sam Brewitt-Taylor, 'From Religion to Revolution: Theologies of Secularisation in the British Student Christian Movement, 1963–1973', *Journal of Ecclesiastical History*, 66 (2015), 792–811; Jay P. Corrin, *Catholic Progressives in England after Vatican II* (Notre Dame, IN: University of Notre Dame Press, 2013).

7   Hugh McLeod, *The Religious Crisis of the 1960s* (Oxford: Oxford University Press, 2007).

8   Arthur Marwick, 'The Cultural Revolution of the Long Sixties: Voices of Reaction, Protest, and Permeation', *International History Review*, 27 (2005), 782.

9   Myra Marx Ferree and Carol McClurg Mueller, 'Feminism and the Women's Movement: A Global Perspective', in David A. Snow, Sarah A. Soule and Hanspeter Kriesi (eds), *The Blackwell Companion to Social Movements* (Chichester: John Wiley & Sons, 2008), p. 576.

and decision-making; in the movement away from uniformity and towards small communities and personal responsibility; in the role of the individual in exploring new ministries; in nuns' and sisters' embodied turn towards modern and secular society and in the exploration of personal femininities. But unlike many social movements that were developed from the bottom up, this one originated from the top down. Massimo Faggioli has argued that 'What emerges clearly is that at Vatican II we have a paradox about the renewal of religious life and religious orders: the movement does not come from the religious orders themselves and not from the bishops belonging to a religious order (see the 1964 debate), but only from the whole ecclesiological debate at Vatican II.'[10] Despite this top-down impetus, women religious made these changes their own. Women religious were rigorous in their modelling of the *aggiornamento* of the Second Vatican Council.[11] Given their vast numbers, they were a significant link to the Catholic laity and world beyond Catholicism. Even in a Protestant Britain, Catholic sisters and nuns would have been a visible workforce in the first half of the twentieth century and they in turn were conscious of the various post-war secular movements. They encountered them in their students, families and in the media. They were influenced by these movements as well as by Council documents; the changing dimensions of religious life reflected the integration of new Church teachings with broader societal shifts.

Transnationalism

The religious institutes discussed here, both active and enclosed, were part of religious families which operated within transnational networks, crossing borders to meet in shared social spaces in Rome or motherhouses and daughterhouses across Europe, exchanging ideas in meetings, seminars and workshops and communicating via epistolary correspondence. Though religious institutes have always been international, the degree of their transnationalism has altered over time. Exchange and sharing of educational praxis were commonplace amongst

---

10 Massimo Faggioli, *Catholicism and Citizenship: Political Cultures of the Church in the Twenty-First Century* (Collegeville, MN: Liturgical Press, 2017), p. 11.

11 Michael P. Hornsby-Smith, 'A Transformed Church', in Michael P. Hornsby-Smith (ed.), *Catholics in England 1950–2000: Historical and Sociological Perspectives* (London: Cassell, 1999), p. 19. One informant told him that the structures of decision-making in female religious orders 'are a million years ahead of the Church generally'.

the larger teaching congregations during the growth and dynamism of the 'teaching age' of nineteenth-century religious life.[12] The first half of the twentieth century, a period virtually unresearched by scholars, suggests an age of consolidation with institutionalisation, what Susan O'Brien calls 'regularisation and greater conformity'.[13] Post-war changes in the ways religious institutes operated internally and externally reinvigorated the scope of transnational exchanges. Expanding participation in governance, the creation of amalgamations and federations, deformalising relationships and encouraging debate on facets of renewal through newsletters, questionnaires, meetings and face-to-face encounters connected sisters and nuns in new ways. Cross-institute interactions were also a feature of transnational exchanges as women religious from different religious institutes interacted in Rome during the 1950s at meetings and conferences. Ideas crossed national boundaries through personal interactions but also through the burgeoning industry of religious life studies, including nun memoirs and a proliferation of sociological and theological writing, often infused with a particular national experience, but read and discussed by women religious from other national contexts.

Post-war transnationalism did not imply uniformity. This transfer and exchange of ideas about renewal highlighted real and imagined national differences. Anecdotal commentaries in participants' recollections, reflected also in documentary sources, evinced a belief that the pace of renewal varied by national context. One London-based sister from an international congregation recollected in speaking of her own congregation:

12 Cada *et al.* call the post-1800 surge in religious life the 'age of the teaching congregations'. Lawrence Cada, Raymond Fitz, Gertrude Foley, Thomas Giardino and Carol Lichtenberg, *Shaping the Coming Age of Religious Life* (New York: Seabury Press, 1979), p. 13; Deirdre Raftery, 'Teaching Sisters and Transnational Networks: Recruitment and Education Expansion in the Long Nineteenth Century', *History of Education*, 44 (2015), 717–28; Nicola Yeates, 'The Irish Catholic Female Religious and the Transnationalisation of Care: An Historical Perspective', *Irish Journal of Sociology*, 19 (2011), 77–9.

13 Susan O'Brien, 'Religious Life for Women', in V. Alan McClelland and Michael Hodgetts (eds), *From without the Flaminian Gate: 150 Years of Roman Catholicism in England and Wales, 1850–2000* (London: Darton, Longman & Todd, 1999), p. 123. Congregation histories often cover this time period, but few delve into it with great depth: it is often sandwiched between the dynamic growth of the nineteenth century and the radical changes of the Second Vatican Council. Further research into religious life in the first half of the twentieth century could potentially alter my assessment.

We would be considered the backwater here. I'm not sure that Ireland would have been any better at that time, very slow to move, d'you know? The Americans would have moved much faster. Australia tends to be on the ball as well and to move fairly fast.[14]

British sisters working in their motherhouses in Rome interacted regularly with their international sisters and suggested a vast array of cultural differences in the uptake of renewal:

> The US was moving faster and I think Latin America was moving faster in some ways because they were already involved in the barrios, in small inserted communities, and we were beginning, um no we didn't begin until the early 1970s, to move into very smaller communities ... other European countries were probably moving more slowly.[15]

Another sister also working in Rome opined: 'The USA was well ahead of us in embracing change, but I was aware of some of the conflict and sufferings that were being experienced, in different regions moving at different speeds.'[16] The correspondence and archives of the Sisters of Charity of Our Lady, Mother of Mercy, whose motherhouse was in the Netherlands, was awash with remarks on the speed of renewal that reflected stereotypes identifying Dutch sisters as 'progressive' and England as 'slow'. British sisters in favour of renewal were sometimes stunned at how quickly experimentation was implemented by the Dutch sisters. In oral histories, there were also references to the 'Dutch mentality', which identified the Dutch as 'more outspoken' and 'more of the world', with a 'world outlook' when compared to the assumed narrow British worldview.[17]

National stereotypes of enthusiasm or rejection of renewal are problematic; they essentialise the many modalities of change within religious life, which, as this book has argued, were met at different speeds even between communities within one religious institute. What follows examines some of these specificities of religious life in the British context in comparison with national contexts discussed in interviews or in the archives of the religious institutes examined for this work.

14   Anonymised interview.
15   Anonymised interview.
16   SSH ENW: 'RSCJ and 1967', Luirard survey, Remembrance 13.
17   SCMM-Tilburg: SCMM 010 interviewed by Annemiek van der Veen (2003).

British Catholic conservatism

British Catholic conservatism has been widely discussed in Catholic scholarship. Literary critic Alison Light has attributed this characteristic more widely: 'conservatism', she writes, 'of the lower case variety, has been … unaccounted for; as one of the great unexamined assumptions of British cultural life its history is all but non-existent'.[18] Writing about Catholicism in England after the Second Vatican Council in the 1970s, sociologist Michael Hornsby-Smith acknowledged that the slow pace of post-conciliar change suggested a Catholic reticence for change.[19] A decade later, he reported a 'steady embracing of the "People of God" model of church with all its implications for priest–lay relationships and lay participation in the life of the Church' and a shift from 'closed Catholicism' to 'open Catholicism'.[20] Alana Harris identified a 'rhetoric of the Reformation' as significant to understanding the liturgical debates of the post-conciliar period. Eamon Duffy wrote of the Catholic Church of the 1950s as 'a community on the crest of a wave of self-confidence and success' and a Church 'intellectually ill-prepared for the Council'. Bishops, he says, were able pastors but even the charismatic Cardinal Archbishop of Westminster John Carmel Heenan (1905–1975) was unable to 'steer the community through the theological white-water of the 1960s and early 1970s'.[21] Heenan's response to the directives of the Second Vatican Council reflected his steadfast obedience, though perhaps, for some changes, little enthusiasm.[22] Like many bishops and clergy, he found it difficult to imagine a post-conciliar world where the laity as the 'people of God' were more self-directed and active in

18   Alison Light, *Forever England: Femininity, Literature and Conservatism between the Wars* (London: Routledge, 1991), p. 14.
19   Michael P. Hornsby-Smith, *Tradition and Change in the Roman Catholic Community in England* (London: SSRC, 1977), pp. 28–9.
20   Michael P. Hornsby-Smith, *Roman Catholics in England: Studies in Social Structure since the Second World War* (Cambridge: Cambridge University Press, 1987), p. 43. I have found no similar research of post-war Welsh or Scottish Catholicism.
21   Eamon Duffy, *Faith of Our Fathers* (London: Continuum, 2004), pp. 141–2.
22   James Hagerty, *Cardinal John Carmel Heenan: Priest of the People, Prince of the Church* (Leominster: Gracewing, 2012), pp. xx–xxi; Alana Harris, 'A Fresh Stripping of the Altars? Liturgical Language and the Legacy of the Reformation in England, 1964–1984', in Kathleen Sprows Cummings, Timothy Matovina, and Robert A. Orsi (eds), *Catholics in the Vatican II Era: Local Histories of a Global Event* (Cambridge: Cambridge University Press, 2017), pp. 250, 260. The paucity of scholarship on the bishops of England, Wales and Scotland suggests more questions rather than answers to their attitudes towards the changes of the Second Vatican Council.

Church life. He voiced concerns about some of the experiments and developments in women's religious life. During the Annual General Meeting of the Council of Major Religious Superiors in March 1965, Heenan warned against what he termed the 'gospel of Holland' (*leer van Holland*).[23] The British members of the Dutch Sisters of Charity found the criticism directed towards the Dutch Church, and indirectly towards them, difficult. One report dated 1974 indicated that the

> attitude of the English Church affects the sisters strongly. The very slow adaptation of customs, etc. within the English Church, the attitude of Bishops, clergy and laity to religious and the absence of much real contact with like-minded religious all make renewal difficult.[24]

The more renewal-oriented of the Sisters of Charity of Our Lady, Mother of Mercy were critical of the church hierarchy. One sister commented in 1965 'Young priests aren't allowed to push it.'[25]

The Sisters of Charity of Our Lady, Mother of Mercy who lived and worked in England and Wales were influenced by their Dutch sisters' understanding of renewal and, like much of the media, saw 'those Dutch nuns' as the forerunners of renewal.[26] As in Britain, Catholics in the Netherlands were a minority, though a more substantial one at 35–40 per cent of the population. By the mid-twentieth century, the tenor of Dutch Catholicism had changed from the separateness of a minority sect to a 'dynamic and vital socio-religious system'.[27] Dutch Catholics from the 1920s were adapting to modern society, and during this time the Dutch Church began engaging with modernity (despite a pronounced rhetoric of opposition).[28] Writing in the Preface to *Those Dutch Catholics*,

23 SCMM-ENK: 949, 'Verslag v/h. Werkbezoek van Zr. Willibalde Aan de Engelse Provincie. Van 12 t/m. 30 Oktober 1965'.

24 SCMM-ENK: 79, 'Reflections on the Meeting between the General Board and the Provincial Board of the Netherlands, Rome, March 11th–15th 1974'.

25 SCMM-ENK: 98, 'Verslag v/h. Werkbezoek van Zr. Willibalde Aan de Engelse Provincie. Van 12 t/m. 30 Oktober 1965'.

26 Marjet Derks, 'The Gospel of the Old: Media, Gender, and the Invisible Conservative Dutch Catholic in the Long 1960s', *Schweizerische Zeitschrift für Religions- und Kulturgeschichte*, 104 (2010), 135–54.

27 Jan Roes and Hans de Valk, 'A World Apart? Religious Orders and Congregations in the Netherlands', in Jan De Maeyer, Sophie Leplae and Joachim Schmiedl (eds), *Religious Institutes in Western Europe in the 19th and 20th Centuries* (Leuven: Leuven University Press, 2004), p. 141.

28 Erik Sengers, '"Because We Are Catholic, We Are Modern": The Adaptation of Dutch Catholicism to modern Dutch Society 1920–1960', *Bijdragen, International Journal in Philosophy and Theology*, 67 (2006), 35–7. See also, Erik Sengers, '"Although We Are

Desmond Fisher acknowledged the reputation of the Dutch, 'suspected at best of indulging in dangerous ideas and practices which are upsetting the whole Church; at worst of risking a schism. Dutch experiments in liturgy, ecumenism and in the pastoral handling of moral problems have caused reactions ranging from doubt to shock.'[29] Renewal had important supporters in the Netherlands. Bishop Wilhelmus Marinus Bekkers of 's Hertogenbosch, a charismatic promoter of the Second Vatican Council, was seen as embodying the spirit of the *aggiornamento*.[30] In contrast, bishops of England, Wales and Scotland were seen as concerned with clerical authority; Gabriel Daly has argued that English ultramontanism 'trivialises theology by reducing all issues to questions of authority and obedience.'[31]

Developing a national voice

The worldwide meetings of female religious organised in Rome in the 1950s encouraged the formation of national bodies of religious. These bodies provided a forum for female religious to meet, to communicate and to discuss common goals; they were to become significant in identifying educational needs of teaching sisters, and later renewal.[32] In Britain, the Conference of Major Religious Superiors in Scotland was formed in 1958 and the next year the Conference of Major Religious Superiors was established for England and Wales.[33] The histories of these organisations have yet to be written though their activities are reflected throughout the archives of religious institutes in the organisation of retreats, seminars and workshops on renewal and, in the 1970s, commissioning research

Catholic, We Are Dutch": The Transition of the Dutch Catholic Church from Sect to Church as an Explanation for its Growth and Decline', *Journal for the Scientific Study of Religion*, 43:1 (2004), 129–39.

29 Desmond Fisher, 'Preface', in Michel van der Plas and Henk Suèr (eds), *Those Dutch Catholics* (London: Geoffrey Chapman, 1967), p. 7.

30 Marjet Derks, 'Debating the Council on the Air: Media, Personality, and the Transformation of the Dutch Church', in Kathleen Sprows Cummings, Timothy Matovina, and Robert A. Orsi (eds), *Catholics in the Vatican II Era: Local Histories of a Global Event* (Cambridge: Cambridge University Press, 2017), pp. 204–44.

31 Gabriel Daly, 'Faith and Theology: The Ultramontane Influence', *The Tablet*, 235 (18 April 1981), pp. 391–2.

32 Amy L. Koehlinger, *The New Nuns: Racial Justice and Religious Reform in the 1960s* (Cambridge, MA: Harvard University Press, 2007), p. 27.

33 In Britain there were other professional associations such as the Association of Catholic Schools and the Association of Religious Nursing Sisters but they did not include members of all religious institutes.

on social work.[34] Their sister institutes in Canada and the United States played a very central role in the changes of pre- and post-conciliar religious life.

Historian Heidi MacDonald charts the development of the Canadian Religious Conference, formed in 1954, as the self-described 'spokesman' of Canadian religious institutes.[35] In its first decade, it addressed issues related to the health and education of women religious. There were concerns over cultures of overwork and the increasing demands on women religious as educators and the lag in women's vocations compared to the growth of population. After the Second Vatican Council, the Canadian Religious Conference took on a variety of additional roles, including identifying itself and religious as part of a 'broader church' and encouraging collective sharing of responsibility and resources amongst Canadian women religious.[36] It took on a 'research role' by organising censuses, surveys and using the sciences of psychology and sociology to examine vocations, new and old. It liaised with ecclesiastical authorities on behalf of women religious.[37] By the 1980s, the Canadian Religious Conference had become more overtly feminist in its support of women's increased role in society and in the Church. MacDonald suggests feminist perspectives were not held by all sisters, but that in the late 1960s a maternal feminism, likened to feminine identities as mothers, carers and nurturers, was the foundation of the feminism of Canadian women religious.[38]

---

34 See Chapter 6.
35 Not all women joined the conference or followed its progressive lead. See Rosa Bruno-Jofré, 'The Process of Renewal of the Missionary Oblate Sisters, 1963–1989', in Elizabeth M. Smyth (ed.), *Changing Habits: Women's Religious Orders in Canada* (Ottawa: Novalis, 2007), p. 249.
36 Heidi MacDonald, 'Smaller Numbers, Stronger Voices: Women Religious Reposition Themselves through the Canadian Religious Conference, 1960s–1980s', in Rosa Bruno-Jofré, Heidi MacDonald and Elizabeth M. Smyth (eds), *Vatican II and Beyond: The Changing Mission and Identity of Canadian Women Religious* (Montreal and Kingston: McGill-Queen's University Press, 2017), pp. 31–5; Ellen Leonard, CSJ, 'The Process of Transformation: Women Religious and the Study of Theology, 1955–1980', in Elizabeth M. Smyth (ed.), *Changing Habits: Women's Religious Orders in Canada* (Ottawa: Novalis, 2007), p. 234.
37 MacDonald, 'Smaller Numbers, Stronger Voices', pp. 37, 44.
38 Rosa Bruno-Jofré, Heidi MacDonald and Elizabeth M. Smyth, 'Introduction', in Rosa Bruno-Jofré, Heidi MacDonald and Elizabeth M. Smyth (eds), *Vatican II and Beyond: The Changing Mission and Identity of Canadian Women Religious* (Montreal and Kingston: McGill-Queen's University Press, 2017), p. 11.

National collaborations in the United States have a more complex history. They began with the Sister Formation Movement established after the First International Congress of Teaching Sisters in Rome in 1951. Its initial remit was the education of teaching sisters and it advised on curriculums for special Sister Formation Colleges. As a national organisation, it also provided research in the form of surveys. The Sisters' Institute of Spirituality (1953) also functioned nationally as a means of exploring the theology of religious life, delving into topics such as the formation of feminine character and spirituality and the psychological effects of community structures.[39] The founding of the Conference of Major Superiors of Women of the USA followed in 1956 (renamed in 1972 the Leadership Conference of Women Religious of the USA). In its first years, like the Canadian Religious Conference, the Conference provided an environment to discuss common issues but particularly addressed the spiritual welfare of women religious and the efficacy of their ministries.[40] It also developed a research arm that sponsored surveys on religious life; provided resources to *aggiornamento* chapters; and hosted annual meetings and special programmes on the spiritual and organisational renewal of religious life.[41] As it evolved, the Conference liaised between US women religious and the Holy See, persistently requesting representations on Vatican commissions that made decisions on female religious life.[42] Two additional national organisations were founded: the National Council of American Nuns (1969) and the National Association of Women Religious (1970). Each of these networks developed its own agendas. Amy Koehlinger argues that they were 'vectors of information, quickly and efficiently disseminating research and ideas about renewal',

---

39   Koehlinger, *The New Nuns*, p. 29.
40   Tensions between the competing (and sometimes contradictory) aims of the Sister Formation Conference and the Conference of Major Superiors of Women led to the absorption of the Sister Formation Conference within the Conference in 1964. At the time of the name change to the Leadership Conference of Women Religious, disagreements led to another group being formed, initially known as Consortium *Perfectae Caritatis* and in 1992 renamed the Council of Major Superiors of Women Religious. Margaret M. McGuinness, *Called to Serve: A History of Nuns in America* (New York: New York University Press, 2013), p. 161. Lora Ann Quiñonez and Mary Daniel Turner, *The Transformation of American Catholic Sisters* (Philadelphia: Temple University Press, 1992), pp. 14–16, 19, 153–4.
41   Koehlinger, *The New Nuns*, p. 28.
42   Mary J. Henold, *Catholic and Feminist: The Surprising History of the American Catholic Feminist Movement* (Durham, NC: University of North Carolina Press, 2012), pp. 102–3.

providing a 'solid infrastructure of reform-oriented collaborative organizations'.[43]

Many of these organisations adopted an explicitly feminist agenda as it pertained to religious life. The National Council of American Nuns sought to 'address their own oppression and then the oppression of others'. Its feminist activism often centred on relationships between women religious and male hierarchy, locating women's oppression in Catholic theology, seminary training, papal encyclicals and Canon Law. By the 1970s, the US Conference of Major Superiors of Women had also become explicitly feminist in its orientation.[44] In the 1970s, many of these national organisations supported religious institutes embroiled in conflicts with the episcopal hierarchy about the pace and content of renewal. Post-conciliar histories of female religious life in the United States often include stories of priests or bishops criticising experimentation and the renewal process. Historian of dress Sally Dwyer-McNulty writes that 'sisters winced at the willingness of religious men to take up the topic of women's clothes and even undergarments'.[45] At a time when women religious were changing governance structures in order to make decisions in more participatory and collaborative ways, they were disconcerted when a bishop would then voice his disagreement and insist a decision be reversed.[46] The best-known incident was the public spat between Anita Caspery, who led the Sisters of the Immaculate Heart of Mary, and Cardinal James McIntyre of Los Angeles. Many of the decisions women religious made, whether in educating sisters or allowing them to staff new ministries, further reduced the already declining level of cost-effective services female religious provided to a diocese, and bishops were concerned about the financial viability of the Catholic infrastructure of schools and hospitals. Their heated debate ended in 1970 with the majority of the sisters asking for dispensation from their vows and forming, under the leadership of Anita Caspery, a non-canonical, ecumenical community not tied to the Catholic Church.[47]

These national comparisons suggest that though transnational exchanges were important to the renewal of religious life, the framing of renewal was shaped by local and national contexts and thus translated

43   Koehlinger, *The New Nuns*, p. 28.
44   Henold, *Catholic and Feminist*, pp. 91–103.
45   Sally Dwyer-McNulty, *Common Threads: A Cultural History of Clothing in American Catholicism* (Chapel Hill: University of North Carolina Press, 2014), pp. 187–8.
46   Koehlinger, *The New Nuns*, pp. 233–4.
47   Anita M. Caspary, *Witness to Integrity: The Crisis of the Immaculate Heart Community of California* (Collegeville, MN: Liturgical Press, 2003).

and applied in distinctive ways by women religious. The unwelcome intrusions of clerical and ecclesiastical authorities were less evident in the diocesan and religious archives and the narratives of British women religious, perhaps because many of the religious congregations were of pontifical right, which gave less authority to the bishops and more to the female governance centred in the motherhouse. National organisations aided the transformation of religious life and have been given a prominent place in the histories of North American female religious. Feminism was explicit in the nature of their renewal, and the sometimes difficult nature of the relationships with bishops makes the circumstances in the United States and Canada appear markedly different from those in Britain. It is difficult to compare the influence of national bodies given the paucity of research on their activities in England, Wales and Scotland. However, as Chapter 7 suggested, feminism was not an explicit factor in the British renewal process through to the 1980s and relationships with bishops and clergy appear much more collegial than they did in North America.

Identities

The Second Vatican Council in *Lumen Gentium* (Dogmatic Constitution on the Church, 1964) identified only two categories of Catholics: clerical (holy orders) and lay. In addressing religious life it firmly stated that 'From the point of view of the divine and hierarchical structure of the Church, the religious state of life is not an intermediate state between the clerical and lay states.'[48] Sociologist James Sweeney noted that the two-tier Catholic hierarchy altered the 'ecclesiastical cosmology' and 'dethroned' religious life from its 'higher calling'. In doing this it tampered with 'a fundamental feature of identity' and destabilised religious life.[49] Women religious began to question centuries of self-identity linked to the belief that women religious had a special place in the hierarchy of the church. Some women religious felt a 'loss' in canonical status and questioned their vocation. Others welcomed the conciliar ecclesiology and theology as a means of reorienting their identities as women religious.

---

48 In 1964, *Lumen Gentium* (Dogmatic Constitution on the Church) made explicit that the vocation of vowed religious was equivalent to that of the married or single laity (§43).

49 James Sweeney, 'Religious Life after Vatican II', in Michael P. Hornsby-Smith (ed.), *Catholics in England 1950–2000: Historical and Sociological Perspectives* (London: Cassell, 1999), p. 273.

Much of the nuts and bolts of shifting identities was structural: within new governance structures, nuns and sisters also shared in decision-making; formal distinctions between choir and lay, 'Mother' and 'Sister' disappeared; personal interactions within communities became more relational, which altered understandings of deference; and importantly reconsideration of religious ministries delinked some identities with schools and hospitals. The changes to the ways religious life was lived as they related to religious identities, were personal, and political. As some women religious became politicised their thinking expanded from the local, reorienting ministries and activism towards the national and global. Individual identities for nuns and sisters were as much a modern construct of liberal selfhood as they were a part of the new theological framing and religious understanding of the role of women religious in the world. One wonders, too, whether the emphatic embrace of the new ways of being female religious was a reaction to a moral rigorism that was part of early experiences of religious life. Collective and institutional identities were in flux as competing and contradictory ideas of authenticity and authority jostled for acceptance. This secular age, influenced as it was by both the social movements of the post-war world and the Second Vatican Council, created for some women and some religious institutes a crisis of identity. Dominican theologian Timothy Radcliffe sees the question of identity as one reflecting the transformation of society. He proposes that such crises of identity are ubiquitous, linked to the weakening of institutional identities in the secular as well as the religious sphere.[50]

Another, more serious crisis of identity has become part of the landscape of religious life: the revelations of emotional, physical and sexual abuse at the hands of priests and male and female religious.[51] Damning revelations of abuse were further compounded by the silence of those aware of the abuse and the lack of accountability of members of the ecclesiastical hierarchy who hid these crimes against children and vulnerable adults. Ireland has been most tainted by the scandals involving women religious. Film and media depictions of brutal treatment in Magdalene laundries, industrial schools and

---

50 Timothy Radcliffe, OP, 'The Identity of Religious Today'. www.dominicans.ca/ Documents/masters/Radcliffe/religious_identity.html, accessed 15 November 2016.

51 This is a worldwide crisis that includes institutions managed by religious as well as non-religious and voluntary organisations. The current inquiries being held in England, Wales and Scotland are the Scottish Child Abuse Inquiry www.childabuseinquiry. scot/, accessed December 2018, and the Independent Inquiry into Child Sexual Abuse www.iicsa.org.uk/, accessed December 2018.

orphanages have featured women religious performing acts of cruelty and humiliation. Historian James Smith has suggested that the Church, state and the larger community in Ireland are all implicated in Ireland's 'architecture of containment'.[52] Literary critic Elizabeth Cullingford has questioned the influence of the 'Jansenist inflected Catholicism' in Irish convents.[53] Theologian Annelies van Heijst's description of the regime of pre-conciliar religious life included its 'restless striving for perfection', a value system that embraced self-punishment, emotional coldness, ritual humiliation and blind obedience. This was part of a spiritual value system of a 'dualistic, sacrificial spirituality' she linked to a patriarchal spirituality that saw suffering as redemptive. Van Heijst argues that the 'hard regime was a *structural* feature' of religious life. Revelations of violence, declares sister and historian Phil Kilroy, have 'exposed the power systems which operated in the Church and in religious life'.[54] Power systems were part and parcel of a patriarchal Church and historian Margaret Susan Thompson, in demonstrating the significance of kyriarchy within the structures of religious communities, maintains that 'women themselves can wield oppressive power or can be complicit (or collaborative) in their own oppression'.[55] Some of the women religious interviewed spoke to the kyriarchy within convent life when explaining punishments that were not physical or sexual but were psychological and emotional. Some admitted to feeling humiliated by acts of penance or the 'psychological

52 James M. Smith, 'The Politics of Sexual Knowledge: The Origins of Ireland's Containment Culture and the Carrigan Report (1931)', *Journal of the History of Sexuality*, 13 (2004), 208–33. See also the Commission to Inquire into Child Abuse (2008), known as the Ryan Report, and the Report by the Commission of the Investigation into the Catholic Archdiocese of Dublin, also known as the Murphy Report (2009). In Ireland, the Mother and Baby Home Inquiry is ongoing: www.mbhcoi.ie/mbh.nsf/page/index-en, accessed December 2018.

53 Elizabeth Butler Cullingford, '"Our Nuns Are Not a Nation": Politicizing the Convent in Irish Literature and Film', in Wanda Balzano, Ann Mulhall and Moynagh Sullivan (eds), *Irish Postmodernisms and Popular Culture* (London: Palgrave Macmillan, 2007), pp. 55–73, p. 14.

54 Phil Kilroy, 'Coming to an Edge in History: Writing the History of Women Religious and the Critique of Feminism', in Deirdre Raftery and Elizabeth M. Smyth (eds), *Education, Identity and Women Religious, 1800–1950: Convents, Classrooms and Colleges* (London: Routledge, 2015), p. 25.

55 Margaret Susan Thompson, 'Circles of Sisterhood: Formal and Informal Collaboration among American Nuns in Response to Conflict with Vatican Kyriarchy', *Journal of Feminist Studies in Religion*, 32 (2016), 63–82. The concept of kyriarchy comes out of theologian Elisabeth Schüssler Fiorenza's earlier work. Her more recent work expands on kyriarchy. Elisabeth Schüssler Fiorenza, *Congress of Wo/Men: Religion, Gender, and Kyriarchal Power* (Indianapolis, IN: Dog Ear Publishing, 2016).

rape', as one sister offered, that came along with punishments meted out
with the admonition 'we don't do things like this here'.[56] Some women
religious' mental and physical wellbeing were irretrievably damaged by
this regime. Van Heijst writes:

> [N]uns were robbed of a value-system that was sensitive to human
> suffering, since suffering was viewed as potentially having a spiritual
> benefit for one's soul. It is tragic that women, who gave up so much
> because they intended to do good for their fellow-men, became the
> ones who inflicted pain and misery upon the weakest members of
> society.[57]

The use of humiliation and sacrificial suffering in the convent
was replicated in some classrooms and orphanages. According to
scholars, this occurred because of 'a failure on the part of the teachers
to distinguish between their own "spiritual formation" as members of
a religious order and what was appropriate in the classroom, or [could
be attributed] to inflicting on pupils the frustration and humiliation
which they themselves experienced within the cloister'.[58] Cullingford
has suggested a social class-based dimension of abuse. Ruminating on
her own happy convent school education in an 'empowering female
community'. she questioned 'Was the difference between the enlightened
and the abusive merely a reflection of money and class?'[59] She suggested
that 'nuns who were selected to teach middle-class children were likely
to be better educated and from more prosperous backgrounds than those
who supervised the washing tub or policed the poor'. As I complete this
volume, the texture of historical abuse crimes is becoming even more
complex, with women religious also coming forward as victims of clerical

56   Anonymised interview.
57   Annelies van Heijst, 'The Disputed Charity of Catholic Nuns: Dualistic Spiritual
     Heritage as a Source of Affliction', *Feminist Theology*, 21 (2013), 155–72, p. 169; Jo-
     Anne Fiske, 'Spirited Subjects and Wounded Souls: Political Representations on an Im/
     Moral Frontier' in Myra Rutherdale and Katie Pickles (eds), *Contactzones: Aboriginal
     and Settler Women in Canada's Colonial Past* (Vancouver: UBC Press, 2005); Nicola
     Yeates, 'The Irish Catholic Female Religious and the Transnationalisation of Care: An
     Historical Perspective', *Irish Journal of Sociology*, 19 (2011), 77–93; David Pilgrim,
     'Child Abuse in Irish Catholic Settings: A Non-Reductionist Account', *Child Abuse
     Review*, 21 (2012), 405–13.
58   Tom O'Donoghue and Stephanie Burley, 'God's Antipodean Teaching Force: An
     Historical Exposition on Catholic Teaching Religious in Australia', *Teaching and
     Teacher Education*, 24 (2008), 180–9.
59   Cullingford, '"Our Nuns Are Not a Nation"', p. 14.

abuse.[60] Abuse scandals are not limited to the religious sphere; they appear with alarming regularity in press headlines of residential care in other types of institutions such as homes for the elderly and psychiatric hospitals.[61] Mark Smith, practitioner and theorist of residential child care, controversially noted that 'it has become fashionable, however, to focus on negative images of care'. Not all who spent time in institutions had negative experiences.[62] This field of conflicting memories and divergent viewpoints between care-givers and care-receivers must be a site of further research in the years to come if we are to ever understand cultures of abuse. Scholars of religious life have a particular obligation to avoid the silence of the past.[63]

In the Catholic Church, the trauma extends past the individual to the complicity of silence of authorities within the religious institutes and within the ecclesiastical hierarchy. It is a silence of denial, but also a silence that suggests reputation and status was more important than human lives. Many have voiced their outrage by either leaving the Church or pressuring for reform. Historian Kathleen Sprows Cummings publicly insisted that the Church must 'come to terms with the sins of its past and reform itself so thoroughly that they will never be repeated in the future'.[64] But as we have seen throughout this volume, reform is difficult and not all will see the need to change.

Diminishment alongside rebirth?

From this crisis of identity and the plummeting of vocations, new ways of being female religious were created. In decentring the binary opposition of 'religion' and 'the world', I have told a particular story of female religious

60   'Pope admits clerical abuse of nuns including sexual slavery' (6 February 2019). www. bbc.co.uk/news/world-europe-47134033, accessed 12 March 2019.

61   Academic projects such as Louise Hide's Wellcome Trust-funded 'Hiding in Plain Sight: Cultures of Harm in Residential Institutions for Long-Term Adult Care, Britain 1945–1980s' address the historical context of the underlying belief systems and practices that normalised abuse practices.

62   Mark Smith, *Rethinking Residential Child Care: Positive Perspectives* (Bristol: Policy Press, 2009), p. 24.

63   Robert Orsi, 'A Crisis about the Theology of Children', *Harvard Divinity School Bulletin*, 30 (2002), 27–33. Kathryn Lofton, 'Revisited: Sex Abuse and the Study of Religion' (24 August 2018). https://tif.ssrc.org/2018/08/24/sex-abuse-and-the-study-of-religion/, accessed 6 December 2018.

64   Kathleen Sprows Cummings, 'For Catholics, Gradual Reform Is No Longer an Option', *New York Times* (17 August 2018). www.nytimes.com/2018/08/17/opinion/catholic-church-reform.html, accessed 1 December 2018.

life. Threaded throughout each chapter was the interrelationship and engagement of religion with the post-war secular age. This post-secular analysis has deliberately engaged with religion as a category of analysis emphasising change rather than decline.[65]

This work could easily have centred on decline, as many of the scholars of religion charting secularisation do.[66] The diminishment in numbers of women religious was a significant change. Former sister and American sociologist Helen Rose Fuchs Ebaugh in her analysis of decline predicted that 'the demise [of religious life] is virtually inevitable.'[67] Camillus Metcalfe, a former sister turned psychoanalyst, ended her psycho-analytically-framed book with the assertion that religious life had 'nothing extra to offer. It has lost its identity and its function.'[68] Even the recent surge, a '25-year high' in British entrants reported in both the Catholic and national press, seemed to reflect the depths of the decline rather than the growth it purportedly addressed. Forty-five women entered convents and monasteries in 2014 in England and Wales (up from fifteen in 2009).[69] These numbers are a far cry from the thousands who entered in the 1890s.[70] Sociologists have analysed the cycles of growth and decline in religious life. The historical arc has been well documented: from the desert fathers and mothers (200 to 500); to the age of monasticism (500–1200); to the mendicants (1200–1500); to the apostolic orders (1500–1800); and the age of teaching congregations (1800–1960s). Each had a height when enthusiasm and fervour led to large numbers of entrants; each had a decline when pundits were claiming an apocalyptic 'The end is nigh'. Sociologists of religion charting religious life as a social movement identify periods of foundation; expansion; stabilisation; breakdown; and a final critical period (which includes

---

65   Timothy W. Jones, 'Postsecular Sex? Secularisation and Religious Change in the History of Sexuality in Britain', *History Compass*, 11 (2013), 918–30.

66   For example, Callum G. Brown, *The Death of Christian Britain: Understanding Secularisation, 1800–2000* (London: Routledge, 2001); Steve Bruce, *Religion and Modernization: Sociologists and Historians Debate the Secularization Thesis* (Oxford: Oxford University Press, 1992).

67   Helen Rose Ebaugh, *Women in the Vanishing Cloister: Organizational Decline in Catholic Religious Orders in the United States* (New Brunswick, NJ: Rutgers University Press, 1993), 158.

68   Camillus Metcalfe, *For God's Sake: The Hidden Life of Irish Nuns* (Dublin: Liffey Press, 2014), p. 242.

69   'Women Becoming Nuns Hits 25-Year High', *BBC News* (23 April 2015). www.bbc. co.uk/news/uk-32417296, accessed 8 November 2018.

70   Carmen M. Mangion, *Contested Identities: Catholic Women Religious in Nineteenth-Century England and Wales* (Manchester: Manchester University Press, 2008), pp. 45–6.

breakdown) that potentially leads to a 'transition' period or extinction. Sixty-four per cent of those religious institutes founded before 1800 are no longer extant.[71] Raymond Hostie's analysis of male religious institutes suggests a life span of 250 to 350 years.[72] The public discourse of decline is often focused on a secularised, industrialised Global North, ignoring the stabilisation and sometimes growth and dynamism of female religious life in the Global South.[73] These seem markedly similar to secularisation debates that posit an 'end of religion' though the non-Anglo/European world remains robustly devout.[74] This says volumes about the self-importance of the Global North.

Those analysing decline point to three primary components. The first relates to the natural decline due to mortality. The second is that fewer women entered as postulants, the 'crisis in vocations' that was evident from the 1940s as discussed in Chapter 1. The third is the departures of women religious. Leave-taking in the 1940s–1960s of postulant and novices who had 'no vocation' remains relatively unstudied. Even those communities that appeared to have bustling novitiates during the 1960s and 1970s deserve a second look. One particularly strict enclosed community in Warwickshire was acclaimed in the press for its attractiveness to youth; archive sources suggest the inflow into a bustling novitiate was offset by a steady outflow of postulants and novices who left before profession.[75] Another aspect of the departures is the post-conciliar accelerated rate of departures of professed sisters. Most concur that women left for numerous reasons, identifying their religious institute's slow pace of renewal, or an overly quick renewal or that ambiguous category 'no vocation'.

---

71 Cada et al., Shaping the Coming Age, pp. 53, 59. Susan O'Brien is rightly sceptical of applying the normative pattern of male religious life to women's religious life. Susan O'Brien, 'A Note on Apostolic Religious Life', in Christopher Jamison, OSB (ed.), The Disciples' Call: Theologies of Vocation from Scripture to the Present Day (London: Bloomsbury, 2013), pp. 155–66.

72 Raymond Hostie, Vie et mort des ordres religieux. Approches psychosociologiques (Paris: Desclée de Brouwer, 1972), p. 312.

73 Helen Rose Ebaugh, Jon Lorence and Janet Saltzman Chafetz, 'The Growth and Decline of the Population of Catholic Nuns Cross-Nationally, 1960–1990: A Case of Secularization as Social Structural Change', Journal for the Scientific Study of Religion, 35 (1996), 172.

74 Jones, 'Postsecular Sex?'. It also ignores faith and spirituality outside of denominational structures.

75 'Historic Warwickshire Convent to Close after 160 years', Birmingham Post (25 February 2011). www.birminghampost.co.uk/news/local-news/historic-warwickshire-convent-close-after-3923982, accessed 8 December 2018.

In Britain, as discussed in Chapter 1, the discourse of a 'crisis of vocations' in female religious life occurred much earlier than in the United States and Canada, where scholars report full novitiates in the 1950s and 1960s. To understand the story of post-war religious life means acknowledging the significance of the secular world and Catholic lay movements. Cardinal John Heenan, writing in 1965, was concerned about an emphasis on lay movements: 'If the priesthood of the laity comes to be regarded as sufficient and our brightest boys no longer look to the priesthood we shall have entered a second dark age.'[76] *Quadragesima Anno*, issued by Pope Pius XI in 1931, called for a reinvigoration of the lay apostolate. Lay movements such as Catholic Action, the Young Christian Worker movement and older organisations such as the St Vincent de Paul Society and Catholic Women's League offered young women and men opportunities to serve their Church alongside their single or married vocation.[77] Heenan, and others, were concerned that this siphoned off vocations from the priesthood and religious life. These concerns were felt in other religious denominations also.[78]

Historian Callum Brown placed the onus of secularisation squarely on women in the 1960s.[79] Many Catholics have similarly made women religious responsible for decline. The decline in numbers and the emphasis on social justice led to departures from education and nursing institutional ministries and altered the 'who'

---

76   AAW: HE1/R2 Religious Vocations Exhibition, 1965 (1964–1965), Letter from Cardinal John Carmel Heenan to Anthony H. Reynolds, dated 18 May 1965.

77   Lay movements too (e.g. Catholic Women's League, Children of Mary, etc.) have experienced the trajectory of growth and decline very similar to that of religious life. For an example of these in other dioceses in England and Wales see Peter Doyle, *Mitres and Missions in Lancashire: The Roman Catholic Diocese of Liverpool, 1850–2000* (Liverpool: Bluecoat Press, 2005), pp. 273–6; Margaret Turnham, *Catholic Faith and Practice in England, 1779–1992: The Role of Revivalism and Renewal* (Woodbridge: Boydell & Brewer, 2015), pp. 137–9. These concerns were international. Father Albert Plé surmised that young women preferred Catholic Action to religious life because it was a direct apostolate. Albert Plé (ed.), *The Doctrinal Instruction of Religious Sisters* (London: Blackfriars Press, 1956), p. 67.

78   Hugh McLeod suggests that the drop in Anglican ordinations in 1967 may have been related to the call of social action and the practical Christianity that could be found outside the Church. He suggests that many privileged 'love thy neighbor' through social welfare work rather than the priesthood. McLeod, *The Religious Crisis of the 1960s*, pp. 84–92. For more on the transition to secular movements see also Brewitt-Taylor, 'From Religion to Revolution' and Kenneth Boyd, *The Witness of the Student Christian Movement* (London: SPCK, 2007).

79   Brown, *The Death of Christian Britain*.

and 'how' of evangelisation. In the North American context, the 'error' of interpretation of the Second Vatican Council has been placed at feminism's door.[80] Recently, two Vatican investigations, both initiated in the papacy of Benedict XVI, the Apostolic Visitation of US communities in 2008 and the Doctrinal Assessment of the US Leadership Conference of Women Religious the following year, claimed that sisters in the United States were overly attentive to issues of the poor and marginalised, ignoring other important church teachings on contraception, abortion and homosexuality.[81] The final report, however, published in 2014 under Pope Francis, commended women religious for their 'selfless' work.[82] These debates brought to the surface the ongoing disagreement between 'traditionalists' and 'progressives' regarding the reception of the Second Vatican Council and concerns about 'secularising influences'.[83]

Religious life today

This work has centred on women who remained in religious life despite the tumult of the post-war changes. Their vocations were tested; many revisited the decision to remain. They persisted despite the trauma of the changes in religious life, fought over and fought for, described within these chapters. Thirty years after the *aggiornamento* chapters, sociologist Gerald Arbuckle noted:

> Many religious congregations today are in chaos. They are not sure about the meaning, contemporary relevance or mission of religious life and, on the practical level, they find it difficult to cope with often

---

80 Ann Carey, *Sisters in Crisis: The Tragic Unraveling of Women's Religious Communities* (Huntington, IN: Our Sunday Visitor Publishing Division, 1997); Ebaugh, *Women in the Vanishing Cloister*, pp. 133–48.

81 Kilroy, 'Coming to an Edge in History', p. 24. 'Final Report on the Apostolic Visitation of Institutes of Women Religious in the United States of America' (16 December 2014). https://press.vatican.va/content/salastampa/it/bollettino/pubblico/2014/12/16/0963/02078.html, accessed 9 December 2018.

82 Robert McClory, 'Pope Francis and Women's Ordination', *National Catholic Reporter* (16 September 2013). http://ncronline.org/blogs/ncr-today/pope-francis-and-womens-ordination, accessed 9 December 2018. Thompson, 'Circles of Sisterhood'.

83 These labels are unhelpful but ubiquitous in the press. Kate Stogdon, '"Nothing Was Taken from Me: Everything Was Given": Religious Life and Second Wave Feminism', in Gemma Simmonds, CJ (ed.), *A Future Full of Hope?* (Dublin: The Columba Press, 2012), pp. 64–9.

rapidly declining numbers, few or no vocations and the rising average ages of membership.[84]

Two decades later, the Vitality Study on female religious life acknowledged in its findings the 'messiness' of diminishment existing alongside vitality, concluding:

> The project finds religious women moving from action to a ministry of presence, witness and relationship, perceiving their presence, even in old age, as prophetic faithfulness. If this 'middle space' between past and future is experienced as messy and sometimes bewildering it is also seen as a move from the socially and ecclesially respectable centre of church and society to the margins, both in terms of status and of apostolic focus.[85]

The move from 'chaos' to 'vitality' was not about increasing numbers or 'bustling' novitiates but about collaborative social action geared towards systemic change, as well as ministerial work that in its 'prophetic faithfulness' was less about action and more about relationship.

The nuns and sisters participating in this project acknowledged diminishment within religious life. Some, speaking of their own communities, were aware numerical decline would lead to the eventual closure of their local community, or their religious institute. Other religious institutes remain open to new entrants, attracting small numbers of vocations, both British and foreign-born. They still experience diminishment in their smaller community size and a reduction in the scope of their ministries. Some sisters voiced an acceptance of their diminishment:

> I don't think as a community we are fretting about dying out. Some are. We know we have a lay group, we have a charism to hand on. We're not looking at, oh my goodness, we're dying out, what do we do about dying, you know, we're living in the present moment, we have a charism to hand on, we'd better get on with it. You know, we're not investing in what happens when we're gone.[86]

---

84 Gerald A. Arbuckle, *Out of Chaos: Refounding Religious Congregations* (London: Geoffrey Chapman, 1988), p. 1.

85 Catherine Sexton and Gemma Simmonds, CJ, *Religious Life Vitality Project: Key Project Findings*, 2015, p. 3. static1.squarespace.com/static/5805fde21b631b4e18960 a1a/t/5850339de6f2e1895e2b601e/1481651155537/RLVP+KEY+FINDINGS+FINAL+ %282%29.pdf, accessed 8 December 2018.

86 Anonymised interview.

Some religious institutes have developed an association of lay associates (sometimes called affiliates) as a means of spreading their charism, the spirit of the founder, into the future.[87] Associates formally constitute a separate body from the religious community but join in prayer and ministry. Some associates operate in a volunteer capacity; others as paid employees working in a congregation's ministries or administration.

Despite diminishment, women religious continue to minister in both individual and corporate ways. Many sisters into their seventies and eighties work passionately in their own individual or congregation ministries for as long as they can. Older sisters whose ministerial outreach is limited remain connected through prayer and presence. Theologian Catherine Sexton's research has acknowledged the significance of what she calls 'an evolving identity of post-institutional apostolic religious life'.[88] Some religious institutes remain invested in their history. One sister spoke of her congregation's willingness to invest in their heritage as a means of leaving a footprint in the future:

> We can't give up. I mean, you know, nobody would want to give up anything, I think. But what is it going to be and what's the mystery? I mean you would never know what your children are going to turn out to be and it's the same mystery, you know, we're here and some people would say, what on earth do you put up the heritage and all that kind of stuff down there, we'll all be dead and buried. And I think that's true. Then on the other hand you think, you know, we only have each day, don't we, to live to the best.[89]

Religious institutes (national and international) have also banded together on large multi-congregational international projects such as the Arise Foundation that combats modern slavery.[90] Collaborative initiatives have a greater impact and presence and utilise the expertise of a larger group of sisters. In examining the vitality of a select group of religious institutes, theologians noted a 'strong sense of resilience as their most significant

---

87 Margaret Susan Thompson, '"Charism" or "Deep Story"? Toward a Clearer Understanding of the Growth of Women's Religious Life in Nineteenth-Century America', *Review for Religious*, 28:3 (1999), 230–50.
88 Catherine Sexton, 'Theologies of Ministry among Older Roman Catholic Sisters in the UK', unpublished PhD dissertation, Anglia Ruskin University, 2018.
89 Anonymised interview.
90 'Religious across the UK Invited to Join a Network for Anti-Trafficking'. www.corew. org/news/, accessed 8 December 2018. Forty institutes are involved in a wide range of ministries, in both antislavery and prevention work; others, not involved in active ministries, are doing something in their own way, such as making financial contributions.

and enduring form of vitality'. In this, sisters model to the Church and to wider society 'ways of living diminishment creatively and witness to the possibility of living loss and relinquishment well'.[91]

The negative facets of diminishment were rarely acknowledged in interviews.[92] Those who recalled the 'chaos' of the past almost always justified their experience with appreciation of their own authentic present as religious:

> The changes can look from the outside as if they were all about getting rid of rules, enclosure, structures and everybody doing their own thing. And obviously that's a risk. And I'm not saying that, you know, that changes never happen in a wonderfully balanced way, but now I'm seventy-four, so many years later … I can honestly say that what I entered for, which was for a life, a spiritual life what would energise a life of service. A relationship with God, and the environment where that relationship could develop and be supported by people who held the same vision, I would say has been greatly strengthened by the changes.[93]

Indirectly, the emotiveness of diminishment was touched upon by some women religious when they recalled with longing and nostalgia the bustling novitiates and the influential schools that they managed; there was a palpable hurt when they recounted feelings of rejection in the current lack of interest in religious life or the departures of aspirants.

Is there a radical paradigm shift in the future? One recent study of new entrants to religious life in the United States suggests that a subculture of millennials who might be open to religious life will be difficult to attract unless extant religious institutes do a better job of understanding their beliefs, values, desires and preoccupations.[94] New types of religious intentional communities seem more attractive to these entrants. They include canonical religious institutes and ecclesial lay communities. Some of the new religious institutes such as the Community of Our Lady of Walsingham founded in 2004 intend to become an ecclesial

91   Sexton and Simmonds, 'Religious Life Vitality Project', p. 9.
92   I did not ask questions about diminishment and it was rarely brought up by narrators. I was aware that it could be a sensitive subject, and aligned with Anderson and Jack's approach of honouring the interviewee's 'integrity and privacy', I wanted to avoid topics that 'the narrator has chosen to hold back'. Kathryn Anderson and Dana C. Jack, 'Learning to Listen: Interview Techniques and Analyses', in Sherna Gluck Berger and Daphne Patai (eds), *Women's Words: The Feminist Practice of Oral History* (New York: Routledge, 1991), p. 25.
93   Anonymised interview.
94   Mary Johnson, Patricia Wittberg and Mary L. Gautier, *New Generations of Catholic Sisters: The Challenge of Diversity* (New York: Oxford University Press, 2014).

family: one juridical entity with diverse types of members – consecrated clergy; consecrated men and women; celibate and married laity; associate members with full rights.[95] Others like the Community of the Franciscan Sisters of Renewal founded in the United States in 1988 and located in Leeds look remarkably similar to pre-conciliar religious life. New ecclesial movements, such as Focolare, Communion and Liberation or the Community of Sant'Egidio, build intentional communities with both lay and vowed religious living and working together. New communities offer a range of options that meet the diversity of human needs. Some have firm structures; others offer flexibility and creativity in their ministries. Sociologist William J. F. Keenan suggests that the future of new monasticism holds 'flexible, eclectic, deregulated modes of postmodern religious lifestyles'.[96] Maybe. New ecclesial movements are part of a particular historical moment adapting to a particular cultural climate. Whether they prosper remains a mystery.

Conclusion

This volume in exploring nuns and sisters in a secular age has provided a means with which to decipher complex, diverse stories of female religious life. Religious tradition, for many of the congregations and orders studied here, had by 1945 become ossified and rigid. Renewal began for some in the 1950s and others in the 1960s after the mandates of the Second Vatican Council and particularly *Perfectae Caritatis* (Adaptation and Renewal of Religious Life, 1965). Renewal was influenced by Church directives and by the 'modern world' and the social movements that have become emblematic of post-war ideas of modernity. This research has been grounded by three core premises: women religious were part of and participated in social movements that dramatically altered how religious life was lived; they were members of transnational entities and were influenced by differing interpretations of renewal; and that the struggles for change were linked to competing and contradictory ideas of individual, collective and institutional identities. Women are at the centre of this history, which is consciously intended to enrich women's history, gender history, social and cultural history and religious history. Women

---

95   The Community of Our Lady of Walsingham. www.walsinghamcommunity.org/ about-us/introduction/ecclesial-family-of-consecrated-life, accessed 10 December 2018.

96   William J. F. Keenan, 'Twenty-First-Century Monasticism and Religious Life: Just Another New Millennium', *Religion*, 32 (2002), 13.

were integral change agents in the social movement within the Catholic Church. This 'storming of the barricades' of the hierarchies of religious life, similar to many social movements in '1968', left behind nostalgia and a memory of 'great women' that has made historical assessment difficult. The focus here has been on the ordinary sister and nun, and on personal testimony that tells us how women religious interpreted their own experience. Making the personal political also means understanding the 'politics' that can be shaped by ordinary people. The more philosophical aims of this work were to raise consciousness, a consciousness that social change came at a price. Later generations may welcome, laud and celebrate the efforts of those men and women 'ahead of their time', but they did not pay the price of the disruption that it brought to personal lives. It also seeks to recall that dialogic relationship between religion and the world. The volume also suggests that the changes to religious life in Britain were evolutionary as well as revolutionary; modest experiments of the 1940s and 1950s informed the post-conciliar experiments that were ongoing through to the 1980s and into the present. Despite diminishment, or maybe because of it, the future of religious life is still evolving.

Select bibliography

Primary sources

Archives of religious institutes

Canonesses Regular of the Holy Sepulchre

Durham University Library and Special Collections, GB-033-CHS, Canonesses Regular of the Holy Sepulchre Archive (DUL CHS), Durham, UK

Congregation of Jesus (formerly Institute of the Blessed Virgin Mary)

Archives of the English Province of the Congregation of Jesus (ACJ/EP), York, UK

Poor Clares

Archives of the Poor Clares Monastery, Much Birch (OSC Much Birch), Much Birch, UK
Francis Pullen Archives (in private hands) (FPA), Much Birch, UK

Sisters of Charity Our Lady, Mother of Mercy

Archief Congregatie Zusters van Liefde (SCMM-Tilburg), Tilburg, the Netherlands
Erfgoedcentrum Nederlands Kloosterleven, Archiefinventaris Zusters van Liefde (SCMM-ENK), Sint Agatha, the Netherlands
Archives of the British Province of the Sisters of Charity of Our Lady, Mother of Mercy, Pantasaph, Wales

Sisters of Mercy

Archives of the Union Sisters of Mercy, Great Britain (RSM Union), Handsworth, UK
Institute of Our Lady of Mercy Archives (RSM Institute), Bermondsey, UK

Society of the Sacred Heart

Archives of the Province of England and Wales (SSH ENW), Roehampton, UK
The General Archives of the Society of the Sacred Heart, Rome, Italy

Syon Bridgettines (The Order of the Most Holy Saviour)

Exeter University Library, Syon Abbey Medieval and Modern Manuscript Collection (EUL), Exeter, UK

Vocation Sisters

West Sussex Record Office (WSRO), Chichester, UK

Diocesan archives

Archdiocese of Liverpool Archives (ALA), Liverpool, UK
Archives of the Archdiocese of Westminster (AAW), London, UK
Arundel and Brighton Diocesan Archives (ABDA), Hove, UK
Birmingham Archdiocesan Archives (BAA), Birmingham, UK
Leeds Diocesan Archives, Headingley, Leeds, UK
Plymouth Diocesan Archives (PDA), Exeter, UK
Wrexham Diocesan Archives, Wrexham, UK

Other archives

Bishopsgate Institute, London, UK
British Film Institute (BFI), London, UK
Elizabeth Rendall Archives (ERA), in private hands, York, UK

Newspapers and periodicals

Annuarium Statisticum Ecclesiae
Catholic Herald
Catholic Pictorial
Clergy Review
Doctrine and Life
Dublin Review
The Furrow
Irish Ecclesiastical Record: A Monthly Journal under Episcopal Sanction
Novena
Poor Soul's Friend
Review for Religious
The Tablet
The Way

Papal documents

All papal and other official documents of the Catholic Church can be located at Papal
Encyclicals Online: www.papalencyclicals.net/

Printed primary sources

'A Brief Account of the Community of the Poor Clares Colettines, Notting Hill, London' (1957)

Anon., *Fishy Tales: Living Memories of New Hall 1930–2012* (Colchester, Essex: Canonesses of the Holy Sepulchre, 2012)

Armstrong, Karen, *The Spiral Staircase* (London: HarperCollins, 2004)

——, *Through the Narrow Gate: A Nun's Story* (London: Flamingo, 1981)

Audience Invisible: Broadcast Address of His Holiness Pius XII by Divine Providence Pope to the Cloistered Nuns of the World (London: Catholic Truth Society, 1958)

Baldwin, Monica, *I Leap over the Wall: A Return to the World after Twenty-Eight Years in a Convent* (London: Hamish Hamilton, 1949)

Beveridge, William Henry, *Voluntary Action: A Report on Methods of Social Advance* (London: George Allen & Unwin, 1948)

Bride of a King (London: Daughters of Our Lady of Good Counsel Vocation Houses, 1958)

Brockett, Lorna, *The Ordination of Women: A Roman Catholic Viewpoint* (London: MOW, 1982)

A Carmelite Nun, *The Nun's Answer* (London: Burns, Oates, 1957)

Carr, John, CSSR, *Grown Up* (Dublin: Clonmore & Reynolds, 1957)

[Carroll, Mary Teresa Austin], *Leaves from the Annals of the Sisters of Mercy* (New York: Catholic Publication Society Company, 1883)

Catherine Thomas of Divine Providence, DC, *My Beloved: The Story of a Carmelite Nun* (New York: McGraw-Hill, 1955)

Committee on Voluntary Organisations, *The Future of Voluntary Organisations: Report of the Wolfenden Committee [on Voluntary Organisations]* (London: Croom Helm, 1978)

Cormack, Una, *The Church and Social Work*, Pastoral Investigation of Social Trends (Liverpool: Liverpool Institute of Socio-Religious Studies [for] the Conference of Major Religious Superiors of England and Wales, 1977)

Courtois, Abbé Gaston, *The States of Perfection* (Dublin: Gill, 1961)

De Frees, Madeline, *The Springs of Silence* (Kingston, Surrey: The World's Work 1913, 1954)

Donnelly, Gertrude Joseph, *The Sister, Apostle* (Tenbury Wells: Fowler Wright Books Ltd, 1964)

Douie, Vera, *Daughters of Britain (An Account of the Work of British Women during the Second World War)* (Oxford: The Author, 1949)

Farrell, Ambrose, Henry St John and F. B. Elkisch, *The Education of the Novice* (London: Blackfriars Press, 1956)

Forrestall, James Patrick, *'Tell me Father' about Vocations* (Sydney, London and New York: St Paul Publications, 1961)

Freeman, Jo, 'The Tyranny of Structurelessness', *Berkeley Journal of Sociology*, 17 (1972), 151–64

Godden, Rumer, *In This House of Brede* (London: Pan Books, 1969)

Gorer, Geoffrey, *Exploring English Character* (London: Cresset Press, 1955)

Griffin, Mary, *The Courage to Choose: An American Nun's Story* (Boston: Little, Brown, 1975)

Hagspiel, Bruno M., 'The Religious Life in the U.S. Is on the Decline Both in Men's and Women's Orders', *Sponsa Regis*, 28 (1956), 29–41

History of the New Hall Community of the Canonesses Regular of the Holy Sepulchre (Roehampton: Manresa Press, 1899)

Hulme, Kathryn, *The Nun's Story* (London: Pan Books, 1959)

In a Great Tradition: Tribute to Dame Laurentia McLachlan, Abbess of Stanbrook (London: John Murray, 1956)

Jephcott, A. P., *A Troubled Area: Notes on Notting Hill* (London: Faber & Faber, 1964)

——, *Girls Growing Up* (London: Faber & Faber, 1942)

Jephcott, Pearl, *Rising Twenty: Notes on Some Ordinary Girls* (London: Faber & Faber, 1948)

——, *Some Young People* (Allen & Unwin, 1954)

——, *Time of One's Own: Leisure and Young People* (London: Oliver & Boyd, 1967)

Klein, Josephine, *Samples from English Cultures*, 2 vols (London: Routledge & Kegan Paul, 1965)

Lodge, David, *How Far Can You Go?* (Harmondsworth: Penguin Books, 1981)

Lord, Daniel A., *Shall I Be a Nun?* (St Louis, MO: The Queen's Work Press, 1927)

Loudon, Mary, *Unveiled: Nuns Talking* (London: Chatto & Windus, 1992)

Morgan, Robin, ed., *Sisterhood Is Global: The International Women's Movement Anthology* (Harmondsworth: Penguin Books, 1984)

Morris, Mary, *Voluntary Organisations and Social Progress* (London: Victor Gollancz, 1955)

Motson, Anna, 'Why I Became a Nun', *Cosmopolitan* (July 1973), 39–41

Myrdal, Alva, and Viola Klein, *Women's Two Roles: Home and Work* (London: Routledge & Kegan Paul, 1956)

Parnell, Nancy Steward, *A Venture in Faith. A History of St. Joan's Social and Political Alliance, Formerly the Catholic Women's Suffrage Society, 1911–1961* (London: St Joan's Alliance, 1961)

Pelzer, Anne Marie, 'St Joan's International Alliance' (1977). www.womenpriests.org/interact/pelzer.asp, accessed 8 November 2018

Plé, Albert, ed., *The Doctrinal Instruction of Religious Sisters* (London: Blackfriars Press, 1956)

——, ed., *Authority in the Cloister: Obedience* (London: Blackfriars Press, 1953)

Pope Paul VI, *Motu Proprio Ecclesiae Sanctae: Establishing Norms for Carrying Out Certain Decrees of the Second Sacred Vatican Council*, trans. J. Leo Alston (London: Catholic Truth Society, 1967)

Rowbotham, Sheila, *Woman's Consciousness, Man's World* (Harmondsworth: Penguin Books, 1973)

Rowntree, B. Seebohm, and G. R. Lavers, *English Life and Leisure: A Social Study* (London: Longmans Green and Co., 1951)

Scott, George, *The R.C.s: A Report on Roman Catholics in Britain Today* (London: Hutchinson, 1967)

Seabrook, Jeremy, *Working-Class Childhood* (London: Victor Gollancz, 1982)

Sebestyen, Amanda, 'Britain', in *Sisterhood Is Global: The International Women's Movement Anthology*, ed.Robin Morgan (Harmondsworth: Penguin Books, 1984), 94–102

Sister Felicity, *Barefoot Journey* (London: Darton, Longman & Todd, 1961)

Sister Giles, *The End and the Beginning* (Stanhope: The Memoir Club, 2007)

Sister M. Catherine Frederic, *… and Spare Me Not in the Making: Pages from a Novice's Diary* (London: Clonmore & Reynolds, 1955)

Sister Mary Francis, *A Right to Be Merry* (London: Sheed & Ward, 1956)

Sister Mary Laurence, OP, *The Convent and the World* (London: Blackfriars Publications, 1955)

——, *Nuns are Real People* (London: Blackfriars Publications, 1955)

——, *One Nun to Another* (London: Blackfriars Publications, 1959)

——, *Prayer and All That* (London: Blackfriars Publications, 1958)

——, *She Takes the Veil* (London: Blackfriars Publications, 1952)

——, *They Live the Life* (London: Blackfriars Publications, 1954)

——, *Within the Walls* (London: Blackfriars Publications, 1953)

Smith, Austin, *Passion for the Inner City: A Personal View* (London: Sheed and Ward, 1983)

Stacey, Margaret, *Tradition and Change: A Study of Banbury* (Oxford: Oxford University Press, 1960)

Stacey, Meg, 'Older Women and Feminism: A Note about My Experience of the WLM', *Feminist Review*, 31 (1989), 140–2

Stansill, Peter, and David Zane Mairowitz, eds, *BAMN (By Any Means Necessary): Outlaw Manifestos and Ephemera, 1965–70* (Harmondsworth: Penguin Books, 1971)

Suenens, Cardinal Leon Joseph, *The Nun in the World: New Dimensions in the Modern Apostolate* (Westminster, MD: Newman Press, 1963)

Wilson, Prue, *My Father Took Me to the Circus* (London: Darton, Longman & Todd, 1984)

Secondary sources

Abrams, L., 'Mothers and Daughters: Negotiating the Discourse on the "Good Woman" in 1950s and 1960s Britain', in *The Sixties and Beyond: Dechristianisation in North America and Western Europe, 1945–2000*, ed. Nancy Christie and Michael Gavreau (Toronto: University of Toronto Press, 2013)

Abrams, Lynn, 'Liberating the Female Self: Epiphanies, Conflict and Coherence in the Life Stories of Post-War British Women', *Social History*, 39 (2014), 14–35

——, *Oral History Theory* (London: Routledge, 2010)

Abrams, Mark, *Teenage Consumers* (London: London Press Exchange, 1959)

Adelman, Sarah Mulhall, 'Empowerment and Submission: The Political Culture of Catholic Women's Religious Communities in Nineteenth-Century America', *Journal of Women's History*, 23 (2011), 138–61

Aidala, Angela A., 'Social Change, Gender Roles, and New Religious Movements', *Sociological Analysis*, 46 (1985), 287–314

Alexander, Sally, 'Becoming a Woman in London in the 1920s and 1930s', in *Metropolis London: Histories and Representations since 1800*, ed. David Feldman and Gareth Stedman Jones (London: Routledge, 1989), pp. 245–71

Allan, Graham, 'Social Structure and Relationships', in *Social Context and Relationships*, ed. Steve Duck (London: Sage, 1993), pp. 1–25

Almeida, João Miguel, 'Progressive Catholicism in Portugal: Considerations on Political Activism (1958–1974)', *Histoire @Politique*, 30 (2016), 1–15

Anderson, Kathryn, and Dana C. Jack, 'Learning to Listen: Interview Techniques and Analyses', in *Women's Words: The Feminist Practice of Oral History*, ed. Sherna Gluck and Daphne Patai (London: Routledge, 1991), pp. 11–26

Anderson, Michael, 'The Social Implication of Demographic Change', in *The Cambridge Social History of Britain 1750-1950*, ed. F. M. L. Thompson (Cambridge: Cambridge University Press, 1990)

Andrews, Donna T., *Philanthropy and Police: London Charity in the Eighteenth Century* (Princeton, NJ: Princeton University Press, 1990)

Appleby, R. Scott, 'From State to Civil Society and Back Again: The Catholic Church as Transnational Actor, 1965-2005', in *Religious Internationals in the Modern World*, ed. Abigail Green and Vincent Viaene (Houndmills: Palgrave Macmillan, 2012), pp. 319–42

Arbuckle, Gerald, *Out of Chaos: Refounding Religious Congregations* (London: Geoffrey Chapman, 1988)

——, *Strategies for Growth in Religious Life* (Middlegreen, Slough: St Paul Publications, 1986)

Armstrong, Neil, '"I Insisted I Was Myself": Clergy Wives and Authentic Selfhood in England *c*. 1960-94', *Women's History Review*, 22 (2013), 995–1013

Aspden, Kester, *Fortress Church: The English Roman Catholic Bishops and Politics 1903–1963* (London: Gracewing, 2002)

Assmann, Jan, 'Collective Memory and Cultural Identity', *New German Critique*, 65 (1995), 125–33

Barlow, Tani E., Madeleine Yue Dong, Uta G. Poiger, Priti Ramamurthy, Lynn M. Thomas and Alys Eve Weinbaum, 'The Modern Girl around the World: A Research Agenda and Preliminary Findings', *Gender & History*, 17 (2005), 245–94

Barlow, Tani, Lynn M. Thomas, Priti Ramamurthy, Uta G. Poiger, Madeleine Yue Dong and Alys Eve Weinbaum, eds, *The Modern Girl around the World: Consumption, Modernity, and Globalization* (Durham, NC: Duke University Press, 2008)

Barnett, Michael N., *Empire of Humanity: A History of Humanitarianism* (Ithaca, NY: Cornell University Press, 2011)

Barnett, Michael N., and Janice Gross Stein, eds, *Sacred Aid: Faith and Humanitarianism* (Oxford: Oxford University Press, 2012)

Barr, Colin, and Rose Luminiello, '"The Leader of the Virgin Choirs of Erin": St Brigid's Missionary College, 1883-1914', in *Ireland in an Imperial World*, ed. Timothy G. McMahon, Michael de Nie and Paul Townend (London: Palgrave Macmillan, 2017), pp. 155–78

Beaumont, Caitríona, 'Citizens Not Feminists: The Boundary Negotiated between Citizenship and Feminism by Mainstream Women's Organisations in England, 1928–39', *Women's History Review*, 9 (2000), 411–29

——, *Housewives and Citizens: Domesticity and the Women's Movement in England, 1928–64* (Manchester: Manchester University Press, 2013)

——, 'Moral Dilemmas and Women's Rights: The Attitude of the Mothers' Union and Catholic Women's League to Divorce, Birth Control and Abortion in England, 1928–1939', *Women's History Review*, 16 (2007), 463–85

——, '"What Is a Wife"? Reconstructing Domesticity in Postwar Britain before *The Feminine Mystique*', *History of Women in the Americas*, 3 (2015), 61–76

Beck, George Andrew, ed., *The English Catholics, 1850-1950* (London: Burns, Oates, 1950)

Bennett, Jackie, and Rosemary Forgan, eds, *Convent Girls*, updated and rev. edn; previously titled *There's Something about a Convent Girl* (London: Virago, 2003)

Bennett, Richard, *The Truth Set Us Free: Twenty Former Nuns Tell Their Stories* (Mukilteo, WA: WinePress Publishing., 1997)

Bennett, Veronica, *Looking Good: A Visual Guide to the Nun's Habit* (London: GraphicDesign&, 2016)

Berman, Marshall, *All That Is Solid Melts into Air: The Experience of Modernity* (New York: Simon & Schuster, 1982)

Bingham, Adrian, '"An Era of Domesticity"? Histories of Women and Gender in Interwar Britain', *Cultural and Social History*, 1 (2004), 225–33

Binhammer, Katherine, 'Female Homosociality and the Exchange of Men: Mary Robinson's *Walsingham* ', *Women's Studies*, 35 (2006), 221–40

Birmingham Feminist History Group, 'Feminism as Femininity in the Nineteen-Fifties?', *Feminist Review*, 80 (1979), 28–65

Bolster, M. Angela, *Mercy in Cork 1837–1987: A Sesquicentennial Commemoration* (Cork: Tower Books, 1987)

Bondy, Renée D., 'Roman Catholic Women Religious and Organizational Reform in English Canada: The Ursuline and Holy Names Sisters in the Diocese of London, Ontario, 1950–1970' (unpublished PhD dissertation, University of Waterloo, 2007)

Bonomo, Bruno, '*Presa della parola*: A Review and Discussion of Oral History and the Italian 1968', *Memory Studies*, 6 (2013), 7–22

Bouchier, David, *The Feminist Challenge: The Movement for Women's Liberation in Britain and the USA* (London: MacMillan Press, 1983)

Boulding, Cecily, *Freedom and Authority: Dangerous Gifts? One Woman's Reflections on a – Fairly Significant – Role in the Church* (Cambridge: Margaret Beaufort Institute of Theology, 1997)

Boulding, Mary, *Contemplative Nuns: Are They Wasting Their Lives?* (London: Catholic Truth Society, 1973)

Bowden, Caroline, 'The English Convents in Exile and Questions of National Identity, c. 1600–1688', in *British and Irish Emigrants and Exiles in Europe, 1603–1688*, ed. David Worthington (Leiden: Brill, 2010), pp. 297–314

Boyd, Robin H. S., *The Witness of the Student Christian Movement: 'Church Ahead of the Church'* (London: SPCK, 2007)

Bracke, Maud Anne, 'One-Dimensional Conflict? Recent Scholarship on 1968 and the Limitations of the Generation Concept', *Journal of Contemporary History*, 47 (2012), 638–46

Bradshaw, Ann, *Lighting the Lamp: The Spiritual Dimension of Nursing Care* (Harrow: Scutari, 1994)

Braybon, Gail, and Penny Summerfield, *Out of the Cage: Women's Experiences in Two World Wars* (London: Pandora, 1987)

Brenton, Maria, *The Voluntary Sector in British Social Services* (London: Longman, 1985)

Brewis, Georgina, *A Social History of Student Volunteering: Britain and beyond, 1880–1980*, Historical Studies in Education (New York: Palgrave Macmillan, 2014)

Brewitt-Taylor, Sam, 'From Religion to Revolution: Theologies of Secularisation in the British Student Christian Movement, 1963–1973', *Journal of Ecclesiastical History*, 66 (2015), 792–811

——, 'The Invention of a "Secular Society"? Christianity and the Sudden Appearance of Secularization Discourses in the British National Media, 1961–4', *Twentieth Century British History*, 24 (2013), 327–50

Brock, Megan P., 'Resisting the Catholic Church's Notion of the Nun as Self-Sacrificing Woman', *Feminism & Psychology*, 20 (2010), 473–90

Bromley, David G., 'Linking Social Structure and the Exit Process in Religious Organizations: Defectors, Whistle-Blowers, and Apostates', *Journal for the Scientific Study of Religion*, 37 (1998), 145–60

Brooke, Stephen, 'Gender and Working Class Identity in Britain during the 1950s', *Journal of Social History*, 34 (2001), 773–95

Brosnan, Kathleen A., 'Public Presence, Public Silence: Nuns, Bishops, and the Gendered Space of Early Chicago', *Catholic Historical Review*, 90 (2004), 473–96

Brown, Callum G., *The Death of Christian Britain: Understanding Secularisation, 1800–2000* (London: Routledge, 2001)

——, 'Gender, Christianity, and the Rise of No Religion: The Heritage of the Sixties in Britain', in *The Sixties and Beyond: Dechristianisation in North America and Western Europe, 1945–2000*, ed. Nancy Christie and Michael Gavreau (Toronto: University of Toronto Press, 2013), pp. 39–59

——, 'The People of No Religion: The Demographics of Secularisation in the English-Speaking World since *c.* 1900', *Archiv für Sozialgeschichte*, 51 (2011), 37–61

——, *Religion and Society in Twentieth-Century Britain* (Harlow: Pearson Longman, 2006)

——, *Religion and the Demographic Revolution: Women and Secularisation in Canada, Ireland, UK and USA since the 1960s* (Woodbridge: Boydell Press, 2012)

——, 'Secularization, the Growth of Militancy and the Spiritual Revolution: Religious Change and Gender Power in Britain, 1901–2001', *Historical Research*, 80 (2007), 393–418

——, 'Women and Religion in Britain: The Autobiographical View of the Fifties and Sixties', in *Secularisation in the Christian World*, ed. Callum G. Brown and Michael Snape (Farnham: Ashgate, 2010)

Browne, Sarah F., 'Women, Religion, and the Turn to Feminism: Experiences of Women's Liberation Activists in Britain in the Seventies', in *The Sixties and Beyond: Dechristianisation in North America and Western Europe, 1945–2000*, ed. Nancy Christie and Michael Gavreau (Toronto: University of Toronto Press, 2013), pp. 84–97

Bruce, Steve, *Religion and Modernization: Sociologists and Historians Debate the Secularization Thesis* (Oxford: Oxford University Press, 1992)

——, *Religion in Modern Britain* (Oxford: Oxford University Press, 1995)

Bruce, Steve, and Tony Glendinning, 'When Was Secularization? Dating the Decline of the British Churches and Locating Its Cause', *British Journal of Sociology*, 61 (2010), 107–26

Bruno-Jofré, Rosa, 'The Process of Renewal of the Missionary Oblate Sisters, 1963–1989', in *Changing Habits: Women's Religious Orders in Canada*, ed. Elizabeth M. Smyth (Ottawa: Novalis, 2007), pp. 247–73

Bruno-Jofré, Rosa, Heidi MacDonald and Elizabeth M. Smyth, *Vatican II and Beyond: The Changing Mission and Identity of Canadian Women Religious* (Montreal and Kingston: McGill-Queen's University Press, 2017)

Buchanan, Kathy, *Charm School: The Modern Girl's Complete Handbook of Etiquette* (Camberwell, VIC: Penguin Group Australia, 2003)

Bühlmann, Walter, 'Mission Today', in *A New Missionary Era*, ed. Padraig Flanagan (Maryknoll, NY: Orbis Books, 1979), pp. 61–74

Burke, Timothy, 'The Modern Girl and Commodity Culture', in *The Modern Girl around the World: Consumption, Modernity, and Globalization*, ed. Tani Barlow, Lynn M. Thomas, Priti Ramamurthy, Uta G. Poiger, Madeleine Yue Dong and Alys Eve Weinbaum (Durham, NC: Duke University Press, 2008), pp. 362–69

Cada, Lawrence, Raymond Fitz, Gertrude Foley, Thomas Giardino and Carol Lichtenberg, *Shaping the Coming Age of Religious Life* (New York: Seabury Press, 1979)

Canning, Kathleen, 'Feminist History after the Linguistic Turn: Historicizing Discourse and Experience', *Signs*, 19 (1994), 368–404

CARA, *Global Catholicism: Trends and Forecasts* (Washington, DC: Center for Applied Research in the Apostolate, 2015)

Caspary, Anita Marie, *Witness to Integrity: The Crisis of the Immaculate Heart Community of California* (Collegeville, MN: Liturgical Press, 2003)

Catholic Women Speak Network, *Catholic Women Speak: Bringing Our Gifts to the Table* (New York: Paulist Press, 2015)

Chaves, Mark, 'Secularization as Declining Religious Authority', *Social Forces*, 72 (1994), 749–74

Chinnici, Joseph P., 'An Historian's Creed and the Emergence of Postconciliar Culture Wars', *Catholic Historical Review*, 94 (2008), 219–44

——, 'Religious Life in the Twentieth Century: Interpreting the Languages', *US Catholic Historian*, 22 (2004), 27–47

Choudhury, Mita, *Convents and Nuns in Eighteenth-Century French Politics and Culture* (Ithaca, NY: Cornell University Press, 2004)

Christie, Nancy, and Michael Gauvreau, *The Sixties and Beyond: Dechristianization in North America and Western Europe, 1945–2000* (Toronto: University of Toronto Press, 2013)

Clancy, Phyl, *A Journey of Mercy: From Birth to Rebirth* (Achonry, Co. Sligo: Congregation of the Sisters of Mercy, 1994)

Clark, J. C. D., 'Secularization and Modernization: The Failure of a "Grand Narrative"', *Historical Journal*, 55 (2012), 161–94

Clark, Mary Ryllis, Heather O'Connor and Valerie Krips, eds, *Perfect Charity: Women Religious Living the Spirit of Vatican II* (Reservoir, VIC: Morning Star Publishers, 2015)

Clear, Caitriona, *Nuns in Nineteenth-Century Ireland* (Dublin and Washington, DC: Gill and Macmillan and Catholic University of America Press, 1987)

——, '"Too Fond of Going": Female Emigration and Change for Women in Ireland, 1946–1961', in *The Lost Decade: Ireland in the 1950s*, ed. Dermot Keogh, Finbarr O'Shea and Carmel Quinlan (Cork: Mercier, 2004), pp. 135–46

Clifford, Rebecca, and Nigel Townson, 'The Church in Crisis: Catholic Activism and "1968"', *Cultural and Social History*, 8 (2011), 531–50

Coburn, Carol K., 'An Overview of the Historiography of Women Religious: A Twenty-Five-Year Retrospective', *US Catholic Historian*, 22 (2004), 1–26

Collins, Sylvia, and Michael P. Hornsby-Smith, 'The Rise and Fall of the YCW in England', *Journal of Contemporary Religion*, 17 (2002), 87–100

Coman, Peter, *Catholics and the Welfare State* (London: Longman, 1977)

Conekin, Becky, Frank Mort and Chris Waters, eds, *Moments of Modernity: Reconstructing Britain, 1945–1964* (London: Rivers Oram, 1999)

Connell, Raewyn W., *Gender and Power: Society, the Person and Sexual Politics* (Cambridge: Polity Press, 1987)

Connolly, Mary Beth Fraser, *Women of Faith: The Chicago Sisters of Mercy and the Evolution of a Religious Community* (New York: Fordham University Press, 2014)

Conway, Rebecca, 'Making the Mill Girl Modern? Beauty, Industry, and the Popular Newspaper in 1930s' England', *Twentieth Century British History*, 24 (2013), 518–41

Corner, John, ed., *Popular Television in Britain: Studies in Cultural History* (London: BFI Publishing, 1991)

Corrin, Jay P., *Catholic Progressives in England after Vatican II* (Notre Dame, IN: University of Notre Dame Press, 2013)

Cox, Jeffrey, 'Master Narratives of Long-Term Religious Change', in *The Decline of Christendom in Western Europe, 1750–2000*, ed. Hugh McLeod and Werner Ustorf (Cambridge: Cambridge University Press, 2003), pp. 201–17

——, 'Provincializing Christendom: The Case of Great Britain', *Church History*, 75 (2006), 120–30

Crockett, Alasdair, and David Voas, 'Generations of Decline: Religious Change in 20th-Century Britain', *Journal for the Scientific Study of Religion*, 45 (2006), 567–84

Cullingford, Elizabeth Butler, '"Our Nuns Are Not a Nation": Politicizing the Convent in Irish Literature and Film', in *Irish Postmodernisms and Popular Culture*, ed. Wanda Balzano, Ann Mulhall and Moynagh Sullivan (London: Palgrave Macmillan, 2007), pp. 55–73

Cummings, Kathleen Sprows, 'For Catholics, Gradual Reform Is No Longer an Option', *New York Times* (17 August 2018)

Cummings, Kathleen Sprows, Timothy Matovina and Robert A. Orsi, eds, *Catholics in the Vatican II Era: Local Histories of a Global Event* (Cambridge: Cambridge University Press, 2017)

Curb, Rosemary, and Nancy Manahan, *Lesbian Nuns: Breaking Silence* (Tallahassee, FL: Naiad Press, 1985)

Currie, Robert, Alan D. Gilbert and Lee Horsley, *Churches and Churchgoers: Patterns of Church Growth in the British Isles since 1700* (Oxford: Clarendon Press, 1977)

Daggers, Jenny, *The British Christian Women's Movement: A Rehabilitation of Eve* (Burlington, VT: Ashgate, 2002)

Daly, Mary, *The Church and the Second Sex* (London: Geoffrey Chapman, 1968)

Daunton, Martin, and Bernhard Rieger, eds, *Meanings of Modernity: Britain from the Late-Victorian Era to World War II* (Oxford: Berg, 2001)

Davidoff, Leonore, Megan Doolittle, Janet Fink and Katherine Holden, *The Family Story: Blood, Contract and Intimacy, 1830–1960* (London and New York: Longman, 1999)

Davie, Grace, *Religion in Britain since 1945: Believing without Belonging* (Oxford: Blackwell, 1994)

Davis, Belinda, 'What's Left? Popular Political Participation in Postwar Europe', *American Historical Review*, 113 (2008), 363–90

Day, Abby, *The Religious Lives of Older Laywomen: The Last Active Anglican Generation* (Oxford: Oxford University Press, 2017)

——, 'The Spirit of "Generation A": Older Laywomen in the Church', *Modern Believing*, 56 (2015), 313–23

Deakin, Nicholas, 'The Perils of Partnership: The Voluntary Sector and the State, 1945–1992', in *An Introduction to the Voluntary Sector*, ed. Justin Davis Smith, Colin Rochester and Rodney Hedley (London: Routledge, 1995), pp. 40–65

Delaney, Enda, *Demography, State and Society: Irish Migration to Britain, 1921–1971* (Liverpool: Liverpool University Press, 2000)

——, 'The Vanishing Irish? The Exodus from Ireland in the 1950s', in *The Lost Decade: Ireland in the 1950s*, ed. Dermot Keogh, Finbarr O'Shea and Carmel Quinlan (Cork: Mercier, 2004), pp. 80–6

Delap, Lucy, 'Conservative Values, Anglicans and the Gender Order in Inter-War Britain', in *Brave New World: Imperial and Democratic Nation-Building in Britain Between the Wars*, ed. Laura Beers and Geraint Thomas (London: Institute of Historical Research, 2011), pp. 121–40

Derks, M. E. B., 'The Gospel of the Old: Media, Gender, and the Invisible Conservative Dutch Catholic in the Long 1960s', *Schweizerische Zeitschrift für Religions- und Kulturgeschichte*, 104 (2010), 135–54

Derks, Marjet, 'Catholicism, Gender and Volcanic Leadership: Controversies around the Grail Movement in the Netherlands, 1920s-1930s', in *Episcopacy, Authority, and Gender: Aspects of Religious Leadership in Europe, 1100–2000*, ed. Jan Wim Buisman, Marjet Derks and Peter Raedts (Leiden: Brill, 2015), pp. 188–209

——, 'Changing Lanes: Dutch Women Witnessing the Second Vatican Council', *Trajecta*, 22 (2013), 81–102

——, 'Debating the Council on the Air: Media, Personality, and the Transformation of the Dutch Church', in *Catholics in the Vatican II Era: Local Histories of a Global Event*, ed. Kathleen Sprows Cummings, Timothy Matovina and Robert A. Orsi (Cambridge: Cambridge University Press, 2017), pp. 204–44

deVries, Jacqueline, 'More than Paradoxes to Offer: Feminism, History and Religious Cultures', in *Women, Gender and Religious Cultures in Britain, 1800–1940*, ed. Sue Morgan and Jacqueline deVries (London: Routledge, 2010), pp. 188–210

Diefendorf, Barbara, 'Rethinking the Catholic Reformation: The Role of Women', in *Women, Religion, and the Atlantic World, 1600–1800*, ed. Daniella Kostroun and Lisa Vollendorf (Toronto: University of Toronto Press, 2009)

Doyle, Peter, *Mitres and Missions in Lancashire: The Roman Catholic Diocese of Liverpool, 1850–2000* (Liverpool: Bluecoat Press, 2005)

Drake, Richard, 'Catholics and the Italian Revolutionary Left of the 1960s', *Catholic Historical Review*, 94 (2008), 450–75

Dries, Angelyn, *The Missionary Movement in American Catholic History* (Maryknoll, NY: Orbis Books, 1998)

Duck, Steve, ed., *Social Context and Relationships*, Understanding Relationship Processes Series (Newbury Park, CA and London: Sage, 1993)

Duffy, Eamon, *Faith of Our Fathers* (London: Continuum, 2004)

Dunn, Marilyn, 'Spaces Shaped for Spiritual Perfection: Convent Architecture and Nuns in Early Modern Rome', in *Architecture and the Politics of Gender in Early Modern Europe*, ed. Helen Hills (Aldershot: Ashgate, 2003), p. 151–76

Dwyer-McNulty, Sally, *Common Threads: A Cultural History of Clothing in American Catholicism* (Chapel Hill: University of North Carolina Press, 2014)

Dyhouse, Carol, *Girl Trouble: Panic and Progress in the History of Young Women* (London: Zed Books, 2013)

——, 'Towards a "Feminine" Curriculum for English Schoolgirls: The Demands of Ideology 1870–1963', *Women's Studies International Quarterly*, 1 (1978), 297–311

Ebaugh, Helen Rose, *Women in the Vanishing Cloister: Organizational Decline in Catholic Religious Orders in the United States* (New Brunswick, NJ: Rutgers University Press, 1993)

Ebaugh, Helen Rose Fuchs, *Out of the Cloister: A Study of Organizational Dilemmas* (Austin: University of Texas Press, 1977)

Ebaugh, Helen Rose Fuchs, and Paul Ritterband, 'Education and the Exodus from Convents', *Sociology of Religion*, 39 (1978), 257–64

Ebaugh, Helen Rose, Jon Lorence and Janet Saltzman Chafetz, 'The Growth and Decline of the Population of Catholic Nuns Cross-Nationally, 1960–1990: A Case of Secularization as Social Structural Change', *Journal for the Scientific Study of Religion*, 35 (1996), 171–83

Eisenstadt, S. N., *From Generation to Generation: Age Groups and Social Structure* (London: Collier-Macmillan, 1956)

Elliott, Kit, '"A Very Pushy Kind of Folk": Educational Reform 1944 and the Catholic Laity of England and Wales', *History of Education*, 35 (2006), 91–119

Ellis, Roger, *Syon Abbey: The Spirituality of the English Bridgettines* (Salzburg: Universität Salzburg, 1984)

Ellis, Sylvia A., 'British Student Protest during the Vietnam War', in *Student Protest: The Sixties and After*, ed. Gerard J. Degroot (London: Longman, 1998), pp. 54–69

Faderman, Lilian, *Surpassing the Love of Men: Romantic Friendship and Love between Women from the Renaissance to the Present* (New York: William Morrow, 1981)

Faggioli, Massimo, *Catholicism and Citizenship: Political Cultures of the Church in the Twenty-First Century* (Collegeville, MN: Liturgical Press, 2017)

——, 'The New Elites of Italian Catholicism: 1968 and the New Catholic Movements', *Catholic Historical Review*, 98 (2012), 18–40

——, *Vatican II: The Battle for Meaning* (Mahwah, NJ: Paulist Press, 2012)

Farrell, James J., *The Spirit of the Sixties: Making Postwar Radicalism* (London: Routledge, 1997)

Fawcett, Hilary, 'Fashioning the Second Wave: Issues across Generations', *Studies in the Literary Imagination*, 39 (2006), 95–113

Feldner, Heiko, Claire Gorrara and Kevin Passmore, eds, *The Lost Decade? The 1950s in European History, Politics, Society and Culture* (Newcastle upon Tyne: Cambridge Scholars Publishing, 2011)

Fellerhoff, Mary Christine, CSA, 'The Ministerial Future of Women Religious', *New Theology Review*, 16 (2013), 13–22

Felski, Rita, *The Gender of Modernity* (London: Harvard University Press, 1995)

Ferree, Myra Marx, and Carol McClurg Mueller, 'Feminism and the Women's Movement: A Global Perspective', in *The Blackwell Companion to Social Movements*, ed. David A. Snow, Sarah A. Soule and Hanspeter Kriesi (Chichester: John Wiley & Sons, 2008), pp. 576–607

Field, Clive D., 'Gradualist or Revolutionary Secularization? A Case Study of Religious Belonging in Inter-War Britain, 1918–1939', *Church History and Religious Culture*, 93 (2013), 57–93

Finlayson, Geoffrey, *Citizen, State, and Social Welfare in Britain 1830–1990* (Oxford: Clarendon Press, 1994)

Fiorenza, Elisabeth Schüssler, *Congress of Wo/Men: Religion, Gender, and Kyriarchal Power* (Indianapolis, IN: Dog Ear Publishing, 2017)

———, *Memory of Her: A Feminist Theological Reconstruction of Christian Origins* (New York: Crossroad, 1983)

Fisher, Desmond, 'Preface' in Michel van der Plas and Henk Suèr, eds, *Those Dutch Catholics* (London: Geoffrey Chapman, 1967)

Fitzpatrick-Behrens, Susan, 'From Symbols of the Sacred to Symbols of Subversion to Simply Obscure: Maryknoll Women Religious in Guatemala, 1953 to 1967', *The Americas*, 61 (2004), 189–216

———, 'Knowledge Is Not Enough: Creating a Culture of Social Justice, Dignity, and Human Rights in Guatemala: Maryknoll Sisters and the Monte María" Girls"', *US Catholic Historian*, 24 (2006), 111–28

———, *The Maryknoll Catholic Mission in Peru, 1943–1989: Transnational Faith and Transformation* (Notre Dame, IN: University of Notre Dame Press, 2012)

Foley, Nadine, ed., *Journey in Faith and Fidelity: Women Shaping Religious Life for a Renewed Church* (New York: Continuum, 1999), pp. 95–123, p. 99

Fowler, David, *The First Teenagers: The Lifestyle of Young Wage-Earners in Interwar Britain* (London: The Woburn Press, 1995)

Frederick, Marla F., *Between Sundays: Black Women and Everyday Struggles of Faith* (Berkeley: University of California Press, 2003)

Garnett, Jane, Matthew Grimley, Alana Harris, William Whyte and Sarah Williams, eds, *Redefining Christian Britain: Post-1945 Perspectives* (London: SCM Press, 2006)

Gass, Marie Therese, *Unconventional Women: 73 Ex-Nuns Tell Their Stories* (Clackamas, OR: Sieben Hill, 2001)

Gatrell, Peter, *Free World? The Campaign to Save the World's Refugees, 1956–1963* (Cambridge: Cambridge University Press, 2011)

Geiringer, David, '"At Some Point in the 1960s, Hell Disappeared": Hell, Gender and Catholicism in Post-War England', *Cultural and Social History*, 15 (2018), 1–17

———, 'Catholic Understandings of Female Sexuality in 1960s Britain', *Twentieth Century British History*, 28 (2017), 209–38

Gerrard, Paul, '"The Lord Said 'Come' ": Why Women Enter a Religious Order', *Oral History*, 24 (1996), 54–8

———, 'St Clare of Assisi and the Poor Clares: A New Spring', *Studies in Church History* 33 (1997), 547–61

Gervais, Christine, 'Alternative Altars: Beyond Patriarchy and Priesthood and towards Inclusive Spirituality, Governance and Activism among Catholic Women Religious in Ontario', *Canadian Woman Studies*, 29 (2011), 8–14

——, *Beyond the Altar: Women Religious, Patriarchal Power, and the Church* (Waterloo, Ont.: Wilfrid Laurier University Press, 2018)

Gilbert, Alan D., *The Making of Post-Christian Britain: A History of the Secularization of Modern Society* (London: Longman, 1980)

Gilbert, Joanna, 'Young People in Search of Religious Vocation', in *A Future Full of Hope?*, ed. Gemma Simmonds, CJ (Dublin: The Columba Press, 2012), pp. 92–105

Gildea, Robert, James Mark and Anette Warring, eds, *Europe's 1968: Voices of Revolt* (Oxford: Oxford University Press, 2013)

Giles, Judy, *The Parlour and the Suburb: Domestic Identities, Class, Femininity and Modernity* (Oxford: Berg, 2004)

Gittins, Diana, *The Family in Question: Changing Households and Familiar Ideologies* (London: Macmillan, 1985)

Gleadle, Kathryn, and Zoë Thomas, 'Global Feminisms, c. 1870–1930: Vocabularies and Concepts – A Comparative Approach', *Women's History Review*, 27 (2017), 1–16

Gleason, Philip, 'A Browser's Guide to American Catholicism, 1950–1980', *Theology Today*, 38 (1981), 373–88

Goltz, Anna von der, 'Generations of 68ers', *Cultural and Social History*, 8 (2011), 473–91

Gorringe, Timothy, 'Liberation Theology', in *Palgrave Dictionary of Transnational History*, ed. Akira Iriye and Pierre-Yves Saunier (Basingstoke: Palgrave Macmillan, 2009), pp. 588–9

Granick, Jaclyn, 'Sacralized Humanitarianism: A Comparison of Three Faith-Based Private Associations', 2011. www.swiss-quakers.ch/ge/library/e-documents/7971-Granick2011. pdf, accessed 26 February 2016

Green, Abigail, and Vincent Viaene, eds, *Religious Internationals in the Modern World: Globalization and Faith Communities since 1750* (Houndmills: Palgrave Macmillan, 2012)

Grey, Mary, '"Expelled Again from Eden": Facing Difference through Connection', *Feminist Theology*, 21 (1999), 8–20

Gwynn, Denis, 'Growth of the Catholic Community', in *The English Catholics, 1850–1950*, ed. George Andrew Beck (London: Burns, Oates, 1950)

Hagerty, James, *Cardinal John Carmel Heenan: Priest of the People, Prince of the Church* (London: Gracewing Publishing, 2012)

Halbwachs, Maurice, and Lewis A. Coser, *On Collective Memory* (Chicago: University of Chicago Press, 1992)

Halvorson, Michael, and Karen Spierling, eds, *Defining Community in Early Modern Europe* (Aldershot: Ashgate, 2008)

Hamer, Edna, *Elizabeth Prout, 1820–1864: A Religious Life for Industrial England* (Oxford: Gracewing, 1994)

Hamilton, Elizabeth, *Cardinal Suenens: A Portrait* (London: Hodder and Stoughton, 1975)

Hamlett, Jane, and Lesley Hoskins, 'Comfort in Small Things? Clothing, Control and Agency in County Lunatic Asylums in Nineteenth- and Early Twentieth-Century England', *Journal of Victorian Culture*, 18 (2013), 93–114

Hanna, Erika, 'Reading Irish Women's Lives in Photograph Albums', *Cultural and Social History*, 11 (2014), 89–109

Hannam, June, *Feminism* (Harlow, Pearson Education, 2012)

Hanson, Eric O., *The Catholic Church in World Politics* (Princeton, NJ: Princeton University Press, 1987)

Harris, Alana, *Faith in the Family: A Lived Religious History of English Catholicism, 1945–1982* (Manchester: Manchester University Press, 2013)

——, '"A Paradise on Earth, a Foretaste of Heaven": English Catholic Understandings of Domesticity and Marriage, 1945–65', in *The Politics of Domestic Authority since 1800*, ed. Lucy Delap, Abigail Wills and Ben Griffin (London: Palgrave Macmillan, 2009), pp. 155–81

——, '"The Writings of Querulous Women": Contraception, Conscience and Clerical Authority in 1960s Britain', *British Catholic History*, 32 (2015), 557–85

Harris, Alana, and Martin Spence, '"Disturbing the Complacency of Religion"? The Evangelical Crusades of Dr Billy Graham and Father Patrick Peyton in Britain, 1951–54', *Twentieth Century British History*, 18 (2007), 481–513

Harrison, Brian, *Seeking a Role: The United Kingdom, 1951–1970* (Oxford: Clarendon Press, 2009)

Hastings, Adrian, *A History of English Christianity 1920–1985* (London: Collins, 1986)

——, 'Some Reflexions on the English Catholicism of the Late 1930s', in *Bishops and Writers: Aspects of the Evolution of Modern English Catholicism*, ed. Adrian Hastings (Wheathampstead: Anthony Clarke, 1977), pp. 107–26

Hastings, Adrian, ed., *Modern Catholicism: Vatican II and After* (New York: Oxford University Press, 1991)

Hastings, Adrian, and Vincent Alan McClelland, 'Greater Britain and Ireland', in *Modern Catholicism: Vatican II and After*, ed. Adrian Hastings (New York: Oxford University Press, 1991), pp. 365–76

Heeney, Brian, *The Women's Movement in the Church of England, 1850–1930* (Oxford: Clarendon Press, 1988)

Heijst, Annelies van, 'The Disputed Charity of Catholic Nuns: Dualistic Spiritual Heritage as a Source of Affliction', *Feminist Theology: The Journal of the Britain & Ireland School of Feminist Theology*, 21 (2013), 155–72

——, *Models of Charitable Care: Catholic Nuns and Children in Their Care in Amsterdam, 1852–2002* (Leiden and Boston: Brill, 2008)

——, 'The Passion-Paradigm: The Religious Caring of "The Poor Sisters of the Divine Child"', *European Journal of Women's Studies*, 5 (1998), 35–46

Heijst, Annelies van, Marjet Derks and Marit Monteiro, *Ex Caritate: Kloosterleven, Apostolaat en Nieuwe Spirit van Actieve Vrouwelijke Religieuzen in Nederand in de 19c en 20c Eeuw* (Hilversum: Uitgeverij Verloren, 2010)

Hemmings, Clare, 'Telling Feminist Stories', *Feminist Theory*, 6 (2005), 115–39

Hennessy, Peter, *Having It So Good: Britain in the Fifties* (London: Allen Lane, 2006)

Henold, Mary, *Catholic and Feminist: The Surprising History of the American Catholic Feminist Movement* (Chapel Hill: University of North Carolina Press, 2012)

Henry, Astrid, *Not My Mother's Sister: Generational Conflict and Third-Wave Feminism* (Bloomington: Indiana University Press, 2004)

Hervieu-Léger, Danièle, *Religion as a Chain of Memory*, trans. Simon Lee (Cambridge: Polity Press, 2000)

Hetherington, Kevin, *The Badlands of Modernity: Heterotopia and Social Ordering* (London and New York: Routledge, 1997)

Hewitt, Nancy A., *No Permanent Waves: Recasting Histories of U.S. Feminism* (New Brunswick, NJ: Rutgers University Press, 2010)

Hickey, John, *Urban Catholics: Urban Catholicism in England and Wales from 1829 to the Present Day* (London: Geoffrey Chapman, 1967)

Higgs, Catherine, and Jean N. Evans, 'Embracing Activism in Apartheid South Africa: The Sisters of Mercy in Bophuthatswana, 1974–94', *Catholic Historical Review*, 94 (2008), 500–21

Hilton, Matthew, 'Politics Is Ordinary: Non-Governmental Organizations and Political Participation in Contemporary Britain', *Twentieth Century British History*, 22 (2011), 230–68

Hobsbawm, Eric, 'The Present as History: Writing the History of One's Own Times', Creighton Lecture, University of London, 1993

Hoefferle, Caroline M., *British Student Activism in the Long Sixties* (London: Routledge, 2013)

Holland, Joe, *Modern Catholic Social Teaching: The Popes Confront the Industrial Age, 1740–1958* (New York: Paulist Press, 2003)

Hollinshead, Janet E., 'From Cambrai to Woolton: Lancashire's First Female Religious House', *Recusant History*, 25 (2001), 461–86

Holloway, Gerry, *Women and Work in Britain since 1840* (London: Routledge, 2005)

Holscher, Kathleen, 'Contesting the Veil in America: Catholic Habits and the Controversy over Religious Clothing in the United States', *Journal of Church and State*, 54 (2012), 57–81

Hopgood, Stephen, *Keepers of the Flame: Understanding Amnesty International* (Ithaca, NY and London: Cornell University Press, 2006)

Horn, Gerd-Rainer, *The Spirit of '68: Rebellion in Western Europe and North America, 1956–1976* (Oxford: Oxford University Press, 2007)

———, *The Spirit of Vatican II: Western European Progressive Catholicism in the Long Sixties* (Oxford: Oxford University Press, 2015)

Horn, Gerd-Rainer, and Emmanuel Gerard, eds, *Left Catholicism 1943–1955: Catholics and Society in Western Europe at the Point of Liberation* (Leuven: Leuven University Press, 2001)

Horn, Gerd-Rainer, and Padraic Kenney, *Transnational Moments of Change: Europe 1945, 1968, 1989* (Lanham, MD: Rowman & Littlefield, 2004)

Hornsby-Smith, Michael P., *An Introduction to Catholic Social Thought* (Cambridge: Cambridge University Press, 2006)

———, *Reflections on a Catholic Life* (Peterborough: Fastprint Publishing, 2010)

———, *Roman Catholic Beliefs in England* (Cambridge and New York: Cambridge University Press, 1991)

———, *Roman Catholics in England: Studies in Social Structure since the Second World War* (Cambridge: Cambridge University Press, 1987)

——, *Tradition and Change in the Roman Catholic Community in England* (London: SSRC, 1977)

Hornsby-Smith, Michael P., ed., *Catholics in England 1950–2000: Historical and Sociological Perspectives* (London: Cassell, 1999)

Hornsby-Smith, Michael P., John Fulton and Margaret Norris, *The Politics of Spirituality: A Study of a Renewal Process in an English Diocese* (Oxford: Clarendon Press, 1995)

Hornsby-Smith, Michael P., and Raymond M. Lee, *Roman Catholic Opinion: A Study of Roman Catholics in England and Wales in the 1970s* (Guildford: University of Surrey, Department of Sociology, 1979)

Hostie, Raymond, *Vie et mort des ordres religieux. Approches psychosociologiques* (Paris: Desclée de Brouwer, 1972)

Houriet, Robert, *Getting Back Together* (New York: Coward, McCann & Geoghegan, 1971)

Hunt, Andrew, "'When Did the Sixties Happen?' Searching for New Directions', *Journal of Social History*, 33 (1999), 147–61

Ingham, Mary, *Now We Are Thirty: Women of the Breakthrough Generation* (London: Eyre Methuen, 1981)

Iriye, Akira, 'Transnational History', *Contemporary European History*, 13 (2004), 211–22

Jansen, Sharon L., *Reading Women's Worlds from Christine de Pizan to Doris Lessing: A Guide to Six Centuries of Women Writers Imagining Rooms of Their Own* (New York: Palgrave Macmillan, 2011)

Jerman, Betty, *The Lively-Minded Women: The First Twenty Years of the National Housewives Register* (London: Heinemann, 1981)

Johnson, Elizabeth A., 'Jesus and Women: "You Are Set Free"', in *Catholic Women Speak: Bringing Our Gifts to the Table*, ed. Catholic Women Speak Network (New York: Paulist Press, 2015), pp. 19–22

Johnson, Mary, SND de N., Patricia Wittberg SC and Mary L. Guatier, *New Generations of Catholic Sisters: The Challenge of Diversity* (Oxford: Oxford University Press, 2014)

Jones, E. A., *Syon Abbey 1415–2015: England's Last Medieval Monastery* (London: Gracewing, 2015)

Jones, Timothy W., 'Postsecular Sex? Secularisation and Religious Change in the History of Sexuality in Britain', *History Compass*, 11 (2013), 918–30

Keenan, William J. F., 'Twenty-First-Century Monasticism and Religious Life: Just Another New Millennium', *Religion*, 32 (2002), 13–26

Kehoe, S. Karly, *Creating a Scottish Church: Catholicism, Gender and Ethnicity in Nineteenth-Century Scotland* (Manchester: Manchester University Press, 2010)

Kenny, Michael G., 'A Place for Memory: The Interface between Individual and Collective History', *Comparative Studies in Society and History*, 41 (1999), 420–37

Kilroy, Phil, 'Coming to an Edge in History: Writing the History of Women Religious and the Critique of Feminism', in *Education, Identity and Women Religious, 1800–1950: Convents, Classrooms and Colleges*, ed. Deirdre Raftery and Elizabeth M. Smyth (London: Routledge, 2015), pp. 6–30

Kim, Sonja, '*The Modern Girl around the World: Consumption, Modernity, and Globalization*. Edited by Alys Eve Weinbaum, Lynn M. Thomas, Priti Ramamurthy, Uta G. Poiger,

Madeleine Yue Dong, and Tani E. Barlow. Durham, NC: Duke University Press, 2008 (Review)', *Journal of World History*, 22 (2011), 411–15

King, Ursula, 'The Catholic Intellectual Tradition and Women Theologians', in *Catholic Women Speak: Bringing Our Gifts to the Table*, ed. Catholic Women Speak Network (New York: Paulist Press, 2015), pp. 11–14

——, 'Women's Contribution to Contemporary Spirituality', *The Way Supplement*, 84 (1994), 26–37

Knight, Barry, *Voluntary Action* (London: CENTRIS, 1993)

Koehlinger, Amy L., 'American Sisters Haven't Strayed. The Vatican Has', *Religion & Politics*, 2012. http://religionandpolitics.org/2012/07/20/american-sisters-havent-strayed-the-vatican-has/, accessed 7 February 2018

——, *The New Nuns: Racial Justice and Religious Reform in the 1960s* (Cambridge, MA: Harvard University Press, 2007)

Kolmer, Elizabeth, 'Catholic Women Religious and Women's History: A Survey of the Literature', *American Quarterly*, 30 (1978), 639–51

——, *Religious Women in the United States: A Survey of the Influential Literature from 1950 to 1983* (Wilmington, NC: Michael Glazier, 1984)

Komonchak, Joseph A., 'Vatican II as Ecumenical Council: Yves Congar's Vision Realized', *Commonweal*, 129 (2002), 12–14

Kuhns, Elizabeth, *The Habit: A History of the Clothing of Catholic Nuns* (New York: Doubleday, 2003)

Kurasawa, Fuyuki, 'A Message in a Bottle: Bearing Witness as a Mode of Transnational Practice', *Theory, Culture & Society*, 26 (2009), 92–111

Kynaston, David, *Modernity Britain: Opening the Box, 1957–1959* (London: A&C Black, 2013)

Lamb, Matthew L., and Matthew Levering, eds, *Vatican II: Renewal within Tradition* (Oxford: Oxford University Press, 2008)

Lamberigts, M., and L. Kenis, eds, *Vatican II and Its Legacy* (Leuven: Leuven University Press, 2002)

Lane, Dermot A., 'Vatican II: The Irish Experience', *The Furrow*, 55 (2004), 67–81

Langhamer, Claire, 'Feelings, Women and Work in the Long 1950s', *Women's History Review*, 16 (2017), 77–92

——, 'Leisure, Pleasure and Courtship: Young Women in England 1920–60', in *Secret Gardens, Satanic Mills: Placing Girls in European History, 1750–1960*, ed. Mary Jo Maynes, Birgitte Søland and Christina Benninghaus (Bloomington: Indiana University Press, 2005), pp. 269–83

——, 'Love and Courtship in Mid-Twentieth-Century England', *Historical Journal*, 50 (2007), 173–96

——, 'Love, Selfhood and Authenticity in Post-War Britain', *Cultural and Social History*, 9 (2012), 277–97

——, 'The Meanings of Home in Postwar Britain', *Journal of Contemporary History*, 40 (2005), 341–62

——, *Women's Leisure in England, 1920–1960* (Manchester: Manchester University Press, 2000)

Leff, Lisa Moses, *Sacred Bonds of Solidarity: The Rise of Jewish Internationalism in Nineteenth-Century France* (Stanford, CA: Stanford University Press, 2006)

Leonard, Ellen M, 'Ecclesial Religious Communities Old and New', *The Way Supplement*, 201 (2001), 119–27

Lewis, Jane, 'Marriage', in *Women in Twentieth-Century Britain*, ed. Ina Zweiniger-Bargielowska (London: Longman, 2001), pp. 69–85

Light, Alison, *Forever England: Femininity, Literature and Conservatism between the Wars* (London: Routledge, 2013)

Linden, Ian, 'The Language of Development: What Are International Development Agencies Talking About?', in *Development, Civil Society and Faith-Based Organizations: Bridging the Sacred and the Secular*, ed. Gerard Clarke and Michael Jennings (London: Palgrave Macmillan, 2008), pp. 72–93

——, 'Social Justice in Historical Perspective', in *Catholics in England 1950–2000: Historical and Sociological Perspectives*, ed. Michael P. Hornsby-Smith (London: Cassell, 1999), pp. 139–57

Linton, Eliza Lynn, 'The Girl of the Period', *Saturday Review* (14 March 1868), 339–40

Little, Anne M., 'Cloistered Bodies: Convents in the Anglo-American Imagination in the British Conquest of Canada', *Eighteenth Century Studies*, 39 (2006), 187–200

Lofton, Kathryn, 'Revisited: Sex Abuse and the Study of Religion' (24 August 2018). https://tif.ssrc.org/2018/08/24/sex-abuse-and-the-study-of-religion/, accessed 6 December 2018

Longden, Bernard, 'Widening Participation in Higher Education', in *The Foundation of Hope: Turning Dreams into Reality*, ed. R. John Elford (Liverpool: Liverpool University Press, 2003), pp. 50–63

Lowe, Rodney, *The Welfare State in Britain since 1945* (Basingstoke: Macmillan, 1993)

Lowndes, Vivien, and Greg Smith, *Mapping the Public Policy Landscape: Faith-Based Voluntary Action* (Swindon: Economic and Social Research Council, 2006)

Luirard, Monique, *The Society of the Sacred Heart in the World of Its Times 1865–2000*, trans. Frances Gimber (Saint Louis, MO: iUniverse, 2016)

Luquet, Wade, 'The Contribution of the Sisters of Mercy to the Development of Social Welfare', *Affilia*, 20 (2005), 153–68

Lyons, Mary, *Governance Structures of the Congregation of the Sisters of Mercy: Becoming One* (Lewiston, NY and Lampeter: Edwin Mellen Press, 2005)

McCarthy, Helen, 'Social Science and Married Women's Employment in Post-War Britain', *Past and Present*, 233 (2016), 269–305

McCarthy, Timothy G., *The Catholic Tradition: Before and After Vatican II, 1878–1993* (Chicago: Loyola University Press, 1994)

——, *The Catholic Tradition: The Church in the Twentieth Century*, 2nd edn (Chicago: Loyola University Press, 1998)

McClelland, V. Alan, and Michael Hodgetts, eds, *From without the Flaminian Gate: 150 Years of Roman Catholicism in England and Wales, 1850–2000* (London: Darton, Longman & Todd, 1999)

McClelland, Vincent Alan, 'John Carmel Heenan, the Second Vatican Council and the Rise and Fall of an English Lumen Vitae', in *Essays in Tribute to J. Valentine Rice, 1935–2006*, ed. Aidan Seery (Dublin: Lilliput Press, 2010), pp. 69–97

MacDonald, Heidi, 'Smaller Numbers, Stronger Voices: Women Religious Reposition Themselves through the Canadian Religious Conference, 1960s-1980s', in *Vatican*

II and Beyond: The Changing Mission and Identity of Canadian Women Religious, ed. Rosa Bruno-Jofré, Heidi MacDonald and Elizabeth M. Smyth (Montreal and Kingston: McGill-Queen's University Press, 2017), pp. 17–54

McEnroy, Carmel, *Guests in Their Own House: The Women of Vatican II* (New York: Crossroad, 1996)

McGuinness, Margaret M., *Called to Serve: A History of Nuns in America* (New York: New York University Press, 2013)

McKenna, Yvonne, 'Embodied Ideals and Realities: Irish Nuns and Irish Womanhood, 1930s–1960s', *Éire-Ireland*, 41 (2006), 40–63

——, 'Entering Religious Life, Claiming Subjectivity: Irish Nuns, 1930s–1960s', *Women's History Review*, 15 (2006), 189–211

——, 'Forgotten Migrants: Irish Women Religious in England, 1930s–1960s', *International Journal of Population Geography*, 9 (2003), 295–308

——, 'A Gendered Revolution: Vatican II and Irish Women Religious', *Irish Feminist Review*, 1 (2005), 75–93

——, *Made Holy: Irish Women Religious at Home and Abroad* (Dublin: Irish Academic Press, 2006)

——, 'Sisterhood? Exploring Power Relations in the Collection of Oral History', *Oral History*, 31 (2003), 65–72

McKibbin, Ross, *Classes and Cultures: England 1918–1951* (Oxford: Oxford University Press, 1998)

McLeod, Hugh, 'The 1960s', in *Religion and the Political Imagination*, ed. Ira Katznelson and Gareth Stedman Jones (Cambridge: Cambridge University Press, 2010), pp. 254–74

——, 'Reflections and New Perspectives', in *The Sixties and Beyond: Dechristianisation in North America and Western Europe, 1945–2000*, ed. Nancy Christie and Michael Gavreau (Toronto: University of Toronto Press, 2013), pp. 453–67

——, *Religion and the People of Western Europe: 1789–1970* (Oxford: Oxford University Press, 1981)

——, *The Religious Crisis of the 1960s* (Oxford: Oxford University Press, 2007)

McNamara, Jo Ann, *Sisters in Arms: Catholic Nuns through Two Millennia* (London: Harvard University Press, 1996)

Maloney, Susan M., 'Obedience, Responsibility, and Freedom: Anita M. Caspary, IHM, and the Post-Conciliar Renewal of Catholic Women Religious', *US Catholic Historian*, 32 (2014), 121–49

Mangion, Carmen M., 'Bad Habits? France's "Burkini Ban" in Historical Perspective', *History Workshop Online* (4 October 2016). www.historyworkshop.org.uk/bad-habits-frances-burkini-ban-in-historical-perspective/, accessed 25 October 2018

——, 'Community Voices and "Community Scripts"', *Studies*, 107 (2018), 302–13

——, *Contested Identities: Catholic Women Religious in Nineteenth-Century England and Wales* (Manchester: Manchester University Press, 2008)

——, ' "It Took a Little While to Get It Right": Women Religious and Family Relationships, 1940–1990', *Catholic Ancestor*, 16 (2016), 60–8

——, 'A New Internationalism: Endeavouring to "Build from This Diversity, Unity", 1940–1990', *Journal of Contemporary History* (2019)

——, '"Shades of Difference": Poor Clares in Britain', in *Le Concile Vatican II et le monde des religieux (Europe occidentale et Amérique du Nord, 1950-1980)*, ed. Christian Sorrell (Lyon: LARHRA, 2019), pp. 317-29

——, 'Syon Abbey's "Second Summer"', 1900-1950', in *Continuity and Change: Papers from the Birgitta Conference at Dartington, 2015*, ed. Elin Andersson, Claes Gejrot, E. A. Jones and Mia Akestam (Stockholm: Kungl. Vitterhets historie och antikvitetsakademien, 2017), pp. 367-88

——, '"To Console, to Nurse, to Prepare for Eternity": The Catholic Sickroom in Late Nineteenth-Century England', *Women's History Review*, 21 (2012), 657-72

——, 'Women Religious and Family Relationships', *Catholic Ancestor*, 16 (2016), 60-8

Mannheim, Karl, 'The Problem of Generations', in *Karl Mannheim: Essays*, ed. Paul Kecskemeti (New York: Routledge, 1972), pp. 276-322

Manuel, Paul Christopher, Lawrence C. Reardon and Clyde Wilcox, *The Catholic Church and the Nation-State: Comparative Perspectives* (Washington, DC: Georgetown University Press, 2006)

Marland, Hilary, *Health and Girlhood in Britain, 1874-1920* (Basingstoke: Palgrave Macmillan, 2013)

Marwick, Arthur, ' "1968" and the Cultural Revolution of the Long Sixties (c. 1958-c. 1974)', in *Transnational Moments of Change: Europe*, ed. Gerd-Rainer Horn and Padraic Kenney (Oxford: Rowman & Littlefield, 2004), pp. 81-118

——, *British Society since 1945* (London: Allen Lane, 1982)

——, 'The Cultural Revolution of the Long Sixties: Voices of Reaction, Protest, and Permeation', *International History Review*, 27 (2005), 780-806

——, *The Sixties: Cultural Revolution in Britain, France, Italy, and the United States, c.1958-c.1974* (Oxford: Oxford University Press, 1998)

——, 'Youth Culture and the Cultural Revolution of the Long Sixties', in *Between Marx and Coca-Cola: Youth Cultures in Changing European Societies, 1960-1980*, ed. Axel Schildt and Detlef Siegfried (New York: Berghahn Books, 2005), pp. 39-58

Melloni, Alberto, and Massimo Faggioli, eds, *Religious Studies in the 20th Century: A Survey on Disciplines, Cultures and Questions* (Münster: Lit Verlag, 2006)

Metcalfe, Camillus, *For God's Sake: The Hidden Life of Irish Nuns* (Dublin: Liffey Press, 2014)

Michelman, Susan, 'Breaking Habits: Fashion and Identity of Women Religious', *Fashion Theory*, 2 (1998), 165-92

Michelman, Susan O., 'Changing Old Habits: Dress of Women Religious and Its Relationship to Personal and Social Identity', *Sociological Inquiry*, 67 (1997), 350-63

Mitchell, Gillian A. M., 'Reassessing "the Generation Gap": Bill Haley's 1957 Tour of Britain, Inter-Generational Relations and Attitudes to Rock'n'Roll in the Late 1950s', *Twentieth Century British History*, 24 (2013), 573-605

Mitchell, Sally, *The New Girl: Girls' Culture in England, 1880-1915* (New York: Columbia University Press, 1995)

Molengraft, Sister Alix van de, *It All Began with Three Beguines: History of Ten Thousand Sisters of Charity* (Preston: Nemco Press, 1992)

Monteiro, Marit, Marjet Derks and Annelies Van Heijst, 'The Stories the Religious Have Lived by since the 1960's', in *Religious Stories We Live by: Narrative Approaches in*

Theology and Religious Studies, ed. R. Ruard Ganzevoort, Maaike de Haardt and Michael Scherer-Rath (Leiden: Brill, 2014), pp. 221–40

Morgan, Sue, 'Theorising Feminist History: A Thirty-Year Retrospective', *Women's History Review*, 18 (2009), 381–407

——, *Women, Religion and Feminism in Britain, 1750–1900* (Basingstoke: Palgrave Macmillan, 2002)

Morris, Jeremy, 'Enemy Within? The Appeal of the Discipline of Sociology to Religious Professionals in Post-War Britain', *Journal of Religion in Europe*, 9 (2016), 177–200

Moruzi, Kristine, *Constructing Girlhood through the Periodical Press, 1850–1915* (Farnham: Ashgate, 2012)

Moutray, Tonya J., *Refugee Nuns, the French Revolution, and British Literature and Culture* (London: Routledge, 2016)

Mumm, Susan, 'Women, Priesthood, and the Ordained Ministry in the Christian Tradition', in *Religion in History: Conflict, Conversion and Coexistence*, ed. John Wolffe (Manchester: Manchester University Press in association with The Open University, 2004), pp. 190–216

Nash, David, 'Reconnecting Religion with Social and Cultural History: Secularization's Failure as a Master Narrative', *Cultural and Social History*, 1 (2004), 302–25

National Office for Vocations of the Roman Catholic Church in England, Compass Project, 'Religious Life in England and Wales' (London: National Office for Vocations, 2010)

Nava, Mica, and Alan O'Shea, eds, *Modern Times: Reflections on a Century of English Modernity* (London: Routledge, 2013)

Nestor, Pauline, *Female Friendships and Communities: Charlotte Brontë, George Eliot, Elizabeth Gaskell* (New York: Oxford University Press, 1985)

Neuhaus, Richard John, *The Catholic Moment: The Paradox of the Church in the Postmodern World* (San Francisco: Harper & Row, 1987)

Neussendorfer, M., 'Modernizing the Religious Habit', *Sponsa Regis*, 36 (1964), 67–79

Norr, James L., and Jeanne Schweickert, 'Organizational Change and Social Participation: Results of Renewal in a Women's Religious Order', *Review of Religious Research*, 17 (1976), 120–33

Nye, Anselm, *A Peculiar Kind of Mission: The English Dominican Sisters, 1845–2010* (Leominster: Gracewing, 2011)

O'Brien, Anne, 'Catholic Nuns in Transnational Mission, 1528–2015', *Journal of Global History*, 11 (2016), 387–408

O'Brien, Peter, *Evacuation Stations: Memoir of a Boyhood in Wartime England* (the author, 2012)

O'Brien, Susan, *Leaving God for God: The Daughters of Charity of St Vincent de Paul in Britain, 1847–2017* (London: Darton, Longman & Todd, 2017)

——, 'A Note on Apostolic Religious Life', in *The Disciples' Call: Theologies of Vocation from Scripture to the Present Day*, ed. Christopher Jamieson (London: Bloomsbury, 2013), pp. 155–66

——, 'Religious Life for Women', in *From without the Flaminian Gate: 150 Years of Roman Catholicism in England and Wales, 1850–2000*, ed. V. Alan McClelland and Michael Hodgetts (London: Darton, Longman & Todd, 1999), pp. 108–41

——, '"Terra Incognita": The Nun in Nineteenth-Century England', *Past and Present*, 121 (1988), 110–40

O'Collins, Gerald, *Living Vatican II: The 21st Council for the 21st Century* (Mahwah, NJ: Paulist Press, 2006)

O'Donoghue, Tom, and Stephanie Burley, 'God's Antipodean Teaching Force: An Historical Exposition on Catholic Teaching Religious in Australia', *Teaching and Teacher Education*, 24 (2008), 180–9

Offen, Karen M., 'Defining Feminism: A Comparative Historical Approach', *Signs*, 14 (1988), 119–57

O'Keefe-Vigneron, Gráinne, 'Irish Nuns and Artichokes: The Experiences of Irish Women Religious in a French Order', in *New Perspectives on the Irish Abroad: The Silent People?*, ed. Mícheál Ó hAodha and Máirtín Ó Catháin (Plymouth: Lexington Books, 2014), pp. 37–53

O'Malley, John W., 'Vatican II: Did Anything Happen?', *Theological Studies*, 67 (2006), 3–33

O'Malley, John W., David G. Schultenover and Stephen Schloesser, *Vatican II: Did Anything Happen?* (London: Continuum, 2007)

Orsi, Robert A., 'A Crisis about the Theology of Children', *Harvard Divinity School Bulletin*, 30 (2002), 27–33

——, 'Everyday Miracles: The Study of Lived Religion', in *Lived Religion in America: Toward a History of Practice*, ed. David A. Hall (Princeton, NJ: Princeton University Press, 1997), pp. 3–21

Osgerby, Bill, *Youth in Britain since 1945* (Oxford: Blackwell, 1997)

O'Shea, Alan, 'English Subjects of Modernity', in *Modern Times: Reflections on a Century of English Modernity*, ed. Mica Nava and Alan O'Shea (London: Routledge, 2013), pp. 7–37

O'Sullivan, Tim, 'Television Memories and Cultures of Viewing, 1950–65', in *Popular Television in Britain: Studies in Cultural History*, ed. John Corner (London: BFI Publishing, 1991), pp. 159–81

Oved, Yaacov, *Globalization of Communes: 1950–2010* (New Brunswick, NJ: Transaction, 2013)

Passerini, Luisa, 'Work Ideology and Consensus under Italian Fascism', *History Workshop Journal*, 8 (1979), 82–108

Passmore, Kevin, 'The 1950s in European Historiography', in *The Lost Decade? The 1950s in European History, Politics, Society and Culture*, ed. Heiko Feldner, Claire Gorrara and Kevin Passmore (Newcastle upon Tyne: Cambridge Scholars Publishing, 2010), pp. 28–39

Pasture, Patrick, 'Beyond the Feminization Thesis: Gendering the History of Christianity in the Nineteenth and Twentieth Centuries', in *Beyond the Feminization Thesis: Gender and Christianity in Modern Europe*, ed. Patrick Pasture, Jan Art and Thomas Buerman (Leuven: Leuven University Press, 2012)

——, 'Dechristianization and the Changing Religious Landscape in Europe and North America since 1950: Comparative, Transatlantic and Global Perspectives', in *The Sixties and Beyond: Dechristianization in North America and Western Europe, 1945–2000*, ed. Nancy Christie and Michael Gauvreau (Toronto: University of Toronto Press, 2013), pp. 367–402

——, 'Religion in Contemporary Europe: Contrasting Perceptions and Dynamics', *Archiv für Sozialgeschichte*, 49 (2009), 319–50

——, 'Religious Globalisation in Post-War Europe: Spiritual Connections and Interactions', *Archiv für Sozialgeschichte*, 51 (2011), 63–108

Paulmann, Johannes, 'Conjunctures in the History of International Humanitarian Aid during the Twentieth Century', *Humanity: An International Journal of Human Rights, Humanitarianism, and Development*, 4 (2013), 215–38

Pereiro, James, 'Who Are the Laity?', in *From without the Flaminian Gate: 150 Years of Roman Catholicism in England and Wales: 1850–2000*, ed. V. Alan McClelland and Michael Hodgetts (London: Darton, Longman & Todd, 1999), pp. 167–91

Perkin, Harold, *The Rise of Professional Society: England since 1880* (London and New York: Routledge, 1989)

Pilcher, Jane, *Age and Generation in Modern Britain* (Oxford: Oxford University Press, 1995)

Pilgrim, David, 'Child Abuse in Irish Catholic Settings: A Non-Reductionist Account', *Child Abuse Review*, 21 (2012), 405–13

Porta, Donatella della, and Mario Diani, *Social Movements: An Introduction* (Oxford: Blackwell, 1999)

Portelli, Alessandro, 'The Peculiarities of Oral History', *History Workshop Journal*, 12 (1981), 96–107

Priestley, J. B., *English Journey* (London: William Heinemann, 1934)

Prochaska, F. K., *Philanthropy and the Hospitals of London: The King's Fund, 1897–1990* (Oxford: Clarendon Press, 1992)

Proctor, Robert, *Building the Modern Church: Roman Catholic Church Architecture in Britain, 1955 to 1975* (Farnham: Ashgate, 2014)

Quinlan, Mary H., *The Society of the Sacred Heart, 1914–1964* (the author, 1995)

Quiñonez, Lora Ann, and Mary Daniel Turner, *The Transformation of American Catholic Sisters* (Philadelphia: Temple University Press, 1992)

Radcliffe, Timothy, OP, 'The Identity of Religious Today'. www.dominicans.ca/Documents/masters/Radcliffe/religious_identity.html, accessed 15 November 2016

Raftery, Deirdre, 'Rebels with a Cause: Obedience, Resistance and Convent Life, 1800–1940', *History of Education*, 42 (2013), 1–16

——, 'Teaching Sisters and Transnational Networks: Recruitment and Education Expansion in the Long Nineteenth Century', *History of Education*, 44 (2015), 717–28

Rahner, Karl, *The Church after the Council* (New York: Herder and Herder, 1966)

Rapley, Elizabeth, *The Lord as Their Portion: The Story of the Religious Orders and How They Shaped Our World* (Cambridge: Eerdmans, 2011)

Rendall, Jane, *The Origins of Modern Feminism: Women in Britain, France and the United States, 1780–1860* (London: Macmillan, 1985)

Rives, Danielle, 'Taking the Veil: Clothing and the Transformation of Identity', *Proceedings of the Western Society for French History*, 33 (2005), 465–86

Robbins, Keith, '1968: Identities – Religion and Nation in the United Kingdom', *Schweizerische Zeitschrift für Religions- und Kulturgeschichte / Revue suisse d'histoire religieuse et culturelle.*, 104 (2010), 35–50

Roberts, Elizabeth, *Women and Families: An Oral History 1940–1970* (Oxford: Blackwell, 1995)

———, *Women's Work, 1840–1940* (Cambridge: Cambridge University Press, 1995)

Roes, Jan, and Hans de Valk, 'A World Apart? Religious Orders and Congregations in the Netherlands', in *Religious Institutes in Western Europe in the 19th and 20th Centuries: Historiography, Research and Legal Position*, ed. Jan De Maeyer, Sofie Leplae and Joachim Schmiedl (Leuven: Leuven University Press, 2004), pp. 135–62

Rogers, Carole G., *Habits of Change: An Oral History of American Nuns* (New York: Oxford University Press, 2011)

Rooney, Miriam, 'Our Block', in *The Vanishing Irish: The Enigma of the Modern World*, ed. John O'Brien (London: W. H. Allen, 1954), pp. 193–201

Rose, Nikolas, 'Assembling the Modern Self', in *Rewriting the Self: Histories from the Renaissance to the Present*, ed. Roy Porter (London: Routledge, 1997), pp. 224–48

———, *Governing the Soul: The Shaping of the Private Self* (London: Routledge, 1990)

Rowbotham, Sheila, *Promise of a Dream: Remembering the Sixties* (London: Allen Lane, 2000)

Rowland, Christopher, ed., *The Cambridge Companion to Liberation Theology* (Cambridge: Cambridge University Press, 2007)

Ruether, Rosemary Radford, *Sexism and God-Talk: Toward a Feminist Theology: With a New Introduction* (Boston: Beacon Press, 1993)

Russell, Polly, 'Using Biographical Narrative and Life Story Methods to Research Women's Movements: Sisterhood and After', *Women's Studies International Forum*, 35 (2012), 132–4

Ryan, Bill, *Catholicism in a Globalizing World: Is Catholic Social Thought Relevant in Today's New Context of Globalization?* (Regina, Sask.: Campion College, 2004)

Sabine, Maureen, *Veiled Desires: Intimate Portrayals of Nuns in Postwar Anglo-American Film* (New York: Fordham University Press, 2013)

Sandbrook, Dominic, *White Heat: A History of Britain in the Swinging Sixties* (London: Little, Brown, 2006)

Sangster, Joan, 'Telling Our Stories: Feminist Debates and the Use of Oral History', *Women's History Review*, 3 (1994), 5–28

Saresella, Daniela, 'Ecclesial Dissent in Italy in the Sixties', *Catholic Historical Review*, 102 (2016), 46–68

Sbardella, Francesca, 'Inhabited Silence: Sound Constructions of Monastic Spatiality', *Etnográfica. Revista do Centro em Rede de Investigação em Antropologia*, 17 (2013), 515–34

Schippers, Mimi, 'Recovering the Feminine Other: Masculinity, Femininity, and Gender Hegemony', *Theory and Society*, 36 (2007), 85–102

Schmiedl, Joachim, 'Reception and Implementation of the Second Vatican Council', in *The Transformation of the Christian Churches in Western Europe (1945–2000) / La Transformation des Églises Chrétiennes en Europe Occidentale*, ed. Leo Kenis, Jaak Billiet and Patrick Pasture (Leuven: Leuven University Press, 2010)

Schneider, Mary L., 'American Sisters and the Roots of Change: The 1950s', *US Catholic Historian*, 7 (1988), 55–72

Schneiders, Sandra M., *Beyond Patching: Faith and Feminism in the Catholic Church* (New York: Paulist Press, 1991)

——, 'Formation for New Forms of Religious Community Life', *The Way Supplement*, 62 (1988), 63–76

——, *New Wineskins: Re-Imagining Religious Life Today* (New York: Paulist Press, 1986)

Schwarz, Walter, *The New Dissenters: The Nonconformist Conscience in the Age of Thatcher* (London: Bedford Square, 1989)

Scott, Joan W., 'The Evidence of Experience', *Critical Inquiry*, 17 (1991), 773–97

Scott, Peter, 'Marketing Mass Home Ownership and the Creation of the Modern Working-Class Consumer in Inter-War Britain', *Business History*, 50 (2008), 4–25

Scull, Margaret M., 'A New Plea for an Old Subject? Four Nations History for the Modern Period', in *Four Nations Approaches to Modern 'British' History: A (Dis)United Kingdom?*, ed. Naomi Lloyd-Jones and Margaret M. Scull (Basingstoke: Palgrave Macmillan, 2018), pp. 3–31

Segal, Lynne, *Out of Time: The Pleasures and the Perils of Ageing* (London: Verso, 2012)

——, 'She's Leaving Home: Women's Sixties Renaissance', in *1968 in Retrospect: History, Theory, Alterity*, ed. Gurminder K. Bhambra and Ipek Demir (Basingstoke: Palgrave Macmillan, 2009), pp. 29–42

Sengers, Erik, '"Although We Are Catholic, We Are Dutch": The Transition of the Dutch Catholic Church from Sect to Church as an Explanation for Its Growth and Decline', *Journal for the Scientific Study of Religion*, 43 (2004), 129–39

——, '"Because We Are Catholic, We Are Modern": The Adaptation of Dutch Catholicism to Modern Dutch Society 1920-1960', *Bijdragen, International Journal in Philosophy and Theology*, 67 (2006), 23–41

Sewell, Dennis, *Catholics: Britain's Largest Minority* (London: Penguin Books, 2001)

Sexton, Catherine, 'Theologies of Ministry among Older Roman Catholic Sisters in the UK', unpublished PhD dissertation, Anglia Ruskin University, 2018

Sexton, Catherine, and Gemma Simmonds, CJ, *Religious Life Vitality Project: Key Project Findings*, 2015. static1.squarespace.com/static/5805fde21b631b4e18960a1a/t/58503 39de6f2e1895e2b601e/1481651155537/RLVP+KEY+FINDINGS+FINAL+%282% 29.pdf, accessed 8 December 2018

Sheehan, Mary Ellen, 'Vatican II and the Ministry of Women in the Church: Selected North American Episcopal Statements and Diocesan Practice', in *Vatican II and Its Legacy*, ed. M. Lamberigts and L. Kenis (Leuven: Leuven University Press, 2002), pp. 469–86

Simmonds, Gemma, CJ, 'Religous Life, a Question of Visibility', in *A Future Full of Hope?*, ed. Gemma Simmonds, CJ (Dublin: The Columba Press, 2012), pp. 116–28

Simmonds, Gemma, CJ, ed., *A Future Full of Hope?* (Dublin: The Columba Press, 2012)

Sinnott, Anneliese, 'Mission and Ministry: The Task of Discipleship', in Nadine Foley, ed., *Journey in Faith and Fidelity: Women Shaping Religious Life for a Renewed Church* (New York: Continuum, 1999), pp. 95–123

Skillen, Fiona, *Women, Sport and Modernity in Interwar Britain* (Bern: Peter Lang, 2013)

Smith, James M., 'The Politics of Sexual Knowledge: The Origins of Ireland's Containment Culture and the Carrigan Report (1931)', *Journal of the History of Sexuality*, 13 (2004), 208–33

Smith, Mark, *Rethinking Residential Child Care: Positive Perspectives* (Bristol: Policy Press, 2009)

Smith-Rosenberg, Carroll, 'The Female World of Love and Ritual: Relations between Women in Nineteenth-Century America', *Signs*, 1 (1975), 1–29

Spencer, Stephanie, '"Be Yourself": Girl and the Business of Growing up in Late 1950s England', in *Women and Work Culture: Britain c.1850–1950*, ed. Krista Cowman and Louise Ainsley Jackson (Farnham: Ashgate, 2005), pp. 141–58

——, *Gender, Work and Education in Britain in the 1950s* (Basingstoke: Palgrave Macmillan, 2005)

——, 'Schoolgirl to Career Girl. The City as Educative Space', *Paedagogica Historica*, 39 (2003), 121–33

——, 'Women's Dilemmas in Postwar Britain: Career Stories for Adolescent Girls in the 1950s', *History of Education*, 29 (2000), 329–42

Stacey, Meg, 'Older Women and Feminism: A Note about My Experience of the WLM', *Feminist Review*, 31 (1989), 140–2

Stark, Rodney, and Roger Finke, 'Catholic Religious Vocations: Decline and Revival', *Review of Religious Research*, 2000, 125–45

Steedman, Carolyn, *Landscape for a Good Woman: A Story of Two Lives* (London: Virago, 1986)

——, 'State-Sponsored Autobiography', in *Moments of Modernity: Reconstructing Britain 1945–1964*, ed. F. Conekin, Frank Mort and Chris Waters (London: Rivers Oram Press, 1999)

——, 'Writing the Self: The End of the Scholarship Girl', in *Cultural Methodologies*, ed. Jim McGuigan (London: Sage, 1997), pp. 106–25

Steele, Francesca, *The Convents of Great Britain and Ireland* (London: Sands, 1924)

Stevenson, George, 'The Women's Movement and "Class Struggle": Gender, Class Formation and Political Identity in Women's Strikes, 1968–78', *Women's History Review*, 25 (2016), 741–55

Stogdon, Kate, '"Nothing Was Taken from Me: Everything Was Given": Religious Life and Second Wave Feminism', in *A Future Full of Hope?*, ed. Gemma Simmonds, CJ (Dublin: The Columba Press, 2012), pp. 63–77

Sullivan, Mary C., *Catherine McAuley and the Tradition of Mercy* (Notre Dame, IN: University of Notre Dame Press, 1995)

Sullivan, Rebecca, 'Celluloid Sisters: Femininity, Religiosity, and the Postwar American Nun Film', *Velvet Light Trap*, 46 (2000), 56–72

——, *Visual Habits: Nuns, Feminism, and American Postwar Popular Culture* (Toronto: University of Toronto Press, 2005)

Summerfield, Penny, 'Dis/Composing the Subject: Intersubjectivities in Oral History', in *Feminism and Autobiography: Texts, Theories, Methods*, ed. Tess Cosslett, Celia Lury and Penny Summerfield (London: Routledge, 2000), pp. 91–106

——, 'Public Memory or Public Amnesia? British Women of the Second World War in Popular Films of the 1950s and 1960s', *Journal of British Studies*, 48 (2009), 935–57

Summers, Anne, *Christian and Jewish Women in Britain, 1880–1940: Living with Difference* (New York: Palgrave Macmillan, 2017)

Summers, Julie, *When the Children Came Home: Stories of Wartime Evacuees* (New York: Simon & Schuster, 2011)

Sutcliffe-Braithwaite, Florence, *Class, Politics, and the Decline of Deference in England, 1968-2000* (Oxford: Oxford University Press, 2018)

Sweeney, James, *The New Religious Order: A Study of the Passionists in Britain and Ireland, 1945-1990 and the Option for the Poor* (London: Bellew, 1994)

———, 'Prophets and Parables: A Future for Religious Orders', *Informationes Theologiae Europae*, 4 (2001), 273-92

———, 'Religious Life after Vatican II', in *Catholics in England 1950-2000: Historical and Sociological Perspectives*, ed. Michael P. Hornsby-Smith (London: Cassell, 1999), pp. 266-87

Taithe, Bertrand, 'Pyrrhic Victories? French Catholic Missionaries, Modern Expertise, and Secularizing Technologies', in *Sacred Aid: Faith and Humanitarianism*, ed. Michael Barnett and Janice Gross Stein (Oxford: Oxford University Press, 2012), pp. 166-87

Taylor, Charles, *The Ethics of Authenticity.* (Cambridge, MA: Harvard University Press, 1992)

———, *A Secular Age* (Cambridge, MA: Harvard University Press, 2007)

———, 'Two Theories of Modernity', *Hastings Center Report*, 25 (1995), 24-33

Taylor, Marilyn, 'Influencing Policy: A UK Voluntary Sector Perspective', in *International Perspectives on Voluntary Action: Reshaping the Third Sector*, ed. David Lewis (London: Earthscan, 1999), pp. 182-201

———, 'Voluntary Action and the State', in *British Social Welfare*, ed. David Gladstone (London: UCL Press, 1995), pp. 214-33

Taylor, Verta, and Nancy E. Whittier, 'Collective Identity in Social Movement Communities: Lesbian Feminist Mobilization', in *Frontiers in Social Movement Theory*, ed. Aldon D. Morris and Carol McClurg Mueller (New Haven, CT and London: Yale University Press, 1992), pp. 104-29

Tentler, Leslie Woodcock, 'Who Are the Catholic Feminists?', *Reviews in American History*, 37 (2009), 315-20

Thane, Pat, 'Family Life and "Normality" in Postwar British Culture', in *Life after Death: Approaches to a Cultural and Social History of Europe during the 1940s and 1950s*, ed. Richard Bessel and Dirk Schumann (Cambridge: Cambridge University Press, 2003), pp. 193-210

Thomas, Barbara Lawler, 'Canon Law and the Constitutions of Religious Congregations', *The Way*, 50 (1984), 47-60

Thomas, Nick, 'Challenging Myths of the 1960s: The Case of Student Protest in Britain', *Twentieth Century British History*, 13 (2002), 277-97

———, 'Will the Real 1950s Please Stand Up?', *Cultural and Social History*, 5 (2008), 227-35

Thompson, Margaret Susan, '"Charism" or "Deep Story"? Toward a Clearer Understanding of the Growth of Women's Religious Life in Nineteenth-Century America', *Review for Religious*, 28 (1999), 230-50

———, 'Circles of Sisterhood: Formal and Informal Collaboration among American Nuns in Response to Conflict with Vatican Kyriarchy', *Journal of Feminist Studies in Religion*, 32 (2016), 63-82

——, 'Of Nuns, Habits, Chainsaws, and Why the Combination is Less Than "Nuntastic"', *Global Sisters Report* (26 September 2017)

Thomson, Alistair, 'Unreliable Memories? The Use and Abuse of Oral History', in *Historical Controversies and Historians*, ed. William Lamont (London: UCL Press, 1998), pp. 23–34

Thomson, Mathew, 'The Popular, the Practical and the Professional: Psychological Identities in Britain, 1901–1950', in *Psychology in Britain: Historical Essays and Personal Reflections*, ed. G. D. Bunn, A. D. Lovie and G. D. Richards (Leicester: BPS Books, 2001), pp. 115–32

Tichenor, Kimba Allie, *Religious Crisis and Civic Transformation: How Conflicts over Gender and Sexuality Changed the West German Catholic Church* (Waltham, MA: Brandeis University Press, 2016)

Tinkler, Penny, '"Are You Really Living?" If Not, "Get With It!"', *Cultural and Social History*, 11 (2014), 597–619

——, *Constructing Girlhood: Popular Magazines for Girls Growing Up in England, 1920–1950* (London: Taylor & Francis, 1995)

——, '"Picture Me As a Young Woman": Researching Girls' Photo Collections from the 1950s and 1960s', *Photography and Culture*, 3 (2010), 261–81

Tinkler, Penny, Stephanie Spencer and Claire Langhamer, 'Revisioning the History of Girls and Women in Britain in the Long 1950s', *Women's History Review*, 26 (2017), 1–8

Tinkler, Penny, and Cheryl Krasnick Warsh, 'Feminine Modernity in Interwar Britain and North America: Corsets, Cars, and Cigarettes', *Journal of Women's History*, 20 (2008), 113–43

Tisdall, Laura, 'Inside the "Blackboard Jungle" Male Teachers and Male Pupils at English Secondary Modern Schools in Fact and Fiction, 1950 to 1959', *Cultural and Social History*, 12 (2015), 489–507

Tobin, Mary Luke, 'Women in the Church since Vatican II', *America*, 155 (1 November 1986), 242–6

Todd, Selina, 'Class, Experience and Britain's Twentieth Century', *Social History*, 39 (2014), 489–508

——, *Young Women, Work, and Family in England 1918–1950* (Oxford: Oxford University Press, 2005)

——, 'Young Women, Work, and Leisure in Interwar England', *Historical Journal*, 48 (2005), 789–809

Todd, Selina, and Hilary Young, 'Baby-Boomers to "Beanstalkers": Making the Modern Teenager in Post-War Britain', *Cultural and Social History*, 9 (2012), 451–67

Tranter, Janice, 'The Irish Dimension of an Australian Religious Sisterhood: The Sisters of Saint Joseph', in *Religion and Identity*, ed. Patrick O'Sullivan (London: Leicester University Press, 1996), pp. 234–55

Trimingham Jack, Christine, *Growing Good Catholic Girls: Education and Convent Life in Australia* (Melbourne: Melbourne University Press, 2003)

Trzebiatowska, Marta, 'Habit Does Not a Nun Make? Religious Dress in the Everyday Lives of Polish Catholic Nuns', *Journal of Contemporary Religion*, 25 (2010), 51–65

Viaene, Vincent, 'International History, Religious History, Catholic History: Perspectives for Cross-Fertilization (1830–1914)', *European History Quarterly*, 38 (2008), 578–607

Viaene, Vincent, ed., *The Papacy and the New World Order (1878–1903)* (Leuven: Leuven University Press, 2005)

Vicinus, Martha, *Independent Women: Work and Community for Single Women, 1850–1920* (Chicago: University of Chicago Press, 1988)

Vinen, Richard, *National Service: Conscription in Britain, 1945–1963* (London: Allen Lane, 2014)

———, 'Where Did You Leave Them? Historians and "Losing the 1950s"', in *The Lost Decade? The 1950s in European History, Politics, Society and Culture*, ed. Heiko Feldner, Claire Gorrara and Kevin Passmore (Newcastle upon Tyne: Cambridge Scholars Publishing, 2010), pp. 10–27

Wall, Barbra Mann, 'Catholic Nursing Sisters and Brothers and Racial Justice in Mid-20th-Century America', *Advances in Nursing Science*, 32 (2009), 81–93

———, 'Catholic Sister Nurses in Selma, Alabama, 1940–1972', *Advances in Nursing Science*, 32 (2009), 91–102

———, *Into Africa: A Transnational History of Catholic Medical Missions and Social Change* (New Brunswick, NJ: Rutgers University Press, 2015)

Walsh, Barbara, *Roman Catholic Nuns in England and Wales, 1800–1937: A Social History* (Dublin: Irish Academic Press, 2002)

Ware, Anne Patrick, ed., *Midwives of the Future: American Sisters Tell Their Story* (London: Sheed and Ward, 1985)

Warren, Heather A., 'The Shift from Character to Personality in Mainline Protestant Thought, 1935–1945', *Church History*, 67 (1998), 537–55

Warsh, Cheryl Krasnick, and Dan Malleck, eds, *Consuming Modernity: Gendered Behaviour and Consumerism before the Baby Boom* (Vancouver: UBC Press, 2013)

Weaver, Mary Jo, *New Catholic Women: A Contemporary Challenge to Traditional Religious Authority* (San Francisco: Harper & Row, 1985)

Welshman, John, *Churchill's Children: The Evacuee Experience in Wartime Britain* (Oxford: Oxford University Press, 2010)

White, Teresa, *A Vista of Years: History of the Society of the Sisters Faithful Companions of Jesus 1820–1993* (privately printed, 2013)

Whittle, Sean, *Vatican II and New Thinking about Catholic Education: The Impact and Legacy of Gravissimum Educationis* (London: Taylor & Francis, 2016)

Wilkinson, Gert, and Ann Denham, *Cloister of the Heart: Association of Contemplative Sisters* (Bloomington, IN: Xlibris Corporation, 2009)

Williams, Margaret, *The Society of the Sacred Heart: History of a Spirit 1800–1975* (London: Darton, Longman & Todd, 1978)

Wilson, Elizabeth, *Only Halfway to Paradise: Women in Postwar Britain, 1945–1968* (London: Tavistock Publications, 1980)

Wilson, Linda, *Constrained by Zeal: Female Spirituality amongst Nonconformists, 1825–75* (Carlisle: Paternoster, 2000)

Withers, Deborah M., 'Women's Liberation, Relationships and the "Vicinity of Trauma"', *Oral History*, 40 (2012), 79–88

Wittberg, Patricia, *The Rise and Fall of Catholic Religious Orders: A Social Movement Perspective* (Albany, NY: SUNY Press, 1994)

Woodhead, Linda, '"Because I'm Worth It": Religion and Women's Changing Lives in the West', in *Women and Religion in the West: Challenging Secularization*, ed. Kristin Aune, Sonya Sharma and Giselle Vincett (Aldershot: Ashgate, 2008), pp. 147–61

Wright, Sheila, '"Every Good Woman Needs a Companion of Her Own Sex": Quaker Women and Spiritual Friendship, 1750–1850', in *Women, Religion and Feminism in Britain, 1750–1900*, ed. Sue Morgan (Basingstoke: Palgrave Macmillan, 2002), pp. 89–104

Wuthnow, Robert, 'Recent Pattern of Secularization: A Problem of Generations?', *American Sociological Review*, 41 (1976), 850–67

Yeates, Nicola, 'The Irish Catholic Female Religious and the Transnationalisation of Care: An Historical Perspective', *Irish Journal of Sociology*, 19 (2011), 77–93

Zuidema, Jason, ed., *Understanding the Consecrated Life in Canada: Critical Essays on Contemporary Trends* (Waterloo: Wilfrid Laurier University Press, 2015)

Index

INDEX

Daughters of Charity of St Vincent de
   Paul, Company of 49, 52, 72,
   106, 111, 120, 138, 168, 197, 210
deference 103, 129, 133–5, 141, 146, 152,
   159, 266, 267, 280
Divine Office 1, 13, 14, 16, 52, 123–4,
   135–40, 161, 195, 255
Dominican sisters and nuns 22, 47, 54,
   75–81, 85, 87, 91, 110, 113, 123,
   124, 184, 189–91, 197, 198, 201,
   227, 244, 280
Dwyer, Bishop George 219

Ecclesiae Sanctae (1966) 99, 104, 111
ecclesial movements, lay 198, 224,
   290–1
ecumenism 94, 147, 194, 195, 199, 202,
   211, 275, 278
education of women religious 47,
   182–7
Evangelii Nuntiandi (1975) 107, 219
Evangelii Praecones (1951) 218

Faithful Companions of Jesus 54, 103
family relationships 187–91
feminism 23, 124, 157, 230–9, 240, 241,
   276, 279, 287
   see also Women's Liberation
   Movement
Fidei Donum (1957) 219
foreign missions 49, 218–27
France 85, 87, 96, 224
Francis, Pope 287
Franciscan Missionaries of the Divine
   Motherhood 90, 179, 229
Friedan, Betty 39

Gaine, Michael 203
Gaudium et Spes (1965) 200, 268
generations 68, 76–7, 86, 90, 96, 107,
   112–13, 122, 127–8, 133, 150–60,
   253
global Catholicism 5, 20–2, 26, 31–4,
   36, 57–60, 78, 94, 192–6, 200,
   227–8

'golden age' 12, 31, 38, 52, 66
governance 1, 15, 32, 57, 93–4, 97, 101–
   26, 138, 179, 192, 230, 246–8,
   269–71, 278–80
grille 44, 89, 166, 188–9, 249–57, 264

habit see religious habit
Heenan, John Carmel, Cardinal
   Archbishop of Westminster 27,
   114–15, 185, 201, 273–4, 286
homelessness 202, 208, 212–14, 217,
   226, 228
homosocial relationships 32, 128–33,
   160
horarium 32, 80, 123–4, 133–6, 138–40,
   144–5, 149, 160

identities 13, 19–21, 134–5, 138, 149–50,
   164, 195, 203, 220, 230, 257–65,
   279–84, 289
individualism 71, 131, 165, 186, 232
Institute of the Blessed Virgin Mary
   14, 17–18, 42, 53–4, 59, 99, 100,
   105, 114, 119, 123, 141, 175
international congresses 31, 36, 58, 59,
   67, 87, 182, 189, 239, 259, 268,
   277
Ireland see Catholicism, Ireland
Irish migration 50
Irish-born women religious 15, 29, 47,
   49–50, 141, 220, 260, 263

Jesuits (Society of Jesus) 43, 59, 60, 81,
   178, 194
John XXIII, Pope 27–8, 242
justice and peace 194–5, 201, 207, 211,
   214, 215, 224

La Retraite, Congregation of 14, 16, 18
La Sagesse (Congregation of the
   Daughters of Wisdom) 202
Latin America 201, 219–24, 272
Latin Mass 115
lay sisters 8, 104, 135, 146, 150, 161, 186,
   280

"Brevity is the Soul of Wit"
William Shakespeare's Hamlet
Act 2, Scene 2 in 1603